Methods in
RECEPTOR RESEARCH

METHODS IN MOLECULAR BIOLOGY

Edited by

ALLEN I. LASKIN
ESSO Research and Engineering
* Company*
Linden, New Jersey

JEROLD A. LAST
Harvard University
Cambridge, Massachusetts

VOLUME 1: Protein Biosynthesis in Bacterial Systems
    edited by Jerold A. Last and Allen I. Laskin

VOLUME 2: Protein Biosynthesis in Nonbacterial Systems
    edited by Jerold A. Last and Allen I. Laskin

VOLUME 3: Methods in Cyclic Nucleotide Research
    edited by Mark Chasin

VOLUME 4: Nucleic Acid Biosynthesis
    edited by Allen I. Laskin and Jerold A. Last

VOLUME 5: Subcellular Particles, Structures, and Organelles
    edited by Allen I. Laskin and Jerold A. Last

VOLUME 6: Immune Response at the Cellular Level
    edited by Theodore P. Zacharia

VOLUME 7: DNA Replication
    edited by Reed B. Wickner

VOLUME 8: Eukaryotes at the Subcellular Level
    edited by Jerold A. Last

VOLUME 9: Methods in Receptor Research (in two parts)
    edited by Melvin Blecher

Methods in
RECEPTOR RESEARCH

(in two parts)

Part II

Edited by Melvin Blecher

Department of Biochemistry
Georgetown University Medical Center
Washington, D.C.

MARCEL DEKKER, INC.   New York and Basel

MARCEL DEKKER, INC.

270 Madison Avenue, New York, New York 10016

LIBRARY OF CONGRESS CATALOG CARD NUMBER: 75-40846

ISBN: 0-8247-6415-3

Current printing (last digit):
10 9 8 7 6 5 4 3 2 1

PRINTED IN THE UNITED STATES OF AMERICA

To Jocelyn

PREFACE

The Editor need not remind the reader of the currency of receptor research; the burgeoning literature is an ample reminder. The reader will also have frequently encountered the frustration arising from sketchy methods often provided in journal articles; hence, the popularity of volumes dealing exclusively with methods. This volume, therefore, is an effort to collect in laboratory manual form a broad spectrum of the detailed methods employed currently by many of the world's foremost receptor research laboratories.

We have elected to exclude from this volume methods involving receptors for steroid and thyroid hormones since we feel that such methods, having much in common with each other but little in common with those used with other hormones, warrant separate treatment in another volume. Therefore we will deal here exclusively with receptors for polypeptide hormones, prostaglandins, catecholamines, opiates, acetylcholine, lectins, and cholera toxins.

The reader will note a certain amount of seeming redundancy and overlap among the chapter titles and methods employed. Thus, more than one chapter is devoted to several of the hormones (insulin, glucagon, prostaglandins and gonadotropins), and many authors use the chloramine-T method for preparing radioiodinated polypeptides. The Editor feels, however, that the redundancy and overlap are more apparent than real. In these instances, different laboratories will have different experimental approaches and will utilize methods and variations unique to their system, even though studying the same ligand.

Finally, while the experimental approaches, laboratory methods, and data-handling techniques described herein are given in terms of specific ligands and receptor macromolecules, many of the chapters provide information which has general applicability. To cite two examples, Catt et al. in Chapter 9 describe general methods for the determination of binding constants and concentrations of receptors, while De Meyts in Chapter 11 deals extensively with general methods for determining the physicochemical parameters of steady-state binding and for studying cooperative interactions among receptor sites.

Melvin Blecher

CONTRIBUTORS TO PART II

JOËL BOCKAERT, Laboratoire de Physiologie Cellulaire, Collège de de France, Paris, France

MAX M. BURGER, Department of Biochemistry, Biocenter of the University of Basel, Basel, Switzerland

PEDRO CUATRECASAS, * Department of Pharmacology and Experimental Therapeutics, Department of Medicine, The Johns Hopkins University School of Medicine, Baltimore, Maryland

GUY FAYET, Laboratoire de Biochimie Médicale et Unité 38 de l'Institut National de la Santé et de la Recherche Médicale, Faculté de Médecine, Marseille, France

PIERRE FREYCHET,† Unité de Recherche de Diabétologie et d'Etudes Radio-Immunologiques des Hormones Protéiques, Institut National de la Santé et de la Recherche Médicale, Hôpital Saint-Antoine, Paris, France

HENRY G. FRIESEN, Department of Physiology, Faculty of Medicine, University of Manitoba, Winnipeg, Manitoba, Canada

MORLEY D. HOLLENBERG, Department of Pharmacology and Experimental Therapeutics, Department of Medicine, The Johns Hopkins University School of Medicine, Baltimore, Maryland

JOHN L. HUMES, Department of Inflammation and Arthritis, Merck Institute for Therapeutic Research, Rahway, New Jersey

---

*Current affiliation: The Wellcome Research Laboratories, Burroughs Wellcome Company, Research Triangle Park, North Carolina.
† Current affiliation: Groupe de Recherche sur les Hormones Polypeptidiques et la Physiopathologie Endocrinienne, Institut National de la Santé et de la Recherche Médicale, Faculté de Médecine, Chemin de Vallombrose, Nice, France.

VILMA K. JANSONS, Department of Microbiology, College of Medicine
and Dentistry of New Jersey, New Jersey Medical School, Newark,
New Jersey

SERGE JARD, Laboratoire de Physiologie Cellulaire, Collège de France,
Paris, France

FREDERICK A. KUEHL, Jr., Department of Inflammation and Arthritis,
Merck Institute for Therapeutic Research, Rahway, New Jersey

SERGE LISSITZKY, Laboratoire de Biochimie Médicale et Unité 38 de
l'Institut National de la Santé et de la Recherche Médicale, Faculté
de Médecine, Marseille, France

CRAIG C. MALBON, * Department of Biology, Case Western Reserve
University, Cleveland, Ohio

HELEN G. OIEN, Department of Inflammation and Arthritis, Merck
Institute for Therapeutic Research, Rahway, New Jersey

RABARY RAJERISON, Laboratoire de Physiologie Cellulaire, Collège
de France, Paris, France

Ch. VENKATESWARA RAO, Departments of Obstetrics-Gynecology and
Biochemistry, University of Louisville, School of Medicine, Louisville,
Kentucky

CHRISTIAN ROY, Laboratoire de Physiologie Cellulaire, Collège de
France, Paris, France

ROBERT P. C. SHIU,† Department of Physiology, Faculty of Medicine,
University of Manitoba, Winnipeg, Manitoba, Canada

ERIC J. SIMON, Department of Medicine, New York University Medical
Center, New York, New York

MELVYN S. SOLOFF, Department of Biochemistry, Medical College of
Ohio, Toledo, Ohio

BERNARD VERRIER, Laboratoire de Biochimie Médicale et Unité 38 de
l'Institut National de la Santé et de la Recherche Médicale, Faculté de
Médecine, Marseille, France

JAMES E. ZULL, Department of Biology, Case Western Reserve University, Cleveland, Ohio

---

*Current affiliation: Section of Physiological Chemistry, Division of
Biological and Medical Sciences, Brown University, Providence, Rhode
Island.
† Current affiliation: Canadian Centennial Fellow at the National Institutes
of Health, Bethesda, Maryland.

CONTENTS

Preface   v

Contributors to Part II   vii

Contents of Part I   ix

Chapter 12: INSULIN RECEPTORS   385

             Pierre Freychet

      I. Introduction   386
     II. Radiolabeled Insulin   387
    III. Receptor Preparations   395
     IV. General Problems in Insulin–Receptor Binding Assays   403
      V. Binding Assays   409
     VI. Applications of Insulin–Receptor Studies   418
          Acknowledgments   421
          References   422

Chapter 13: METHODS FOR THE BIOCHEMICAL IDENTIFICATION
             OF INSULIN RECEPTORS   429

             Morley D. Hollenberg and Pedro Cuatrecasas

      I. Introduction   430
     II. General Properties of Ligand–Receptor Interactions
          and Technical Considerations   431
    III. Measurements of the Interaction of Insulin with
          Membrane Receptors   442
     IV. Summary   471
          References   472

Chapter 14: LECTIN RECEPTORS   479

             Vilma K. Jansons and Max M. Burger

      I. Introduction   480
     II. Assays for WGA–Receptor Activity   480

III. Isolation of WGA Receptor   482
IV. Isolation of Receptors for Other Lectins   490
 V. Discussion   493
       References   494

Chapter 15: METHODS USED IN THE STUDY OF OPIATE
                    RECEPTORS   497

                    Eric J. Simon

   I. Introduction   498
  II. Preparation and Purification of Labeled Ligands   498
 III. Tissue Preparations for Binding Studies   499
 IV. Assay of Stereospecific Opiate Binding on Membranes   502
  V. Assay for Agonist and Antagonist Properties of Opiates   506
 VI. Preparation of Affinity Chromatography Beads for
         Receptor Purification   506
VII. Affinity Labeling   508
         Acknowledgments   509
         References   509

Chapter 16: OXYTOCIN RECEPTORS IN THE MAMMARY
                    GLAND AND UTERUS   511

                    Melvyn S. Soloff

   I. Introduction   512
  II. Materials   512
 III. Uptake of [^{3}H]Oxytocin by Tissues in Vitro   514
 IV. Autoradiographic Localization of Oxytocin Receptors   517
  V. Binding of [^{3}H]Oxytocin to Subcellular Particles   518
 VI. Oxytocin Binding by Isolated Mammary Gland Cells   523
VII. Oxytocin Binding to Other Mammalian Tissues   528
         Acknowledgments   528
         References   529

Chapter 17: PARATHYROID HORMONE RECEPTORS   533

                    James E. Zull and Craig C. Malbon

   I. Introduction   534
  II. Purification of Parathyroid Hormone   535
 III. Preparation of Radioactive Parathormone   538
 IV. Receptor Preparations   550
  V. Binding Methodology   556
         Acknowledgments   562
         References   562

Chapter 18: PROLACTIN RECEPTORS   565

            Robert P. C. Shiu and Henry G. Friesen

     I. Introduction   566
    II. Studies on Prolactin Receptors Using a Particulate
         Cell Membrane Preparation   567
   III. Studies on the Soluble Prolactin Receptors   579
    IV. Concluding Remarks   592
         Acknowledgments   595
         References   596

Chapter 19: PROSTAGLANDIN RECEPTORS IN ADIPOSE TISSUE   599

            John L. Humes, Helen G. Oien, and
               Frederick A. Kuehl, Jr.

     I. Introduction   600
    II. Preparation of Lipocytes   600
   III. Binding to Intact Lipocytes   601
    IV. Binding to the Receptor Preparation   601
     V. Receptor Preparation for PG Quantitation   606
    VI. Properties of the PGE Receptor Preparation   608
   VII. Application of the Binding Reaction   609
         References   613

Chapter 20: PROSTAGLANDIN E RECEPTORS IN CORPORA
            LUTEA   615

            Ch. Venkateswara Rao

     I. Introduction   616
    II. Preparation of Cell Membranes   616
   III. Binding Assay for $[^3H]$ Prostaglandin E_1 617
    IV. Thin Layer Chromatography of $[^3H]$ Prostaglandin E_1 620
     V. Binding Conditions   622
    VI. Binding Constants for $[^3H]$ PGE_1-Membrane Interaction   626
   VII. Specificity of PGE Receptors   631
  VIII. Macromolecular Nature of PGE Receptors   632
    IX. Effect of Chemical Modification of Membrane
         Proteins on $[^3H]$ PGE_1 Binding   635
         Acknowledgments   636
         References   637

Chapter 21: THYROTROPIN RECEPTORS   641

            Serge Lissitzky, Guy Fayet, and Bernard Verrier

     I. Introduction   642
    II. Radiolabeled Thyrotropin   642

III.   Receptor Preparations   651
IV.   Binding Assays   656
 V.   Quantitative Aspects of TSH–Receptor Interaction   658
       References   663

Chapter 22: VASOPRESSIN RECEPTORS   667

       Serge Jard, Joel Bockaert, Christian Roy, and
          Rabary Rajerison

  I.   Introduction   668
 II.   Preparation of Labeled Neurohypophyseal Peptides   669
III.   Characterization of Oxytocin Receptor(s) on Intact
       Epithelial Cells   675
IV.   Characterization of the Vasopressin Receptor in
       Membrane Fractions   681
 V.   Solubilization of Membrane Vasopressin Receptors   693
       Acknowledgments   700
       References   701

Author Index   705

Subject Index   743

CONTENTS OF PART I

Chapter 1: METHODS OF ISOLATION AND CHARACTERIZATION
OF THE ACETYLCHOLINE RECEPTOR
Arthur Karlin, Mark G. McNamee, Cheryl L. Weill, and
Ramon Valderrama

Chapter 2: PREPARATION OF ACTH-SENSITIVE ADRENOCORTICAL
MEMBRANES
Francis M. Finn and Klaus Hofmann

Chapter 3: [^{3}H] (-)-ALPRENOLOL: A NEW TOOL FOR THE STUDY
OF BETA-ADENERGIC RECEPTORS
Robert J. Lefkowitz

Chapter 4: CHOLERA TOXIN RECEPTORS
Vann Bennett and Pedro Cuatrecasas

Chapter 5: FOLLICLE-STIMULATING HORMONE: MEASUREMENT
BY A RAT TESTES TUBULE TISSUE RECEPTOR ASSAY
Leo E. Reichert, Jr.

Chapter 6: ISOLATION OF GLUCAGON RECEPTOR PROTEINS
FROM RAT PLASMA MEMBRANES
Steven Goldstein and Melvin Blecher

Chapter 7: METHODS TO CHARACTERIZE THE CARDIAC GLUCAGON
RECEPTOR
Gerald S. Levey, Mary A. Fletcher, and S. Ramachandran

Chapter 8: THE GLUCAGON RECEPTOR IN PLASMA MEMBRANES
PREPARED FROM RAT LIVER
Stephen L. Pohl

Chapter 9: RECEPTORS FOR GONADOTROPIC HORMONES
Kevin J. Catt, Jean-Marie Ketelsleges, and Maria L. Dufau

Chapter 10: GONADOTROPIN RECEPTORS
Brij B. Saxena

Chapter 11: INSULIN AND GROWTH HORMONE RECEPTORS IN HUMAN
            CULTURED LYMPHOCYTES AND PERIPHERAL BLOOD
            MONOCYTES
            Pierre De Meyts

Methods in
RECEPTOR RESEARCH

Chapter 12

INSULIN RECEPTORS

Pierre Freychet*

Unité de Recherche de Diabétologie et
d'Etudes Radio-Immunologiques des Hormones Protéiques
Institut National de la Santé et de la Recherche Médicale
Hôpital Saint-Antoine
Paris, France

I. INTRODUCTION   386

II. RADIOLABELED INSULIN   387

    A. Preparation and Properties of Monoiodoinsulin   388
    B. Preparation of [^{125}I] Insulin for Receptor-Binding Studies   389
    C. Other Methods of Labeling   394

III. RECEPTOR PREPARATIONS   395

    A. Intact Organs and Tissue Pieces   395
    B. Isolation and Use of Intact Cells   396
    C. Isolation and Use of Cell Membranes   399
    D. Solubilization of Membrane Receptors   402

---

*Current affiliation: Groupe de Recherche sur les Hormones Polypep-
tidiques et la Physiopathologie Endocrinienne, Institut National de la
Santé et de la Recherche Médicale, Faculté de Médecine, Chemin de
Vallombrose, Nice, France.

IV. GENERAL PROBLEMS IN INSULIN-RECEPTOR
      BINDING ASSAYS   403

      A. Assessment of Specificity   403
      B. Kinetic and Quantitative Aspects of Insulin Binding   406

 V. BINDING ASSAYS   409

      A. Binding Assays Using Intact Cells   409
      B. Binding Assays Using Cell Membranes   412
      C. Binding Assays Using Solubilized Material   415
      D. Expression of Results   415

VI. APPLICATIONS OF INSULIN-RECEPTOR STUDIES   418

      A. Structure-Function Relationships   419
      B. The Insulin Receptor in Pathological States   420

      ACKNOWLEDGMENTS   421

      REFERENCES   422

I. INTRODUCTION

During the past several years, both new methods and adaptation of previously described approaches have permitted extensive studies of interactions between peptide hormones and their receptors [1-4]. In 1969, two groups, using [^{125}I]ACTH [5] and [^{125}I]angiotensin [6], respectively, developed methods that were applicable generally for the direct study of the interaction between a peptide hormone and its specific receptors on target cells. This direct approach has rapidly been extended to insulin, glucagon, and many other peptide hormones [1-4]. With the use of radiolabeled peptide hormone and receptor-containing intact cells or cell membranes for direct studies, the peptide hormone-receptor interaction has become a quantifiable biochemical reality.

The concept that insulin was able to act while on the surface of the cell was first suggested by studies with antihormone antibody: Anti-insulin serum was found to reverse the action of insulin on diaphragm [7], suggesting that the hormone, even at the time it was acting, was still exposed to the extracellular medium, i.e., on the plasma membrane of the cell. This was also suggested by the observation that trypsin-treated fat cells lost their ability to respond to insulin stimulation [8] without losing their cellular integrity and their ability to utilize glucose or to respond to other hormones. Insulin coupled to insoluble agarose particles was shown to be biologically active [9]. Since under this form the hormone could not enter the intact cell, it was concluded that the biological effect can be generated through the sole interaction of the hormone with receptors on the cell surface; the interpretation and validity of the latter studies, however, has been questioned [10]. Although specific insulin-binding sites have been found on intracellular organelles [11-13], direct studies of insulin-receptor interactions have demonstrated the plasma membrane fraction of the cell as the predominant location of the receptor sites [14]. Along with the discovery of cAMP as an intracellular "second messenger" of hormone action and the localization of hormone-stimulated adenylate cyclase to the plasma membrane of the cell, these results have substantiated the concept of cell-surface membrane receptors for insulin and other peptide hormones.

Since peptide hormone receptors have not been isolated in "pure" form, they are defined by their functional properties [3]. The major, and minimal, property of the receptor is its specificity for a given hormone, i.e., the ability to selectively recognize a hormone in a specific binding reaction. When the recognition function is strictly dependent on the biologically active structure of the hormone, as is the case for insulin (see Sec. IV. A), this requirement is largely fulfilled, and this also provides some indirect evidence that binding of the hormone to receptor can be related to the biological effects of the hormone. In this chapter, the term receptor will be used to refer only to that component of the membrane which selectively discriminates and binds insulin. This functional definition does not preclude that the receptor may or may not be separate from that part of the membrane which translates the hormone signal that eventually results in a biological effect [3].

The basic methods and techniques for the direct study of insulin-receptor interactions are similar to those used in other competitive binding assays. They have largely benefited from the work of Berson and Yalow[15] on the interactions between insulin and its specific antibodies. They require isotopically labeled insulin, a suitable receptor preparation, and an appropriate means for separating the insulin-receptor complex from free insulin. It is the purpose of this chapter to review these methodological aspects and to present some applications of insulin-receptor binding assays.

II. RADIOLABELED INSULIN

The use of radioactively labeled insulin to study the interaction of the hormone with its receptor must fulfill two requirements. (1) The labeled insulin must retain the biological activity of the native (unlabeled) insulin. Since, however, the binding affinity of hormone to receptor and the efficacy of the hormone-receptor complex in activating cellular processes represent two functions which may be structurally separate, the retention

of binding affinity is a minimal but sufficient requirement for the labeled
hormone to be a valid tracer of the native hormone in studies of hormone
binding to receptor in vitro. (2) The specific radioactivity of the labeled
insulin must be high enough to permit the use of low concentrations, i.e.,
near the physiological values.

A. Preparation and Properties of Monoiodoinsulin

When the first direct studies of insulin binding to target tissues were
attempted with the use of radioiodinated hormone [16-19], uncertainties
about the biological activity of the iodoinsulin [20] and the specificity of
the binding process [21] limited the validity and interpretation of the
results. Several studies [22-24] had shown that, in contrast to a recent
observation with glucagon [25], increasing the degree of iodine incorporation into the insulin molecule resulted in a loss of biological activity, but
it was not certain whether monoiodoinsulin retains biological activity per
se.

The preparation, isolation, and characterization of monoiodoinsulin
has been described elsewhere [26]. Only the general principles of the
method and a few remarks which are relevant to the preparation of [^{125}I]-
insulin for receptor-binding studies will be presented. It is essential to
use (or prepare) highly purified insulin, e.g., "monocomponent" [27] or
"single component" [28] insulin in order to remove both proinsulin or
proinsulin-like components and desamido-insulin(s). Removal of the latter is particularly important to achieve separation between iodoinsulin
and uniodinated insulin on ion-exchange chromatography [26] since des-
amidation, like iodination, increases negative charges. To obtain large
quantities of iodinsulin for chemical and biological analysis, milligrams
of highly purified insulin are iodinated with $K^{127}I$, to which is added a
trace (5-10 μCi) of $Na^{125}I$. Iodination is performed with insulin:I in
molar equivalents of 10:1 in order to minimize the introduction of more
than one atom of I per insulin molecule. Iodination involves oxidation
of the iodide with subsequent incorporation into the ortho positions of
tyrosine; chloramine-T [29] is used as the oxidant and is added in multiple small additions. In the final mixture, Insulin:I:chloramine-T is
~ 10:1:1-2. Under these conditions, ~ 10% of the insulin is iodinated.
Iodoinsulin is separated from uniodinated insulin by gradient chromatography on DEAE-cellulose at pH 9 to 9.4 in 7 M urea. At these pHs,
the difference between the pKs of monoiodotyrosine and uniodinated tyrosine [30] allows the separation of monoiodoinsulin from uniodinated insulin [26]. Spectrophotometric titration [30] reveals that nearly one
out of the four (22%) tyrosines of the insulin molecule in the iodoinsulin peak is in the form of monoiodotyrosine; whereas the content
of diiodotyrosine is trivial, indicating that the iodoinsulin peak con-

sists mainly of monoiodoinsulin [26]. This preparation is indistinguishable from native insulin in its capacity to stimulate glucose oxidation by isolated fat cells [26]. Thus, monoiodoinsulin retains biological activity unaccounted for by its small (~12%) content of uniodinated insulin.

Other studies [31] have shown that certain tyrosine residues are preferentially iodinated and that, in monoiodoinsulin, most of the iodine incorporations occur on the A chain (Tyr A_{14} and Tyr A_{19}). Previous reports on the loss of biological activity of monoiodoinsulin [20, 32], which contrasted with the retention of binding ability of the monoiodohormone in one of these studies [32], have not been fully confirmed [33] or substantiated. The biological activity of monoiodoinsulin has been amply confirmed [34-36]; in the latter study [36], incorporation of iodine predominantly involved Tyr A_{14}. Because Tyr A_{19} is engaged in interactions which may be important in maintaining the three-dimensional structure of the insulin molecule [37], and in view of possible conformation change(s) induced by iodine incorporation, the position of iodination may influence the biological activity of monoiodoinsulin. It has, however, been shown that, except at extreme pHs, monoiodination of insulin is likely to predominantly involve A_{14}, and this should not substantially affect the hormone conformation [36]. It has now become evident that, under certain conditions, one can prepare iodinated insulin that is highly suitable for direct studies of insulin-receptor interactions. These conditions imply iodinating at pH 6 to 8, with an average iodination level of one iodine atom (or less) per insulin molecule and, preferably in the author's opinion, the chromatographic isolation of monoiodoinsulin (see Sec. II. B. 2. c).

B. Preparation of [^{125}I] Insulin for Receptor-Binding Studies

As already mentioned, studies of insulin-receptor interactions require a labeled hormone of high specific radioactivity, which implies the use of radioactive (^{125}I of ^{131}I) iodide. Theoretically, ^{131}I would yield monoiodohormone with higher specific activity (~16,200 Ci/mmol) than ^{125}I (~2,300 Ci/mmol) if both were available isotopically pure. However, ^{125}I is preferred for the following reasons: It can be obtained virtually carrier-free, i.e., close to 100% isotopic abundance, whereas the maximal isotopic abundance of ^{131}I does not exceed 30% [15]; it has a longer half-time (60 vs 8 days) than ^{131}I; and it is counted with greater efficiency in most gamma counters. Two types of modifications [1, 3, 14, 26, 38-43] of the Hunter and Greenwood method [29] have been introduced in the labeling of insulin with ^{125}I and the use of chloramine-T for receptor studies. These modifications were designed to yield mostly monoiodoinsulin and to minimize hormone damage by the oxidant.

1. The First Modification

This is very similar to that already described (Sec. II. A) for the preparation of mono [^{127}I] insulin, except that Na^{125}I (instead of K^{127}I), and micrograms of insulin (instead of milligrams) are used [26]. In this method,
only ~ 10% of the insulin is iodinated using mild conditions.

a. Iodination Procedure

Typically, the iodination mixture contains in a total volume of 100 to 150
μl, insulin at 0.5 mM and Na^{125}I at 0.03 to 0.05 mM i.e., in 100 μl
final volume, ~300 μg of insulin (mol wt $\cong$ 6,000) and 8 to 10 mCi of
^{125}I (specific activity of carrier-free ^{125}I $\cong$ 18 mCi/μg). Chloramine-T
is added stepwise in several small aliquots, each being equimolar to
iodide, i.e., ~1.1 μg of chloramine-T in 100 μl final volume, until the
desired degree of iodination (usually 60 to 80% incorporation of the iodide
into the protein) is achieved. Iodine incorporation is measured after each
addition of chloramine-T by 10% (vol/vol) trichloroacetic precipitation
and by adsorption of [^{125}I] insulin to silicate [15]. In the final mixture,
insulin:I:chloramine-T is ~10:1:2-4. Because insulin is used in excess
of chloramine-T, addition of the reducing agent sodium metabisulfite may
be omitted.

b. Purification Procedure

The iodination mixture is then chromatographed on DEAE-cellulose [26].
As indicated (Sec. II. A), the chromatographic step is designed to separate
the [^{125}I] insulin from unlabeled insulin, thereby enriching the specific
activity of the labeled hormone; it also separates free iodide, as well as
damaged and diiodinated hormone, from the monoiodohormone.

c. Comments

The separation of [^{125}I] insulin from unlabeled insulin is, however, much
more difficult to achieve when very small quantities of hormone are used,
which precludes obtention of "carrier-free" mono[^{125}I] insulin with the
expected specific activity of 380 μCi/μg [26]. This may be due, in part,
to contamination of the insulin with desamido-insulin [26] but is difficult
to avoid even when insulin is purified shortly before iodination. The
specific radioactivity of the [^{125}I] insulin prepared by this method is
difficult to predict and may be quite low (e.g., 20-50 μCi/μg), which
impairs its use if very low concentrations of hormone are desired.

2. The Second Modification

This consists of iodinating insulin directly with 0.7 to 0.9 I atom per molecule by using ^{125}I in equimolar amount to insulin and by reducing the
volume of reaction [38-43].

a. Iodination Procedure

Typically, the following are successively added to the iodination tube:
20 μl of 0.3 M phosphate buffer, pH 7.5; 5 μl of 1 mg/ml insulin (i.e.,
5 μg) in 0.01 N HCl; 10 μl of carrier-free Na^{125}I (I-S$_4$, purchased from
Commissariat à l'Energie Atomique, Saclay, France), which represents
~2 mCi (or ~0.11 μg of ^{125}I); 5 μl of a freshly prepared solution of
chloramine-T at 2.5 mg/ml (i.e., 12.5 μg) in 0.3 M phosphate buffer; after 30 to 40 sec, 5 μl of a 5 mg/ml (i.e., 25 μg) solution of sodium metabisulfite in 0.3 M phosphate buffer. Concentrations of reactants in the
iodination tube are ~20 μM insulin, 20 μM iodide, 900 μM chloramine-T
and 2,500 μM sodium metabisulfite, i.e., ~1:1:45:125. Under these conditions, 70 to 90% of the iodide is incorporated into the insulin, which
yields a calculated specific activity of 280 to 360 μCi/μg, i.e., an average
incorporation of ~0.7 to 0.9 iodine atom per molecule of insulin; 90% of
the iodine is on the A chain [43]. Immediately after the sodium metabisulfite, 100 μl of 2.5% (wt/vol) albumin in 0.3 M phosphate buffer is added
to the iodination mixture; albumin picks up residual reactive I and prevents
[^{125}I] insulin from damage and adsorption to glass.

b. Purification Procedures

Two procedures can be used to purify the [^{125}I] insulin. One of them
simply consists of separating the labeled and unlabeled insulin from free
iodide and from some of the damaged components by adsorption of [^{125}I] –
insulin to cellulose following the procedure of Yalow and Berson [44].
The other consists of purifying the iodination mixture by chromatography
on DEAE-cellulose as described [26], except that urea is omitted in this
case, because of the small quantity of insulin applied and the risk of peptide damage by carbamylation through the formation of cyanate. The
chromatographic procedure removes free iodide as well as damaged and
diiodinated insulin. It also separates, to a certain extent, uniodinated
hormone from [^{125}I] insulin, thereby enriching slightly the specific activity
of the [^{125}I] hormone [26]. The elution patterns of [^{125}I] insulin and
[^{125}I] proinsulin on DEAE-cellulose chromatography are shown in Figure 1.
The main peak of [^{125}I] insulin is eluted at the same ionic strength as
biologically active monoiodoinsulin (see Sec. II. A and Ref. 26). This
preparation of [^{125}I] insulin exhibits the same kinetic of binding in liver
plasma membranes whether used alone at increasing concentrations or
diluted, at a tracer dose, in increasing concentrations of native (unlabeled)
insulin (Fig. 2), suggesting that the labeled insulin possesses a binding
affinity to receptor which is similar, or very close, to that of unlabeled
insulin.

c. Comments

Both purification procedures have produced labeled insulin that is suitable
for receptor studies. [^{125}I] Insulin purified by the first procedure, i.e.,

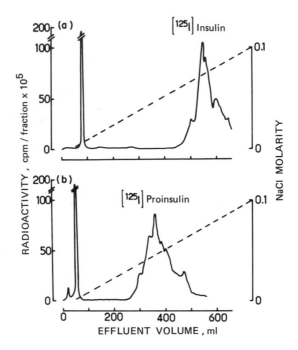

FIG. 1. Elution profiles for [125I] insulin (a) and [125I] proinsulin (b) on
DEAE-cellulose chromatography. Iodination mixtures (5 μg of peptide
with an average of 0.7-0.8 I atom per molecule) were applied to 0.9 ×
20-cm columns of DEAE-Cellulose that had been equilibrated in 50 mM
tris-HCl, pH 9.4, at 4°C. After 100 ml of buffer had passed over the
columns, a gradient to 0.1 M NaCl was applied. The first narrow peaks
represent damaged components. Reprinted from Ref. 41, by courtesy
of the American Society for Clinical Investigation, Inc.

adsorption to cellulose or silicate, has been widely employed in receptor-
binding studies [1-3, 38, 45-54, 57-69]. Commercially available labeled
insulins have also been used [70-77]; they often have a lower specific
radioactivity, which may preclude their utilization if low concentrations
of hormone are to be used. In the author's opinion, there are, however,
three reasons to prefer the second purification procedure, i.e., the
DEAE-cellulose chromatography. (1) The main peak of [125I] insulin is
eluted at the same ionic strength as biologically active monoiodoinsulin,
and its binding affinity is very close, if not identical, to that of native
insulin (Fig. 2). (2) At the level of iodination attained by this procedure,
i.e., 0.7 to 0.9 iodine atom per molecule, the proportion [22] of diiodinated insulin, whose biological activity is presumably altered, cannot

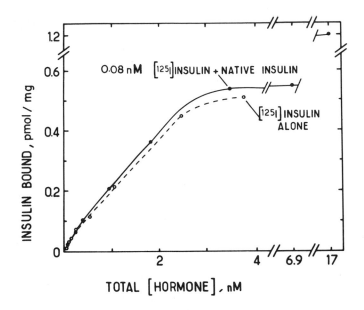

FIG. 2. Insulin binding in liver plasma membranes. The amount of
insulin bound is plotted as a function of insulin concentration. The specific binding of $[^{125}I]$ insulin used alone at increasing concentrations has been
compared to that of a fixed concentration of $[^{125}I]$ insulin diluted in increasing concentrations of native (unlabeled) insulin. The amount of
hormone bound was calculated from the percent of $[^{125}I]$ insulin specifically
bound at each concentration of total (labeled alone or labeled plus unlabeled)
hormone (see text, Sec. V. D). [Reprinted from Ref. 4, by courtesy of
Médecine et Hygiène.]

be neglected ($\sim$ 20%). The DEAE-cellulose chromatography allows the
exclusion of this species, which is eluted after monoiodoinsulin [26].
(3) Damaged component(s), which do not bind to receptors [38], are
separated from intact $[^{125}I]$ insulin more completely by the DEAE-cellulose
chromatography than by the simple adsorption of the labeled hormone to
cellulose or silicate. The latter point is important in view of the hormone
degradation that may occur during iodination and may vary between iodina-
tions. In our experience this method of purification has proved very reliable to yield $[^{125}I]$ insulins which behave towards receptors in a highly
reproducible manner.

    d. Quality Control and Storage of Labeled Insulin

The integrity of $[^{125}I]$ insulin may be estimated by conventional techniques
such as its precipitability by trichloroacetic acid, its ability to adsorb to

silica, and to bind to anti-insulin antibody [38]. The most sensitive and appropriate technique is, however, the ability of the labeled hormone to bind to insulin-specific receptors [38]. It is possible to bind up to 70 to 80% of the mono[^{125}I] insulin using a large concentration of liver plasma membranes. However, because degradation [38] and nonspecific adsorption of [^{125}I] insulin are favored by high concentrations of membranes (see Sec. IV. B), this type of control is not adequate. It is preferable to test the [^{125}I] insulin under standardized and reproducible conditions of the binding assay, i.e. (see Sec. V. B), incubation of the hormone with liver membranes at 0.20 to 0.25 mg of protein per ml for 60 min at 30°C. A standard inhibition curve of [^{125}I] insulin binding [41, 52, 78] is run in the presence of unlabeled insulin over a wide range (0.17-17 nM) of hormone concentration and includes a great excess of unlabeled insulin (3.5-20 μM) in order to determine the nonspecific binding (see Sec. IV. B). This binding assay allows the testing of freshly prepared [^{125}I] insulin, and may be repeated every 10 to 15 days in order to assess the integrity of [^{125}I] insulin during storage. A single batch of liver plasma membranes (i.e., 40 to 50 mg of membrane protein if the starting amount of liver is 80 g) permits the testing of successive preparations of [^{125}I] insulin every 10 to 15 days over a period of 8 to 12 months. Alteration of the labeled hormone is suspected when the specific binding decreases and the nonspecific binding increases. With this control, we have observed that [^{125}I] insulin prepared following the second modification of the chloramine-T method and purified on DEAE-cellulose can be used for at least four weeks and occasionally for 5 to 6 weeks after iodination. The [^{125}I] insulin is distributed into 200- to 500-μl samples that are stored at -20°C in Krebs-Ringer phosphate buffer containing 1% (wt/vol) bovine serum albumin (fraction V), pH 7.5; the albumin prevents adsorption of the labeled hormone to glass and may improve the stability of the preparation. Samples are used only once.

C. Other Methods of Labeling

Iodination may also be performed enzymatically with the use of lactoperoxidase to catalyze the oxidation of iodide in the presence of H_2O_2. This method has been employed to iodinate a variety of peptide hormones used in receptor studies, especially the glycoproteins [3]. It has also been utilized for insulin [32, 33, 35, 36], but a systematic comparison of this method and the modified chloramine-T method(s) has not been made thus far. Iodination of insulin with the use of the iodine monochloride reagent [79] has also been employed in receptor studies [80, 81].

Other isotopes (e.g., ^{3}H, ^{14}C) would yield labeled insulin of much lower specific radioactivity [3]. Receptor-binding studies have been conducted with [³H] insulin at 84 Ci/mmol [82]. The theoretical specific activity of tritiated insulin with one ³H substituted per hormone molecule is 29 Ci/mmol, i.e., about 80 times less than the specific activity of mono[¹²⁵I] insulin ($\cong$ 2,300 Ci/mmol), which limits the suitability of [³H] insulin when low concentrations of hormone are to be used. Furthermore, the potential advantage of tritiation which, in contrast to iodination, is a substitution rather than an addition, is opposed by the rather harsh conditions of the procedure itself [3]. ³H labeling, however, has proven most useful with the smaller peptide hormones such as vasopressin and oxytocin [3].

Attempts have recently been made to prepare labeled insulins suitable for ultrastructural studies of the hormone-receptor interactions. Insulin linked to horseradish peroxidase through reaction with glutaraldehyde retains very little (0.6%) immunological reactivity [83] and presumably is biologically inactive. In contrast, insulin linked to ferritin through a soluble, low-molecular-weight dextran appears to retain both immunological reactivity and binding affinity to receptor and, thus, represents an appropriate marker for ultrastructural studies [84]. The use of insulin-ferritin for ultrastructural studies has also been reported [85]. Insulin "immobilized" on a solid, macroscopically visible matrix (agarose insulin) has been used in an attempt to visualize the binding of insulin to intact fat cells and their ghosts [86].

III. RECEPTOR PREPARATIONS

A. Intact Organs and Tissue Pieces

Attempts have been made to measure the binding of radioiodinated insulin to small tissue slices or pieces, or to small organs such as isolated intact muscle [16, 18, 19, 21, 32; author's unpublished observations]. The theoretical advantages of this procedure (i.e., minimal alteration of the cells and more "physiological" conditions) are usually largely impaired by the high proportion of nonspecific binding and adsorption of the labeled hormone [21], the trapping and degradation of insulin, and by the fact that such preparations represent diffusion barriers as well as mixed cell populations. This type of preparation, however, may be employed to provide qualitative or semiquantitative data when the amount of tissue is too small [87] to permit cell isolation or fractionation, or when the target organ is exposed to labeled insulin prior to tissue fractionation [17].

Receptor preparations usually fall into three classes: isolated intact cells, particulate fractions of cells, and solubilized fractions of cells.

B. Isolation and Use of Intact Cells

Two types of cell have been employed in studies of insulin binding to
receptors. The first type consists of cells obtained from major target
organs of the hormone, e.g., the adipose tissue and the liver. The
second type is represented by cells that have thus far not been recognized
as major targets for insulin but which are more accessible and do not
require isolation from a compact organ, e.g., peripheral blood mononuclear cells and thymic lymphocytes.

Cells of the first type have usually been isolated by enzymatic digestion of the tissue or organ. Isolated fat cells have been prepared following the method of Rodbell [88]. This involves the use of crude collagenase, which is contaminated by proteolytic enzymes. Since the insulin
receptor is highly susceptible to trypsin [14, 47, 72, 89, 90] and other
proteases, and because the contamination of crude collagenase by proteolytic enzymes may vary between different lots, it is recommended
that each lot be tested by measuring the ability of isolated cells to bind
insulin. Similar and even more crucial problems are encountered with
the use of isolated fat cells in insulin bioassay. In this regard, it is
evident that a lot of collagenase which has been recognized as suitable
for the isolation of cells that are sensitive to insulin in a bioassay is
quite appropriate for the preparation of cells for receptor-binding studies.
The converse, however, may not be true, since the insulin-stimulated
glucose transport and antilipolysis may be altered without significant
damage of the hormone receptor itself [60]. The albumin used in the
buffer during the isolation procedure should be tested like the collagenase.
In addition to the careful selection of collagenase and albumin and to the
control of the physical chemical parameters (buffer, pH, temperature),
shortening the time of exposure to the collagenase with the help of mechanical disruption (e.g., more vigorous and faster shaking) and/or decreasing
the concentration of collagenase have generally proved useful in minimiz-
ing alteration of receptors on the cell surface. The procedure of cell
isolation also depends on the collagenase employed, the amount of tissue
treated, the intensity of shaking, and the time of exposure to the enzyme.
Isolated rat fat cells have been the most widely used in studies of insulin-
receptor interactions [26, 57, 60, 64, 65, 67, 72, 74, 89, 90]. Adipocytes isolated from surgically obtained subcutaneous abdominal adipose
tissue in humans have also been employed to measure the binding of
[125I]insulin [56, 81].

Enzymatic perfusion of the liver with collagenase and hyaluronidase
has been used to isolate liver cells which consist mostly of parenchymal
cells (hepatocytes) and are suitable for studies of hormone-receptor
interactions [11, 42, 91]. The isolation procedure is derived from that
described by Berry and Friend [92] with various modifications [11, 42,

43]. Briefly, the method that we have used consists of perfusing the liver in situ through the portal vein with Ca^{2+}-free Locke's solution containing 27 mM sodium citrate, then with Hank's solution containing enzymes (collagenase at 0.5 mg/ml or less and hyaluronidase* at 0.5 mg/ml) and 4% (wt/vol) bovine serum albumin. The digested liver is filtered through 100-mesh silk screen, and cells are collected by low speed (200 rpm for 1 min) centrifugation, then washed twice in Krebs-Ringer phosphate buffer containing 2 to 3% (wt/vol) albumin. As estimated in phase scope microscopy, the cells obtained by this method consist mostly of free hepatocytes (~90% of the total). These are 85 to 95% viable as judged by their ability to exclude trypan blue. The periphery of intact cells is highly refractive [43]. Isolated hepatocytes maintain their ATP content, their ability to bind insulin and glucagon [42], and their capacity to respond to these hormones [93] for at least 2 to 3 hr. They are stored in flat-bottom vials (at room temperature or at 5°C) under a thin (4-5 mm) layer of buffer to avoid cell death by anoxy [43]. The yield ranges between 250 and 350 × 10^6 cells for a 5-g liver, which represents the recovery of ~40 to 50% of the parenchymal cells. Mechanical disruption to increase the yield should be avoided. The remarks concerning the use of collagenase and albumin for the isolation of fat cells are also applicable to that of liver cells. Isolated mammary cells [94, 95] prepared by treating freshly excised mouse mammary gland with collagenase, and isolated chondrocytes [64], have also been used in studies of [^{125}I] insulin binding.

Both circulating and cultured human lymphocytes have been employed as a source for insulin receptors [45, 47, 49-51, 53, 55, 66, 96, 97]. Two methods have been utilized to isolate lymphocytes from peripheral blood. In the first method [45, 47, 49-51, 53, 55, 96, 97], a Ficoll-Hypaque gradient is used to separate the mononuclear leucocytes and granulocytes [98] obtained in the white cell layer (buffy coat) of peripheral blood (300-500 ml). In the second method [55, 66], passage of blood (200-500 ml) through a nylon-fiber column is used to separate lymphocytes from other leucocytes. The method used appears to be crucial, since insulin-specific binding sites have been observed in a highly reproducible manner in freshly isolated cells prepared by the first method [45, 47, 49-51, 53, 55, 96, 97], whereas essentially no specific insulin binding has been detected in cells freshly isolated by the second method [55, 66]. As has been pointed out [2, 55], the latter procedure produces small lymphocytes which are predominantly nonimmunoglobulin-bearing (T) cells, whereas the first method provides a mixed population of immunoglobulin-bearing (B) and nonimmunoglobulin-bearing (T) cells, suggesting that lymphocytes of the B-type may be primarily involved in binding insulin. On the other hand, it has been reported that monocytes rather than lymphocytes are essentially responsible for the specific binding of insulin by peripheral blood mononuclear cells [99, 100]. The

---

*Hyaluronidase may be omitted.

precise identification of the cell type involved is of obvious importance in view of the accessibility of the circulating blood cells for the study of insulin-receptor interactions in pathological states [49, 50] (see also Sec. VI. B). Cultured human lymphocytes [45, 47, 53, 96, 97] and lectin-transformed lymphocytes [66] have also been used as a source for insulin receptors. Insulin-specific binding sites have been observed in cultured human skin fibroblasts obtained by biopsy [45], and in rat [46] and mouse [54] thymocytes.

Isolated intact cells possess a major potential advantage over other receptor preparations: They are metabolically active and hence it is possible to measure both the binding of insulin and a biological effect of the hormone in the same preparation. This is of particular interest in the case of insulin because of the lack of consistent direct effect of this hormone on plasma membrane-bound enzymes (see Sec. III. C). Insulin-stimulated glucose oxidation [57, 60, 72, 76], lipogenesis [72, 74, 76, 101], and antilipolysis [60] have thus been measured in the same fat cell preparations as those used to study the specific binding of insulin. Insulin-stimulated uridine incorporation and α-aminoisobutyric acid uptake have been measured, together with insulin binding, in isolated mammary cells [95] and in isolated thymocytes [46, 54], respectively. It has often been difficult, however, to establish a direct correlation between the binding and the biological effect(s) of the hormone. Such difficulty rests on several factors. The simple models of hormone action usually employed to relate the hormone binding and the biological response may not be appropriate [3]. Insulin-specific binding sites may be present in cells which, at a certain stage of organ development [87] or function [95], do not respond to the hormone, or which do not seem to be a major target for insulin [45, 47]. Under certain conditions of study, only a minority of the binding sites appear to be involved in the maximal biological response [72, 74, 101]. Moreover, the comparison between binding and biological effect(s) in isolated intact cells is made difficult in practical terms because the optimal experimental conditions (temperature, time, cell and hormone concentrations, incubation medium) for measuring binding often differ from those for measuring biological effect(s); the most adequate conditions for studying binding are not always the most "physiological" ones. For example, measurement of binding at steady-state often requires lower temperatures of incubation than those employed to measure biological effect(s) (see Sec. IV. B). Because of the relatively limited number of receptor sites on the cell surface, the cell concentrations which are necessary to measure a significant binding of insulin are usually higher [46, 54, 57, 72] than those required to observe a biological effect. A higher cell concentration in the binding assay results in a higher risk of hormone degradation (see Sec. IV. B), which can be minimized by decreasing the temperature at which the binding assay is performed. This is especially true with cells that have high enzymatic activities, such as liver cells [42, 43], but also exists with most isolated cell preparations [38, 74], although fat cells [38, 57, 74] and lymphocytes [45, 47, 49, 54] degrade less insulin than do hepatocytes under similar experimental conditions. Furthermore, high cell concentrations may complicate the quantitative analysis of the binding data because they favor nonspecific adsorption and trapping of the labeled hormone.

Another advantage of isolated cells in insulin-receptor binding studies is the possibility of measuring and expressing the binding directly per cell. This is of special interest in studies comparing the insulin-binding affinities and capacities (i.e., the number of receptor sites per cell) between various physiological or pathological states. These studies are, however, limited by the heterogeneity of cells which compose most tissues. Cultured cells may be homogeneous if cloned populations are used. These cells, however, usually are tumor or transformed cells and this itself may modify the insulin receptor population [66]. There is a wide range of insulin-binding affinities and capacities among various human lymphoid cell lines in culture [47]. Heterogeneity is also encountered within a given cell type. For example, the size of isolated fat cells is quite variable even when cells are prepared from animals in apparently consistent metabolic and/or nutritional state. The isolation procedure (filtration and washing steps, centrifugation speed and duration) may favor the selection of fat cells of a certain size. Furthermore, the larger fat cells (especially those obtained from obese animals and human subjects) are quite fragile and may be partly eliminated through breakage during the isolation procedure. For all of these reasons, careful attention must be paid to the isolation procedure in terms of interexperimental reproducibility and comparison (cell type and size) among different metabolic, nutritional, and clinical states. Although isolated cells offer the unique advantage of permitting direct quantitation of the binding parameters per cell and, possibly, that of measuring a biological effect of insulin, the demonstration that the receptor is altered requires the use of cells from various tissues or organs as well as that of specific subcellular fractions (see Sec. VI. B).

C. Isolation and Use of Cell Membranes

A variety of cell membrane preparations has been used to study insulin-receptor interactions. Their practical advantages over most isolated intact cells rest on the fact that they can be stored for several weeks or months in the frozen state, that the same preparation can be repeatedly used if prepared in sufficient quantity, and that hormone degradation and nonspecific adsorption may be controlled or minimized since the most purified subcellular fraction with respect to receptors, i.e., the plasma membrane, can be used at low concentration in the binding assay.

Two types of cell membranes have been employed. One type consists of relatively crude preparations which represent, in fact, microsomal fractions [102]. In brief, these are prepared by differential centrifugation of homogenates (usually in 0.25 M sucrose). The 40,000 g pellet of liver [61, 103] or the 24,000 g (or 45,000 g, see Ref. 61) pellet of fat cell [58] homogenates have been used. A 100,000 g microsomal membrane preparation has been employed in binding studies of insulin to human placenta [68] and to a variety of tissues or organs from a number of animal species [69]. The second type is represented by partially or highly purified plasma membranes such as those obtained from the liver following the method of Neville [104, 105]. In this method, cell rupture in hypotonic media (e.g., 1 mM $NaHCO_3$) with a Dounce-type homogenizer releases intact sheets of plasma membranes which constitute the largest fragments in the homogenate and can be concentrated by a low-speed (1,500 g) centrifugation. Plasma membranes are floated in sucrose just above their isopycnic density and thus separated from the more dense mitochondria and microsomal fragments. The larger plasma membrane fragments are then isolated by zonal centrifugation stabilized by a sucrose gradient. This method allows both morphological and biochemical evaluations of purity of the plasma membrane fraction [104-107[. To ensure reproducibility, careful attention must be paid to the critical steps of the procedure, i.e., the homogenization, the low-speed (1,500 g) centrifugation of the homogenate, the accuracy in adjusting the various sucrose solutions (this requires the use of a refractometer), and the monitoring of each step by phase microscopy [105, 107]. Plasma membranes prepared by this method retain insulin-binding ability and other properties such as glucagon-binding and basal or stimulated adenylate cyclase activity after storage for several months at -70°C in multiple small pellets, which are used only once. They have been used extensively in studies of insulin binding to receptors [3, 4, 11, 14, 26, 38-41, 48, 52, 75, 78, 82, 108-110]. Modifications of this and other methods have also been applied to insulin-receptor binding studies [70, 71, 73, 80, 81]. Plasma membranes prepared from isolated fat cells following the method of McKeel and Jarett [111] and that of Laudat et al. [112] have been used in studies of insulin binding to receptors [39, 62, 113]. A specific binding of [^{125}I] insulin has been characterized in membranes prepared from rat and mouse cardiac muscle [13, 114] following the method of Kidwai et al. [115].

Even the most highly purified types of membrane preparations often contain 5 to 10% contamination by mitochondrial and microsomal proteins [107], while less purified preparations may be composed of up to 90% of these contaminants [3]. The less purified fractions are usually faster to prepare than purified plasma membranes. Speed may be critical, at least with certain tissues, to avoid or minimize loss of membrane-bound enzyme activity, such as adenylate cyclase. However, the latter is still present at a rather high specific activity even in the most highly purified plasma membrane fraction of the liver [106]. Two points deserve mention here. (1) An inhibitory effect of insulin on the basal and the glucagon-stimulated adenylate cyclase activity has been reported in a crude mouse liver particulate fraction [116] and in rat fat cell and liver microsomal membranes [103]. In contrast, insulin has not been found to significantly inhibit the basal and the glucagon-stimulated adenylate cyclase activity in partially or highly purified liver plasma membranes [106, 117, 118]. It is uncertain whether this discrepancy points to the lack of direct effect of insulin on the plasma membrane adenylate cyclase or is related to the loss of some membrane component during the purification procedure. A stimulatory effect of insulin on the plasma membrane-bound phosphodiesterase activity in a purified plasma membrane fraction of rat liver has been reported [119]. (2) Very little, if any, degradation of insulin has been observed [59] with rat liver microsomal membranes.

In the author's opinion, the use of the most purified plasma membrane preparation available to study insulin receptors outweighs that of less purified membrane fractions for the following reasons. (1) Since, for many organs, the plasma membrane protein represents only ~ 0.3 to 5% of the total cell protein [3, 107], the specific activity of insulin binding is much higher in purified plasma membranes than in less purified fractions. Serial purification of liver plasma membranes, for example, results in a 30- to 50-fold increase in the concentration of insulin receptors per milligram of protein [3, 11, 14]. (2) The nonspecific binding (see Sec. IV. B) represents a lower proportion of the total binding in the most purified plasma membrane fraction. (3) The use of low concentrations of membrane protein minimizes the degradation of insulin (see Sec. IV. B). (4) Certain cellular organelles other than the plasma membrane may possess insulin-specific binding sites [11, 12, 114]. These, however, may be of different affinity or concerned with different function(s) with respect to insulin [107]. For example, the marked difference in insulin-binding capacity observed between the purified liver plasma membranes of obese hyperglycemic (ob/ob) mice and of their thin littermates has not been found in fractions of smooth or rough endoplasmic reticulum of livers from these two types of mice [11]. Therefore, in less purified membranes (e.g., a microsomal fraction), contamination with these organelles would lead to an underestimation of the difference in insulin-binding capacity which is observed between the obese and the thin mouse in purified plasma membranes [11, 13, 114]. In this respect, the insulin receptor defect in certain pathological states (see Sec. VI. B) may represent an additional marker of plasma membrane purification.

It should be pointed out that, even with purified plasma membranes, several problems [3, 107] are encountered in assessing the nature and

the purity of the preparation. These are related to the frequent heterogeneity of the starting material with respect to cell type, which may
result in a significant portion of the membrane isolated from a cell type
other than the one of major interest in the organ or tissue investigated.
Within a given cell type, the isolation procedure may favor the selection
of a specialized area of the plasma membrane and the final preparation
may not be representative of the total plasma membrane. The problem
of selection becomes particularly important in doing comparative studies
between various physiological or pathological states in which quantitation
of membrane receptors is attempted [11, 13, 39, 107-109, 114]. In these
cases, particular attention must be paid to assessing and comparing the
degree of purification of the membrane preparations. This requires the
determination of membrane yield and the measurement of marker enzymes
as well as comparison of morphology. It may also be useful to determine
the protein-subunit structure by acrylamide gel electrophoresis [3, 11,
107] and to compare receptor concentrations for several hormones in a
given plasma membrane preparation [3, 11, 107, 113]. Quantitation of
membrane receptors in comparative studies between physiological or
pathological states undoubtedly requires the use of the most purified and
best characterized plasma membrane preparation since, as pointed out,
the receptor defect on the plasma membrane will be underestimated, or
even missed, if the plasma membrane is diluted in other subcellular
organelles which bind insulin specifically but may not have the defect.
More generally, there appears to be a distinct value in using a purified
and well-characterized plasma membrane preparation in order to ensure
consistency and reproducibility of the binding data when different batches
of membranes are used.

D. Solubilization of Membrane Receptors

Insulin receptors have been solubilized from cell membranes and from
intact cells. The criteria used to ascertain solubilization have usually
included the absence of significant sedimentation under a force of 200,000
g or more, the passage through membrane filters having a pore diameter
of 0.2 μm, and exclusion on gel filtration [61, 63, 96, 97]. Nonionic
detergents such as Triton X-100 [61, 63] and NP-40 [96] have been employed to extract insulin-binding macromolecules in "soluble" form from
rat liver and fat cell membranes [61, 63] and from human lymphocytes in
culture [96]. Extraction with Lubrol-PX has also permitted the solubilization along with glucagon-binding specific proteins, of an insulin-binding
material from rat liver plasma membranes [120]. Insulin receptors have
also been obtained in a soluble form without the use of detergents in the
incubation medium of human lymphocytes in culture [97]. Solubilized
insulin receptors retain many, if not all, of the insulin-binding characteristics of receptor sites on intact cells or plasma membranes.

Solubilized insulin receptors offer major advantages in terms of attempts to purify and further characterize [61, 63] the receptor molecule. Combination of various purification procedures, including affinity chromatography, have afforded a purification of the receptor of ~250,000 [2]. It has been calculated that the molecular weight of the insulin-binding macromolecular complex is ~300,000, but this does not correct for the amount of detergent bound to the proteins [2]. A number of problems have thus far hampered both the practical use of solubilized receptors and the achievement of their purification. First, the problems of heterogeneity and contamination of the original preparation are still present in the solubilized material. Second, the continuous presence of the detergent, usually required to maintain the binding proteins in a "soluble" state, does not allow precise physical measurements. Furthermore, the labeled hormone may associate with micelles of the detergent and form a complex which, on gel chromatography, may be mistaken for the hormone-receptor complex [120]. Finally, the extraordinary scarcity of the insulin-binding proteins in biological tissues ($\sim 10^{-4}\%$ of the protein of a rat liver homogenate, see Ref. 2) has made it difficult to prepare and purify the insulin receptor in sufficient quantity for further physical chemical characterization.

IV. GENERAL PROBLEMS IN INSULIN-RECEPTOR BINDING ASSAYS

A. Assessment of Specificity

The major property, and minimal requirement, of the receptor is its hormonal specificity. This implies that only unlabeled insulin (and no other protein or peptide hormone) is capable of competing with [^{125}I]-insulin for binding to receptor. Moreover, since very high concentrations of unlabeled insulin may prevent adsorption of [^{125}I] insulin [21], the binding of [^{125}I] insulin must exhibit sensitivity to low concentrations of unlabeled insulin, and a complete displacement curve of the labeled hormone should be obtained with unlabeled insulin concentrations within reasonable limits (Fig. 3).

The biological specificity of the insulin-binding sites as highly selective discriminators for the insulin molecule has been established with the study of insulins, insulin analogs, and derivatives which offer a wide spectrum of structural and functional modifications [14, 40, 42, 78, 114]. As seen in Table 1, the relative potencies of insulins, proinsulin, and insulin derivatives to compete for the insulin-binding sites in liver plasma membranes are in direct proportion to their relative biological potencies in isolated fat cells. These observations have been extended to other insulin-binding systems with intact cells [42, 45-47, 54-57, 74], cell membranes [58, 59, 62, 68, 69, 114], and solubilized binding material

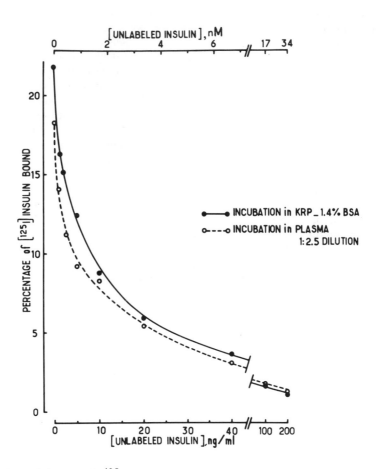

FIG. 3.   Inhibition of [^{125}I] insulin binding to liver plasma membranes
by unlabeled insulin.   Membrane-bound [^{125}I] insulin, expressed as percentage of total radioactivity, is plotted as a function of unlabeled insulin
concentration.   The nonspecific binding has not been subtracted.   Experimental conditions were as described in the text (Sec. V. B) for the
sensitized radioreceptor assay, i.e., two sequential steps at 4°C with
membranes at 0.15 mg protein per ml exposed to varying concentrations
of unlabeled insulin for 8 hr prior to the addition of [^{125}I] insulin at 0.04
nM for a subsequent incubation of 16 hr.   A parallel experiment was
performed in the presence of insulin-free (i.e., < 10 μU/ml by radioimmunoassay) human plasma.   All samples contained 1 mM N-ethyl-
maleimide as inhibitor of insulin degradation.

TABLE 1. Relative Potencies[a] of Insulins and Insulin Derivatives in Binding to Liver Membranes, Stimulating Glucose Oxidation by Fat Cells, and Reacting in Insulin Radioimmunoassay[b]

Preparation	Liver membranes	Fat cells	Radioimmunoassay
Porcine insulin	100	100	100
Bovine insulin	100	100	70
Guinea pig insulin	1.1	1.0	0.001
Chicken insulin	180	190	See Ref. 122
Fish insulin	53	50	0.2
Porcine proinsulin	3.3	2.1	48
Bovine desoctapeptide insulin	1.9	1.5	11
Bovine desalanine, desasparagine insulin	1.7	1.4	15

[a] In each case, the numbers in the table equal

$$100 \times \frac{\text{Molar concentration of porcine insulin to achieve 50\% effect}}{\text{Molar concentration of insulin or derivative to achieve 50\% effect}}$$

[b] From Refs. 14, 41, and 122.

[61, 63, 96, 97] from various tissues and animal species. A close correlation between the receptor-binding affinity and the biological potency in
vitro has also been observed with a variety of chemically modified insulins
[40, 76] and with proinsulin-like and insulin-like molecules [41, 64, 121]
(see also Sec. VI. A). In contrast to the receptor-binding affinity, the
immunological reactivity often does not correlate with the biological
potency (Table 1). Three conclusions can be drawn. (1) The binding
affinity is strictly dependent on the biologically active structure of the
insulin molecule. Therefore, the basic requirement regarding the biological specificity of the receptor is largely fulfilled. (2) No competitive
antagonist has been found among the insulin analogs and derivatives tested,
since, in all cases, the decrease in biological potency has been entirely
accounted for by the decrease in binding affinity. With the exception of
chicken insulin, which behaves as a "superagonist" of porcine insulin (at
least in the rat [122]), all other insulins and insulin derivatives tested
are agonists of lower potency (Table 1). (3) The high degree of biological
specificity demonstrated by the receptor is in marked contrast to the
specificity of antibody-binding sites which are often not related to bioactivity (Table 1).

In summary, it is essential to assess specificity by: (1) measuring
the ability of low concentrations of unlabeled insulin to inhibit the binding
of labeled insulin and (2) screening insulins and insulin derivatives of
varying biological potency in order to establish the biospecificity of the
binding system.

B. Kinetic and Quantitative Aspects of Insulin Binding

With virtually all systems for the study of insulin interaction with specific
receptors, there are several problems that are encountered in the quantitative analysis of kinetic properties of the interaction. These have been
reviewed in detail [3, 52]; they will be considered here inasmuch as they
are concerned with the characterization and use of insulin-receptor binding assays.

1. Nonspecific Binding

In most systems with intact cells, cell membranes, or solubilized
material, insulin binding has been considered to consist of at least two
processes, one of which is saturable with respect to hormone, or
"specific," and the other of which is nonsaturable or "nonspecific."
Since the latter behaves as unsaturable over the range of insulin concentrations experimentally practical, binding to this nonspecific site may be
considered as a constant percentage of the tracer [^{125}I] insulin. This
percentage has usually been measured as the radioactivity associated with

cells, membranes, or extracts in the presence of a great excess, e.g.,
20 to 100 μg/ml (i.e., ~3.5-17 μM) of unlabeled insulin, and has been
subtracted from the total of [^{125}I] insulin binding to yield specific binding
[11, 39, 41, 42, 45-47, 52-54, 57-65, 67-69, 89, 114]. Using this
definition, the nonspecific binding represents < 5% of the total binding
with purified liver plasma membranes. The nonspecific binding is often
higher (usually, between 5 and 20% of the total binding, occasionally
more) when binding is measured in intact cells [42, 45, 46, 49, 54], in
plasma membranes of fat cell [39, 62], and in less purified cell fractions
[11, 114]. The nonspecific binding increases when the labeled insulin
has been damaged during storage (see Sec. II. B) or degraded after exposure to cells or cell membranes. Two points should be kept in mind
regarding nonspecific binding. (1) Subtraction of nonspecific binding is
a useful simplification in the analysis of the data, but it is not clear that
this binding is nonspecific in a biological sense. It is evident that the
proportion of nonspecific binding subtracted from total will depend on
that concentration of unlabeled insulin which is arbitrarily assigned as
"excess." This problem can be minimized by using a great excess
(i.e., at least 50/μg ml, or ~10 μM) of unlabeled hormone: This usually
results in a nonspecific binding which represents only 10% or less of
total binding. (2) It may be difficult to accurately determine the contribution of nonspecific binding to total binding of [^{125}I] insulin above high
concentrations of unlabeled hormone, because of the low level of radioactivity bound at high concentrations of unlabeled insulin. This may
significantly affect the determination of the maximum insulin-binding
capacity of the system, depending on how much nonspecific binding is
subtracted from total binding of [^{125}I] insulin.

2. Hormone and Receptor Degradation

In addition to the interaction of insulin with its receptors, two other reactions are occuring which influence the quantitative study of the interaction, namely, insulin degradation and receptor degradation. Virtually
all preparations that contain insulin-specific receptors also contain system(s)
which degrade(s) insulin [38, 42, 52, 74, 78]. In liver membranes, insulin
binding to receptors and hormone degradation appear to be largely independent processes* [38]: the degradation process affects native insulin and biologically inactive insulin derivatives to a similar extent, and there is no correlation between the binding affinity of an insulin derivative to receptor and
its ability to inhibit insulin degradation [3, 38]. The degrading enzyme(s)
exhibit(s) lower apparent affinity for insulin than does the receptor [38].

---

*These results do not preclude the possibility that binding of insulin to re-
ceptor may be the initial step of the degrading process in the intact cell
[see S. Terris and D. F. Steiner, J. Biol. Chem., 250:8389 (1975)].

Physical chemical parameters such as pH, ionic strength, and temperature affect binding to receptor and insulin degradation in a different manner [38, 52, 78]; thus, the degradation reaction is decreased at low temperature where insulin binding is actually increased. The labeled insulin recovered by dissociation of the hormone-receptor complex in liver membranes has been found to be intact [38, 57, 58], and it may actually possess improved properties over the [^{125}I] insulin originally used [38], indicating that the receptor-binding process may serve as a purification procedure for the hormone. The reaction of insulin degradation is very dependent on the conditions of incubation in the binding assay, more particularly on the temperature and the concentration of membranes [52] or cells [74]. The degradation of [^{125}I] insulin does not exceed 5 to 15% after a 60-min exposure to purified liver plasma membranes at 0.2 to 0.3 mg protein per ml [40, 52, 122]. At higher membrane concentrations, insulin degradation can be almost totally inhibited by the sulfhydryl-blocking agent, N-ethyl-maleimide (1 mM) which, at this concentration, has no inhibitory effect on the binding of insulin to receptor [38, 78]. The apparent amount of degradation is also dependent on the method used to measure degradation, hormone binding to receptor being the most sensitive [38]. Like hormone degradation, receptor "degradation" is a function of time, temperature, ionic strength, and membrane concentration [52]. At 30°C, the insulin receptor of purified liver plasma membranes is degraded with a half-time of ~4 hr [52]. Since the ability to degrade insulin and, presumably, the stability of receptor may differ in varying receptor preparations, it is essential to measure hormone and receptor degradation when characterizing a new insulin-receptor binding system. The quantitative analysis of the binding data also requires knowledge of the amount of hormone degraded [52].

3. Kinetic Aspects of Insulin Binding to Receptors

Insulin binding to receptor is a rapid reaction whose variables are the time, temperature, and concentrations of the reacting species, i.e., hormone and receptor. Both the amount of binding and the rate of binding are temperature-dependent, with a slower but higher binding of insulin achieved at lower temperature [42, 47, 52, 114]. Thus, the maximum value of receptor-bound insulin is two and one-half to three times higher at 4°C than that observed at 30°C. This, however, requires 12 to 24 hr vs 30 to 60 min at 30°C. The higher binding at lower temperature is related, in part, to a decrease in insulin degradation and also to an increase in both the apparent affinity constants and in the number of receptor sites [52]. The insulin-receptor complex can be dissociated by dilution, with a mean half-time of dissociation of ~15 min at 30°C [52]. In many insulin-binding systems, the addition of unlabeled insulin increases the rate of dissociation; this has been interpreted as suggestive of negative cooperativity between the binding sites [51].

When establishing the optimal conditions for a binding assay, all of the parameters discussed must be considered. Insulin and receptor degradation may be minimized by decreasing the temperature and membrane concentration. This in turn requires longer times of incubation to reach equilibrium. Since the competitive binding assay is done at steady-state of binding, it is necessary to perform a time course of association to define the optimal time and temperature conditions of the assay. One also needs to know the speed of dissociation in order to avoid or minimize dissociation of the hormone-receptor complex during the procedure of isolation of receptor-bound insulin.

V. BINDING ASSAYS

The reagents that we have usually employed in binding assays are as follows (variations will be given with each procedure when appropriate).

Buffer: Ca^{2+}-free Krebs-Ringer phosphate (KRP) without and with 5, 10, or 30 mg/ml bovine serum albumin, Fraction V (BSA), pH 7.5.

[^{125}I] insulin: 3 to 6 ng/ml in buffer with 10 mg/ml BSA.

Unlabeled insulin: stock solutions from 10 ng/ml to 10 μg/ml, e.g., 10, 20, 50, 100, 200, 400 ng/ml and 1, 2, 4, and 10 μg/ml, in buffer with 10 mg/ml BSA. Solutions are stored at -15°C in 200- 500-μl samples which are used only once. They are stable for at least three months.

Unlabeled insulin: 0.5 or 1 mg/ml in 0.01 N HCl

Isolated cells or cell membranes.

A. Binding Assays Using Intact Cells

1. Incubation Procedure

For a standard insulin-binding assay with isolated liver cells [42], 200-μl samples of a cell suspension in buffer with 30 mg/ml BSA are dispensed to 95 × 15-mm plastic tubes to give a final concentration of ~1.5 × 10⁶* cells per ml, and are then gassed for ~1 min with 95% O_2-5% CO_2. Tubes are capped with rubber stoppers and allowed to stand at 30°C for 10 min with continuous shaking at 130 cycles per min. Unlabeled insulin is then added (25 μl) to give final concentrations ranging from 1 ng/ml (~25 μU/ml or ~0.17 nM) to 400 ng/ml (~10 mU/ml or ~68 nM). Each

---

*Lower concentrations of liver cells (e.g., ~0.5 × 10⁶/ml) may be employed, especially to reduce hormone degradation.

point is done in triplicate. $[^{125}I]$ Insulin (25 μl) is added to each tube immediately after the unlabeled hormone to give a fixed final concentration ("tracer") of 0.3 to 0.6 ng/ml ($\sim$7.5 to 15 $\mu U/ml$ or $\sim$0.05 to 0.1 nM). Unlabeled hormone is omitted in 4 or 5 tubes and is replaced by buffer (25 μl); these allow the measurement of the amount of labeled insulin bound in the absence of unlabeled insulin, which is usually referred to as initial binding of $[^{125}I]$ insulin or B_0. To measure non-specific binding, $[^{125}I]$ insulin is also incubated in the presence of un-labeled insulin at 50 to 100 $\mu g/ml$. After the addition of unlabeled and labeled insulin, incubation is continued for 30 min at 30°C.

2. Isolation of Cell-Bound Insulin

The cell-bound hormone is isolated by filtration of incubation mixtures on cellulose acetate EAWP (1.0 μm) Millipore filters as follows: Two milliliters of chilled buffer containing 5 mg/ml BSA are rapidly added to the tubes, whose contents are immediately filtered. Tubes are rinsed with 4 ml of buffer that are rapidly transferred onto filters; cells on filters are further washed with another 4 ml of buffer. The radio-activity on the filters is then counted in a gammacounter. The filtration and washing procedure does not consume more than 30 sec for each tube. It is possible to filter several samples in rapid succession (Sampling Manifold, Millipore).

3. Comments

The KRP can be replaced by a Krebs-Ringer bicarbonate buffer containing 1.2 mM $CaCl_2$ (KRB). In studies comparing hormone binding and cAMP accumulation in isolated liver cells [93], KRB containing 30 mg/ml BSA and 10 mM alanine (with or without 1 mM theophylline), pH 7.4, has been used in both studies; at these concentrations, alanine and/or theophylline do not affect insulin binding significantly [42]. Krebs-Ringer bicarbonate [57, 74], Krebs-Ringer-N-2-hydroxyethylpiperazine-N'2-ethanesulfonic acid (KR-HEPES) [72] and 25 mM tris-HCl, pH 7.5 [56], have also been used in studies of insulin binding to isolated fat cells. Studies of insulin binding to lymphocytes [47, 49, 55] or thymocytes [46, 54] have been performed in 25 (or 50) mM tris-HCl buffer containing 120 mM NaCl; 1.2 (or 2.5) mM Mg SO_4, 2.5 (or 5) mM KCl; 10 mM glucose; 1 mM EDTA; and 10 (or 20) mg/ml BSA, pH 7.4 to 7.6; or in Hank's balanced salt solution containing 1 mg/ml BSA [66].

The optimal time and temperature conditions of the assay vary with the type of cell and the concentrations of the reactive species (hormone and receptor). With isolated liver cells at 1.4×10^6 cells per ml, a steady state of binding of $[^{125}I]$ insulin at 1 nM is reached by 20 to 30 min and persists for 60 to 120 min at 30°C [42]. With isolated fat cells, incubations have been performed for 20 [72] or 30 min at 24°C [57], or for 45 min at 37°C [74, 76], and with lymphocytes for 70 to 150 min at 15°C [46, 47, 49, 54, 55]. As pointed out (Sec. IV. B), it is essential to make sure that, under the conditions used, the steady state of binding is reached for all of the concentrations of insulin used. In time-course experiments, the mixture of [^{125}I] insulin and cells is distributed into aliquot samples which are rapidly filtered (or centrifuged, see following discussion) at appropriate time intervals to isolate cell-bound [^{125}I] hormone as indicated. Since the proportion of nonspecific binding may increase with time, it is necessary to determine the nonspecific binding throughout in a simultaneous experiment where [^{125}I] insulin is incubated in the presence of an excess of unlabeled hormone [41, 42].

Either the filtration or centrifugation procedure can be used to isolate cell-bound hormone. To avoid, or minimize, dissociation, the separation must be done rapidly at low temperature. The filtration procedure may be more convenient for the rapid assay of large numbers of samples. It is also possible to rapidly separate cells from cell suspensions by centrifugation through oils. Since [^{125}I] insulin adsorbs strongly to most cellulose derivatives, the choice of membrane for filtration is a critical factor [57]. Cellulose acetate filters (EAWP, 1.0-μm pore diameter) that have been soaked in buffer containing 30 mg/ml BSA for 2 to 3 hr at room temperature before use adsorb < 0.1 to 0.2% of total [^{125}I] insulin and are adequate for studies of [^{125}I] insulin binding to cells [42, 57, 95]. The filtration rate may be impaired if cell concentration is too high. Centrifugation has also been employed to separate cell-bound from free hormone. This method is preferred when large concentrations of cells are required in the assay, as is the case with lymphocytes [45, 47, 49, 55] and thymocytes [46, 54]. As described by Rodbell et al. [123], aliquot samples (100-200 μl) of incubation mixtures are layered onto 200 μl of chilled buffer containing 10 to 20 mg/ml BSA in plastic microtubes. After centrifugation in a microcentrifuge (e.g., Microfuge model 152, Beckman Instruments) at ~10,000 g for 5 min (1-2 min is sufficient for liver cells), the supernatants are removed by aspiration, the surface of the pellet is promptly washed with 200 μl of chilled 10% (wt/wt) sucrose, and the tip of the plastic microtube (with the cell pellet) is excised and counted in a gammacounter. Of special interest for rapid isolation of fat cell-bound hormone is the method described by Gliemann et al. [124], in which cells are rapidly separated from the buffer by centrifugation for 30 sec at 10,000 g through dinonyl phthalate [56, 74, 76]. A similar technique has been described for rapid separation of thymocytes from medium by centrifugation through dibutylphthalate or silicone oil [125]. In addition to rapidity, these techniques minimize the amount of extracellular medium trapped within the cell pellet, which may not be negligible when large concentrations of cells are used.

B. Binding Assays Using Cell Membranes

1. Incubation Procedure

Insulin-binding assays with cell membranes have been performed under conditions which are similar to those used with intact cells. They are listed in Table 2 for liver plasma membranes. With the concentrations of $[^{125}I]$ insulin and membrane used, a steady-state of binding is reached by 30 to 60 min and persists for another 60 to 120 min [41, 52] at 30°C. Degradation of $[^{125}I]$ insulin is < 10 to 15% [52, 122] after 60 min at 30°C. Although a 30-min incubation period has been sufficient, in most instances, to reach steady-state, there has been some variability between time-course experiments regarding the time at which steady-state is achieved. Incubations for 60 min at 30°C allow achievement of a steady-state of binding with virtually all of the $[^{125}I]$ insulin concentrations used. Lower temperatures of incubation require longer periods of time to reach steady state (Sec. V. B. 3).

2. Isolation of Membrane-Bound Insulin

Membrane-bound insulin is isolated by centrifugation in microfuge tubes or by filtration as described (Sec. V. A).

3. Comments

As with intact cells, various buffers have been employed for the study of insulin binding to cell membranes. Krebs-Ringer phosphate has been widely used [11, 14, 26, 38-41, 48, 52, 70, 71, 75, 78, 108, 109, 114, 122, Table 2]), as well as KRB [12, 58, 59, 62, 73]. The use of 0.1 M phosphate buffer and that of 25 mM tris-HCl (pH 7.4) have been reported [68, 69]. The concentration of albumin in the incubation mixture has ranged from 0.8 mg/ml [69] to 35 mg/ml [73] and has been 10 to 15 mg/ml (Table 2) in most studies. Although it has been reported that glucose, Na^+, and K^+ increase maximum binding of insulin by fat pad membranes [73], binding of insulin to cell membranes is virtually unaffected by the nature of the buffer used or by a number of different ionic species, heavy metals, or metal-complexing agents [2; author's unpublished observations]. The pH optimum of binding is between 7.4 and 8, with a rapid falloff on the acid side: At pH 7, the binding is decreased by 60% [78, 109]. Most studies have been conducted at pH 7.5. Very high ionic strength media such as 2 M NaCl have been reported to increase insulin binding to receptors in cell membranes [52, 58, 59]. This has been interpreted as resulting from the "unmasking" of binding sites [2, 58, 59] that are otherwise "buried" and inaccessible to the

TABLE 2. Incubation Conditions for Insulin–Binding Assay in Liver Plasma Membranes

Reagent or buffer	Volume (μl)	Final concentration
Krebs–Ringer phosphate (KRP) with 30 mg/ml bovine serum albumin (BSA), pH 7.5	200	14 mg/ml BSA
Membranes: 100–150 μg protein in KRP	200	0.2–0.3 mg/ml
Unlabeled insulin in KRP with 10 mg/ml BSA, pH 7.5	50	0.17–34 nM[a]
^{125}I-insulin in KRP with 10 mg/ml BSA, pH 7.5	50	0.05–0.15 nM

[a] An excess of unlabeled insulin (10–17 μM) is also used to measure nonspecific binding (see text).

hormone. It has also been shown, however, that insulin degradation is decreased and that the apparent affinity constants of binding are increased in 2 M NaCl [52]; furthermore, insulin receptors in liver plasma membranes are degraded at a faster rate in high ionic strength media [52].

Although most studies have been conducted at 30°C [11, 14, 26, 38-41, 48, 52, 75, 78, 108, 109, 122] or at 24°C [12, 58, 59, 62, 68, 69] for 30 to 60 min, higher temperatures, e.g., 37°C [70, 73] and, more often, lower temperatures, e.g., 20°C [110, 126, 127] or 4°C [52, 114] have been used. As already pointed out (Sec. IV. B) there is a distinct value in measuring insulin binding at lower temperatures, since this decreases insulin degradation [38] and also increases the amount of insulin bound [52]. This requires, however, a longer period of incubation due to the slower rate of binding, e.g., 5 to 6 hr at 20°C [110, 114, 127] or 12 to 24 hr at 4°C [52, 114].

A sensitized insulin-binding assay has been developed [author's unpublished data] by incubating liver plasma membranes with insulin in two sequential steps at 4°C. In step 1, varying concentrations of unlabeled insulin (or unknown samples) are incubated with membranes for 8 hr. Step 2 is initiated with the addition of [^{125}I] insulin and incubation is continued for 16 hr. Medium and reagents are as indicated in Table 2, and plasma (200 μl in 500 μl incubation volume, i.e., 1:2.5 diluted) can be substituted to the KRB-BSA buffer (Fig. 3). This assay detects unlabeled insulin at 0.5 ng/ml (i.e., about 12.5 μU/ml or ~0.1 nM). Insulin-free plasma does not alter the [^{125}I] insulin binding to a very large extent, nor does it impair the sensitivity of the system to insulin (Fig. 3). Thus, unlabeled insulin at 1 ng/ml and at 5 ng/ml displaces 20 to 25% and 40 to 50% of the [^{125}I] insulin, respectively, regardless of the presence of plasma (Fig. 3). The sensitivity of this assay, which combines the effects of incubation at 4°C and preincubation of membranes with unlabeled insulin, is improved by a factor of three to five over that of the usual one-step binding assay conducted for 30 to 60 min at 30°C.

The final volume of incubation mixtures is usually 0.5 ml. Smaller volumes (e.g., 0.25 ml) have been preferred when membranes are in limited amount [39, 114]. The membrane concentration in the assay usually ranges from 0.1 to 0.3 mg protein per ml. Incubation can be performed directly in the microfuge tubes [127]. Care must be taken in using centrifugal methods to isolate membrane-bound hormone that the force and duration of centrifugation are sufficient to recover all of the membranes; this is of particular importance if the membrane preparation consists mostly of small vesicles. Membrane-bound insulin has also been isolated by filtration of incubation mixtures. Filters of smaller pore size than that for intact cells are employed, e.g., cellulose acetate EGWP (0.2 μm) Millipore filters [41, 58, 59, 62, 68, 69]. The filtration and washing procedure is similar to that described for the isolation of cell-bound insulin (Sec. V. A).

C. Binding Assays Using Solubilized Material

The effect of the detergent on the hormone binding must be evaluated, and the concentration of solubilized material should be adjusted accordingly [61]. As in binding assays with intact cells or cell membranes, unlabeled insulin at 25 to 50 $\mu g/ml$ is added to control tubes to determine the nonspecific binding [63]. Separation of receptor-bound from free hormone has been accomplished by selective precipitation [128] of the insulin-receptor complex [61, 63] by polyethylene glycol (Carbowax 6000). Separation of bound and free insulin can be performed by gel filtration; however, $\sim$20 to 30% less binding is measured by this method, presumably due to some dissociation of the hormone-receptor complex during chromatography [61]. In contrast to solubilized material from fat cell and liver membranes, insulin-binding material solubilized from cultured lymphocytes by the nonionic detergent NP-40 does not precipitate upon extensive dialysis against 10 mM phosphate-buffered saline (PBS), pH 7.6 [96]. Incubations with this material have been performed for 70 to 90 min at 23°C in PBS, pH 7.6, and separation of bound from unbound insulin has been accomplished [96] by gel filtration on Sephadex G-50 or by adsorption of unbound hormone to talc [129]. Water-soluble insulin receptors obtained from human lymphocytes in culture [97] have also been used, and the insulin-receptor complex has been isolated by the polyethylene glycol precipitation method [128].

D. Expression of Results

1. Expression of Binding Data

Binding data have been expressed in a variety of manners. It is beyond the scope of this chapter to present and discuss all of them. Many of the studies cited in the reference list, and more particularly Refs. 52 and 130, will provide the reader with detailed and critical analysis of the quantitative aspects of the binding data. The binding of $[^{125}I]$ insulin has usually been expressed as counts per minute (cpm) bound or as percent of total radioactivity bound, and plotted as a function of the concentration of unlabeled insulin (or total insulin) in the incubation mixture. This results in a "displacement" curve with decreasing radioactivity bound in the presence of increasing concentrations of unlabeled hormone (Fig. 3). The percent of $[^{125}I]$ insulin bound is measured as $100 \times B/T$, where B is the radioactivity (cpm) bound and T is the total radioactivity (cpm) in the corresponding sample. Binding of $[^{125}I]$ insulin has also been expressed (Fig. 4) as percent of initial binding $100 \times B/B_0$ where B_0 represents the binding of $[^{125}I]$ insulin in the absence of unlabeled hormone. The binding may also be plotted as the ratio of bound (B) to free (F) insulin, or B/F. In most instances, binding has been expressed as specific binding, i.e., after subtraction of nonspecific (NS) binding.

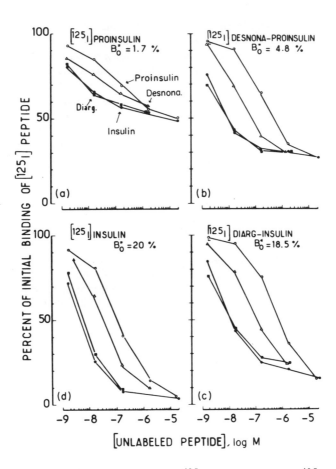

FIG. 4. Binding and displacement of [^{125}I] proinsulin (a), [^{125}I] desnonapeptide proinsulin (b), [^{125}I] diarginine insulin (c) and [^{125}I] insulin (d)
by unlabeled proinsulin (open circles), desnonapeptide proinsulin (open
triangles), diarginine insulin (closed squares), and insulin (closed circles).
Binding is expressed as percent of initial binding (see text, Sec. V. D) of
[^{125}I] peptide and is plotted as a function of unlabeled peptide concentration.
The percentage of total radioactivity initially bound (B_0*) is indicated for
each [^{125}I] peptide. The nonspecific binding has not been subtracted.
Reprinted from Ref. 41, by courtesy of the American Society for Clinical
Investigation, Inc.

Thus, the specific binding of [^{125}I] insulin has been expressed as $100 \times$ B - NS/T (percent bound) or as B - NS/F (bound-to-free ratio), where NS is the counts per minute bound in the presence of a great excess of unlabeled insulin (see Sec. IV. B). Under conditions where insulin degradation must be accounted for, the fraction of intact free hormone has been determined [38, 52]; then [52]

$$\frac{B}{F} \text{ (corrected)} = \frac{B - NS}{F \times \text{fraction intact}}$$

2. Quantitative Analysis of Binding Data

The amount of insulin bound, expressed on a mole basis (e.g., picomoles or femtomoles) or a weight basis (e.g., nanograms or picograms), can be obtained by multiplying the percent of [^{125}I] insulin bound by the corresponding total concentration of hormone. The value thus obtained represents the concentration of bound insulin. By dividing this value by the concentration of cells, membrane protein, or solubilized material protein in the incubation mixtures, one obtains the amount of insulin bound per cells (e.g., per 10^5 or 10^6 cells) or per weight unit (usually milligrams) of membrane or solubilized protein. The amount of insulin bound is plotted as a function of total hormone concentration (Figs. 2 and 5); this permits an approximation of the maximum insulin-binding capacity [41, 42, 57-59, 61, 63, 109, 110, 114, 127]. Using this type (Michaelis-Menten) of plot to determine the apparent dissociation constant of the hormone-receptor complex requires expression of the amount bound as a function of free (rather than total) hormone concentration, unless the total concentration of receptor is much smaller than the dissociation constant [130]. Scatchard treatment of the binding data has also been widely employed [11, 39, 47, 54-56, 62, 63, 68, 72, 75, 78, 114, 126, 127]. In this analysis, the B/F ratio is plotted as a function of the concentration (or amount) of bound insulin. In most studies where the specific binding of insulin to cell membranes, as well as to intact cells, has been analyzed by this method, the resultant points have been found to fit a model with two orders of binding sites: a high affinity-low capacity site and a low affinity-high capacity site [11, 39, 47, 54-56, 62, 68, 75, 78, 114, 126, 127]. Scatchard plots permit the calculation of affinity constants and binding capacities. However, the use of this and other methods of analysis requires several important assumptions [52]. It has been shown [51] that progressive saturation of the receptors by insulin reduces their affinity for the hormone, which suggests that the insulin-receptor interaction exhibits negative cooperativity. In this case, the upward concavity of the Scatchard plot would reflect the continuously decreasing affinity of the insulin receptor, rather than a true heterogeneity of the receptor population. In the presence of cooperativity, Hill analysis provides a useful means of comparing average affinities and quantifying

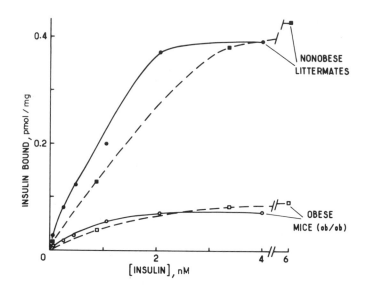

FIG. 5. Binding of insulin to fat cell plasma membranes from obese
hyperglycemic (ob/ob) mice and from their nonobese littermates. The
nonspecific binding has been subtracted and amounts of insulin specifically
bound are plotted as a function of insulin concentration. Results of
separate experiments with two different preparations of membranes for
each group of mice are depicted by solid lines and dashed lines. Replotted
from data shown in Ref. 39 and from Ref. 4, courtesy of Médecine et Hygiène.

cooperative interactions [127]. The Lineweaver-Burk plot has also been
used to determine the apparent dissociation constant of the hormone-
receptor complex and the binding capacity of receptors in studies of
insulin binding to isolated fat cells [56, 74]. The limitations of this type
of analysis (Scatchard, Lineweaver-Burk) when two or more orders of
binding sites, or when cooperativity between the sites, are present must
be reemphasized [3, 52, 130, 131], and it should be kept in mind that, in
most cases, the numbers (affinity constants, binding capacities) derived
from these analyses represent only approximations.

VI. APPLICATIONS OF INSULIN-RECEPTOR STUDIES

Two types of studies will be presented as examples of direct applications.
One type is concerned with the use of insulin-receptor binding systems to
study hormone structure-function relationships. The other type deals
with the search for a defect of the insulin receptor in pathological states.

A. Structure-Function Relationships

In studies compa ring insulin activity to the hormone structure, five
functional properties of the hormone may be considered: (1) the binding
affinity to receptor; (2) the ability to induce negative cooperativity between the receptor sites; (3) the ability to react with the degrading site(s);
(4) the biological potency and efficacy; and (5) the immunological reactivity. Properties (1), (2), and (3) can be directly explored by investi-
gating interactions between insulin and intact cells or cell membranes.
Properties (4) and (5) are tested by bioassays and immunoassays. A
large number of insulins, insulin analogs, and derivatives have been
studied for binding, biological activity, and induction of negative cooperativity. As pointed out (Sec. IV. A), there has been a close parallel
between the binding affinity to receptor and the biological potency in all
cases, but not between binding and negative cooperativity [132]. The
structural requirements for binding to receptor and expression of biological activity are strictly dependent on the three-dimensional structure
of insulin. Any substantial modification of this structure has caused a
parallel loss of binding affinity and biological potency [14, 37, 40, 76].
In this respect, certain residues (Gly A_1, Asn A_{21}, the C-terminal
octapeptide $B_{23}-B_{30}$ sequence of the B chain), and the neighboring regions
in the three-dimensional structure are of particular importance [37].

The relative binding affinity of an insulin analog or derivative for the
insulin receptor has been estimated from displacement curves in which
the ability of the analog or derivative to inhibit the binding [^{125}I] insulin
is compared to that of native insulin. Each analog or derivative is tested
at varying concentrations and binding data, expressed as percent of
initial binding of [^{125}I] insulin (see Sec. V. D), are plotted as a function
of unlabeled peptide concentration (Fig. 4). The concentration of insulin
analog or derivative that produces 50% inhibition of the [^{125}I] insulin
binding has been taken to approximate its binding affinity relative to that
of native insulin [40, 41]. The binding affinity has also been expressed
as inhibition constant (Ki) derived from the displacement of [^{125}I] insulin
by insulin derivatives [76]. Logit transformation of the [^{125}I] insulin
binding has been employed to linearize the data [122].

Direct studies of binding of [^{125}I] labeled insulin analogs allow one
to investigate the possibility that an insulin analog (e.g., proinsulin or
proinsulin-like components) might also interact with specific receptors
distinct from the insulin receptors, i.e., with receptors whose affinity
for analog would be equal to or greater than their affinity for insulin.
This has not been found to be the case for proinsulin and proinsulin-like

components [41], which exhibit the same order of relative potency in all
of the binding systems studied and whose direct binding is in close proportion to their relative potency in inhibiting the binding of [^{125}I] insulin

(Fig. 4). Since the immunological reactivity of proinsulin (and proinsulin-like components) is usually much higher, with most anti-insulin sera, than their binding affinity to receptor and their biological potency (Table 2), radioreceptor assay (see Fig. 3 and Refs. 133 and 134) of endogenous insulins and proinsulin components is of great interest in certain pathological states [135]. Radioreceptor assays for insulin complement the conventional radioimmunoassay and bioassay and offer a unique advantage in that they are based on affinity for a biospecific receptor rather than on immunospecificity. With this technique, it is also possible to screen rapidly and specifically a variety of natural and synthetic insulins and insulin-like molecules.

B. The Insulin Receptor in Pathological States

The insulin receptor is not a static structure. It has been shown that the binding of insulin to fat cell [39], liver [11, 108, 109], and heart muscle [13, 114] plasma membranes is reduced by 60 to 85% in obese hyper-glycemic (ob/ob) mice as compared to their thin littermates (Fig. 5). Analyses of these data have revealed that the decrease in insulin binding in ob/ob mice is mainly, if not exclusively, accounted for by a decrease in the insulin receptor concentrations [3, 11, 39, 54, 108, 109, 126, 127]. A similar defect of the insulin receptor has been observed in db/db mice [109, 127; author's unpublished observations with M. H. Laudat and P. Laudat], in the acquired obesity of gold-thioglucose-treated mice [109, 127], and in states of glucocorticoid excess in the rat [48, 109]. Impairment of insulin binding has also been reported in circulating mononuclear cells from obese human subjects [49] and from insulin-resistant patients [50], and in fat cell membranes [81, author's unpublished observations with M. H. Laudat and P. Laudat] from obese human subjects.

In these comparative studies, it is essential to accurately determine the purity of the membrane preparations [107]. Accordingly, the studies of insulin binding in plasma membranes of the ob/ob mouse have included several kinds of controls. Thus, with the obese mouse liver, in spite of the increased volume and weight of the organ, the yield and purity of the plasma membrane fraction was comparable to that of the thin mouse as judged by protein content, membrane marker enzymes (5'-nucleotidase and adenylate cyclase), and contamination by other organelles [3, 11, 107, 108]. Furthermore, the protein subunit compositions were remarkably similar for both groups of purified membranes [11, 107]. Another way to minimize the risk of differential plasma membrane selection between two groups has been to study other cell-surface receptors. It has thus been found that, in contrast to the marked reduction (70-80%) in insulin receptors in liver membranes of the ob/ob mouse, there is little. (~20%) or no change in the membrane binding of glucagon, growth hormone, or isoproterenol [3, 11]. Similarly, the binding of norepinephrine in fat cell membranes of the ob/ob mouse is decreased by ~30%, whereas insulin binding in the same membranes is decreased by 80% [113]. It has also been found that, despite their increased size, hepatocytes from the ob/ob mouse bind significantly less insulin than do hepatocytes from the thin littermates [11]. Therefore, the decrease in insulin receptors in the ob/ob mouse is observed whether the data are expressed per cell, per unit of surface area, per milligram of membrane protein, per unit of plasma membrane marker enzymes, or per receptor site for other hormones such as glucagon, growth hormone, and catecholamine [11]. The insulin receptor defect has also been demonstrated in thymocytes [54] and in heart muscle membranes [13, 114] of the ob/ob mouse, which excludes the complications related to the cell size and organ volume, since the mean cell size of thymocytes and the heart weight are similar in the obese and thin mice. Finally, there is no increase in hormone degradation, which might explain the defect in binding observed [11, 54, 114, 127]. In addition to paying a particular attention to these points, it is necessary to perform binding experiments with membranes that have had identical previous history in terms of preparation, evaluation of purification, and storage conditions. It is also imperative to use the same preparation of labeled insulin and the same standards of unlabeled hormone when comparing binding in membranes from two groups of animals. Attempts should be made to use similar membrane protein (or cell) concentrations for the two groups. Studies with circulating blood mononuclear cells also require precise identification of the cell types which are compared, since considerable variation has been observed among various circulating mononuclear cells in their ability to bind insulin, as already mentioned (Sec. III. B).

The possibility of directly and quantitatively studying insulin-receptor interactions in states of altered sensitivity to insulin will probably yield valuable information regarding both the pathophysiology of these syndromes and the factors which regulate the insulin receptor.

ACKNOWLEDGMENTS

The author is deeply indebted to the many friends and colleagues who participated in various aspects of the work covered in this chapter and to those who provided preprints of unpublished articles. The careful preparation of the manuscript by D. Lhenry and the skillful technical assistance of N. Grenier-Brossette are gratefully acknowledged. The personal work covered in this chapter was supported mainly by the Institut National de la Santé et de la Recherche Médicale (INSERM, Paris, France), and by the National Institutes of Health (NIH, Bethesda, Md., U.S.A.).

REFERENCES*

1. J. Roth, Metabolism, 22:1059 (1973).

2. P. Cuatrecasas, in Annual Review of Biochemistry (E. E. Snell, ed.),
   Vol. 43, Annual Review Inc., Palo Alto, 1974, pp. 169-214.

3. C. R. Kahn, in Methods in Membrane Biology (E. D. Korn, ed.),
   Vol 3, Plenum, New York, 1975, pp. 81-146.

4. P. Freychet, G. Rosselin, D. Bataille, F. Rançon, M. Fouchereau,
   and Y. Broer, in Cyclic AMP, New Antidiabetic Drugs, Parasitosis
   Chemotherapy (B. Glasson and A. Benakis, eds.), Médecine et Hygiène
   Geneva, 1974, pp. 7-26 (in French).

5. R. J. Lefkowitz, J. Roth, W. Pricer, and I. Pastan, Proc. Natl.
   Acad. Sci. U.S.A., 65:745 (1970).

6. S. Y. Lin and T. L. Goodfriend, Am. J. Physiol., 218:1319 (1970).

7. I. Pastan, J. Roth, and V. Macchia, Proc. Natl. Acad. Sci. U.S.A.,
   56:1802 (1966).

8. T. Kono, J. Biol. Chem., 244:1772 (1969).

9. P. Cuatrecasas, Proc. Natl. Acad. Sci. U.S.A., 63:450 (1969).

10. H. M. Katzen and G. J. Vlahakes, Science, 179:1142 (1973).

11. C. R. Kahn, D. M. Neville, Jr., and J. Roth, J. Biol. Chem., 248:
    244 (1973).

12. J. J. M. Bergeron, W. H. Evans, and I. I. Geschwind, J. Cell.
    Biol., 59:771 (1973).

13. P. Freychet and E. Forgue, Diabetes, 23 (Suppl. 1):354, Abstract
    (1974).

14. P. Freychet, J. Roth, and D. M. Neville, Jr., Proc. Natl. Acad.
    Sci. U.S.A., 68:1833 (1971).

15. S. A. Berson and R. S. Yalow, in Methods in Investigative and
    Diagnostic Endocrinology (S. A. Berson and R. S. Yalow, eds.),
    Vol. 2A, North Holland, Amsterdam, 1973, pp. 84-125.

16. W. C. Stadie, N. Haugaard, and M. Vaughan, J. Biol. Chem., 200:
    745 (1953).

17. P. M. Edelman, S. L. Rosenthal, and I. L. Schwartz, Nature, 197:
    878 (1963).

---

*Review of the literature as of December 1974.

18. C. J. Garratt, R. J. Jarrett, and H. Keen, Biochim. Biophys. Acta, 121:143 (1966).

19. H. J. Wohltmann and H. T. Narahara, J. Biol. Chem., 241:4931 (1966).

20. E. R. Arquilla, H. Ooms, and K. Mercola, J. Clin. Invest., 47:474 (1968).

21. K. Newerly and S. A. Berson, Proc. Soc. Exptl. Biol. Med., 94: 751 (1957).

22. L. W. De Zoeten and R. Van Strick, Rec. Trav. Chim. (Pays-Bas), 80:927 (1961).

23. C. J. Garratt, Nature, 201:1324 (1964).

24. J. L. Izzo, A. Roncone, M. J. Izzo, and W. F. Bale, J. Biol. Chem., 239:3749 (1964).

25. W. W. Bromer, M. E. Boucher, and J. M. Patterson, Biochem. Biophys. Res. Commun., 53:134 (1973).

26. P. Freychet, J. Roth, and D. M. Neville, Jr., Biochem. Biophys. Res. Commun., 43:400 (1971).

27. J. Schlichtkrull, J. Brange, A. H. Christiansen, O. Hallund, L. G. Heding, and K. H. Jorgensen, Diabetes, 21 (Suppl. 2):649 (1972).

28. R. E. Chance, Diabetes, 21 (Suppl. 2):461 (1972).

29. W. M. Hunter and F. C. Greenwood, Nature, 194:495 (1962).

30. H. Edelhoch, J. Biol. Chem., 237:2778 (1962).

31. L. W. De Zoeten and E. Havinga, Rec. Trav. Chim. (Pays-Bas), 80:917 (1961).

32. B. Lambert, B. Ch. J. Sutter, and Cl. Jacquemin, Hormone Metab. Res., 4:149 (1972).

33. B. Lambert, J. M. Félix, and Cl. Jacquemin, C.R. Acad. Sci. Paris, 275:711 (1972).

34. D. A. Bihler and J. W. S. Morris, Biochem. J., 130:321 (1972).

35. J. C. Sodoyez, F. Sodoyez-Goffaux, M. M. Goff, A. E. Zimmerman, and E. R. Arquilla, J. Biol. Chem., 250:4268 (1975).

36. J. L. Hamlin and E. R. Arquilla, J. Biol. Chem., 249:21 (1974).

37. T. L. Blundell, J. F. Cutfield, S. M. Cutfield, E. J. Dodson, G. G. Dodson, D. C. Hodgkin, and D. A. Mercola, Diabetes, 21 (Suppl. 2):492 (1972).

38. P. Freychet, R. Kahn, J. Roth, and D. M. Neville, Jr., J. Biol. Chem., 247:3953 (1972).

39. P. Freychet, M. H. Laudat, P. Laudat, G. Rosselin, C. R. Kahn, P. Gorden, and J. Roth, FEBS Lett., 25:339 (1972).

40. P. Freychet, D. Brandenburg, and A. Wollmer, Diabetologia, 10:1 (1974).

41. P. Freychet, J. Clin. Invest., 54:1020 (1974).

42. P. Freychet, G. Rosselin, F. Rançon, M. Fouchereau, and Y. Broer, Hormone Metab. Res., (Suppl. Series) 5:72 (1974).

43. A. Le Cam, P. Freychet, and P. Lenoir, Diabetes, 24:566 (1975).

44. R. S. Yalow and S. A. Berson, J. Clin. Invest., 39:1157 (1960).

45. J. R. Gavin, III, J. Roth, P. Jen, and P. Freychet, Proc. Natl. Acad. Sci. U.S.A., 69:747 (1972).

46. I. D. Goldfine, J. D. Gardner, and D. M. Neville, Jr., J. Biol. Chem., 247:6919 (1972).

47. J. R. Gavin, III, P. Gorden, J. Roth, J. A. Archer, and D. N. Buell, J. Biol. Chem., 248:2202 (1973).

48. I. D. Goldfine, C. R. Kahn, D. M. Neville, Jr., J. Roth, M. M. Garrison, and R. W. Bates, Biochem. Biophys. Res. Commun., 53:852 (1973).

49. J. A. Archer, P. Gorden, J. R. Gavin, III, M. A. Lesniak, and J. Roth, J. Clin. Endocrinol. Metab., 36:627 (1973).

50. J. A. Archer, P. Gorden, C. R. Kahn, J. R. Gavin, III, D. M. Neville, Jr., M. M. Martin, and J. Roth, J. Clin. Invest., 21:4, Abstract (1973).

51. P. De Meyts, J. Roth, D. M. Neville, Jr., J. R. Gavin, III, and M. A. Lesniak, Biochem. Biophys. Res. Commun., 55:154 (1973).

52. C. R. Kahn, P. Freychet, J. Roth, and D. M. Neville, Jr., J. Biol. Chem., 249:2249 (1974).

53. J. R. Gavin, III, J. Roth, D. M. Neville, Jr., P. De Meyts, and D. N. Buell, Proc. Natl. Acad. Sci. U.S.A., 71:84 (1974).

54. A. H. Soll, I. D. Goldfine, J. Roth, C. R. Kahn, and D. M. Neville, Jr., J. Biol. Chem., 249:4127 (1974).

55. J. Olefsky and G. M. Reaven, J. Clin. Endocrinol. Metab., 38:554 (1974).

56. J. M. Olefsky, P. Jen, and G. M. Reaven, Diabetes, 23:565 (1974).

57. P. Cuatrecasas, Proc. Natl. Acad. Sci. U.S.A., 68:1264 (1971).

58. P. Cuatrecasas, J. Biol. Chem., 246:7265 (1971).

59. P. Cuatrecasas, B. Desbuquois, and F. Krug, Biochem. Biophys. Res. Commun., 44:333 (1971).

60. P. Cuatrecasas and G. Illiano, J. Biol. Chem., 246:4938 (1971).

61. P. Cuatrecasas, Proc. Natl. Acad. Sci. U.S.A., 69:318 (1972).

62. J. M. Hammond, L. Jarett, I. K. Mariz, and W. H. Daughaday, Biochem. Biophys. Res. Commun., 49:1122 (1972).

63. P. Cuatrecasas, J. Biol. Chem., 247:1980 (1972).

64. R. L. Hintz, D. R. Clemmons, L. E. Underwood, and J. J. Van Wyk, Proc. Natl. Acad. Sci. U.S.A., 69:2351 (1972).

65. V. G. Bennett and P. Cuatrecasas, Science, 176:805 (1972).

66. U. Krug, F. Krug, and P. Cuatrecasas, Proc. Natl. Acad. Sci. U.S.A., 69:2604 (1972).

67. J. N. Livingston, P. Cuatrecasas, and D. H. Lockwood, Science, 177:626 (1972).

68. B. I. Posner, Diabetes, 23:209 (1974).

69. B. I. Posner, P. A. Kelly, R. P. C. Shiu, and H. G. Friesen, Endocrinology, 95:521 (1974).

70. P. D. R. House and M. J. Weidemann, Biochem. Biophys, Res. Commun., 41:541 (1970).

71. P. D. R. House, FEBS Lett., 16:339 (1971).

72. T. Kono and F. W. Barham, J. Biol. Chem., 246:6210 (1971).

73. C. A. Robinson, Jr., B. R. Boshell, and W. J. Reddy, Biochim. Biophys. Acta, 290:84 (1972).

74. S. Gammeltoft and J. Gliemann, Biochim. Biophys. Acta, 320:16 (1973).

75. C. Freeman, K. Karoly, and R. C. Adelman, Biochem. Biophys. Res. Commun., 54:1573 (1973).

76. J. Gliemann and S. Gammeltoft, Diabetologia, 10:105 (1974).

77. F. Haour and J. Bertrand, J. Clin. Endocrinol. Metab., 38:334 (1974).

78. P. Freychet, C. R. Kahn, J. Roth, and D. M. Neville, Jr., in

Endocrinology (R. O. Scow ed.), Excerpta Medica, Amsterdam, 1973, International Congress Series No. 273, pp. 335-340.

79. J. L. Izzo, W. F. Bale, M. J. Izzo, and A. Roncone, J. Biol. Chem., 239:3743 (1964).

80. L. Shlatz and G. V. Marinetti, Science, 176:175 (1972).

81. G. V. Marinetti, L. Shlatz, and K. Reilly, in Insulin Action (I. B. Fritz, ed.), Academic Press, New York, 1972, pp. 207-276.

82. C. Y. Yip, in Insulin Action (I. B. Fritz, ed.), Academic Press, New York, 1972, pp. 115-135.

83. J. Biener, F. K. Jansen, and D. Brandenburg, Diabetologia, 9:53 (1973).

84. L. Orci, D. P. Bataille, P. Freychet, and G. Rosselin, Diabetes, 24 (Suppl. 2), 393 (1975) (abstract).

85. L. Jarett and R. M. Smith, J. Biol. Chem., 249:7024 (1974).

86. D. D. Soderman, J. Gemershausen, and H. M. Katzen, Proc. Natl. Acad. Sci. U.S.A., 70:792 (1973).

87. H. J. Eisen, I. D. Goldfine, and W. H. Glinsmann, Proc. Natl. Acad. Sci. U.S.A., 70:3454 (1973).

88. M. Rodbell, J. Biol. Chem., 235:375 (1964).

89. P. Cuatrecasas, J. Biol. Chem., 246:6522 (1971).

90. R. M. M. El-Allawy and J. Gliemann, Biochim. Biophys. Acta, 273:97 (1972).

91. J. M. Olefsky, J. Johnson, F. Liu, P. Edwards, and S. Baur, Diabetes, 24:801 (1975).

92. M. N. Berry and D. S. Friend, J. Cell. Biol., 43:506 (1969).

93. G. Rosselin, P. Freychet, M. Fouchereau, F. Rançon, and Y. Broer, Hormone Metab. Res., (Suppl. Series) 5:78 (1974).

94. T. Oka and Y. J. Topper, Proc. Natl. Acad. Sci. U.S.A., 68:2066 (1971).

95. E. O'Keefe and P. Cuatrecasas, Biochim. Biophys. Acta, 343:64 (1974).

96. J. R. Gavin, III, D. L. Mann, D. N. Buell, and J. Roth, Biochem. Biophys. Res. Commun., 49:870 (1972).

97. J. R. Gavin, III, D. N. Buell, and J. Roth, Science, 178:168 (1972).

98. A. Boyum, Scand. J. Clin. Lab. Invest., Suppl., 1:109 (1968).

99. A. R. Bianco, R. H. Schwartz, and B. S. Handwerger, Diabetologia, 10:359, Abstract (1974).

100. R. H. Schwartz, A. R. Bianco, B. S. Handwerger, and C. R. Kahn, Proc. Natl. Acad. Sci. U.S.A., 72:474 (1975).

101. J. Gliemann, S. Gammeltoft, and J. Vinten, J. Biol. Chem., 250:3368 (1975).

102. B. Desbuquois, F. Krug, and P. Cuatrecasas, Biochim. Biophys. Acta, 343:101 (1974).

103. G. Illiano and P. Cuatrecasas, Science, 175:906 (1972).

104. D. M. Neville, Jr., J. Biophys. Biochem. Cytol., 8:413 (1960).

105. D. M. Neville, Jr., Biochim. Biophys. Acta, 154:540 (1968).

106. S. L. Pohl, L. Birnbaumer, and M. Rodbell, J. Biol. Chem., 246:1849 (1971).

107. D. M. Neville, Jr. and C. R. Kahn, in Methods in Molecular Biology (A. I. Laskin and J. A. Last, eds.), Vol. 5, Dekker, New York, 1974, pp. 57-88.

108. C. R. Kahn, D. M. Neville, Jr., P. Gorden, P. Freychet, and J. Roth, Biochem. Biophys. Res. Commun., 48:135 (1972).

109. C. R. Kahn, A. H. Soll, D. M. Neville, Jr., I. D. Goldfine, J. A. Archer, P. Gorden, and J. Roth, in Fogarty International Proceedings, Conference on Obesity (G. Bray, ed.), Bethesda, 1974.

110. D. M. Neville, Jr., C. R. Kahn, A. Soll, and J. Roth, in Protides of the Biological Fluids (H. Peeters, ed.), Pergamon Press, New York, 1973, pp. 269-273.

111. D. W. McKeel and L. Jarett, J. Cell. Biol., 44:417 (1970).

112. M. H. Laudat, J. Pairault, P. Boyer, N. Martin, and P. Laudat, Biochim. Biophys. Acta, 255:1005 (1972).

113. P. Laudat, M. H. Laudat, and P. Freychet, in VIII Congress of the International Diabetes Federation, Excerpta Medica, Amsterdam, International Congress Series No. 280, p. 75 (abstract).

114. M. E. Forgue and P. Freychet, Diabetes, 24:715 (1975).

115. A. M. Kidwai, M. A. Radcliffe, G. Duchon, and E. E. Daniel, Biochem. Biophys. Res. Commun., 45:901 (1971).

116. K. D. Hepp, Eur. J. Biochem., 31:266 (1972).

117. G. Rosselin and P. Freychet, Biochim. Biophys. Acta, 304:541 (1973).

118. F. Leray, A. M. Chambaut, M. L. Perrenoud, and J. Hanoune, Eur. J. Biochem., 38:185 (1973).

119. P. D. R. House, P. Poulis, and M. J. Weidemann, Eur. J. Biochem., 24:429 (1972).

120. N. A. Giorgio, C. B. Johnson, and M. Blecher, J. Biol. Chem., 249:428 (1974).

121. K. Megyesi, C. R. Kahn, J. Roth, E. R. Froesch, R. E. Humbel, J. Zapf, and D. M. Neville, Jr., Biochem. Biophys. Res. Commun., 57:307 (1974).

122. J. Simon, P. Freychet, and G. Rosselin, Endocrinology, 95:1439 (1974).

123. M. Rodbell, H. M. J. Krans, S. L. Pohl, and L. Birnbaumer, J. Biol. Chem., 246:1861 (1971).

124. J. Gliemann, K. Østerlind, J. Vinten, and S. Gammeltoft, Biochim. Biophys. Acta, 286:1 (1972).

125. P. A. Andreasen, B. P. Schaumburg, K. Østerlind, J. Vinten, S. Gammeltoft, and J. Gliemann, Anal. Biochem., 59:610 (1974).

126. A. H. Soll, C. R. Kahn, and D. M. Neville, Jr., J. Biol. Chem., 250:4702 (1975).

127. A. H. Soll, C. R. Kahn, D. M. Neville, Jr., and J. Roth, J. Clin. Invest., 56:769 (1975).

128. B. Desbuquois and G. D. Aurbach, J. Clin. Endocrinol., 33:732 (1971).

129. G. Rosselin, R. Assan, R. S. Yalow, and S. A. Berson, Nature, 212:355 (1966).

130. D. Rodbard, in Receptors for Reproductive Hormones (B. W. O'Malley and A. R. Means, eds.), Plenum, New York, 1973, pp. 289–326.

131. E. E. Baulieu and J. P. Raynaud, Eur. J. Biochem., 13:293 (1970).

132. P. De Meyts, J. Roth, D. M. Neville, Jr., and P. Freychet, in 56th Meeting of the Endocrine Society, Atlanta, June 1974 (abstract).

133. P. Gorden, J. R. Gavin, III, C. R. Kahn, J. A. Archer, M. Lesniak, C. Hendricks, D. M. Neville, Jr., and J. Roth, Pharmacol. Rev., 25:179 (1973).

134. F. Rançon, M. Laburthe, G. Rosselin, and P. Freychet, Hormone Metab. Res., 6:489 (1974).

135. P. Gorden, J. Roth, P. Freychet, and R. Kahn, Diabetes, 21 (Suppl. 2):673 (1972).

Chapter 13

METHODS FOR THE BIOCHEMICAL IDENTIFICATION
OF INSULIN RECEPTORS

Morley D. Hollenberg
Pedro Cuatrecasas*

Department of Pharmacology and Experimental Therapeutics
Department of Medicine
The Johns Hopkins University School of Medicine
Baltimore, Maryland

I. INTRODUCTION   430

II. GENERAL PROPERTIES OF LIGAND–RECEPTOR
INTERACTIONS AND TECHNICAL CONSIDERATIONS   431

   A. Number and Affinity of Receptors   431
   B. Preparation of Radioactive Insulin Derivatives   431
   C. Rates of Association and Dissociation   433
   D. The Problem of Receptor Identification and
      Nonreceptor Insulin Interactions   434
   E. Methods for the Measurement of Insulin-Receptor
      Interactions   439
   F. Analysis of Binding Data   440

III. MEASUREMENTS OF THE INTERACTION OF INSULIN
WITH MEMBRANE RECEPTORS   442

   A. Insulin Receptors in Fat and Liver   442

*Current affiliation: The Wellcome Research Laboratories, Burroughs
Wellcome Company, Research Triangle Park, North Carolina.

B. Enzymatic Probes of Insulin-Receptor Interactions   451
C. Solubilization of Insulin Receptors   455
D. Macromolecular Insulin Derivatives and Receptor Studies   460
E. Insulin Receptors in Cultured Cells   464

IV. SUMMARY   471

    REFERENCES   472

I. INTRODUCTION

During the past decade, considerable progress has been made in the study, identification, and purification of a variety of membrane-localized hormone receptors, many of which are dealt with in this work. The studies of the interaction of insulin with receptor structures, to be described in this chapter, can serve not only to illustrate a general approach to the elucidation of ligand-membrane interactions, but also to reveal some of the limitations and pitfalls of these approaches. Each polypeptide may present special technical problems in such studies; this chapter will elaborate on the specific experimental procedures which have been used in the work with insulin.

In general, the approach has been to measure interaction (binding) of radioactively labeled insulin with intact target cells or with isolated intact or solubilized membrane preparations derived from such cells. The binding is surmised to reflect a "specific" receptor* interaction if it exhibits: (1) strict structural and steric specificity; (2) saturability, indicating a finite and limited number of binding sites; (3) tissue specificity in accord with insulin's known biological target cell sensitivity; (4) high affinity, in harmony with the low physiological concentration of insulin; and (5) reversibility, which is kinetically consistent with the reversal of the physiological effects observed upon removal of insulin from the medium. Even when all of these criteria are met, the data can be difficult to interpret unless the binding measurements can be evaluated in a system where biological activity can be simultaneously monitored. In this respect, it is instructive to consider data obtained from nonreceptor systems, which exhibit many of the above binding criteria. Both receptor and nonreceptor systems will be presented in connection with the studies on insulin receptors.

---

*The term "receptor" as used in this chapter is taken to represent that membrane-associated structure which performs the function of insulin recognition, so as to initiate the chain of events leading to a hormonal response.

II. GENERAL PROPERTIES OF LIGAND-RECEPTOR INTERACTIONS
AND TECHNICAL CONSIDERATIONS

A. Number and Affinity of Receptors

In general, hormone receptors exhibit remarkably high ligand affinities, with dissociation constants on the order of 10^{-8} M or lower. In addition, the number of such binding sites found on any given cell are vanishingly small. Early estimates based on pharmacologic data [1, 2] of the numbers of specific drug receptors present on responsive cells ($\sim 10^5$/cell) are in excellent agreement with recent direct measurements, e.g., 1.5×10^5 atropine receptors per smooth muscle cell [3], $\sim 10^4$ insulin receptors per fat cell [4], and $\sim 8 \times 10^4$ epidermal growth factor receptors per fibroblast [5]. The small number of sites and the low concentrations over which range measurements must be made necessitate the use of highly sensitive radioisotopic techniques. It can be calculated that compounds possessing specific activities in the range 10 to 20 Ci/mmol (a value usually attainable for ^{3}H-labeled compounds) would restrict measurements (e.g., in the fat cell, with 10^6 cells per sample and 10^4 binding sites per cell) to a maximum binding of a few hundred counts per minute above background. Since experiments with large quantities of cells or membranes are both impractical and subject to special kinds of complications, it is, thus, desirable to work with ^{125}I- or ^{131}I-labeled or comparable derivatives which possess specific activities of $\sim 1,000$ to 3,000 Ci/mmol. Such iodinated derivatives of insulin have proved most useful both in radioimmunoassay and in receptor studies.

B. Preparation of Radioactive Insulin Derivatives

Iodinated insulin derivatives for use in receptor studies can be conveniently prepared by procedures employing the chloramine-T-sodium metabisulfite technique, as originally described by Greenwood and Hunter [6], with minor modifications [4 and unpublished observations]. Carrier-free Na^{125}I (1 to 3 mCi in a volume of 5 to 10 μl) is added to 100 μl 0.25 M sodium phosphate buffer, pH 7.5 (0.51 g Na$_2$HPO$_4 \cdot$H$_2$O + 4.15 g NaH$_2$PO$_4$ per 100 ml), and insulin (5 μl of a solution 1 mg/ml in 0.05 M NaHCO$_3$) is then added with a glass capillary, so as to avoid bubbling the solution. Immediately, 20 μl of a freshly prepared solution of chloramine-T (0.5 mg/ml in distilled H$_2$O) is added with gentle agitation; and the oxidation reaction is allowed to proceed 20 to 30 sec, at which time sodium metabisulfite (20 μl of 1 mg/ml in distilled H$_2$O) is added and the consequent reduction step allowed to proceed for a period of 5 to 10 sec. The reaction misture is then diluted with 200 μl of 0.1 M sodium phosphate buffer, pH 7.5, containing 0.1% wt/vol crystalline bovine albumin. An

aliquot (10 μl) is quickly withdrawn so as to quantitate by crystal scintillation counting the amount of radioactive iodine present in the reaction
medium. The remaining solution is then transferred with 2 to 3 ml of
albumin-containing buffer to a heavy-walled, 12-ml, conical centrifuge
tube containing a talc pellet (25 mg; Ormont Drug and Chemical Co.,
Englewood, N. J.), which is then crushed and triturated with a Pasteur
pipet so as to adsorb the iodinated peptide. The small amount of solution remaining in the reaction vessel (12 × 75-mm glass test tube) is
diluted with ~ 0.5 ml albumin-containing buffer and saved for the measurement of the percent of ^{131}I or ^{125}I incorporated into peptide.

The talc-adsorbed insulin is suspended in ~ 10 ml albumin-containing
buffer, pelleted by centrifugation and the pellet washed four more times
in this manner. Insulin is eluted from the final pellet by suspension in
2 to 3 ml of a solution comprised of 3 ml N HCl, 2.5 ml H_2O, and 0.5 ml
20% crystalline albumin (either in H_2O or in Krebs-Ringer bicarbonate
buffer, pH 7.4). The suspension is clarified by centrifugation (3,000
rpm for 40 min) and the ^{125}I-labeled insulin is transferred to a tared vial
and the exact volume determined by weight. Several drops of 0.25 M
sodium phosphate buffer, pH 7.5, are added, and the solution is adjusted
to near neutrality (pH 4 to 7, indicator paper) by the dropwise addition of
N NaOH up to an amount just under half the original volume. Should the
solution inadvertently become alkaline, a drop of N HCl is added and the
pH then readjusted to near neutrality. An aliquot (20 μl) of the neutralized solution is withdrawn to measure the radioactivity and the precipitability of the preparation by trichloroacetic acid. A typical experiment
yields ~ 3 ml of a solution containing 300 to 600 ng/ml insulin having a
specific activity of 100 to 300 Ci/g. The solution is frozen in 1-ml
aliquots for further use.

The incorporation of ^{125}I is estimated in the following manner: An
aliquot, e.g., 50 μl, of the residual diluted reaction mixture is mixed
into 1.0 ml of 0.1 M phosphate buffer, pH 7.5, containing 1% wt/vol
bovine albumin. An equal aliquot (50 μl) is withdrawn for measurement
of radioactivity. Trichloroacetic acid (0.5 ml of a 10% wt/vol solution
in H_2O) is then added, the precipitate chilled in ice, and then sedimented
in a clinical centrifuge. An aliquot of the supernatant (50 μl) is withdrawn and the radioactivity measured. It is assumed that the radioactivity remaining in the supernatant represents nonincorporated [125]I.
The fraction (f) of ^{125}I incorporated into insulin is given by the formula

$$f = \frac{R.A. \text{ initial} - 1.5 \text{ R.A. final}}{R.A. \text{ initial}} \qquad (1)$$

where R.A. initial and R.A. final refer to the radioactivity in aliquots
before and after the addition of trichloroacetic acid, respectively. If,

in the initial reaction mixture containing 5 μg insulin, there were C μCi present, the specific activity (S.A.) of the insulin preparation is given by the equation

$$S.A. = \frac{f \cdot C}{5} \ \mu Ci/\mu g \qquad (2)$$

In a procedure identical to the one described in the previous paragraph, the fraction of ^{125}I-labeled insulin precipitated by trichloroacetic is determined for an aliquot of the final neutralized talc eluate. In practice, 95 to 99% of the radioactivity is precipitated for a preparation of [125I] insulin which is fully active biologically and which yields good binding data. The number of radioactive iodine molecules, on average, which are incorporated into insulin can be calculated using a value of 1.62×10^7 mCi/matom for ^{131}I and 2.17×10^6 mCi/matom for [125]I.

The use of the lactoperoxidase technique [7] also yields highly radioactive ^{125}I-substituted insulin. However, this method employs H_2O_2 in the reaction to generate free iodine and, thus, does not avoid exposure of insulin to a strong oxidizing agent. The enzymatic procedure, thus, does not offer a fundamentally distinct chemical iodination procedure. Nonetheless, the enzymatic method has been found to yield ^{125}I derivatives of prolactin better suited to receptor studies than derivatives prepared by the chloramine-T method [8].

C. Rates of Association and Dissociation

While most measurements of ligand-receptor interactions are done under equilibrium (or steady-state) conditions, it is useful to consider the rates of association (k_1) and dissociation (k_{-1}) of ligand. Not only do such measurements provide an independent estimate of the affinity ($K_D = k_{-1}/k_1$), but the rates determined may reveal serious limitations in the techniques whereby it is desired to measure ligand binding. For example, most measurements require efficient and complete separation of membrane-bound from free ligand. How rapidly must such separations be achieved? It has been observed for insulin (at 24°C) that $k_1 = 1.5 \times 10^7$ M^{-1} sec^{-1} and that $k_{-1} = 7.4 \times 10^{-4}$ sec^{-1} [4]. Since the half-life (at 24°C), $t_{1/2} = 0.693/k_{-1}$, can be caldulated to be about 16 min, a variety of methods can be used to isolate the membrane-bound insulin, especially if the procedures are performed at 4°C, where the dissociation rate is reduced by about 10-fold. However, should the affinity of a ligand for the membrane be less than that of insulin (e.g., $K_D = 10^{-9}$ M), and if the rate of association be similar to that of insulin (or other diffusion-limited processes), then the half-life of the receptor-ligand complex

could be as short as 46 sec. In practice, it is likely that both k_1 and
k_{-1} will alter to yield the quotient or K_D of 10^{-9} M. However, even with
a ligand-receptor association limited solely by diffusion (i.e., $k_1 \cong 10^{10}$
M^{-1} sec^{-1}), it can be calculated that, given a K_D of 10^{-8} M, the maximal
half-life for the ligand-receptor complex could be ~ 7 msec. Since, in
most receptor systems, the diffusion rate constants will be much lower,
because of the large size of the interactants (cells, membranes, ligand
macromolecule), the experimental half-life can be expected to be much
longer. From such calculations it is evident that in many instances it
may be necessary to use very rapid techniques, e.g., oil floatation or
centrifugation [9] or filtration [4] to separate the free from membrane-
bound ligand for further analysis. Techniques employing columns, or
the washing of centrifugally pelleted material may not suffice. Since
the rate of dissociation will, in general, be highly dependent on temperature, it is advisable to perform the separation procedures at 4°C, where
the dissociation rate is considerably lowered. For studies with insulin,
the high affinity and relatively long (16 min) half-life of the hormone-
receptor complex permit one to choose from several techniques to perform binding studies (see Sec. II. E).

D.   The Problem of Receptor Identification and
Nonreceptor Insulin Interactions

1. Specific Versus Nonspecific Binding

As indicated previously, for purposes of this chapter, the insulin receptor is taken to mean that membrane-associated moiety which "recog-
nizes" insulin in the external cellular milieu. However, all measurements of the interaction of insulin with cell material must be interpreted
in the context of the whole biological system in which the receptor functions. It is frequently difficult, in studies of the binding of ligands at
very low concentrations, to determine the quantity of total binding which
relates specifically to the polypeptide's biological action. For insulin,
measurements in biological systems either in whole animals or in vitro
indicate a saturation of the dose-response relationships in the range of
150 to 220 μU/ml (~ 6 ng/ml or 10^{-9} M). Further, estimates of the
serum levels of insulin suggest a working range for the receptor in the
region 10 to 100 μU/ml ($\sim 10^{-11}$ to 10^{-9} M). It is therefore assumed
that insulin, at concentrations of 10^{-8} M or higher, will saturate fully
all binding sites related to its biological action. Consequently, for
practical purposes it is assumed in binding studies that the amount of
radioactive insulin not "displaced" from the membrane by such high
($\sim 10^{-8}$ M) concentrations of unlabeled insulin (when added before or
together with isotopically labeled insulin), is bound in a "nonspecific
manner" (e.g., to glass, filters, connective tissue, nonreceptor mem-

brane structures, radioisotope-exchange, etc.). Conversely, the radioactivity displaced by nonradioactive insulin and insulin analogs at low
(10^{-11} to 10^{-9} M) concentrations, is considered to reflect "specific"
insulin binding. It is necessary, but not sufficient in this regard, to
demonstrate that insulin analogs with lowered biological activity also
possess a reduced ability to compete with native insulin for binding.

The nonspecific binding may in some cases exhibit very high affinity,
e.g., comparable to or higher than that of the receptor-related insulin
binding, and may thus constitute a substantial amount of the total binding
even when very low concentrations of insulin are used. Nonspecific
binding, however, will nearly always exhibit a large capacity, such that
it is difficult, if not impossible, to demonstrate saturability of binding.
Additionally, the nonspecific binding is in most cases an extremely
rapid process which does not exhibit the longer time course (20 to 60
min for equilibrium at 24°C) of receptor binding. As a rule, the criteria
of saturability, chemical and target tissue specificity, high affinity, and
reversibility can serve to distinguish the specific binding of radioactively
labeled insulin from nonspecific interactions.

2. Nonreceptor Specific Insulin Interactions

While these criteria are generally useful, it is salutary to consider the
interaction of insulin with nonreceptor materials (talc, test tubes,
agarose derivatives), where many of the binding criteria are fulfilled
[10]. Under appropriate conditions, apparently specific insulin binding
can be observed simply by shaking vigorously in glass test tubes (B-D
× 75-mm RTU tubes) solutions of ^{125}I-labeled insulin in 0.1% wt/vol
albumin-containing buffer, pH 7.4, in the presence and absence of native
insulin. When the solutions are filtered over Millipore EAWP or EGWP
membranes, more radioactivity is trapped in the absence than in the
presence of native insulin (Table 1). The "specific" binding is not observed
either in the absence of shaking or, if the solution is shaken in the tubes,
before the addition of insulin. Furthermore, the "specific" binding exhibits a high affinity and appears to be saturable (Fig. 1). The binding
does not appear to occur on heavy particulate matter, since centrifugation techniques (to be discussed later) fail to demonstrate sedimentable
radioactivity. Further studies with talc (Fig. 2) and dodecadiamine-
agarose [10] indicate not only that insulin derivatives can cause appropriate (i.e., lowered efficacy) and specific displacement of ^{125}I-labeled
insulin from inert materials, but that such "displacement" can exhibit
complicated "cooperative" behavior [10]. It is clear that native insulin
competes for the binding of [^{125}I] insulin to talc (Fig. 2) in a way not too
dissimilar from binding to plasma membrane preparations (Sec. III).
As in the plasma membrane systems, insulin competes for binding more

TABLE 1.   Specific Binding of Insulin in the Absence of Tissue by Vigorous Shaking of Assay Mixtures[a,b]

| | Binding (cpm) | | | |
| | Glass tubes | | Plastic tubes | |
Addition	Shaking	No shaking	Shaking	No shaking
None	$25,300 \pm 2500$	3260 ± 380	3230 ± 290	2880 ± 310
Native insulin, 5 μg/ml	$14,800 \pm 1500$	2940 ± 760	3100 ± 110	2500 ± 200

[a]Incubation media (0.2 ml) consisting of Hanks' buffer containing 0.1% albumin were incubated with and without vigorous agitation at 24°C for 40 min in the presence of $[^{125}I]$ insulin (2×10^5 cpm, 1.1 Ci/μmol), with and without native insulin. Glass or plastic tubes (12 × 75 mm) were used as indicated, and binding (cpm ± 1/2 range of duplicates) was determined by filtration over EA cellulose acetate Millipore filters. Similar results are obtained if the buffer used is Krebs-Ringer bicarbonate, 0.1% albumin.

[b]Data from Ref. 10.

effectively than proinsulin, at least at low concentrations. A variety of other peptide hormones unrelated to insulin inhibit very poorly (Fig. 2). However, unlike the findings with biological insulin receptors, the growth hormone derivative (peptide 1-39), desoctapeptide insulin and reduced carboxymethylated insulin (but not the separated chains) compete nearly as well as native insulin. Binding to talc is time- and temperature-dependent, requiring ~ 1 hr at 24°C to reach near steady state. Studies on the effect of increasing the concentration of $[^{125}I]$ insulin on binding give complex data suggestive of "positive cooperativity," and Scatchard plots [11] of these data are not readily interpretable.

The studies with nonreceptor materials demonstrate that the basic properties (or criteria) of ligand binding by biological receptors can also be exhibited, at least in part, by nonreceptor interactions. Saturability by itself simply implies a finite or limited number of "acceptor" molecules, assuming that true steady-state binding is achieved. Furthermore, it is not surprising that nonspecific adsorptive interactions should exhibit some degree of chemical or steric specificity, especially under conditions which display very high affinity and must therefore involve the simultaneous formation of several bonds to achieve the necessary energies of interaction. Other examples of nonreceptor interactions exist which, at least superficially, resemble those expected for true biological receptors: $[^{125}I]$ glucagon can bind specifically to certain

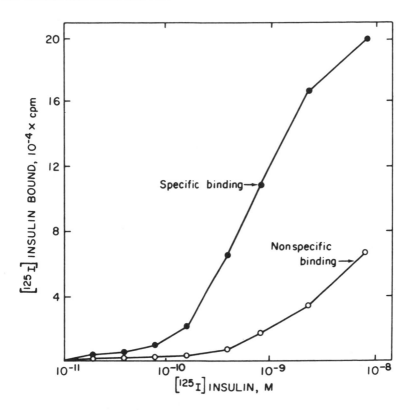

FIG. 1. Dependence on insulin concentration of "specific" binding of insulin during vigorously agitated assays in glass tubes in the absence of tissue. Incubations consisting of Hanks' buffered saline containing 0.1% albumin (0.2 ml) were shaken vigorously for 50 min at 24°C in the presence of varying concentrations of ^{125}I-labeled insulin (1.6 Ci/ μmol), and in the presence and absence of native insulin (50 μg/ml). Binding was determined [4] by filtration over EG cellulose acetate Millipore filters. "Specific" binding (●) was calculated by subtracting the binding observed in the presence of native insulin ("nonspecific" binding, ○) from the total binding (not shown) in the absence of native insulin. Data from Ref. 10.

Millipore filters [12], [3H] naloxone binds stereospecifically to glass filters [13], and opiate drugs bind to cerebroside sulfate stereospecifically and with a relative affinity reflecting potencies observed in vivo [14]. Numerous "foreign" drugs interact highly specifically with naturally occurring macromolecules [15].

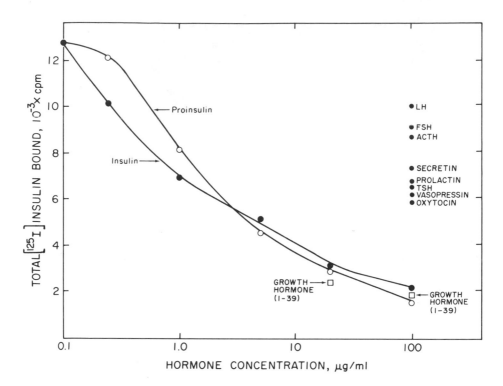

FIG. 2. Specificity of binding of insulin to talc. Samples (0.2 ml) containing 100 μg/ml talc were incubated at 24°C for 30 min with 2.4 × 10⁵ cpm [¹²⁵I] insulin (1.1 Ci/μmol) in the presence of various unlabeled hormones. The latter were added 5 min before addition of [¹²⁵I] insulin. Binding was determined by Millipore (EG, cellulose acetate) filtration. Data from Ref. 10.

It is, however, important to emphasize that bringing attention to the nonreceptor systems is not intended to discourage or mitigate the use of binding methodology (Sec. II. E) to identify and study true biological receptors. In the cases described, as well as others that have been studied, the properties of the nonreceptor systems, when studied in sufficient detail, can be clearly and readily distinguished from those of true receptors. A number of receptor interactions have now been studied which satisfy relatively convincingly the necessary criteria for true or biologically significant receptors [16, 17]. However, since biological tissues will surely also exhibit some of the specific types of interactions described here for simple nonreceptor systems, awareness of such interactions should encourage greater scrutiny, particularly for those interactions observed with high concentrations of insulin, where the results are frequently interpreted to indicate "second" or "multiple" classes of receptors.

E. Methods for the Measurement of Insulin-Receptor Interactions

One of the simplest techniques of measuring insulin binding cells or membranes employs centrifugation as a means of separating bound from free ligand. The binding reaction is allowed to proceed to equilibrium at 24°C (30 to 40 min), and aliquots of the cell or membrane suspension are rapidly chilled to 4°C and pelleted. The resulting pellet is rapidly rinsed with cold buffer without resuspension, and the cellular material solubilized for measurement of radioactivity. The experiment is usually performed in sets of four or six samples, with all samples containing [^{125}I]insulin at the desired concentration, and half of the samples in each set containing $\sim 1 \mu$g/ml native insulin. Provided the trapping of fluid in the pellet is minimal and identical for all samples, the difference in radioactivity between samples without and those with 1 μg/ml native insulin reflects the specific insulin binding. Because of the relatively long ($\sim$ 16 min at 24°C, longer at 4°C) half-life of the insulin-receptor complex, many variations of this technique can yield good data.

The centrifugation technique can be refined with the use of mixtures of water immiscible oils [9, 18, 19] of a density appropriate for the cell or membrane preparation studied. With mixtures of dinonyl- and dibutyl-phthalate, 1:2 vol/vol, layered in the bottom of a conical polyethylene centrifuge tube, most cell preparations can be pelleted below the oil/water interface. The bottom of the tube can then be cut off below the oil/water interface, free from the contaminating aqueous medium, so as to measure the membrane-bound radioactivity. Alternatively, with fat cells, use of the dinonylphthalate oil alone or silicone oil permits flotation of fat cells above the water/oil interface, and measurements of insulin binding to fat cells can be readily performed. With small, high-velocity, rapidly accelerating centrifuges (e.g., Beckman 152 or 152B Microfuge), the separation of free from bound ligand is achieved extremely rapidly; this procedure is particularly useful for the study of binding to "low-affinity" sites, where a dissociation half-life on the order of 60 sec may obtain.

Filtration of cellular material on synthetic polymer filters provides another method to separate free from membrane-bound insulin. The choice of filter is critical, since insulin and other polypeptides such as glucagon [12] can at very low concentrations bind in a "displaceable" manner to materials such as microporous glass or cellulose acetate. In the concentration range ($\leq 10^{-8}$ M) usually studied with ^{125}I-labeled insulin, membrane filters composed of cellulose acetate (e.g., Millipore series E) yield low "background" binding. Filters (2.5-cm diam) are immobilized in a multiple-manifold (50 sample spaces) apparatus, with a tight-fitting silicone-rubber washer sealing the membrane against its support. The seal must be free of dead space around the periphery so that radioactive medium will not be trapped. The membrane or cell suspension (0.5 ml) is filtered (1 micron filter pore size for cells; 0.2 micron pore size for cell membranes) under reduced pressure, and the collected material rapidly (< 10 to 15 sec) washed with 10 ml ice-cold buffer containing 0.1% wt/vol albumin. The radioactivity trapped on the filter is then measured; if so desired, the filtrate can also be collected for further analysis. Similar techniques using filters are employed for studies of solubilized receptors (see Sec. III. C). In brief, the solubilized receptor-hormone complex is precipitated by the addition of polyethylene glycol, and the particulate material is collected and washed on filters.

F. Analysis of Binding Data

The affinities of hormones for their binding sites (e.g., receptors) are very frequently assessed by the competitive displacement of the labeled ligand which binds to the same site. However, the fraction of labeled ligand displaced by a given concentration of unlabeled ligand depends both on the binding site and the labeled ligand concentrations, as well as on the affinity of the ligand. Unless this is appreciated, the calculated ligand affinity can be seriously underestimated [20].

Competitive displacement curves accurately reflect the affinity of the hormone only if the concentrations of labeled hormone and binding sites are substantially less (10-fold at least) than the dissociation constant for the labeled ligand [20]. For an ideal bimolecular reaction, it has been shown [20] that the apparent (from displacement curve) dissociation constant actually exceeds the true dissociation constant by an amount equal to the labeled ligand concentration, plus the binding site concentration, minus three halves the concentration of labeled ligand that would be bound in the absence of unlabeled ligand. For both epidermal growth factor and insulin, the concentration of unlabeled hormone, at which a given fraction of bound labeled hormone is displaced from placenta membranes, is increased by increasing the labeled hormone concentration or the placenta membrane concentration [20]. Competitive-displacement curves will give spuriously high estimates of the K_D for these hormones if they are measured at high labeled-hormone or binding-site concentrations. These considerations are especially important if the apparent affinity of a receptor interaction is to be compared between different tissues, between the same tissue in different species, or between different metabolic states (e.g., diabetes, obesity) of the same species. Unless the conditions (including labeled hormone and receptor concentrations) of assay are identical, artifactual differences may be observed.

Because of limitations on the magnitude of the specific activity of labeled hormones (e.g., even for ^{125}I-labeled hormones), it may not be practical to assess the affinity of very high affinity systems by means of competitive displacement. For example, considering a system with a dissociation constant of 10^{-11} M, the ligand concentration required to displace 50% of the bound labeled will reflect the dissociation constant with accuracy only if both the binding-site and labeled-ligand concentrations are 10^{-12} M or less. Under these conditions the concentration of bound, labeled hormone would be about 5×10^{-14} M. If the hormone were labeled with carrier-free ^{125}I at a molar ratio of one, this would represent only $\sim$ 100 dpm/ml.

Provided that the unlabeled and labeled ligands have the same affinity, the data used to plot competitive displacement curves can be evaluated by the method of Scatchard [11]. Estimations of affinity by Scatchard plot analyses are not invalidated by high concentrations of labeled ligand or binding sites. This method should be used in preference to competitive-binding curves whenever it is suspected that either of these concentrations are not small compared to the dissociation constant. Under conditions of high ligand- or binding-site concentrations, however, other serious methodological problems may arise which can complicate proper analysis by Scatchard plots. For example, with relatively high concentrations of labeled ligand, where only a very small fraction (e.g., $\sim$ 2 to 5%) of the total ligand is bound, the errors in estimating small changes in the concentration of the bound ligand may be large and magnified on Scatchard representations. On the other hand, if the binding-site concentration is very high, such that a very large proportion of the labeled ligand is bound, accurate estimates of small changes in the concentration of free ligand may be prohibited by the presence of even small amounts of unbound, labeled ligand, which may be chemically damaged or altered such that it does not bind properly. The latter situation may be encountered commonly in studies of labeled peptide hormones.

When the unlabeled and labeled ligands do not have the same affinities, there is no simple way of determining the free, unlabeled ligand concentration. Under this condition, Scatchard plots will not be linear [21]. Other conditions exist where Scatchard plots will not be linear. These include heterogeneity of binding sites [22], ligand-ligand interactions [10, 23], binding site-binding site interactions [10], heterogeneity of labeled ligand [11], nonspecific binding [10], inactivation or chemical transformation of the ligand or binding site during the binding reaction, and reactions of the ligand with the binding site which are not of the form A + B = AB [24]. An alternative, relatively simple method of estimating affinity constants from data obtained only with the labeled hormone has been described [25].

III. MEASUREMENTS OF THE INTERACTION OF
INSULIN WITH MEMBRANE RECEPTORS

In the following sections, examples drawn from the experience with
insulin-receptor studies done in this laboratory are used to illustrate
some of the practical difficulties and successes of the approach outlined
in the precious section.

A. Insulin Receptors in Fat and Liver

1. Measurements in Fat Cells

The isolated rat epididymal fat cell, as prepared by the method of Rodbell [26], has proved a useful system in which to study the action of
insulin and other hormones. Briefly, fat cells from the epididymal fat
pad are dissociated by collagenase digestion (0.5 mg/ml, $37°C \times 30$ min
with rapid agitation), and freed from tissue stroma by filtration through
fine silk gauze. Care must be taken to ensure that intact nucleated cells
are obtained. Microscopic examination with the aid of phase contrast
optics and methylene blue stain reveals that fat pads from some animals
(e.g., obese-hyperglycemic mice) may yield only a very small fraction
of whole cells, along with a large number of nonnucleated, globular,
lipid structures which, by simple phase microscopy, may be mistakenly
identified as being fat cells [27]. It is difficult to interpret binding data
for such preparations.

The isolated fat cells are resuspended (0.5 to 5×10^5 ml) in Krebs-
Ringer bicarbonate buffer containing 1% (wt/vol) bovine albumin (KRB-
1% albumin)* and incubated in 0.5-ml aliquots for 30 min at 24°C in the
presence of varying amounts of [^{125}I]insulin, with or without the addition
of 1 μg/ml unlabeled insulin. Either filtration over Millipore EAWP
filters or centrifugal flotation into silicone or dinonylphthalate oil can be
used to isolate cells free from incubation buffer.

The specific binding, obtained by subtracting, from the total radioactive uptake, the amount not displaced by native insulin, is related
linearly to the concentration of iodoinsulin (Fig. 3a) and is linear with
cell concentrations up to at least 6×10^5 cells per ml. The saturable
binding curve parallels closely the biological dose-response curve (increased conversion of [U-^{14}C]glucose to $14CO_2$) both for native and
^{125}I-labeled insulin (Fig. 3b) [4]. The binding-competition curve

---

*Abbreviations used: KRB, Krebs-Ringer bicarbonate buffer, pH 7.4;
Con A, Concanavalin A; EGF, epidermal growth factor; WGA, wheat
germ agglutinin.

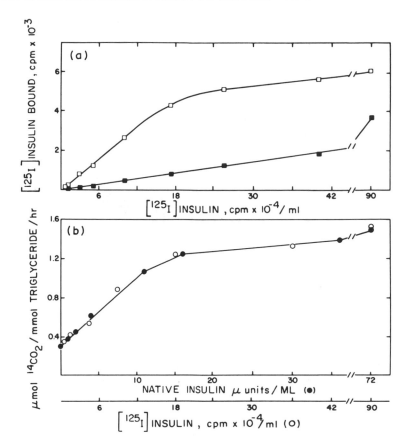

FIG. 3. Ability of native (●) and [^{125}I] insulin (○) to enhance the rate
of glucose oxidation by isolated fat cells (b), correlated with the specific
binding of [^{125}I] insulin (□) to fat cells (a). For each concentration of
[^{125}I] insulin studied, control incubations were done in the presence of
a displacing amount of native insulin. The nonspecific binding, not
represented in the curve for specific binding, is plotted in the upper
graph (■). From Cuatrecasas [4].

(Fig. 4) demonstrates that [^{125}I] insulin bound in small amounts to fat
cells is displaced by increasing amounts of native insulin in a manner
suggesting a near-identity in the binding of these two molecules. It is
of interest that very high concentrations of insulin will further "displace"
substantial amounts of [^{125}I] insulin, perhaps suggesting the presence on
the fat cell of lower-affinity binding sites. The significance of such
sites, which are difficult to relate to the observed concentrations at
which insulin acts on the fat cell, is open to question.

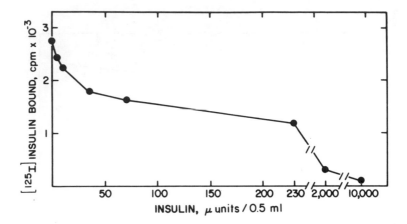

FIG. 4.   Displacement by native insulin of $[^{125}I]$ insulin bound to isolated fat cells.   Fat cells were incubated at 24°C for 30 min with 1.9×10^{-11} M $[^{125}I]$ insulin and increasing amounts of native insulin.   From Cuatrecasas [4].

Unrelated polypeptides and biologically inactive insulin derivatives do not compete for binding of $[^{125}I]$ insulin (Table 2).   However, proinsulin, desoctapeptide insulin and desalanine-insulin, all of which possess reduced but significant biological activity, are observed to compete with $[^{125}I]$ insulin for binding, approximately in step with their measured biological potencies [28–32].   The binding curve indicates an apparent dissociation-equilibrium constant of about 10^{-10} M.

Measurements of the rates of association and dissociation can also yield estimates of the dissociation constant.   For association rate measurements, a relatively small $(7 \times 10^{-11}$ M) amount of $[^{125}I]$ insulin is added to fat cell suspensions, which are rapidly collected and washed on Millipore filters.   The amount of insulin bound at a given time is corrected for the amount of radioactivity bound to aliquots preincubated with high concentrations of native insulin.   The specific insulin binding (Fig. 5) is a time-dependent process, much slower than the almost instantaneous nonspecific binding.   The data from the association-rate binding curve can be substituted into the second-order rate equation:

$$k_1 = 2.303 \frac{1}{t} \cdot \frac{1}{a - b} \cdot \log \frac{b(a - x)}{a(b - x)} \tag{3}$$

in which derivation it is implicit that for the reverse reaction (dissociation), $k_{-1} \ll k_1$.   In the equation, a is the concentration of insulin, b is the concentration of receptor, and x is the concentration of hormone-

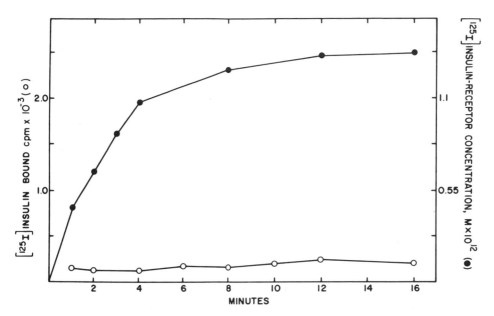

FIG. 5. Rate of binding of [^{125}I] insulin to isolated fat cells at 24°C. Fat cells were incubated with 6.8×10^{-11} M [^{125}I] insulin in the presence (O) and absence (●) of native insulin. The left ordinate describes the uptake of radioactivity, the right ordinate the corresponding concentration of the complex used to calculate the kinetic constants. Data from Cuatrecasas [4].

receptor complex formed at the time t. To solve the equation for k_1, it is essential to know the maximum binding capacity per cell, so that b, the concentration of receptor present, can be calculated. Based on the data in Figure 3, one fat cell binds 11,000 molecules of insulin; this value is used to convert the value for cell concentration into a concentration of receptor. The value obtained for k_1 is $1.5 \pm 0.4 \times 10^7$ M^{-1} sec^{-1}. This rate probably approaches that of a diffusion-controlled process, particularly in view of the large size of one of the diffusing species. It is of interest that the rate equation (3) may not hold for all systems, and in particular for studies with human prolactin (this work, Chap. 18 and Ref. 8); the complete reversible second-order rate equation best fits the experimental data.

The rate of dissociation can also be readily measured with the use of a filter technique. Cell suspensions (0.2 to 0.5 ml) are first equilibrated (20 to 30 min) in KRB-1% albumin containing about 5×10^{-11} M [^{125}I] insulin. A control sample, containing 1 μg/ml native insulin is

TABLE 2. Displacement of [^{125}I] Insulin Binding by Peptide Hormones[a,c]

Tissue	Peptide	Concentration ($\mu g/ml$)	Specific binding [^{125}I] insulin ($10^6 \times$ nmol)
Fat cells	None		2.4
	Insulin	0.002	1.4
	Insulin	0.012	0.7
	Adrenocorticotropin	40	2.4
	Growth hormone	40	2.4
	Prolactin	40	2.5
	Vasopressin	40	2.4
	Oxytocin	40	2.4
	Glucagon	40	2.5
	Carboxymethyl chains of insulin	0.2	2.3
	Oxidized chains of insulin	0.2	2.2
	Reduced insulin[b]	0.3	2.2
Liver membranes	None		4.2
	Insulin	0.002	3.0

Insulin	0.008	2.1
Insulin	0.4	0.1
Proinsulin	0.2	3.4
Proinsulin	10	0.9
Desoctapeptide insulin	5	4.0
Glucagon	50	4.3
Growth hormone	50	4.2

[a]The ability of each peptide to affect the specific binding of [^{125}I] insulin (2.8 × 10^{-11} M for fat cells, 2 × 10^5 cells in 0.5 ml; 1.7 × 10^{-11} M for liver membranes, 71 μg protein in 0.2 ml) was determined at 24°C by filtration methods.

[b]Treated for 90 min at 24°C with 20 mM dithiothreitol in 0.1 M NaHCO$_3$ buffer, pH 8.1.

[c]Data for liver membranes from Cuatrecasas et al. [28]; data for fat cells from Cuatrecasas [29].

included to estimate the net nonspecific insulin binding, presumed to be
the same for all other samples. The dissociation-rate experiment is
then initiated by rapidly collecting and washing cell samples (duplicate
or triplicate for each desired time point) with buffer at 4°C under reduced
pressure on EAWP filters. Excepting the samples which serve as the
"zero-time" estimates of binding, warm buffer (24°C) is then allowed to
percolate through the trapped cells (~ 0.5 ml/min). At timed intervals,
by increasing the vacuum, the buffer is rapidly removed from some
samples, while fresh buffer is continually added to the remaining filter
wells. Finally, filters are removed for measurement of radioactivity.

The dissociation rate data (Fig. 6) can be used to solve for k_{-1} from
the first-order rate equation, which in integrated form, when a, the
amount of hormone-receptor complex dissociated (i.e., free insulin), is
zero at zero time, is given by the expression:

$$k_{-1} = \frac{1}{t} \; 2.303 \log \frac{x}{x - a} \tag{4}$$

where x, in this case, represents the amount of insulin-membrane complex trapped on the filters at zero time, and x - a is given by the amount
of complex remaining on the filters at the indicated times. From Eq. (4)
it can be seen that, when half of the complex has dissociated

$$k_{-1} = \frac{0.693}{t_{1/2}} \tag{5}$$

where $t_{1/2}$ is the half-time of dissociation.

The filter technique gives perhaps the most direct estimate of the
spontaneous dissociation rate. Another approach is, however, possible.
Cell suspensions are first equilibrated with [125 I] insulin, as indicated,
and a high concentration of insulin is added to all samples. At timed
intervals thereafter, suspensions are rapidly diluted with 3 ml cold
buffer (4°C) and harvested (filter or centrifugation method). It is presumed that the radioactive ligand dissociating from the membrane will
be diluted more than 1,000-fold by the high concentration of native insulin,
so that the rebinding of dissociated radioactive material is negligible.
This technique yields good results for a ligand such as glucagon. However, it can be observed with insulin that concentrations of native polypeptide as low as 10^{-9} can enhance the rate of dissociation of 125 I-labeled
insulin from cultured permanent cell line lymphocytes or from liver and
placenta membranes [10, 32, 33, and DeMeyts, this work, Chap. 11].
The interpretation of these data is open to question. It has been suggested
that this phenomenon indicates negatively cooperative receptor interactions [33 and De Meyts, this work, Chap. 11]. Nonetheless, this
phenomenon can also be seen in the inert (talc) binding systems already

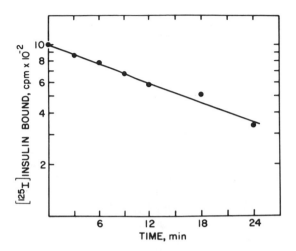

FIG. 6. Semilog plot of the dissociation of $[^{125}I]$ insulin bound to fat cells as a function of time at 24°C. Fat cells were equilibrated at 24°C with $[^{125}I]$ insulin (4.6×10^{-11} M), collected, and washed at 4°C on Millipore filters; and the dissociation at 24°C of the bound insulin was then measured. From Cuatrecasas [4].

discussed, and it has been suggested [10] that the results may also be explained on the basis of insulin dimer formation. Clearly, measurements of the insulin dissociation rate performed in the presence of an excess of unlabeled insulin will overestimate the value of k_{-1} and thus yield falsely high values for the K_D calculated from rate data. The technique is best used for ligands not known to display self-aggregation.

The binding studies in the whole fat cell serve to fulfill most, if not all, of the criteria required for the physico-chemical identification of a hormone receptor. The interaction is insulin-specific, saturable, of high affinity, reversible, and parallels the known biological dose-response relationship. From studies established in the whole cell, one can proceed to examine in an appropriate context insulin interactions in membrane preparations.

2. Insulin Receptors in Fat and Liver Membranes

The experiments outlined previously can be done with membrane fractions from fat and liver, isolated by differential centrifugation. Isolated fat cells prepared by collagenase digestion as outlined (Sec. III. A), and described in detail by Rodbell [26], are homogenized in 0.25 M sucrose with a rotary-knife homogenizer (Polytron PT-10, Brinkman Instruments) and then centrifuged (45,000 g for 30 min) to obtain a particulate fraction ("membrane fraction") which contains virtually all of the specific insulin-binding activity measurable in intact cells. With these membranes, binding curves for [^{125}I] insulin can be obtained which parallel exactly those obtained for intact cells. Either filtration (EGWP filters) or centrifugation techniques yield good results.

Liver membranes can also be demonstrated to contain $\sim$ 80 to 90% of the total specific insulin-binding activity detectable in crude liver homogenates. Liver microsomal membranes from Sprague-Dawley rats (80-200 g) are obtained by differential centrifugation of homogenates (10% wt/vol in 0.25 M sucrose) prepared with a rotary-knife homogenizer (Polytron PT-10, Brinkmann, setting 2.2, 75 sec). The homogenate is centrifuged for 10 min at 650 g, the pellet discarded, and the supernatant centrifuged at 10,000 g for 30 min. The resulting supernatant is then made 0.1 M in NaCl and 0.2 mM in MgSO$_4$ by the addition of small volumes of concentrated solutions of these reagents, and the suspension centrifuged at 37,000 g for 45 min. The resulting pellet is suspended (1 mg/ml membrane protein) in 0.1 M NaHCO$_3$, pH 8, and centrifuged at 37,000 g for 30 min. The supernatant is discarded and the procedure repeated three more times. The resulting pellet is resuspended in 5 mM NaHCO$_3$ (5 to 15 mg protein per ml), divided in equal aliquots, and stored in liquid nitrogen for further analysis. Electron micrographs of membranes prepared in this manner reveal closed, single membrane-limited vesicles with attached ribosomes; no nuclei or mitochondria are present.

Studies with liver membranes prepared by this procedure yield a binding isotherm as shown in Figure 7 [28], indicating an apparent dissociation-equilibrium constant of about 7 $\times$ 10^{-11} M. Measurements of the association/dissociation-rate constants yield the same value for this K_D.

It is evident that in both fat cells [34] and in liver membranes [32], apparently insulin-specific binding sites with lower affinity can be detected ($K_D > 10^{-9}$ M). Since such estimates are based on studies which use native insulin as a competitive ligand, and since the values are extrapolated from Scatchard plots, the limitations (described in Sec. II. F) inherent in these methods will tend to underestimate the true affinity constants. The significance of such low-affinity binding sites—which are difficult to relate to the biologically appropriate concentrations of insulin, which acts at concentrations in the range below 10^{-9} M—is difficult to interpret. It is noteworthy in this regard that minimal proteolysis of insulin receptor structures in fat cells yields binding sites with an identical chemical specificity, but with lowered affinity for insulin (see Sec. III. B). Low-affinity sites in membranes could thus represent either

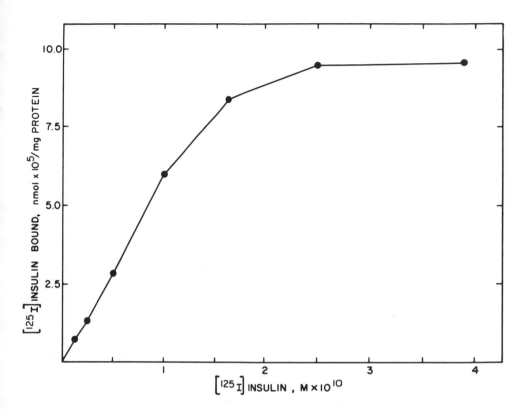

FIG. 7. Binding of [^{125}I] insulin to rat liver membranes. Membranes (50 μg of protein) were incubated with increasing amounts of [^{125}I] insulin, and binding was measured by filtration methods. Values are corrected for nonspecific adsorption of insulin. From Cuatrecasas et al. [28].

"damaged" receptors or binding sites related to an as yet unexplored aspect of insulin physiology.

B. Enzymatic Probes of Insulin-Receptor Interactions

Enzymatic [34-43] and chemical [44-46] procedures have long been used to deduce the properties of the insulin receptor. It is, however, only relatively recently [39, 40, 42] that direct measurements of insulin binding have been coupled to such studies to obtain information specifically about the recognition site.

Digestion with trypsin lowers the sensitivity of fat cells to insulin [36-39, 41, 43], while the cellular response to epinephrine is retained

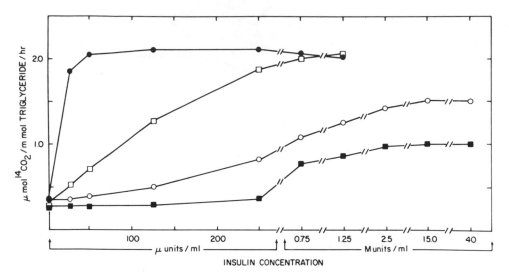

FIG. 8. Effect of increasing the concentration of insulin on the conversion
of [^{14}C] glucose to ^{14}CO$_2$ by isolated fat cells treated with various concentrations of trypsin. The fat cells from 14 rats were divided equally
into four 5-ml samples using Krebs-Ringer bicarbonate buffer containing
1% (wt/vol) albumin. These were incubated in the absence (●) or presence of 10 μg per ml (□), 30 μg per ml (○), and 200 μg per ml (■) of
trypsin for 15 min at 37°C. Soybean trypsin inhibitor equal to three
times the weight of trypsin was added. Each cell fraction was washed
three times with 10 ml of the albumin buffer, and the fractions were resuspended in a total bolume of 23 ml. Samples (0.5 ml) of these cells
were used to measure the specific binding of insulin as a function of the
concentration of [^{125}I] insulin in the medium. Other cell camples (0.25
ml) were used to examine insulin-dependent [^{14}C] glucose oxidation. The
cells were incubated for 60 min at 37°C in Krebs-Ringer bicarbonate
buffer containing 1% (wt/vol) albumin, 0.2 mM [^{14}C] glucose and varying
concentrations of native insulin as indicated in the figure. Data from
Ref. 39.

[36]. Under very mild conditions of trypsin digestion, e.g., 10 μg/ml
trypsin for 15 min at 37°C in the presence of 1% albumin, with the reaction
stopped by the addition of soybean trypsin inhibitor, the cellular response
(conversion of [U-^{14}C] glucose to ^{14}CO$_2$) to insulin is retained, whereas
the cellular sensitivity is reduced (Fig. 8). Studies of the binding of
[^{125}I] insulin to cells so treated reveals a lowered receptor site affinity,
which closely parallels the reduced cellular responsiveness (Fig. 9).
More drastic digestion with trypsin leads to a more complete loss of

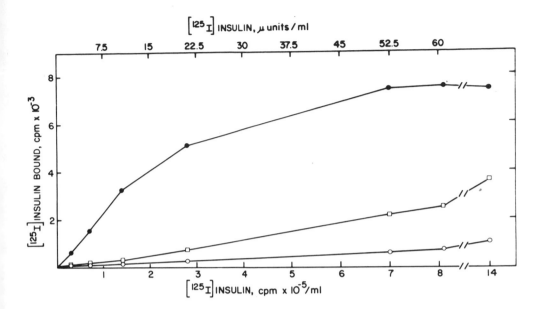

FIG. 9.   Effect of increasing the concentration in the medium of $[^{125}I]$ - insulin on the specific binding to isolated fat cells treated with various concentrations of trypsin.   The fat cells used in this experiment were the same as those that were used in the experiment depicted in Figure 8. The ability of these cells to increase the $[^{14}C]$ glucose oxidation in response to various insulin concentrations is described in Figure 8.   The cells were undigested by enzymes (●), or treated with 10 μg per ml (□), or 30 μg per ml (○) of trypsin for 15 min at 37°C.   Varying amounts of $[^{125}I]$ insulin were added to 0.5 ml suspensions containing 2.5×10^6 cells.   These were incubated at 24°C for 25 min following filtration and washing on Millipore filters.   Data from Ref. 39.

insulin responsiveness and insulin binding [36, 39, 41, 43].   The exquisite sensitivity of insulin receptor structures to trypsin (Fig. 10) must be taken into account during procedures designed to isolate and to study this structure from various tissues.   The presence of even low concentrations of tissue cathepsins would predictably lower the tissue affinity for insulin. This consideration is particulatly a problem in studies on cultured cells (see Sec. III. E), where trypsin is often used to dissociate cells for subculture.

Whereas the studies with trypsin establish the protein nature of the insulin receptor, studies with neuraminidase [42], β-galactosidase [102], and phospholipases [40, 48] have proved useful in assessing the roles

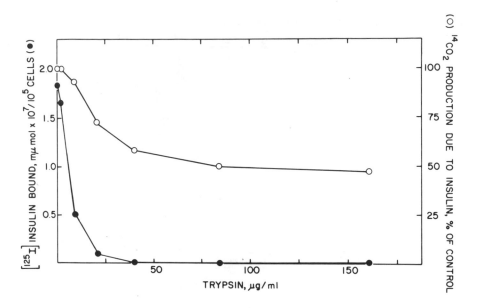

FIG. 10. Effects of tryptic digestion of isolated fat cells on the ability
of insulin to stimulate the conversion of [^{14}C] glucose to ^{14}CO$_2$ (○),
and on the specific binding of [^{125}I] insulin to fat cells (●). Two-milliliter suspensions of fat cells, containing about 8×10^5 cells per ml of
Krebs-Ringer bicarbonate buffer, 1% (wt/vol) albumin, were incubated
at 37°C for 15 min with various concentrations of trypsin. Soybean
trypsin inhibitor equal to three times the amount of trypsin by weight
was added. The cells were washed three times with 10 ml of the same
albumin buffer, and the cells were suspended in 6 ml of this buffer.
Samples (0.25 ml) of these suspensions were incubated at 37°C in Krebs-
Ringer bicarbonate buffer (1.0 ml) containing 2% (wt/vol) albunim and
0.2 mM [^{14}C] glucose (specific activity, 5.1 μCi/μmol) in the absence
and presence of 10 munits of insulin. The production of ^{14}CO$_2$ was
measured during a 60-min incubation period (○). The specific binding
of [^{125}I] insulin to samples (0.5 ml) of the digested and washed cells
was studied using 2.3×10^{-11} M [^{125}I] insulin. Data from Ref. 39.

of phospholipids, galactose, and sialic acid in receptor recognition of
insulin and the consequent response. Neuraminidase, which at low
concentrations (< 1 mU/ml) has an insulin-like action in fat cells, at
high concentrations causes a fall in the basal rate of glucose transport,
and abolishes the effects of insulin on glucose transport and lipolysis
[42]. The enzymatic digestion does not, however, affect the binding of
insulin (affinity, number of binding sites unchanged). It can be concluded

that sialic acid residues are in some way involved in the transmission of the binding signal to structures adjacent to the recognition site. Nonetheless, further (or simultaneous) digestion of neuraminidase-treated cells with β-galactosidase leads to a loss of insulin binding in addition to the loss of biological responsiveness [29, 47]. This finding suggests that galactose groups are involved in the recognition function of the receptor and may constitute a part of this molecule. The glycoprotein nature of the insulin receptor is further corroborated with the use of the plant lectins Concanavalin A and wheat germ agglutinin, which compounds both possess insulin-like activities and bind to insulin receptor structures [49] (see Sec. III. D).

Digestion of fat cells with phospholipases A and C (but not D), while abolishing insulin responsiveness, leads to a three- to sixfold increase in insulin binding to fat cells [40]. The "new" exposed binding sites are kinetically indistinguishable from those initially present in the membrane. If cells are first digested with trypsin, so as to destroy the available insulin-binding sites, subsequent phospholipase digestion unmasks further binding sites. Conversely, treating cells first with phospholipase and then with trypsin leads to a loss of all insulin binding. It thus appears that some insulin-binding sites are normally "covered" by phospholipid and, thus, inaccessible to macromolecules in the medium.

These examples indicate how an enzymatic approach, coupled with parallel measurements of insulin binding and insulin responsiveness, can be of use in elucidating the chemical nature of the receptor structure.

C. Solubilization of Insulin Receptors

Treatment of membranes from fat cells or liver with the nonionic detergent, Triton X-100, leads to a dissolution of the membrane, and a disappearance of insulin binding from the particulate residue [47, 50, 51]. At a Triton X-100 concentration of ~ 1% vol/vol, more than 80% of the binding activity of fat- or liver-membrane suspensions is removed from the particulate matter. The binding activity can be recovered in the clear supernatant after centrifugation at 300,000 $\underline{g}$ for 70 min at 4°C.

Gel filtration of the solubilized protein in the presence of 0.5% vol/vol Triton X-100 at 4°C indicates that [^{125}I]insulin can associate with material eluted in the column void volume (Sephadex G-50) (Fig. 11). If the material from the high-molecular-weight fraction is subsequently incubated with native insulin at 37°C, and then rechromatographed, the radioactivity no longer migrates with the high-molecular-weight component, but appears in the lower-molecular-weight fraction [Fig. 11(c)]. It is evident that even in the presence of 0.5% vol/vol Triton X-100, insulin binds in an insulin-specific and reversible manner to soluble membrane

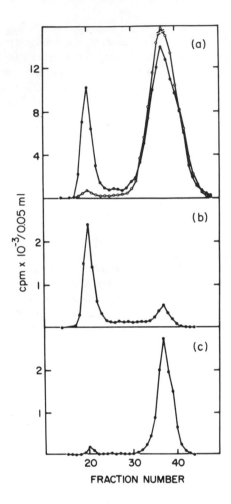

FIG. 11. Gel filtration patterns demonstrating specific and reversible binding between [^{125}I]insulin and material solubilized from liver-cell membranes with Triton X-100. Liver cell membranes (6 mg of protein per ml) suspended in 0.5 M tris-HCl buffer (pH 7.4) were incubated for 20 min at 24°C with 0.5% Triton X-100 and centrifuged at 300,000 g for 70 min. The supernatant (0.5 ml) was incubated for 30 min at 24°C with 1.6 nM [^{125}I]insulin, cooled in ice, and applied to a column (45 × 1 cm) of Sephadex G-50 (medium), equilibrated, and run at 4°C with Krebs-Ringer bicarbonate-0.1% albumin (wt/vol)-0.5% Triton X-100 [(a), ●—●]. The flow rate was 4.5 ml/hr, and each fraction contained 0.8 ml. A separate sample (0.5 ml) was processed identically, except that it was incubated with native insulin (50 μg/ml) for 3 min before addition of [^{125}I]-insulin [(a), O—O]. The effluent buffer containing the first radioactive

constituents. It is important to note that even at 4°C, appreciable spontaneous dissociation of [^{125}I] insulin from the high-molecular-weight
material occurs during chromatography [Fig. 11(c)].

An alternative to column techniques for the measurement of the interaction of insulin with soluble macromolecules employs polyethylene glycol
(Carbowax 6000) to precipitate selectively the insulin-receptor complex,
while free insulin is left in the supernatant. This approach has proved
useful for selective protein fractionation and has been applied to the
radioimmunoassay of peptide hormones [52]. For measurement of insulin
binding, 5 to 50 μl of detergent-extracted supernatant is added to 0.2 ml
Krebs-Ringer bicarbonate buffer-0.1% wt/vol albumin, containing [^{125}I] -
insulin with (control tubes only) or without 25 to 50 μg/ml native insulin.
Equilibration of binding is achieved in ~20 to 50 min at 24°C, at which
time 0.5 ml of ice-cold 0.1 M sodium phosphate buffer (pH 7.4) containing 0.1% wt/vol bovine γ-globulin is added and tubes placed in ice. One-
half milliliter of cold 25% wt/vol polyethylene glycol is added (final
concentrations, 10% wt/vol), the tubes thoroughly mixed, and placed in
ice for 10 to 15 min. The suspension is then filtered under reduced
pressure on cellulose acetate (Millipore EH) filters and the collected
precipitate washed with 3 ml of 8% wt/vol polyethylene glycol in 0.1 M
tris-HCl buffer (pH 7.4) before measurement of trapped radioactivity by
crystal scintillation counting. As for the measurements of binding with
cells and membranes, the specific binding is determined by subtracting,
from the total radioactivity bound, that which remains in the presence of
a high concentration (25 to 50 μg/ml) of native insulin. Under these conditions, < 0.5% of the total free [^{125}I] insulin is precipitated or adsorbed
nonspecifically; nearly quantitative precipitation of the insulin-receptor
complex occurs.

Concentrations of polyethylene glycol < 8% (wt/vol) incompletely
precipitate the complex; concentrations > 12% significantly precipitate
free insulin. The presence of γ-globulin is essential as a carrier for
the precipitation reaction, but concentrations > 0.1% (wt/vol) cause

---

FIG. 11 (continued)
peak (tubes 18-21 in (a), ●─●), which corresponds to the column void
volume, was pooled. One milliliter of this material, containing 126,000
cpm, was immediately rechromatographed on the same column (b); the
first radioactive peak in this column contained a total of 92,000 cpm.
Another 1 ml of the pooled material of the first peak was incubated with
10 μg of native insulin for 50 min at 37°C before chromatography (c).
The material appearing in the void volume of this column, after incubation for 30 min at 37°C with fresh [^{125}I] insulin (1.7 nM), followed by
chromatography, was capable of again binding [^{125}I] insulin. (From Ref. 51).

precipitation of free insulin. If the pH of the buffer containing the γ-globulin is > 8 or < 7, the complex is less effectively precipitated; phosphate buffers (0.1 M, pH 7.4) can be used effectively in the incubation medium. A final concentration of Triton X-100 in the assay mixture in excess of 0.2% vol/vol results in decreased insulin binding. The membrane extracts are, therefore, diluted before assay so that the final concentration of Triton X-100 is usually < 0.1% and always < 0.2% (vol/vol). For the estimation of rate data (see Sec. II. C) (association/dissociation) it is assumed that the addition of the cold polyethylene glycol/γ-globulin solutions stop the binding reaction at the timed intervals.

Another nonionic detergent, Lubrol-PX, can also be used effectively to solubilize the insulin-receptor structures from liver or fat cell membranes. However, the presence of this detergent interferes with the formation of the insulin-receptor complex, as determined by the polyethylene glycol binding assay; a concentration of Lubrol of 0.5% vol/vol inhibits 85% of the insulin binding. Other agents which are much less successful in solubilizing receptors than these two detergents are sodium dodecylsulfate, dimethylsulfoxide, dimethyl formamide, hexafluoroisopropanol, and pyridine. About 10% of the binding activity of liver cell membranes can be extracted by vigorous agitation in distilled water; ~ 20 to 30% of insulin binding activity of liver or fat cell to membranes is extracted with lithium diiodosalicylate, an agent used to solubilize glycoproteins from red cell membranes [53]. Insulin-binding proteins have also been isolated from lymphocyte membranes by use of the detergent NP-40 [54].

It is remarkable that, even when solubilized, the receptor retains its affinity and specificity for insulin (Table 3 and Fig. 12) [47, 51]. From the binding curve (Fig. 12) and from rate data obtained as for the particulate receptor, a dissociation constant of about 10^{-10} M can be estimated for the soluble insulin-receptor complex.

Chromatography of the soluble insulin-receptor complex on the columns of Sepharose 6B in the presence of Triton X-100 (0.75%) yields some information concerning the molecular size of the complex (Fig. 13). Based on the behavior of other proteins under the same conditions, and the correlation of Stokes radius with elution volume according to Laurent and Killander [55], a molecular diameter of ~70 Å can be estimated for the insulin-receptor complex.

The sedimentation behavior of the hormone-receptor complex can be studied on sucrose gradients [5-20% sucrose in 0.1 M sodium phosphate buffer, pH 7.4, containing 0.1% wt/vol bovine albumin and 0.2 % vol/vol Triton X-100 (Fig. 14)]. A sucrose sedimentation coefficient of ~ 11S is observed for the insulin-binding protein. With the reservation that the interaction of nonionic detergents can modify the physico-chemical

TABLE 3. Displacement of $[^{125}I]$ Insulin from Soluble Insulin-Receptor Complex by Insulin Derivatives and Peptide Hormones[a, b]

Addition	Specific binding of $[^{125}I]$ insulin (cpm)	
	Fat cell	Liver
No additions	7210 ± 320	5890 ± 430
Insulin		
5 ng/ml	3030 ± 104	2710 ± 350
0.5 µg/ml	110 ± 30	70 ± 25
Desalanine-insulin, 5 ng/ml	3140 ± 78	2940 ± 280
Desoctapeptide-insulin		
50 ng/ml	7010 ± 240	5690 ± 610
200 ng/ml	4840 ± 310	4230 ± 410
Reduced and carboxymethylated insulin, 5 µg/ml	6970 ± 206	5740 ± 350
Proinsulin, 0.1 µg/ml	3560 ± 260	2990 ± 170
Glucagon, 0.1 mg/ml	7440 ± 340	5970 ± 280
ACTH, 0.1 mg/ml	7510 ± 420	5620 ± 350
Oxytocin, 0.1 mg/ml	7320 ± 304	5750 ± 290
Growth hormone, 0.1 mg/ml	7450 ± 220	5730 ± 220

[a]Samples of Triton X-100-solubilized material from fat (30 µg of protein) or liver (35 µg of protein) membranes were incubated for 60 min at 24°C in 0.25 ml of Krebs-Ringer bicarbonate buffer containing 0.1% albumin, 61 pM $[^{125}I]$ insulin, and the indicated hormone. Insulin binding was determined with polyethylene glycol. Values are means ± standard error (n = 3).

[b]Data from Ref. 51.

behavior of membrane proteins [56] one can, from the estimated values of Stokes radius and sedimentation coefficient (assuming a partial specific volume of 0.725 cm^3/g) calculate a molecular weight of ~ 300,000 for the insulin-binding protein. The true molecular weight may be lower (perhaps by 20-30%), since no correction is made for the amount of detergent bound to the protein. Similar molecular parameters have been described for the acetylcholine-binding protein solubilized from Electrophorus electricus [57].

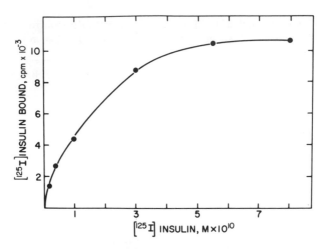

FIG. 12. Effect of the concentration of [^{125}I] insulin on the specific bind-ing to Triton X-100-solubilized material from liver membranes. Assays contained 100 μg of solubilized protein per ml, and binding was deter-mined by the polyethylene glycol method as described in the text. (From Ref. 51).

D. Macromolecular Insulin Derivatives and Receptor Studies

1. Biological Properties of Macromolecular Derivatives

Part of the evidence to indicate that insulin receptors are localized at the cell surface has been obtained using insoluble inert supports derivatized with insulin. In these derivatives, insulin is covalently coupled via the alpha amino groups of the A- and B chains, or the ϵ-NH$_2$ group of lysine in the B chain. In controlled experiments, where the problem of cleavage of the bound insulin from the inert support is minimized or accounted for, such derivatives can be shown to possess biological activity in isolated cell systems. For instance, insulin-agarose can enhance the conversion of [U-^{14}C] glucose to ^{14}CO$_2$ [58] in isolated fat cells. Soluble insulin-dextran derivatives are active in whole animals in reducing blood sugar levels and inducing hepatic enzymes [59, 60]. It has been known for some time that molecules bound covalently to CNBr-activated agarose display "leakage" into the medium [61, 62]. For this reason, it is very difficult to design conditions of assay such that the quantity of ligand which is leaked off the support during the assay is not sufficiently large by itself to stimulate the biological response, since this complicates greatly the interpretation. It is generally helpful in these experiments to utilize agarose beads which have very low degrees of substitution,

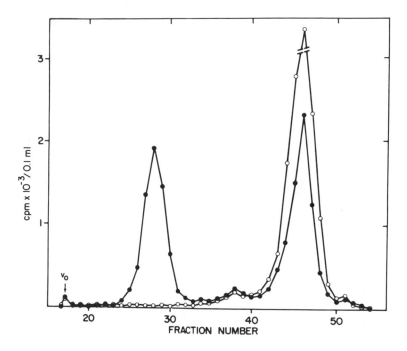

FIG. 13. Sepharose 6B chromatography of water-soluble insulin receptor
of liver membranes. Liver membranes (4.1 mg of protein per ml of
0.05 M tris-HCl buffer, pH 7.4) were incubated with 0.75% (vol/vol)
Triton X-100 for 20 min at 4°C, followed by centrifugation for 2 hr at
300,000 g. The supernatant (0.5 ml) was adjusted with NaCl to 0.1 M
and albumin to 3% (wt/vol). $[^{125}I]$ Insulin (5×10^5 cpm) was added alone
(●) or after the addition of native insulin (20 μg/ml) (○), and the
samples, after incubation for 30 min at 24°C, were placed in ice. The
samples were then chromatographed at 4°C on a column (1.5×87 cm)
of Sepharose 6B which had been equilibrated for four weeks with Krebs-
Ringer bicarbonate buffer containing 0.5% (vol/vol) Triton X-100 and 0.1%
(wt/vol) albumin. The flow rate was ~ 6 ml/hr. The small radioactive
peak appearing in Fraction 38, which represents ~ 4% of the total radioactivity applied on the column, was essentially unchanged in the absence
of membrane extract, in the absence of detergent in the buffer, in the
presence of native insulin in the sample, and after reducing the albumin
concentration in the sample to 0.1% (wt/vol). Rechromatography of the
rapidly migrating peak results in the reappearance of a major peak in
the same position (Fraction 28) and a small peak in the retarded position
(Fraction 46); no significant radioactivity was present in the region of
Fractions 36 to 40. The elution of insulin-binding protein was compared
with the elution of protein of known molecular dimensions under identical
conditions. (From Ref. 47).

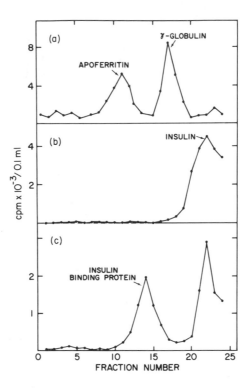

FIG. 14. Sedimentation behavior of insulin-binding protein of fat cell membranes on 5 to 20% sucrose gradients. Fat cell membranes were extracted with 1% (vol/vol) Triton X-100 and centrifuged for 70 min at 44,000 rpm as described in the text. The supernatant was dialyzed for 16 hr at 4°C against 0.1 M sodium phosphate buffer containing 0.2% (vol/vol) Triton X-100. The supernatant (0.2 ml, containing 0.5 mg of protein) was incubated at 24°C for 20 min with [^{125}I] insulin (3.5 × 10^4 cpm) before being subjected to gradient centrifugation for 16 hr. Another sample of supernatant was processed identically, except that native insulin (20 μg) was added 5 min before incubating with [^{125}I] insulin (b). A sample (0.2 ml) of the dialysis buffer described above was also centrifuged (a) under identical conditions after addition of [^{14}C]acetyl apoferritin (6.1 × 10^4 cpm) and [^{14}C]acetyl γ-globulin (7.2 × 10^4 cpm). The broader appearance of the insulin peak in (b) compared to that in (c) probably results from aggregated forms of insulin which form in the former because of its high concentration. (From Ref. 47).

since the quantity that can leak off will then be small. In addition, such mildly derivatized beads may have a very substantial portion of the total ligand on the bead surface [63] rather than distributed throughout the bead interior. Such a situation may be mandatory for properly examining insulin-agarose derivatives, since the substituted hormone is, thus, accessible to the cell and the total quantity of hormone which serves as a "reservoir" for potential leakage is reduced. An alternative method for preventing leakage, and thus showing the biological activity of hormone-agarose derivatives is to utilize agarose beads which contain macro-molecular "arms" (e.g., branched polyamino acid polymers) which are attached to the agarose backbone by multiple points [62, 64, 65]. Insulin-agarose derivatives of this type have been shown to be biologically active under conditions where negligible leakage of the free hormone occurs [58]. In these studies, insulin-agarose was active on fat cells, while the bead-free incubation medium which had been used for these studies was incapable of stimulating freshly prepared cells. It is of particular importance to note that, in some experiments, the observed effects can be attributed to insulin cleaved from the support. For example, in studies of the action of insulin-Sepharose on hepatoma tissue culture (HTC) cells in culture, a large proportion of the observed induction of tryosine amino transferase could be accounted for by free insulin in solution [66]. Likewise, in experiments with highly derivatized beads (sufficient for amino acid analysis, [67]) leakage of insulin from the bead interior undoubtedly masks the effects of covalently bound insulin.

It is of interest that, while the macromolecular derivatives exhibit biological activities on the whole similar to free insulin, in some instances qualitative and quantitative differences can be observed. Insulin-agarose, which in fat cells mimics the action of insulin, may act via fewer contacts at the fat cell surface than does soluble insulin and may, thus, in some respects be more potent than insulin itself. Similarly insulin-dextran derivatives administered i.v. in alloxan-diabetic rats appear more potent than soluble insulin in their ability to lower blood sugar and induce hepatic enzyme synthesis [60]. Mammary gland cells from virgin mice, which do not respond (uptake of α-aminoisobutyric acid) to soluble insulin, do respond to insulin-agarose in the way by which insulin-sensitive mammary cells from pregnant mice respond. Strikingly, the effects of insulin-agarose in cells from virgin mice can be blocked by soluble insulin [68].

With insulin-agarose derivatives, it is possible to infer the presence of receptors in whole cells by direct microscopic observation. Fat cells, which normally float on aqueous buffers, can be seen to stick to insulin-agarose beads. Depending on the degree of derivatization of the beads with insulin, the cells either sink with the beads, or cause the beads to float [69]; the addition of soluble insulin reverses the binding of cells to the beads.

2. Macromolecular Derivatives and Receptor Isolation

Macromolecular insulin derivatives have also proved extremely useful in the isolation of insulin-binding proteins by affinity chromatographic techniques [50]. Passage of Triton X-100-solubilized liver membrane preparations over columns of diamino-dipropylaminosuccinyl-N-phenyl-alanyl-insulin-agarose leads to considerable adsorption of the insulin-binding activity. Subsequently, the insulin-binding proteins can be eluted at pH 6.0 in the presence of 4.5 M urea. A purification of receptor of ~ 8,000-fold with respect to the membrane extract, and ~ 250,000-fold with respect to the original liver homogenate is achieved [50].

The plant lectins, Concanavalin A (Con A) and wheat germ agglutinin (WGA) have insulin-like action in fat cells and bind to insulin-receptor structures [49]. Agarose derivatives of these lectins also adsorb the insulin-binding proteins from detergent-solubilized preparations. At present, technical problems appear to limit somewhat the "capacity" of the derivatized agarose solumns, and thus, so far, prevent the isolation of large amounts of receptor protein. Nonetheless, it is expected that improvements on the approach outlined, will yield amounts of receptor sufficient for chemical characterization.

E. Insulin Receptors in Cultured Cells

The majority of studies in vitro concerning the action of insulin have been done with isolated tissue preparations (e.g., diaphragm, fat, liver). It has proved difficult, if not impossible, with such systems to obtain certain kinds of information (e.g., receptor turnover, biosynthesis) about insulin-receptor function. It is evident that cultured, propagable cell lines may provide an alternative system to provide such data. It has for many years been known that insulin at high concentrations (1 μg/ml) functions as a growth-promoting factor for cells in culture [70, 71]. Nonetheless, early experiments with cultured human fibroblasts [72] failed to show an action of insulin at concentrations within the physiological range (10^{-11} to 10^{-9} M). The development of the techniques described for the measurement of specific insulin-cell interactions makes possible an independent approach to the study of insulin receptors in cultured cells.

1. Insulin Receptors in Human Lymphocytes

Human peripheral white blood cells possess specific binding sites for insulin [73-75]. However, the studies of Krug et al. [73] reveal that,
whereas macrophages and, perhaps, other leukocytes can bind considerable amounts of insulin, nylon-column-purified lymphocytes free from
macrophages polymorphs and platelets possess less than one insulin binding site per cell. This finding has been confirmed by Olefsky and Reaven
[76].

   When nylon-column-purified lymphocytes are stimulated by a phyto-
mitogen such as Concanavalin A, there is a dramatic appearance of binding sites for insulin in step with the onset of DNA synthesis [73] (Figs. 15

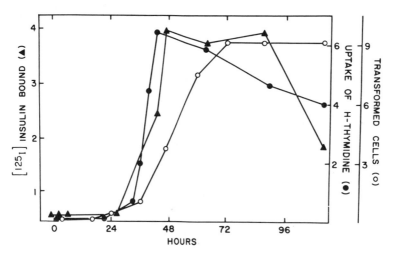

FIG. 15. Binding of insulin to lymphocytes during transformation.
Column-purified human peripheral-blood lymphocytes (5×10^5 cells per
ml) were cultured with Concanavalin A (40 μg/ml). Specific binding of
[^{125}I] insulin (10^{16} mol), incorporation of [^{3}H] thymidine into DNA (10^4
cpm), and the number of transformed cells ($\times 10^5$) are expressed per
10^6 cells. For thymidine incorporation into nuclear DNA, samples were
incubated with 1 μCi/ml [^{3}H] thymidine (6.7 mCi/μmol) for 3 hr at 37°C
in 5% CO_2 in air. The cells, chilled and washed with cold saline, were
precipitated with 5% Cl_3CCOOH. The precipitate, washed with cold 5%
Cl_3CCOOH and methanol, was dissolved (15 min at 70°C) in hydroxide of
hyamine before counting. [^{3}H] Thymidine uptake by unstimulated control
culture cells was always < 500 cpm per 10^6 cells and was, therefore,
neglected. All data represent mean values of three determinations.

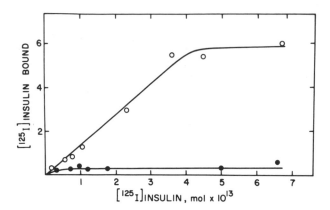

FIG. 16.   Binding of [^{125}I] insulin to lectin-transformed ($\bigcirc$) and untrans-
formed ($\bullet$) lymphocytes as a function of [^{125}I] insulin concentration.
Binding, in $10^{16} \times$ mol per 10^6 cells, is corrected for nonspecific adsorption of insulin. Measurements were made on aliquots of cells (3-4 $\times 10^6$)
in 0.2 ml of Hanks' buffer at 24°C. From [73].

and 16). The binding sites are not detected before stimulation by techniques (phospholipase digestion, triton-X solubilization) which in other
cells unmask cryptic insulin-binding sites. Cell division per se is not
required for the appearance of insulin-binding sites, since in the presence of cytochalasin B, which blocks mitosis, Concanavalin A-stimulated
multinucleated cells possess increased numbers of insulin-binding sites
in proportion to their increased surface area compared with untreated
Concanavalin A-stimulated cells. It is presumed either that the emergent insulin-binding sites are synthesized de novo or that, before Concanavalin A-stimulation, they are present in a form not readily detected.
The emergence of the insulin-binding site is not dependent on the nature
of the mitogenic stimulus; either phytohemagglutinin or periodate stimulated cells possess insulin-binding sites [77].

The lymphocyte insulin-binding sites share many characteristics in
common with those detected in fat cells, i.e., specificity for insulin,
saturability, increase in number on treatment with phospholipase. The
binding affinity (K_D about 10^{-9} M), however, appears to be about an
order of magnitude lower than that observed in liver and fat cells. Insulin-
binding sites are not the only "new" sites to appear. Specific binding sites
for nerve growth factor [77, 78] and growth hormone [79] can also be detected on lectin-stimulated lymphocytes. Binding sites for glucagon and
epidermal growth factor cannot, however, be detected [77 and unpublished
observations].

As yet it has not been possible reproducibly to demonstrate biological responses (glucose transport, protein, DNA, or glycogen synthesis) to physiological insulin concentrations with either the lectin-stimulated cells or the RPMI 6237 permanent cell line lymphocytes, which also possess insulin receptors [73 and unpublished observations]. Effects of insulin on α-aminoisobutyric acid transport in suckling rat thymocytes have been measured [80]. However, insulin is active in these cells only at concentrations (10^{-9} to 10^{-6} M) well above those which obtain for serum ($\sim 10^{-10}$ M). Thus, no physiological function can yet be ascribed to the emergent insulin receptors; and it is not possible to obtain biological measurements in parallel with the binding measurements, so as to interpret the significance of the lymphocyte receptors. It has been suggested [77] that the emergent receptors may be required either for completion of the mitogenic process itself or for some new function of the activated lymphocyte.

2. Insulin Receptors in Human Fibroblasts

In explanted human fibroblasts monolayers, it is possible to measure simultaneously the biological activity (stimulation of DNA synthesis and of α-aminoisobutyrate uptake) and binding of insulin [81-84]. Compared with epidermal growth factor (EGF), insulin is a relatively poor fibroblast mitogen (Fig. 17). In the presence of insulin alone, it is difficult to estimate with confidence an apparent K_m for stimulation of thymidine incorporation. However, if cells are simultaneously "primed" with EGF at a dose insufficient in itself to cause significant DNA synthesis, the insulin effect (thymidine incorporation) is magnified and a dose-response relationship can be obtained with greater precision (Fig. 18). An apparent K_m for insulin of about 10^{-9} M can be measured.

Insulin also stimulates the uptake of α-aminoisobutyric acid in identical confluent fibroblast monolayers (1.5-cm diam). Cells are first changed from the growth medium to an amino acid-free buffer [85, 86] containing 0.1% albumin. After equilibrating 1 to 2 hr at 37°C in an atmosphere of 5% CO_2 in air, fresh buffer containing insulin at the desired concentrations is added, and the incubation continued for 1 to 3 more hr. The action of insulin is maximal after ~ 1 hr. At the end of the insulin stimulation period, the uptake of α-aminoisobutyric acid in replicate monolayers is determined during a 12-min period in room air. The stimulation by insulin is dose-related, with a half-maximal effect at about 10^{-9} M; the action of insulin in this regard can be compared with that of EGF, which causes half-maximal stimulation at about 5×10^{-11} M (Fig. 19). The measurements of insulin-stimulated α-aminoisobutyric acid uptake provide a more precise estimate of the apparent K_m for insulin in the fibroblasts than do the measurements of insulin-mediated thymidine incorporation.

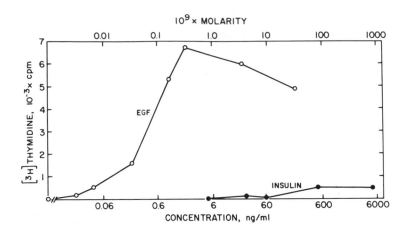

FIG. 17. Stimulation of thymidine incorporation by EGF and insulin in human fibroblasts. Confluent cells were refed with serum-free growth medium containing 0.1% (wt/vol) bovine albumin and either EGF or insulin. [^{3}H] Thymidine incorporation, measured at 23 hr is expressed as cpm/100 μg protein and is corrected for the amount incorporated in the absence of stimulant (390 ± 100 cpm for insulin; 900 ± 180 cpm for EGF) From Hollenberg and Cuatrecasas [81].

The binding of [^{125}I] insulin to the same fibroblasts is saturable and corresponds to the pharmacologic activity of insulin in these cells (Fig. 18). Binding measurements are performed on intact monolayers (1.5 cm) grown in multidish trays (Linbro Chemical Co., New Haven, Conn.). Cells are rinsed free from growth medium, and incubated with [^{125}I] insulin for 40 min at 24°C in 0.1% wt/vol albumin-buffer (Earle's or Hanks', pH 7.4), with or without native insulin (1 to 2 μg/ml). Monolayers are rinsed free from the supernatant with four 2-ml portions of ice-cold albumin-free buffer, and dispersed in 0.2 N NaOH (70°C for 10 min) for measurement of radioactivity and protein content. There are about 4,000 insulin-binding sites per cell, with an apparent K_D of approximately 10^{-9} M.

It may be pertinent that the affinity of insulin for receptors on fibroblasts and on lectin-stimulated lymphocytes differs significantly from that measured in the fat and liver cell: the K_D is approximately 10^{-9} M for fibroblasts and lymphocytes, versus 10^{-10} M in fat and liver tissue. The presence of receptors with an even lower affinity ($K_D \geq 10^{-8}$ M) for insulin can be inferred from other studies on cultured cells [74, 87, 89].

What might be the significance of receptor sites which at physiological insulin concentrations would be only minimally occupied? It is

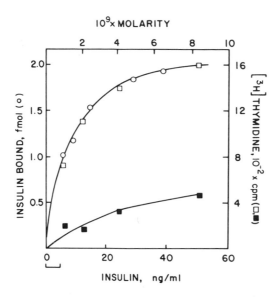

FIG. 18. Insulin binding and stimulation of thymidine incorporation in fibroblasts. Human skin-derived fibroblasts were grown to confluency ($\sim 3 \times 10^5$ cells; 100 μg protein) in 1.5-cm wells. Incorporation of thymidine (1 μCi/ml) during a 1 hr pulse, 24 hr after the addition of insulin, with (□) or without (■) EGF (40 pg/ml), is expressed as cpm per monolayer. Values, representing the mean incorporation in three replicate monolayers, are corrected for incorporation observed in the absence of insulin. The addition of EGF alone (40 pg/ml) led to the incorporation of 2,950 ± 60 cpm, with 2,580 ± 200 cpm incorporated in the absence of either EGF or insulin. In the experiment without EGF, 1,720 ± 30 cpm were incorporated in the absence of insulin. Insulin binding (O), determined for duplicate monolayers is corrected for non-specific binding of [^{125}I] insulin in the presence of native insulin (2 μg/ml) and is expressed as femtomoles bound per monolayer. The bar below the abscissa represents the physiological range of serum insulin concentrations (< 6 ng/ml or 150 μ per ml). From Ref. 83.

possible that the artificial conditions of tissue culture lead to a lowering of the insulin-receptor affinity. Evidence has been presented concerning the marked sensitivity of insulin receptors to trypsin and presumably to tissue cathepsins. While care is taken to eliminate completely the trypsin used in dispersing fibroblasts in culture, the possibility remains that residual tryptic action leads to a functional fibroblast receptor with lowered insulin affinity. It is important to point out, however, that

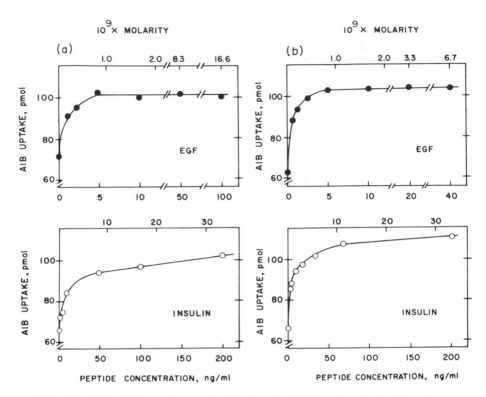

FIG. 19. Stimulation of α-aminoisbutyrate (AIB) uptake by insulin and EGF in fibroblasts derived from newborn foreskin (a) and from adult female forearm skin (b). Confluent monolayers were rinsed free from growth medium and incubated for 1 hr under 5% CO_2 in air at 37°C in Hanks' buffer pH 7.4 containing 25 mM tris-HCl, 0.1% bovine albumin, and increasing amounts of either EGF or insulin. At 1 hr, the uptake per monolayer of α-aminoisobutyrate (8 μM) was measured at 37°C in room air during a 12-min pulse as described in the text; values represent the average of duplicate determinations. (From Ref. 83).

under identical conditions of culture, the EGF receptor, which is also trypsin-sensitive [90], retains a high peptide affinity ($K_D \cong 10^{-10}$ M).

Alternatively, it is possible that insulin receptors exist in the cultured cells in a very large excess of those required for biological activation, such that maximal effects would occur with occupancy of only a small portion of receptors. It should be noted that receptor studies performed in recent years indicate that one should rigorously question previous data suggesting that some systems have a large proportion of "spare" receptors for endogenous hormones [16]. It is also possible that the lymphocyte- and fibroblast-binding sites interact with a noninsulin impurity present in small amounts, even in the best available insulin preparations. For example, contamination of 1% by an unrelated peptide having a $K_D = 10^{-11}$ M could account for the binding and biological data. Nonetheless, experiments with highly purified "single component" insulin yield dose-response curves in fibroblasts identical to those obtained with less pure recrystallized preparations. It is perhaps more likely that the lymphocyte- and fibroblast-binding sites do indeed interact specifically with insulin, but that the receptors may be intended for another, as yet unidentified, peptide.

Other peptides (somatomedin, multiplication stimulating activity, Con A, and WGA) are thought to interact with insulin-receptor structures [49, 91-94]. Is it not also possible that insulin will be found to cross-react with the physiological receptors for other, perhaps similar or related anabolic peptides? For instance, it is known that oxytocin can at high concentrations elicit an antidiuretic response, presumably interacting with vasopressin receptors; the action of vasopressin on the uterus at pharmacological concentrations is also well-documented. Other examples of cross-reactivity of peptides at receptor sites are becoming apparent. Vasoactive intestinal polypeptide (VIP) and secretin can interact at a common receptor site in liver membranes [95, 96]. This is an especially instructive example, since the binding sites which were originally discovered using ^{125}I-labeled secretin were assumed to be specific receptors for this hormone despite a relatively low apparent affinity for secretin. Actually, liver membrane receptors demonstrate a much greater affinity for VIP and are, therefore, likely to be the true receptors for this hormone. Human growth hormone and prolactin are thought to compete for receptor sites in pregnant rabbit breast and liver tissue [97, 98]. It may be of particular importance in view of the discussion that polypeptides from serum with insulin-like activities, which are not neutralized by anti-insulin antibodies (the so-called nonsuppressible insulin-like polypeptides, e.g., NSILA-S [99-100], appear to be more potent than insulin in stimulating DNA synthesis in human fibroblasts [101]. The meticulous analysis of the interaction of membrane-binding sites with peptide hormones of known structure may, thus, unexpectedly yield information germane to the action of other as yet unidentified, but physiologically important, polypeptides. It will be of considerable importance to compare the fibroblast affinity for insulin with the affinity for other insulin-related polypeptides.

IV. SUMMARY

It is felt that the studies outlined in this chapter to exemplify the methods employed in this and other laboratories for the study of insulin-receptor interactions illustrate some of the difficulties and successes of such an approach. A background is thereby provided for evaluating studies of a similar nature with other biologically active ligands.

Studies on insulin binding in fat and liver cells undoubtedly do reflect a true hormone-receptor interaction; there is a clear correlation between the biological (dose-response, serum level) and physico-chemical data. On the other hand, studies of the interaction of insulin with fibroblasts and lymphocytes reveal significant quantitative discrepancies between the K_D in the cultured cells and both the K_D observed in liver and fat cells and the known serum levels of insulin. These observations suggest interesting possibilities which can be elucidated by further work.

Methods in addition to measurements of ligand binding afford a more complete picture of the insulin receptor. The use of enzymatic probes complements studies of insulin binding, so as to provide information not only about the chemical structure of the insulin receptor itself, but also about the nature of those constituents involved in the translation of the binding signal into a cellular response. The solubilization and physico-chemical characterization of the insulin receptor has yielded information regarding the size of the insulin binding species. Macromolecular insulin derivatives prove useful both in localizing the insulin receptor at the cell membrane, and also in the isolation of receptors. Additionally, the macromolecular insulin derivatives possess interesting pharmacologic properties which warrant further study.

On the whole, the application of the general approach outlined has yielded some answers, as well as many interesting questions concerning the interaction of insulin with plasma membrane receptors. New approaches are needed to explore further the events coincident with and consequent to insulin binding. Hopefully this chapter may serve as a small stimulus for the development of such techniques.

REFERENCES

1. A. J. Clark, J. Physiol., 61:530 (1926).

2. A. J. Clark, J. Physiol., 61:547 (1926).

3. W. D. M. Paton and H. P. Rang, Proc. Roy. Soc. B, 163:1 (1965).

4. P. Cuatrecasas, Proc. Natl. Acad. Sci. U.S.A., 68:1264 (1971).

5. M. D. Hollenberg and P. Cuatrecasas, Proc. Natl. Acad. Sci. U.S.A., 70:2964 (1973).

6. F. C. Greenwood and W. M. Hunter, Biochem. J., 89:114 (1963).

7. J. I. Thorell and B. G. Johansson, Biochim. Biophys. Acta, 251: 363 (1971).

8. R. P. C. Shiu and H. G. Friesen, Biochem. J., 140:301 (1974).

9. J. Gliemann, K. Osterlind, J. Vinten, and S. Gammeltoft, Biochim. Biophys. Acta, 286:1 (1973).

10. P. Cuatrecasas and M. D. Hollenberg, Biochem. Biophys. Res. Commun., 62:31 (1975).

11. G. Scatchard, Ann. N.Y. Acad. Sci., 51:660 (1949).

12. P. Cuatrecasas, M. D. Hollenberg, K.-J. Chang, and V. Bennett, Recent Progr. Hormone Res., 31:37 (1975).

13. S. H. Snyder, personal communication 1973.

14. H. H. Loh, T. M. Cho, Y. C. Wu, and E. L. Way, Life Sci., 14: 2231 (1974).

15. A. Goldstein, L. Aronow, and S. M. Kalman, Principles of Drug Action, Wiley, New York, 1974, pp. 00-00.

16. P. Cuatrecasas, Ann. Rev. Biochem., 43:169 (1974).

17. M. D. Hollenberg and P. Cuatrecasas, in Biochem Actions of Hormones, (G. Litwack, ed.), Vol. 3, Academic Press, N.Y., 1975, p. 41.

18. J. N. Livingston, P. Cuatrecasas, and D. H. Lockwood, J. Lipid Res., 15:26 (1974).

19. K.-J. Chang and P. Cuatrecasas, J. Biol. Chem., 249:3170 (1974).

20. S. Jacobs, K.-J. Chang, and P. Cuatrecasas, Biochem. Biophys. Res. Commun., 66:687 (1975).

21. S. I. Taylor, Biochemistry, 14:2357 (1975).

22. I. M. Klotz and D. L. Munston, Biochemistry, 10:3065 (1971).

23. L. W. Nichol, G. D. Smith, and A. G. Ogston, Biochim. Biophys. Acta, 184:1 (1969).

24. S. Swillens, E. Van Cauter, and J. E. Dumont, Biochim. Biophys. Acta, 364:250 (1974).

25. K.-J. Chang, S. Jacobs, and P. Cuatrecasas, Biochim. Biophys. Acta, 406:294 (1975).

26. M. Rodbell, J. Biol. Chem., 239:375 (1964).

27. K.-J. Chang, D. Huang, and P. Cuatrecasas, Biochem. Biophys. Res. Commun., 64:566 (1975).

28. P. Cuatrecasas, B. Desbuquois, and F. Krug, Biochem. Biophys. Res. Commun., 44:333 (1971).

29. P. Cuatrecasas, Diabetes, 21 (Suppl. 2):396 (1972).

30. P. Freychet, J. Roth, and D. M. Neville, Jr., Proc. Natl. Acad. Sci. U.S.A., 68:1833 (1971).

31. P. Freychet, J. Roth, and D. M. Neville, Biochem. Biophys. Res. Commun., 43:400 (1971).

32. R. Kahn, P. Freychet, J. Roth, and D. M. Neville, Jr., J. Biol. Chem., 249:2249 (1974).

33. P. DeMeyts, J. Roth, D. M. Neville, Jr., and J. R. Gavin, III, Biochem. Biophys. Res. Commun., 55:154 (1973).

34. J. M. Hammond, L. Jarett, I. K. Mariz, and W. H. Daughaday, Biochem. Biophys. Res. Commun., 49:1122 (1972).

35. J. R. Kuo, C. E. Holmlund, I. K. Dill, and N. Bohonos, Arch. Biochem. Biophys., 117:269 (1966).

36. (a) T. J. Kono, J. Biol. Chem., 244:1772 (1969); (b) T. J. Kono, J. Biol. Chem., 244:5777 (1969).

37. J. N. Fain and S. C. Loken, J. Biol. Chem., 244:3500 (1969).

38. M. P. Czech and J. N. Fain, Endocrinology, 87:191 (1970).

39. P. Cuatrecasas, J. Biol. Chem., 246:6522 (1971).

40. P. Cuatrecasas, J. Biol. Chem., 246:6532 (1971).

41. T. Kono and F. W. Barham, J. Biol. Chem., 246:6210 (1971).

42. P. Cuatrecasas and G. Illiano, J. Biol. Chem., 246:4938 (1971).

43. R. M. M. El-Allawy and J. Gliemann, Biochim. Biophys. Acta, 273:97 (1972).

44. E. H. Cadenas, H. Kaji, C. R. Park, and H. Rasmussen, J. Biol. Chem., 236:PC 63 (1961).

45. H. Carlin and O. Hechter, J. Biol. Chem., 237:1371 (1962).

46. V. R. Lavis and R. H. Williams, J. Biol. Chem., 245:23 (1970).

47. P. Cuatrecasas, J. Biol. Chem., 247:1980 (1972).

48. J. W. Rosenthal and J. N. Fain, J. Biol. Chem., 246:5888 (1971).

49. P. Cuatrecasas and G. P. E. Tell, Proc. Natl. Acad. Sci. U.S.A., 70:485 (1973).

50. P. Cuatrecasas, Proc. Natl. Acad. Sci. U.S.A., 69:1277 (1972).

51. P. Cuatrecasas, Proc. Natl. Acad. Sci. U.S.A., 69:318 (1972).

52. B. Desbuquois and G. D. Aurbach, J. Clin. Endocrinol., 33:732 (1971).

53. V. T. Marchesi and E. D. Andrews, Science, 174:1247 (1971).

54. J. R. Gavin, III, D. N. Buell, and J. Roth, Science, 178:168 (1972).

55. T. C. Laurent and J. Killander, J. Chromatog., 14:137 (1964).

56. C. Tanford, Y. Nozaki, J. A. Reynolds, and S. Makino, Biochemistry, 13:2639 (1973).

57. J.-C. Meunier, R. W. Olsen, A. Menez, P. Fromageot, P. Boquet, and J.-P. Changeux, Biochemistry, 11:1200 (1972).

58. P. Cuatrecasas, Proc. Natl. Acad. Sci. U.S.A., 63:450 (1969).

59. K. J. Armstrong, M. W. Noall, and J. E. Stouffer, Biochem. Biophys. Res. Commun., 47:354 (1972).

60. F. Suzuki, Y. Dakuhara, M. Ono, and Y. Takeda, Endocrinology, 90:1220 (1972).

61. P. Cuatrecasas, in Advances in Enzymology (A. Meister, ed.), Vol. 36, Wiley, New York, 1972, p. 29.

62. V. Sica, E. Nola, I. Parikh, G. A. Puca, and P. Cuatrecasas, Nature, New Biol., 244:36 (1973).

63. G. S. David, T. H. Chino, and R. A. Reisfeld, FEBS Lett., 43:264 (1974).

64. P. Cuatrecasas, Science, 179:1143 (1975).

65. I. Parikh, S. March, and P. Cuatrecasas, in Methods in Enzymology (W. B. Jakoby and M. Wilchek, eds.), Academic Press, New York, 1974, p. 77.

66. J. L. Garwin, and T. D. Gelehrter, Arch. Biochem. Biophys., 164:52 (1974).

67. H. J. Kolb, R. Renner, K. D. Hepp, L. Weiss, and O. Wieland, Proc. Natl. Acad. Sci. U.S.A., 72:248 (1975).

68. T. Oka and Y. J. Topper, Proc. Natl. Acad. Sci. U.S.A., 68:2066 (1971).

69. D. D. Soderman, J. Germershausen, and M. Katzen, Proc. Natl. Acad. Sci. U.S.A., 70:792 (1973).

70. G. O. Gey and W. Thalhimer, J. Amer. Med. Soc., 82:1609 (1924).

71. H. M. Temin, R. W. Pierson, Jr., and N. C. Dulak, in Growth, Nutrition and Metabolism of Cells in Culture (V. I. Cristofalo and G. Rothblat, eds.), Vol. I, Academic Press, New York, 1972, p. 50.

72. S. Goldstein and J. W. Littlefield, Diabetes, 18:545 (1969).

73. U. Krug, F. Krug, and P. Cuatrecasas, Proc. Natl. Acad. Sci. U.S.A., 69:2604, (1972).

74. J. R. Gavin, Jr., J. Roth, P. Jen, and P. Freychet, Proc. Natl. Acad. Sci. U.S.A., 69:747 (1972).

75. J. R. Gavin, III, P. Gorden, J. Roth, J. A. Archer, and D. N. Buell, J. Biol. Chem., 248:2202 (1973).

76. J. Olefsky and G. M. Reaven, J. Clin. Endocrinol. Metab., 38:554 (1974).

77. M D. Hollenberg and P. Cuatrecasas, in Control of Proliferation in Animal Cells (B. Clarkson and R. Baserga, eds), Cold Spring Harbor, N.Y., 1974, pp. 423-434.

78. S. P. Banerjee, S. H. Snyder, P. Cuatrecasas, and L. A. Greene, Proc. Natl. Acad. Sci. U.S.A., 70:2519 (1973).

79. R. S. Bockman and M. Sonenberg, personal communication 1973.

80. I. D. Goldfine, J. D. Gardner, and D. M. Neville, Jr., J. Biol. Chem., 247:6919 (1972).

81. M. D. Hollenberg, and P. Cuatrecasas, Proc. Natl. Acad. Sci. U.S.A., 70:2964 (1973).

82. M. D. Hollenberg and P. Cuatrecasas, J. Clin. Invest., 53:33a (1974).

83. M. D. Hollenberg and P. Cuatrecasas, J. Biol. Chem., 250:3845 (1975).

84. M. D. Hollenberg, Life Sciences, 18:521 (1976).

85. J. H. Hanks, and R. E. Wallace, Proc. Soc. Exptl. Biol. Med., 71:196 (1949).

86. W. R. Earle, J. Natl. Cancer Inst., 4:165 (1974).

87. N. D. Goldberg, M. K. Haddox, E. Dunham, C. Lopez, and J. W. Hadden, in Control of Proliferation in Animal Cells (B. Clarkson and R. Baserga, eds.), Cold Spring Harbor, N.Y., 1974, p. 609.

88. W. L. Risser, T. D. Gelehrter, J. Biol. Chem., 248:1248 (1973).

89. A. Vaheri, E. Ruoslahti, T. Hovi, and S. Nordling, J. Cell. Physiol., 81:355 (1973).

90. E. O'Keefe, M. D. Hollenberg, and P. Cuatrecasas, Arch. Biochem. Biophys., 164:518 (1974).

91. R. L. Hintz, D. R. Clemmons, L. E. Underwood, and J. J. Van Wyk, Proc. Natl. Acad. Sci. U.S.A., 69:2351 (1972).

92. R. W. Pierson, Jr. and H. M. Temin, J. Cell. Physiol., 79:319 (1972).

93. N. C. Dulak and H. M. Temin, J. Cell. Physiol., 81:153 (1973).

94. N. C. Dulak and H. M. Temin, J. Cell. Physiol., 81:161 (1973).

95. B. Desbuquois, M. H. Laudet, and Ph. Laudet, Biochem. Biophys. Res. Commun., 53:1187 (1973).

96. B. Desbuquois, Eur. J. Biochem., 46:439 (1974).

97. R. P. C. Shiu, P. A. Kelly, and N. G. Friesen, Science, 180:968 (1973).

98. T. Tsushima and H. G. Friesen, J. Clin. Endocrinol. Metab., 37:334 (1973).

99. O. Oelz, E. R. Froesch, H. F. Bunzli, R. E. Humbel, and W. J. Ritschard, in Handbook of Physiology (D. F. Steiner and N. Freinkel, eds.), Vol. 1, Williams and Wilkins, Baltimore, 1971, pp. 685–702.

100. R. E. Humbel, H. Bunzli, K. Mully, O. Oelz, E. R. Froesch, and W. J. Ritschard, in Proceedings of the VII Congress of the International Diabetes Federation (R. R. Rodriguez and J. Valance-Owen, eds.), Excerpta Medica, Amsterdam, 1971, 306–317.

101. M. M. Rechler, J. M. Podskalny, I. D. Goldfine, and C. A. Wells, J. Clin. Endocrinol. Metab., 39:512–521 (1974).

102. P. Cuatrecasas, in Proc. Symp. on Insulin, Academic Press, N. Y., 1972, p. 137.

Chapter 14

LECTIN RECEPTORS

Vilma K. Jansons

Department of Microbiology
College of Medicine and Dentistry of New Jersey
New Jersey Medical School
Newark, New Jersey

and

Max M. Burger

Department of Biochemistry
Biocenter of the University of Basel
Basel, Switzerland

I. INTRODUCTION   480

II. ASSAYS FOR WGA-RECEPTOR ACTIVITY   480

    A. Inhibition of Agglutination   480
    B. Inhibition of Binding   481

III. ISOLATION OF WGA RECEPTOR   482

    A. Preparation of Receptor-Containing Subcellular Fractions   482
    B. Solubilization   486
    C. Fractionation   488

IV. ISOLATION OF RECEPTORS FOR OTHER LECTINS   490

    A. General Survey   490
    B. Mitogenic Lectin Receptors in Lymphocytes   490

V. DISCUSSION   493

    REFERENCES   494

I. INTRODUCTION

Derived from plants and invertebrates, lectins are proteins that can interact with carbohydrates present in mammalian cell membranes [1, 2]. The
sequelae to lectin-cell interactions are varied and complex. To mention
some examples, a lectin may preferentially agglutinate transformed cells
[3], influence growth of neoplastic cells [4], or stimulate lymphocytes to
transform [5]. The first step always is the binding of the lectin to a receptor in the plasma membrane. The number of purified lectins is increasing
continuously. An extensive bibliography is presented in a recent review
[3], and detailed procedures for the purification of several lectins are
compiled in a volume on methods [6].

The isolation and purification of lectin receptors is still a new field
with many problems and uncertainties. Of the methods reported so far,
none has been totally satisfactory. In this chapter, several procedures
will be discussed for each phase of isolation and purification, since at
this time an eclectic approach might be the most fruitful. The emphasis
will be on the isolation of the receptor(s) for wheat germ agglutinin (WGA).
Since the WGA receptor(s) has been isolated using all the major procedures, it provides a common basis for comparison of the methods described
by different laboratories for other lectin receptors.

II. ASSAYS FOR WGA-RECEPTOR ACTIVITY

A. Inhibition of Agglutination

To test for WGA-receptor activity, the inhibition of agglutination is most
commonly used. The agglutinating titer of a particular WGA preparation
is determined as follows. Twofold serial dilutions of WGA are set up in
small test tubes, the first tube containing usually 100 μg of WGA per 0.1
ml in 0.154 M NaCl-0.01 M phosphate buffer, pH 7.2 (PBS). To each
WGA concentration, test cells are added in 0.05 ml PBS. Agglutination
is cell type- and cell number-dependent. A good response with susceptible
cells is usually obtained with 10^7 cells per ml but quite often 2×10^6 cells
are sufficient. Tube contents are mixed, then a drop is transferred to a
hemagglutinating tray on a rocking platform at room temperature, where
mixing is allowed to proceed for 4 min. Agglutination is scored from 0
to +4, corresponding to the following percentage of single cells remaining:

100-88% = 0; 63-44% = +1; 32-23% = +2; 15-10% = +3; and 3-0% = +4.
Intermediate values are recorded in brackets [7]. To test for inhibition,
twofold serial dilutions of WGA receptor are carried out in small test
tubes, starting with 50 μg per 0.05 ml PBS. A concentration of WGA to give
+3 agglutination is added in 0.05 ml PBS to each test tube, mixed, and
allowed to stand for 10 min; then 0.05 ml of cells in PBS are added. Agglutination is scored as previously described. The inhibitory capacity
of the WGA-receptor fraction is obtained calculating the minimum concentration of the receptor which fully inhibits +3 agglutination.

B. Inhibition of Binding

The ability of an isolated receptor to inhibit binding between a lectin and
cell surface is a more direct test for receptor activity than inhibition of
agglutination. Adair and Kornfeld [8] have studied the inhibition of binding of [^{125}I] WGA to human erythrocyte ghosts by membrane glycoproteins
solubilized in Triton X-100. The authors feel that although whole cells
could not be used since they would lyse, the presence of the detergent did
not interfere significantly in their binding assay.

1. Preparation of [^{125}I] WGA

WGA is iodinated following the procedure of Hunter [9], as follows: 25 μl
of chloramine-T (100 μg) is added to 200 μl of WGA solution (200 μg) containing 2 mCi of carrier-free Na^{125}I (New England Nuclear) in 0.1 M
sodium phosphate-0.1 M N-acetyl glucosamine, pH 7.4, and after 20 sec
at 25°C, 100 μl of sodium metabisulfite (240 μg) is added, followed by 200
μl of potassium iodide (2 mg). The reaction mixture is passed over a
column of Sephadex G-25 and the [^{125}I] WGA is recovered in the excluded
volume. The specific activity is 10^5-10^6 cpm/μg [10].

2. Inhibition of Binding

A standardized assay mixture containing 250 μg of bovine serum albumin
(BSA), 1 to 20 μg of [^{125}I] WGA, an aliquot of the solubilized receptor,
and 0.15 M NaCl-0.01 M NaHCO$_3$ to a total volume of 0.2 ml is incubated
for 15 min at room temperature, then 50 μl of ghosts (equivalent to 5×10^6
cells) are added, and the incubation continued for an additional 30 min.
Five milliliters of 0.15 M NaCl are added, and the diluted mixture is
filtered through a Millipore filter (PHWP, 0.3 μ) which has been presoaked
in 0.5% BSA solution for at least 2 hr before use. The presoaking is
important, to prevent WGA from sticking to the Millipore membrane. The
filters are washed twice with 5-ml portions of saline, then placed in
counting tubes, and counted in a Packard Autogamma counter. Control
samples are set up, omitting the receptor [8].

III. ISOLATION OF WGA RECEPTOR

WGA receptor has been isolated from nucleated cells and human erythrocytes by several methods which differ in the way the receptor-containing
subcellular fractions are prepared and also in further steps in isolation.
A summary on methods utilized to isolate WGA receptor is presented in
Table 1.

A. Preparation of Receptor-Containing Subcellular Fractions

Three procedures have been used to prepare the starting material: (1)
hypotonic extraction, (2) controlled surface hydrolysis by proteolytic
enzymes, and (3) isolation of membranes. The selection of a method
would depend on the type of subsequent investigation planned. For example, a study on the relationships between receptor and membrane glycoproteins in general would require as a first step the isolation of whole
membranes. It should be realized, however, that markers reacting exclusively with outer surface glycoproteins should be included to identify
the WGA receptors exposed on the intact cell surface. The use of proteolytic enzymes to obtain surface glycopeptides must be carefully monitored to ensure that only surface material has been released. Studies on
surface glycopeptides can contribute to the identification and structural
analysis of the oligosaccharides which react with WGA, but they cannot
produce information on the whole protein structure, nor can they ascertain
if the glycopeptides originated from one or several membrane glycoproteins. In yet another method, cells are subjected to a slight hypotonic
shock, which causes the release of cell-surface material. The short-
coming of this method is that, while certain cells, e.g., L1210, release
WGA receptor-containing fractions very easily while 90% of cells remain
viable, other types of cells, e.g., L5178Y, bind the receptors more
tightly. Under conditions in which the viability of such cells is maintained,
there is only a partial release of WGA receptor; WGA continues to agglutinate the treated cells. Furthermore, one has to be aware that during
such an extraction procedure, new WGA-receptor sites may become
available.

1. Hypotonic Extraction

This method has been used to isolate WGA receptor from L1210 cells [11].

a. Propagation of Cells

L1210 cells are maintained in DBA/2 mice by weekly i.p. injections
(5×10^4 cells per mouse). If long-range experiments are planned, stock
suspensions of tumor cells should be stored at -70°C in 12.5% dimethyl-

TABLE 1. Representative Methods for Isolation of WGA Receptor

Cell type	Assay for receptor activity	Subcellular fraction utilized for isolation of receptor	Solubilizing agent	Fractionation	Recovery	Ref.
Human erythrocytes	Inhibition of binding	RBC ghosts	Triton X-100	Affinity chromatography	6%	[8]
Mouse leukemia L1210	Inhibition of agglutination	Plasma membrane fraction	Lithium diiodosalicylate (LIS), phenol, pyridine, guanidine HCl	Conventional column chromatography; affinity chromatography	n.d.[a]	[11]
In vitro cultured L1210	Inhibition of agglutination	Isolated plasma membrane	LIS	---	n.d.[a]	[12]
Rat ascites hepatoma AS-30 D	Inhibition of agglutination	Papain-labile glycopeptides	---	Conventional column chromatography	n.d.[a]	[14]

[a] n.d.: Not determined.

sulfoxide. Not more than 15 transfers from a stock suspension of L1210 cells should be done in DBA/2 mice. From these mice, the hybrid BDF$_1$ can be injected for weekly harvest of material. Since the L1210 line has been carried for many years in different laboratories under varying conditions, it is likely that variations in the susceptibility to the hypotonic shock as well as in the composition and content of membrane glycoproteins might be found.

It is also possible to use L1210 cells adapted for growth in tissue culture. Large quantities of cells can be obtained from commercial sources, e.g., Associated Biomedic Systems, Inc. (Buffalo, N.Y.). L1210 cells will grow in suspension culture in MEM (Grand Island Biologicals (GIBCO), N.Y.), supplemented with 10% calf serum, 10% fetal calf serum, 20% NCTC (GIBCO), and 1% penicillin (10,000 units/ml) streptomycin (10,000 μg/ml), or in supplemented RPMI 1640 (GIBCO) [12]. Saturation density for L1210 cells in supplemented MEM is 2×10^6 cells per ml. In our laboratory we have not observed differences in agglutinability of L1210 cells by WGA as a function of cell density.

b. Labeling of Cells

L1210 cells adapted to growth in tissue culture are labeled with [^{3}H] glucosamine by the following procedure: 2×10^6 cells are seeded in 75-cm^2 Falcon flasks containing 20 ml of the supplemented MEM described in the preceding discussion. After incubation for 24 hr at 37°C, 200 μCi of [^{3}H] glucosamine, (D-glucosamine-6-^{3}H; New England Nuclear, 6 mCi/mg) are added to each flask. Cells are allowed to grow for an additional 72 hr before being harvested. A method for incorporation of isotope into L1210 cells grown intraperitoneally in mice has also been described [13].

c. Harvesting and Extraction

L1210 cells propagated in mice are harvested on day seven after i.p. injection. Optimally, a BDF mouse will yield 0.3 to 0.5 ml packed cells. Cells are immediately washed by centrifugation at 25°C in 30 volumes of 0.15 M NaCl. This ratio is necessary to wash off material adsorbed to cell surface. Washing is repeated three times. Single cell suspensions without clumps are obtained more easily if cell sediments after centrifugation are at first suspended in small quantities of 0.15 M NaCl, (1:1 vol/vol) and gently dispersed by pipetting. The final 1:30 dilution is done only after a smooth homogeneous cell suspension has been obtained. Contaminating red blood cells can be removed from the cell sediment by aspiration. A preferential lysis of red blood cells after the first wash in 0.15 M NaCl can also be achieved by incubation for 10 min at ambient temperature in 0.8% NH$_4$Cl. Under these conditions, red blood cells are lysed while L1210 cells show only a slight loss of viability.

Tissue culture cells for isolation of WGA receptor can be harvested when maximal density has been reached. It might be relevant in this context to point out that agglutinability by Concanavalin A (Con A), however, has been reported to decrease with increase in cell density [12]. Cells are washed in calcium-magnesium-free phosphate buffered saline. We prefer to carry out the washing procedure as fast as possible after cells have been harvested, using solutions at ambient temperatures.

Washed cells ($1\text{-}5 \times 10^8$ cells per 5 ml) are incubated in 0.8% NaCl for 20 min at 37°C under slow rotatory shaking. At the end of the incubation period, the supernatant fluid is collected by centrifugation at 400 $\underline{g}$ for 5 min and stored at 5°C, while the cell pellet is resuspended in 0.7% NaCl ($1\text{-}5 \times 10^8$ cells per 5 ml) and reextracted again for 20 min at 37°C. Washing of cells, as well as separation of cells and supernatant fluids, should be done in plastic tubes, using swinging bucket rotors to decrease loss in cell viability. Both supernatant fluids are combined and centrifuged for 90 min at 105,000 $\underline{g}$ to obtain the sediment which contains the receptor fraction. The nucleic acid associated with the sediment is removed by treatment with ribonuclease (Ribonuclease A; Worthington Biochemicals). Sediment originating from 1 ml of packed cells is suspended in 1 ml of 0.1 M tris-HCl buffer, pH 8.5, 0.01 M $CaCl_2$. RNase (20 μg) is added, and the reaction mixture is incubated for 1 hr at 37°C. Digestion of the nucleic acid is followed by monitoring the increase in absorption of the soluble fraction at 260 nm. Upon completion, the samples are diluted with cold distilled water, and sediments are collected and washed twice in cold distilled water by centrifugation for 1 hr at 100,000 $\underline{g}$. If possible, the sediment should be solubilized without freezing. However, in order to accumulate large quantities of material, storage is sometimes necessary. In that case, sediments are stored frozen at -20°C.

2. Isolation of Surface Material Using Proteolytic Enzymes

Both papain and trypsin have been used to release surface glycopeptides.

a. Papain

Smith and co-workers have described a procedure for obtaining papain-labile glycopeptides from rat ascites hepatoma cells, AS-30D [14]. Cells were washed in calcium- magnesium-free phosphate-buffered saline, pH 7.5; then 4×10^7 cells per ml were incubated for 40 min at 37°C in the presence of papain, 3 units per ml of cell suspension. This concentration of enzyme was found to be optimal for release of glycopeptides containing WGA-receptor sites. Similar papain treatment has also been used to release WGA-receptor sites from Ehrlich ascites cells [15].

b. Trypsin

Trypsin also releases glycopeptides containing WGA-receptor sites [18]. Erythrocytes from 3 liters of outdated bank blood were washed three times with three volumes of 0.15 M NaCl-0.01 M $NaHCO_3$ to remove the plasma and buffy coat. Then red blood cells were trypsinized for 1 hr at 37°C by incubating one volume of packed cells in one volume of 0.15 M NaCl-0.05 M phosphate buffer containing 0.25 mg trypsin per ml. After incubation, cells were removed by centrifugation. The supernatant fluid was chilled and one-eighth volume of cold 50% trichloroacetic acid was added. The precipitate was removed by centrifugation. The supernatant fluid, which contains the glycopeptides, was neutralized with NaOH, dialyzed overnight at 4°C, and lyophilized.

3. Isolation of Membranes

Since lectin receptors are plasma membrane glycoproteins, any method which yields clean plasma membrane preparations could be used as a starting point for the isolation of lectin receptors. Erythrocyte ghosts are most commonly isolated by the procedure of Dodge et al. [17]. Detailed methods for preparation of membranes from several types of nucleated cells have been compiled recently [18]. Membranes from 1210 cells, subsequently used to isolate glycoproteins containing WGA receptors, have been prepared by Hourani and co-workers [12]. L1210 cells were allowed to swell in a hypotonic buffer, then homogenized. The membranes were isolated by partition in a two-phase system of polyethylene glycol and Dextran.

B. Solubilization

If membrane fractions or whole membranes are used as starting material for the isolation of WGA receptor, the next step in the isolation procedure is solubilization. Complete solubilization of membrane glycoproteins presents a difficult problem which has not yet been resolved. Glycoprotein fractions containing WGA-receptor activity have been obtained following solubilization with several reagents as discussed in the following sections.

1. Lithium Diiodosalicylate [LIS]

Originally described by Marchesi et al. [19] for isolation of sialoglycoprotein from red blood cells, this method has also been used to isolate WGA receptor(s) from L1210 cells [11].

The sediment described in Sec. III. A. 1. c is suspended (2 mg protein per ml) in 0.05 M tris-HCl buffer, pH 7.4. Freshly recrystallized LIS [19] is added at a concentration of 120 mg/ml. The mixture is stirred for 15 min at room temperature, then a double volume of distilled water is added, and stirring continued for an additional 20 min at 4°C. The soluble fraction is collected after centrifugation for 90 min at 45,000 g, 4°C, an equal volume of cold 50% phenol is added (vol/vol), and the mixture is stirred for 20 min at 4°C. Phase separation is achieved by centrifugation for 1 hr at 4,000 g. The water layer is carefully collected and dialyzed exhaustively against distilled water, whereupon the sample is lyophilized. The lyophilized material is further extracted by suspending (1 mg/ml) in absolute alcohol at 0°C, stirring for 1 hr at 0°C, and centrifuging (10,000 g, 30 min) to collect the precipitate. This procedure is repeated three times, whereupon the sediment is dissolved in distilled water and dialyzed overnight. The water-soluble glycoprotein fraction is collected after centrifugation for 1 hr at 100,000 g. It is advisable to carry out further fractionation without lyophilization, since reaggregation might occur. A similar LIS extraction procedure has also been used to solubilize WGA receptor from L1210 cell membranes [12].

2. Pyridine, Guanidine HCl, Phenol

In addition to the LIS solubilization procedure, the hypotonic "shockate" from L1210 cells has also been extracted by other methods used for solubilization of erythrocyte membrane glycoproteins [11]. These are: pyridine [20], guanidine HCl [21], and phenol [22]. Removal of the solubilizer by dialysis in each case resulted in reaggregation of the glycoproteins.

3. Triton X-100

Triton X-100 has been used by Adair and Kornfeld [8] to solubilize ghosts of human erythrocytes. The soluble fraction contained 70 to 75% of the WGA-receptor activity.

Ghosts were extracted with Triton X-100 following the procedure of Yu et al. [23]. One hundred seventy-five milliliters of ghosts were mixed with 800 ml ice-cold 0.5% Triton X-100 in 0.056 M sodium borate buffer, pH 8. The suspension was kept for 20 min at 4°C with occasional stirring, then centrifuged for 1 hr at 12,000 g. The supernatant fluid contained the solubilized receptors. Removal of the detergent at this point would result in reaggregation.

C. Fractionation

The procedures that can be used to further purify the solubilized fractions depend on previous steps employed to obtain the material. If glycoproteins are solubilized using detergents, the same detergents would also have to be included in the fractionation to prevent reaggregation. On the other hand, when cells have been treated with proteolytic enzymes, glycopeptides which are water-soluble have been collected. Further fractionation can then be achieved with gel filtration and ion-exchange chromatography, which has resulted in a partial resolution of the glycopeptides. Even here reaggregation cannot be excluded.

1. Conventional Column Chromatography

a. Surface Glycopeptide Fraction

The papain-labile glycopeptides from AS-30D hepatoma cells (see Sec. III. A. 2) were resolved into three fractions upon gel filtration on Sephadex G-50, eluted with 0.1 N acetic acid [14]. Each of these fractions was further digested with pronase and chromatographed on Sephadex G-200. The highest WGA-receptor activity was found in a broad peak not completely resolved from the void. This material was chromatographed on a DEAE-cellulose column equilibrated in 0.002 M pyridine-acetic acid buffer, pH 5.3. A fraction possessing WGA-receptor activity was separated from a fraction with Concanavalin A activity.

b. Plasma Membrane Fraction

Partial purification of WGA-receptor fraction obtained from L1210 cells by hypotonic extraction (see Sec. III. A. 1) has been achieved by chromatography on Sephadex G-200, equilibrated in 33% pyridine, 0.0014 M mercaptoethanol [11]. This method was originally described by Blumenfeld et al. [20] for separation of erythrocyte membrane glycoproteins. In the presence of pyridine, partial resolution of both the pyridine- and the phenol-extractable fraction was achieved. For example, the phenol-extractable fraction of L1210 cells containing [3H]glucosamine-labeled glycoproteins resolved into two peaks bearing the [3H]label. Both peaks contained WGA-receptor activity, the lower-molecular-weight material (mol wt 40,000-60,000 daltons) had a fourfold higher receptor activity than the higher-molecular-weight fraction eluting right after the void volume. Upon removal of pyridine, reaggregation was sometimes observed [11].

2. Affinity Chromatography

To date, the most successful use of affinity chromatography for the isolation of WGA receptor has been reported by Adair and Kornfeld [8], who used Triton X-100-solubilized erythrocyte glycoproteins, described in Sec. III. B. 2. These authors show that glycoproteins solubilized by the detergent bind to the affinity column in presence of the detergent and can be eluted with the specific hapten, N-acetylglucosamine.

a. Preparation of WGA Affinity Column

Sepharose 2B is activated with cyanogen bromide following the method of Cuatrecasas et al. [24]. Five milliliters of the activated Sepharose beads are washed with 200 ml of 0.1 M NaHCO$_3$ in a Buchner funnel, then suspended in 50 ml of 0.01 M NaHCO$_3$-0.15 M NaCl containing 40 mg WGA and 0.1 M N-acetylglucosamine to protect the active site. The pH is adjusted to 7.4, and the mixture is stirred gently overnight at 4°C, then packed into a column. The column is washed with 0.15 M NaCl-0.01 M NaHCO$_3$, followed by 0.056 M sodium borate buffer, pH 8.0, and 0.1 M N-acetylglucosamine.

b. Elution

(1) In the Presence of Detergent. Before use, the affinity column is equilibrated with 0.5% Triton X-100 in 0.056 M sodium borate buffer, pH 8.0 [8]. The glycoproteins from erythrocytes, solubilized in Triton X-100, are applied to the column at room temperature. The column is washed with 1 M NaCl in 0.5% Triton X-100, then with 0.5% Triton X-100 in borate buffer, and finally eluted with 0.1 M N-acetylglucosamine. The eluate is dialyzed exhaustively against 0.002 M phosphate buffer, pH 8.0. The dialyzed material should not be lyophilized, but can be concentrated by an Amicon pressure concentrator and stored for a short time (a week) at 4°C, since there is a continuous slow reaggregation. Only 6% of the WGA-receptor activity present in the solubilized erythrocyte ghosts was recovered. The authors advised to overload the column, since then "the glycoproteins with higher affinity will displace those with lower and the fraction eluted finally with the hapten will be more homogenous" [8].

(2) Elution Without Detergent. LIS-solubilized WGA receptor from L1210 cells, as described in Sec. III. B. 1, has also been further fractionated by affinity chromatography. The affinity column is prepared and washed as already described, except that no detergent is used. Best results are obtained if affinity chromatography is done on freshly prepared material which has not been lyophilized. A fraction which is eluted by 0.1 M N-acetylglucosamine has WGA-receptor activity [11].

IV. ISOLATION OF RECEPTORS FOR OTHER LECTINS

A. General Survey

A summary on isolation procedures for receptors of several lectins is presented in Table 2. In general, these methods are similar to those already described for the isolation of WGA receptor. Cell-surface glycopeptides are most often used as a starting material [14, 16, 25, 26]; in one study, the carbohydrate sequence of the PHA receptor isolated from human erythrocytes has been determined [16]. Several lectin receptors have been isolated from human erythrocyte ghosts following solubilization in Triton X-100. Glycoprotein fractions containing lectin receptors for Ricinus communis and Abrus precatorius were separated from receptors for Agaricus bisporus, Lens culinaris, PHA, and WGA by sequential elution on two lectin-Sepharose columns with different affinities [8].

B. Mitogenic Lectin Receptors in Lymphocytes

Crumpton and co-workers have conducted a systematic study on the receptors for Con A [27], PHA [28], and Lens culinaris lectin [29] in pig lymphocytes.

1. Isolation Procedures

Pig lymphocyte membranes were isolated and solubilized in 1% sodium deoxycholate. The glycoprotein receptors for Con A and Lens culinaris lectin were fractionated by affinity chromatography on the respective lectin-Sepharose column [27, 29]. The PHA receptor was isolated by first incubating [^{125}I] PHA with pig lymphocytes, then solubilizing the lectin-cell complex in 1% sodium deoxycholate. The [^{125}I] PHA-membrane-receptor complex was isolated by gel filtration on Sepharose 6B in the presence of 1% sodium deoxycholate [28].

2. Assay for Receptor Activity of Mitogenic Lectins

Since one of the sequelae to mitogenic lectin-lymphocyte interactions is stimulation of DNA synthesis, the inhibition of [^{3}H]thymidine incorporation can be used to assay for receptor activity. The control system contains lymphocytes, lectin, and [^{3}H]thymidine. In the experimental system, several concentrations of the receptor are first preincubated with the lectin. The differences in the [^{3}H]thymidine incorporation between the control and test system are recorded [28].

TABLE 2. Procedures for Isolation of Lectin Receptors

Lectin and source	Specific inhibitor	Cell type	Assay for receptor activity	Subcellular fraction utilized for isolation of the receptor	Solubilizing agent	Fractionation	Ref.
Con A (Concanavalin A); Canavalia ensiformis	D-mannoside D-glucoside	Pig lymphocytes	Inhibition of [³H] thymidine incorporation	Plasma membrane	1% sodium deoxycholate	Affinity chromatography	[27]
		L1210	Inhibition of agglutination	Plasma membrane	Lithium diiodo-salicylate	---	[12]
		Rat ascites hepatoma AS-30D	Inhibition of agglutination	Papain-labile glycopeptides	---	Conventional column chromatography	[14]
		Normal and transformed hepatic cells (Zajdela's hepatoma) in rat	Inhibition of agglutination; inhibition of cell growth	Trypsin-labile glycopeptides	---	Conventional column chromatography	[25]
PHA (Phytohemagglutinin); Phaseolus vulgaris	N-acetyl-D-galactosamine	Human erythrocytes	Inhibition of agglutination	Trypsin-labile glycopeptides	---	Conventional column chromatography	[16]
		Pig lymphocytes thymus cells	Lectin-receptor complex formation	[¹²⁵I] PHA-cell complex	1% sodium deoxycholate	Sepharose 6B; sucrose density gradient	[28]

(continued)

491

TABLE 2 (continued)

Lectin and source	Specific inhibitor	Cell type	Assay for receptor activity	Subcellular fraction utilized for isolation of the receptor	Solubilizing agent	Fractionation	Ref.
Common lentil agglutinin; Lens culinaris	Mannose, N-acetyl- D-glucosamine	Human erythrocytes	Inhibition of binding	RBC ghosts	Triton X-100	Affinity chromatography	[8]
		Pig lymphocytes	Inhibition of [³H] thymidine incorporation	Plasma membrane	1% sodium deoxycholate	Affinity chromatography	[29]
Castor bean agglutinin; Ricinus communis							
a. Ricin	N-acetyl- galactosamine Lactose	Human erythrocytes	Inhibition of binding	RBC ghosts	Triton X-100	Affinity chromatography	[8]
b. RCA	Galactose						
Abrus precatorius lectin	Galactose						
Common mushroom lectin; Agaricus bisporus	Galactose, N-acetyl- galactosamine						
Pea phyto- hemagglutinin; Pisum sativum	D-glucosides D-mannosides D-fructose	Human erythrocytes	Inhbition of agglutination	Pronase-labile glycopeptides	---	Gel filtration; preparative paper electrophoresis	[26]

V. DISCUSSION

One of the most challenging problems in lectin receptor research is to
solubilize the glycoprotein receptors and prevent reaggregation. Even
if receptors are isolated as trypsin- or papain-labile glycopeptides, reaggregation occurs unless the glycopeptides are further hydrolyzed by
pronase. However, when WGA receptor, isolated as a glycoprotein, was
treated with pronase, 98% of the receptor activity was lost [8] .

The recent progress in lectin receptor isolation from erythrocytes
is due to the finding that Triton X-100, a nonionic detergent, preferentially
releases membrane glycoproteins [23] and does not significantly interfere
with the subsequent binding of a lectin to its glycoprotein receptor. Nevertheless, a modification of the general method might be necessary in order
to find the conditions best suited for a particular cell type and lectin.

At this time, most, if not all, isolated receptors must be considered
heterogeneous. Yields are small in most cases, therefore, also qualita-
tively distinct receptors might be missed. The receptor glycoproteins
may also represent a functionally heterogeneous population, including
virus and hormone receptors as well as enzymes. Among the latter may
even be degradative enzymes, e.g., proteases and glycosidases which can
contribute to the unequal degradation of the receptor fraction and alter the
functional groups in affinity chromatography. Unfortunately, the detergents used to improve the efficiency of the fractionation of membrane
glycoproteins quite often not only restrict the investigator in his choice
of biological assays, but even influence the outcome of the few remaining
less sensitive biological assays. It is obvious that inhibition of mitogenic
effects by detergent-containing receptor fractions may turn out to be a
serious problem, since this test requires metabolically active cells and
prolonged incubation periods. But even the inhibition of agglutination,
which is a short assay and is not so dependent on metabolically undamaged
cells, can be influenced by small amounts of detergents or chaotropic
agents like lithium diiodoslicylate. Since the effect of these agents varies
not only from cell to cell, but also depends on the lectin type, one should
run a series of exploratory tests.

It is generally assumed that a lectin reacts with membrane carbohydrates, since the interaction between the cell and the lectin can be blocked
by a carbohydrate hapten. However, nonspecific interactions and "allo-
steric" effects have to be considered. Indeed, we have found that both
Con A and WGA bind tightly to glass and other noncarbohydrate surfaces,
but can be easily removed with appropriate doses of carbohydrate "haptens."
Furthermore, almost all isolation procedures used so far are designed to
selectively purify glycoproteins and remove glycolipids. Although the lower
concentration of potential glycolipid receptors in many cell membranes, as
well as the better availability of the branched carbohydrate portions of the

long glycoprotein extensions, may have justified this neglect; one will have to consider the glycolipids in further evaluations and precise analyses of the detailed makeup of the lectin-receptor molecule population.

Lectins are very useful tools in the study of membrane carbohydrates. However, it would be an oversimplification to imply that all solubilized glycoproteins which bind to a lectin represent lectin receptors on the intact cell surface.

REFERENCES

1. W. C. Boyd, Ann. N.Y. Acad. Sci., 169:168 (1970).

2. N. Sharon and H. Lis, Science, 177:949 (1972).

3. A. M. C. Rapin and M. M. Burger, Advan. Cancer Res., 20:1 (1974).

4. M. M. Burger and K. D. Noonan, Nature, 228:512 (1970).

5. C. K. Naspitz and M. Richter, Progr. Allergy, 12:1 (1968).

6. V. Ginsburg, ed., Methods in Enzymology, Vol. 28, Sec. III, Articles 34 through 46 (S. P. Colowick and N. O. Kaplan, eds.), Academic Press, New York, 1972, p. 313.

7. T. L. Benjamin and M. M. Burger, Proc. Natl. Acad. Sci. U.S.A., 67:929 (1970).

8. W. L. Adair and S. Kornfeld, J. Biol. Chem., 249:4696 (1974).

9. W. M. Hunter, in Handbook of Experimental Immunology (D. M. Weir, ed.), Blackwell Scientific Publishers, Oxford, England, 1967, p. 608.

10. W. R. Redwood, V. K. Jansons, and B. C. Patel, Biochim. Biophys. Acta, 406:347 (1975).

11. V. K. Jansons and M. M. Burger, Biochim. Biophys. Acta, 291:127 (1973).

12. B. T. Hourani, N. M. Chace, and J. H. Pincus, Biochim. Biophys. Acta, 328:520 (1973).

13. J. G. Bekesi, G. St. Arneault, L. Walter, and J. F. Holland, J. Natl. Cancer Inst., 49:107 (1972).

14. D. F. Smith, G. Neri, and E. F. Walborg, Jr., Biochemistry, 12: 2111 (1973).

15. V. P. Wray and E. F. Walborg, Jr., Cancer Res., 31:2072 (1971).

16. R. Kornfeld and S. Kornfeld, J. Biol. Chem., 245:2536 (1970).

17. J. T. Dodge, C. Mitchell, and D. J. Hanahan, Arch. Biochem. Biophys., 100:119 (1963).

18. S. Fleischer and L. Packer, eds., Methods in Enzymology, Vol. 31, Sec. II, Articles 5 through 16 (S. P. Colowick and N. O. Kaplan, eds.), Academic Press, New York, 1974, p. 75.

19. V. T. Marchesi and E. P. Andrews, Science, 174:1247 (1971).

20. O. O. Blumenfeld, P. M. Callop, C. Howe, and L. T. Lee, Biochim. Biophys. Acta, 211:109 (1970).

21. J. T. Gwyne and C. Tanford, J. Biol. Chem., 245:3269 (1970).

22. R. H. Kathan, R. J. Winzler, and C. A. Johnson, J. Exptl. Med., 113:37 (1961).

23. J. Yu, D. A. Fischman, and T. L. Steck, J. Supramol. Struct., 1:233 (1973).

24. P. Cuatrecasas, M. Wilchek, and C. B. Anfinsen, Proc. Natl. Acad. Sci. U.S.A., 61:636 (1968).

25. J. C. Dievard and R. Bourrillon, Biochim. Biophys. Acta, 345:198 (1974).

26. J. Kubanek, G. Entlicher, and J. Kocourek, Biochim. Biophys. Acta, 304:93 (1973).

27. P. Allan, J. Auger, and M. J. Crumpton, Nature, New Biol., 236:23 (1972).

28. D. Allan and M. J. Crumpton, Exptl. Cell Res., 78:271 (1973).

29. M. J. Haymand and M. J. Crumpton, Biochem. Biophys. Res. Comm., 47:923 (1972).

Chapter 15

METHODS USED IN THE STUDY OF OPIATE RECEPTORS

Eric J. Simon

Department of Medicine
New York University Medical Center
New York, New York

I.   INTRODUCTION   498

II. PREPARATION AND PURIFICATION OF LABELED LIGANDS   498

III. TISSUE PREPARATIONS FOR BINDING STUDIES   499

IV. ASSAY OF STEREOSPECIFIC OPIATE BINDING
     ON MEMBRANES   502

     A. Centrifugation Techniques   502
     B. Morphine-Receptor Assay in Cultured Cells   503
     C. Filtration Technique   503
     D. Assay of Stereospecific Binding in Lipid Extracts   504
     E. Assay of Stereospecific Narcotic Binding to Brain
        Cerebrosides   504

V.   ASSAY FOR AGONIST AND ANTAGONIST PROPERTIES
     OF OPIATES   506

VI. PREPARATION OF AFFINITY CHROMATOGRAPHY BEADS
     FOR RECEPTOR PURIFICATION   506

     A. Preparation of Morphine-Sepharose Beads   507
     B. Preparation of Opiates Covalently Attached to Glass
        Beads by Diazotization   507

VII. AFFINITY LABELING   508

      ACKNOWLEDGMENTS   509

      REFERENCES   509

I. INTRODUCTION

The methods used in the studies of opiate receptors may appear relatively primitive when compared to techniques utilized for the study of other receptors discussed in this work. It must be remembered, however, that the existence of stereospecific binding sites for narcotic analgesic drugs in animal brain was demonstrated only recently [1-3]. Even more recently we have demonstrated the existence of such binding sites in human brain obtained at autopsy [4]. Evidence accumulated in several laboratories since that time is consistent with the hypothesis that the stereospecific binding sites represent pharmacologically important opiate recognition sites. They are frequently referred to as opiate receptors, and we will continue this tradition for the sake of brevity. It should be pointed out, however, that the correct definition of a receptor requires the presence of a recognition and binding site as well as a transducer which permits receptor-ligand interaction to trigger the biochemical events that lead to the pharmacological response. The latter has not yet been demonstrated for opiate receptors, but, except for the possible implication of adenyl-cyclase in certain hormone receptors, nothing conclusive is known about the transducing element for any receptor.

Goldstein and his collaborators [5] have reported the existence of other stereospecific opiate-binding sites which are extractable into lipid solvents. They differ from the receptors already mentioned in localization, affinity for opiates, and sensitivity to a variety of enzymes and reagents.

This chapter will review methods which have been used to date for the study of both types of receptors, in a variety of systems ranging from animal and human brain, to cells in culture, and cerebrosides obtained from commercial sources.

II. PREPARATION AND PURIFICATION OF LABELED LIGANDS

Tritium-labeled etorphine (20 Ci/mmol) and naltrexone (15.3 Ci/mmol) are now available in excellent purity upon request from Dr. Robert Willette, Biochemical Research Branch, National Institute on Drug Abuse, Rockville, Md. Tritium-labeled naloxone and morphine can now be purchased from New England Nuclear Corporation, Boston, Mass. Other opiates or antagonists labeled with tritium at high specific activity can be readily obtained by custom labeling from one of the radioisotope supply houses. The preparations are carried out by standard methods of catalytic exchange or reduction of a double bond and will, therefore, not be described here.

The radio purity of labeled ligands is assayed by thin layer chromatography (TLC). Purification is generally done by preparative TLC on silicic acid plates. Table 1 lists a number of solvent systems used in our laboratory and the R_f values for a number of opiates and opiate antagonists.

I will illustrate purification procedures by the manner in which [³H]-etorphine is purified in our laboratory. Labeled etorphine (10-100 μCi) is spotted on silica gel plates containing fluorescent indicator (E. Merck 60 F 254) under a stream of nitrogen. Unlabeled etorphine (10-30 μg) is spotted in lanes on both sides of the lane containing the radioactive material. The unlabeled etorphine is readily visualized under u.v. light by the quenching of the fluorescence of the indicator. The plates are developed in a suitable solvent system, usually sytem 1 (Table 1), which requires 4 to 5 hr (solvent front moves 12-15 cm from origin). Plates are removed from the tank and dried in a stream of nitrogen. When barely dry, the etorphine zones are visualized and marked. The silica in the corresponding zone on the [³H] etorphine lane is scraped off the plate and placed overnight in the dark in 5 ml of chloroform-ethanol (3:1). The extract is counted, and purity is checked by chromatography in at least two solvent systems. The solvent is removed from the silica gel by decantation or filtration and evaporated to dryness in a stream of nitrogen. The residue is dissolved in water and diluted to appropriate concentration. The specific activity can be estimated by measuring u.v. absorption of a suitable solution at 285 nm.

III. TISSUE PREPARATIONS FOR BINDING STUDIES

Initially, all binding studies were carried out in whole brain homogenates. These were prepared from a variety of animals, but most commonly from rats. Male Sprague-Dawley rats (200-300 g) were decapitated by guillotine. The brain was dissected and, once it was established that the cerebellum was devoid of binding capacity, the cerebella were removed. The brain was homogenized at 2°C in 6 to 10 volumes of 0.32 M sucrose per gram, wet weight, of brain in a motor-driven tissue homogenizer (teflon pestle). These homogenates are readily stored at -20°C for 1 to 2 weeks with little loss in binding activity. For binding experiments, the homogenates are thawed and diluted to suitable tissue concentrations (usually

ERIC J. SIMON

TABLE 1. TLC Solvent Systems for Opiates

Solvent system	Opiate R_f values				
	Etorphine	Naltrexone	Naloxone	Levorphanol	Morphine
1. Butanol:acetic acid:water[a] (60:15:25)	0.53	0.38	0.30	0.53	0.37
2. Ethanol:acetic acid:water[b] (60:30:10)	0.73	0.75	–	–	0.54
3. Methanol:benzene:butanol:water[c] (60:10:15:15)	0.90	0.48	0.80	0.34	–
4. Ethanol:pyridine:dioxane:water[b] (50:20:25:15)	0.84	0.72	0.86	–	0.22
5. Methanol:chloroform:ammonium hydroxide[d] (25:75:3 drops)	0.85	0.56	0.07	0.85	0.21

[a] Courtesy of Reckitt and Coleman, Ltd., Hull, England.
[b] From Cochin and Daly [6].
[c] Courtesy of New England Nuclear Corporation, Boston, Mass.
[d] Courtesy of Research Triangle Institute, Research Triangle Park, N.C.

10-40 mg wet weight per ml) with 0.05 M tris-HCl buffer, pH 7.4. The hypotonicity breaks the synaptosomes, but the binding sites remain sedimentable and are presumed to be tightly bound to membranes.

More recently in our laboratory, most binding studies have been performed using rat brain synaptosomal-mitochondrial fractions (P_2), prepared essentially as described by Gray and Whittaker [7]. A rat brain homogenate (1:10, wt/vol) in 0.32 M sucrose is centrifuged at 1,000 g for 10 min. The supernatant fluid is removed and the pellet washed once with 0.32 M sucrose at the same centrifugal force. The wash is added to the supernatant, and the combined supernatant (S_1) is centrifuged at 17,000 g for 15 min. The supernatant is discarded, and the pellet (P_2) is resuspended in the original volume of sucrose. Upon dilution with tris buffer it is ready for use. This fraction contains over 90% of the binding capacity of the whole homogenate and is equally stable at -20°C.

Pert et al. [8] use a washed homogenate prepared as follows: Rat brains, after removal of cerebella, are homogenized in ice-cold 0.05 M tris-HCl buffer, pH 7.4 (100 ml/g wet weight), for 20 sec in a Polytron PT-10 homogenizer, 3,000 rpm. After centrifugation at 10,000 g for 10 min, the supernatant fluid is discarded and the pellets reconstituted in the original volume of tris buffer.

We have recently found that a synaptosomal membrane fraction isolated from the olfactory lobes of the brain of the smooth dog fish (Mustelus canis) is a very convenient and rich source of opiate receptors [E. J. Simon, H. Sher, and H. Meilman, unpublished data]. These fractions can be prepared in very pure form in a single centrifugation step as follows: Olfactory lobes are homogenized in 0.7 M sucrose (10% homogenate wt/vol). The homogenate is centrifuged at 17,000 g for 15 min. Nuclei, mitochondria, and some broken synaptosomes sediment into a tight pellet, while intact synaptosomes float at the top of the sucrose as a pellicle which can be skimmed or poured off. It is then freed of supernatant fluid, rinsed with sucrose, and resuspended by mild homogenization in tris buffer to break the synaptosomes. The synaptosomal membranes can be purified further, if desired, by sedimentation and washing.

Goldstein and his collaborators [5] perform their binding studies in lipid extracts of mouse brain prepared as follows: Each mouse brain (~500 mg wet weight) is homogenized at room temperature in 9.5 ml of chloroform-methanol (2:1, vol/vol). After centrifugation, the extract is washed once with 0.2 volume of distilled water, then precipitated with four volumes of cold ether. The precipitate is sedimented by centrifugation at 8,000 g for 5 min and redissolved in chloroform-methanol.

IV. ASSAY OF STEREOSPECIFIC OPIATE BINDING ON MEMBRANES

A. Centrifugation Techniques

The first use of stereospecific binding as an assay for putative opiate receptors was reported by Goldstein et al. [9] in 1971. These authors incubated mouse brain homogenate with labeled levorphanol in the presence of a 100-fold excess of either unlabeled levorphanol or its inactive enantiomorph dextrorphan. Since levorphanol will block both specific and nonspecific binding of [^{3}H]levorphanol, while dextrorphan would be expected to block only nonspecific binding, the difference in binding observed should be a measure of stereospecific binding. The binding assay was carried out as follows: A mouse brain homogenate (10%, wt/vol) in 0.32 M sucrose in .01 M tris-HCl, pH 7.0, was prepared and diluted to give concentrations of 50 to 150 μg protein per ml. Five-milliliter aliquots were incubated at 25°C in 10-ml polypropylene tubes with 50 μg/ml of unlabeled dextrorphan or levorphanol. Tritiated levorphanol (37.6 μCi/mg, 0.5 μg/ml) was added to the tubes 5 min later and incubation continued for 15 min. Tubes were centrifuged for 1 hr at 105,000 g. The supernatant fluid was discarded, and adhering moisture was removed with absorbent cotton. Pellets were dissolved in 0.1 M NaOH or in Hyamine hydroxide and counted by liquid scintillation. By this technique, only ~2% of total radioactivity adhering to the tissue pellet represented stereospecific binding.

Modifications of this technique, which resulted in 50 to 80% of total binding being stereospecific, were adopted independently in three laboratories [1–3]. These consist of (1) the use of labeled opiates or antagonists with very high specific activities (2–30 Ci/mmol), which permit use of very low drug concentrations (10^{-10} M to 10^{-8} M); and (2) washing of the homogenates after incubation with cold buffer to remove contaminating unbound and loosely bound radioactivity. The modified sedimentation technique is done as follows: Brain homogenate, 2 ml containing 1 to 2 mg of protein per ml, is incubated at 37°C for 5 min with either unlabeled dextrorphan or levorphanol (10^{-7} or 10^{-6} M). Labeled opiate or antagonist (10^{-10} to 10^{-8} M) is added and incubation continued for 15 min. The homogenate is then sedimented at 20,000 g for 15 min. The supernatant is removed, and the pellets washed twice with cold 0.05 M tris-HCl buffer, pH 7.4, by resuspension and centrifugation at the same centrifugal force. The washed pellets are transferred to counting vials provided with teflon-lined screwcaps, using 0.3 ml of water in two portions. Protosol (1 ml) is added, and digestion is allowed to proceed at 55°C for at least 3 hr. Samples are allowed to cool, and 10 ml of toluene counting fluid and three drops of glacial acetic acid (to minimize chemoluminescence) are added. Samples are counted by liquid scintillation, preferably in a refrigerated counter.

B. Morphine-Receptor Assay in Cultured Cells

Recently, Klee and Nirenberg [10] have reported the presence of high-affinity receptors for morphine in a neuroblastoma x glioma hybrid cell line with well-developed neural properties. Neither of the parental lines had receptors. Specific binding was assayed as follows: Cells were centrifuged at 500 g for 5 min at room temperature, and the pellets were washed twice with D-1 salt solution (137 mM NaCl, 5.4 mM KCl, 0.17 mM Na_2HPO_4, 0.22 mM KH_2PO_4, 5.5 mM glucose) and suspended in 0.32 M sucrose, 0.01 M tris-HCl buffer, pH 8.0, at a concentration of ~0.5 mg protein per ml. This cell suspension was added to a plastic test tube containing either 10 μl of water or 10 μl of 10^{-4} M morphine sulfate. A solution (100 μl) of [^{3}H]dihydromorphine (10^{-8} M, 51.2 Ci/mmol) in 0.32 M sucrose was added to each tube. Samples were mixed on a vortex mixer and incubated at 37°C for 10 min. Tubes were centrifuged at 19,000 rpm (45,000 g) for 10 min in a Sorvall centrifuge at 0°C, and supernatants were removed and discarded. Each tube and surface of pellet was washed with 1 ml of 0.32 M sucrose, and the washed pellet was resuspended in 1 ml of 1% Triton X-100 and assayed for radioactivity after addition of 7.5 ml of Triton-toluene scintillation fluid. All operations were carried out in very dim light because morphine and dihydromorphine are readily photo-oxidized. The difference between binding in the presence and absence of morphine is considered to be receptor binding.

C. Filtration Technique

A rapid filtration technique was introduced by Pert and Snyder [2], which has been found useful for a variety of brain homogenates and fractions. For a given tissue, it is necessary to compare the results of filtration with those of sedimentation. Thus, in our studies of opiate receptors in the brain of dog fish (Mustelus canis), the filtration technique gave low and erratic results, and sedimentation had to be used (Simon, Sher, and Meilman, unpublished results).

Brain homogenates or P_2 fractions are diluted with 0.05 M tris buffer to give protein concentrations of 0.2 to 2 mg/ml. Two-milliliter aliquots are incubated as described for the sedimentation assay. Samples are then filtered through Whatman GF/B glass-fiber filters, 24-cm in diameter, and washed twice with 4 ml volumes of ice-cold tris buffer. Filters are dried under an infrared lamp and counted in toluene scintillation cocktail (10 ml) in a liquid scintillation counter. Proteins are determined by the method of Lowry et al. [11]. Results are reported as picomoles of drug bound stereospecifically per milligram of brain protein.

With the pure, labeled drugs of very high specific activity obtained from NIDA, stereospecific binding now constitutes 80 to 90% of total binding. Typical results obtained recently in our laboratory by the filtration technique are presented in Table 2. The results obtained by centrifugation are comparable.

D. Assay of Stereospecific Binding in Lipid Extracts

The technique used by Lowney et al. [5] for studying stereospecific opiate binding in lipid extracts was adapted from the method used in the laboratory of deRobertis [12]. To tissue extract in chloroform-methanol (50-100 μl), or an equivalent volume of the solvent, is added 1 ml of n-heptane and 1 ml of 0.1 M tris-HCl, pH 7.4. [^{14}C] Levorphanol or [^{3}H] dextrorphan (aqueous phase concentration 10^{-7} to 10^{-6} M) is added to separate samples and allowed to equilibrate between the two phases by three treatments, for 10 sec each, on a vortex mixer. The tubes are centrifuged for 1 min at 1,000 g at room temperature to separate the phases before sampling each phase for radioactivity. The increase in the apparent partition coefficient (organic/aqueous) caused by the tissue extract is the measure of binding. The binding of [^{3}H] dextrorphan is subtracted from the binding of [^{14}C] levorphanol to obtain the amount of stereospecific binding.

E. Assay of Stereospecific Narcotic Binding to Brain Cerebrosides

Recently, Loh et al. [13] have reported high-affinity stereospecific binding of etorphine and naloxone to cerebrosides (from bovine brain) obtained from Sigma Chemical Company. Stereospecific binding was assayed in cerebroside liposomes as follows: Cerebroside (200 mg) was dissolved in 20 ml of chloroform to which 200 ml of 50 mM sodium phosphate buffer (pH 7.4) was added with stirring. After removal of chloroform at 60 to 65°C with stirring, 1.0-ml aliquots containing 1 mg of cerebroside in suspension were added to polypropylene tubes containing an appropriate amount of either nonradioactive dextrorphan, levorphanol, etorphine, or morphine (usually $1-2 \times 10^{-5}$ M) dissolved in 0.5 ml of 50 mM sodium phosphate buffer, pH 7.4. Each tube was incubated for 2 hr at 37°C, and after addition of 0.5 ml of 0.8 μM [^{3}H] naloxone (3.6 Ci/mmol) or 0.08 μM [^{3}H] etorphine (3.4 Ci/mmol), the incubation was continued for another hour. The tubes were cooled in ice, centrifuged at 40,000 g for 30 min, and the supernatant was discarded. The pellet was washed twice by resuspension in 5 ml of cold 50 mM phosphate buffer and centrifugation at the same centrifugal force. The washed pellet was suspended in 1 ml of water, and radioactivity was determined by liquid scintillation counting after addition of 10 ml of toluene-Triton X-100 cocktail.

TABLE 2. Stereospecific Binding Assays by Filtration Procedure[a]

Drug	Concentration (M)	d (cpm)	l[b] (cpm)	d-l (cpm)	pmoles bound per mg protein
Etorphine	4.0×10^{-10}	4,100	540	3,560	0.09
	1.6×10^{-9}	7,800	2,000	5,800	0.15
Naltrexone	1.0×10^{-9}	3,013	560	2,453	0.08
	2.3×10^{-9}	5,360	1,340	4,020	0.13

[a]Two milliliters of rat brain P_2 fraction (1 mg protein per ml) were incubated with [^{3}H]etorphine (20 Ci/mmol) or [^{3}H]naltrexone (15.3 Ci/mmol) for 15 min, after preincubation for 5 min with either 10^{-6} M dextrorphan (d) or 10^{-6} M levorphanol (l). Samples were filtered, washed and counted as described in the text. Stereospecific binding is given as the difference (d-l) and as pmol/mg protein bound stereospecifically.

[b]Filtration of labeled etorphine or naltrexone in the absence of brain fraction indicated that ~70 to 80% of the nonspecific binding (l) is to the filter, not to the tissue.

V. ASSAY FOR AGONIST AND ANTAGONIST

PROPERTIES OF OPIATES

We reported profound inhibition of stereospecific etorphine binding by increasing concentrations of salt [1], while no such effect was observed by Pert and Snyder [2] on naloxone binding. On the basis of these observations, we suggested that this may represent a general difference in the manner in which opiate agonists and antagonists are bound. Pert et al. [8] subsequently showed that indeed all agonists tested exhibit reduced binding in the presence of salt, whereas the binding of antagonists is significantly enhanced. They also found that this discriminatory effect is specifically exerted by sodium ions.

When competition of opiate drugs is studied using a labeled "pure" antagonist as the ligand ([^{3}H] naloxone or [^{3}H] naltrexone), the ED_{50} concentration of the competing opiate is increased only slightly or not at all, in the presence of 0.1 M NaCl, if the latter is also an antagonist. If the competing drug is an agonist, its ED_{50} concentration increases from 10- to 60-fold in 0.1 M sodium chloride, while drugs which exhibit mixed agonist-antagonist properties show an intermediate (3- to 7-fold) increase [8, 14].

It is, therefore, possible to obtain an idea of the pharmacology of a new drug with respect to its opiate agonist and/or antagonist potencies by assaying its stereospecific binding to rat brain homogenate in the absence and presence of salt. If the new drug is not available in labeled form, this is done by measuring its competition for binding with a known labeled antagonist, such as [^{3}H] naloxone or [^{3}H] naltrexone. Binding assays are carried out as described previously, both in the presence and absence of 0.1 M NaCl, using five to six concentrations of the unknown drug. Percent of control binding of labeled antagonist is plotted on probit paper against the log of the drug concentration. The concentration of the unknown, which reduces the binding of the labeled antagonist by 50% (ED_{50}), is determined from the plot.

VI. PREPARATION OF AFFINITY CHROMATOGRAPHY BEADS

FOR RECEPTOR PURIFICATION

Purification of receptors is most readily accomplished once the receptor molecules are solubilized in aqueous medium. This has not been achieved at the time this chapter is being written. We have, however, some preliminary results suggesting that membranes containing opiate receptors may be purified by affinity chromatography. Moreover, once opiate-binding molecules are obtained in water solution, affinity beads will be of considerable usefulness for purification. We will, therefore, describe

several preparations of opiates linked covalently to solid beads, suitable
for affinity chromatography.

A. Preparation of Morphine-Sepharose Beads [15]

It is best to couple a drug to its support via a functional group known not
to be required for pharmacological activity. The hydroxyl group in position 6 of morphine is such a group. The specific esterification of the 6-
position with a succinyl group is readily achieved by refluxing morphine
(free base) with excess succinic anhydride for 3 hr in a solvent (20 ml/g)
such as benzene. (Pyridine was used in earlier experiments, but yields
and purity of product are better in benzene.) After decantation of benzene,
the residue is dissolved in water. Unreacted morphine is removed by
filtration at pH 9, where succinylmorphine remains in solution. The pH
is then adjusted to 5, where 6-succinylmorphine crystallizes at 4°C overnight. The yield is 60 to 70% of theoretical.

The 6-succinylmorphine is coupled via the free carboxyl group to
agarose beads containing side arms ending in free amino groups. Sepharose 4B with hexylamine side arms is now available from Pharmacia
(AH-Sepharose 4B). The coupling is done by a procedure similar to that
described by Cuatrecasas [16] for coupling succinylestradiol to agarose,
except that the reaction is carried out in aqueous medium. Fifty milligrams of 6-succinylmorphine (usually tritium-labeled to facilitate determination of bound residues) are dissolved in 20 ml of H_2O. The solution
is added to 12 ml of AH-Sepharose 4B beads. The pH is adjusted to 5
and 250 mg of 1-ethyl-3-(3-dimethylaminopropyl) carbodiimide is added
slowly over 5 min. The pH is monitored frequently and readjusted to 5
with 0.1 N HCl. The reaction is allowed to proceed at room temperature
for 20 hr. The beads are washed in a column successively with 1 liter
of 0.1 M NaCl-0.01 M tris-HCl, pH 7; 100 ml of 1 M NaCl, and again
with 1 liter of NaCl-tris buffer. The yield of morphine bound is 0.1 to
0.3 μmol/ml of settled beads. The beads are stored with sodium azide
(0.025%), and washed extensively immediately before use to remove the
azide and small amounts of released morphine.

Morphine-glass beads have been made in an identical manner by using
glass beads with alkylamino side arms (GAO-3940; Pierce Chemical Co.).

B. Preparation of Opiates Covalently Attached to Glass
Beads by Diazotization

The use of glass beads with side arms which terminate in aromatic amine
groups allows the coupling by diazotization of a variety of morphine derivatives. The drugs can be used directly without previous derivatization.

The method used is essentially that described by Venter et al. [17] for immobilizing catecholamines.

Glass beads containing alkylamine side chains are obtained from Pierce Chemical Company (GAO-3940). Arylamino groups are added by the introduction of nitrobenzene groups and subsequent reduction with sodium dithionite as follows: To 1 g of the GAO glass, add 10 ml of a chloroform solution containing 100 mg of p-nitrobenzoyl chloride and 50 mg of triethylamine. The reaction mixture is refluxed for 1 hr; the solution is then decanted, and the glass washed three times with chloroform. The glass can be air dried or heated for 30 min at 80°C to remove the chloroform.

The nitrated glass is reduced by adding 10 ml of a 1% aqueous sodium dithionite solution and refluxing for 30 to 60 min. The reaction solution is decanted and the aromatic amine product washed three times with water.

The resulting arylamine glass is diazotized and coupled to a drug in the following manner: 10 ml of 2 N HCl are added to 1 g of glass beads in an ice bath followed by 0.25 g of sodium nitrite. The nitrous oxide gas evolved is evacuated by placing the reaction mixture in a vacuum dessicator attached to a water pump for 30 min. The solution is decanted, and the beads are washed on a coarse, sintered glass filter with large quantities of cold distilled water, followed by cold 1% sulfamic acid and again by cold water.

The diazotized beads are coupled to a drug by adding 5 ml of a solution of the drug (10 mg/ml) to the beads and incubating in ice for 60 min, by which time the beads will assume a deep yellow-to-red color. The color frequently intensifies upon overnight incubation in the refrigerator. The beads are washed on a coarse glass filter with 1 liter of HCl (pH 1) and 1 liter of water. Under these conditions ~50 μmol of drug are bound per gram of beads. The beads are stored at 4°C in 0.1 N HCl as a slurry. This procedure has been used to attach morphine, levorphanol, dextrorphan, and etorphine to the glass beads.

VII. AFFINITY LABELING

One method, which has proved powerful in the isolation of a variety of biological macromolecules, and may eventually be exceedingly useful in the isolation and purification of opiate receptors, is affinity labeling. This technique involves the synthesis of molecules closely related to the ligands, in our case opiates, but containing an active chemical group able to form a covalent bond with functional groups at the active binding sites of the receptors. An even more elegant technique is photoaffinity labeling, developed by Westheimer and his collaborators [18], in which

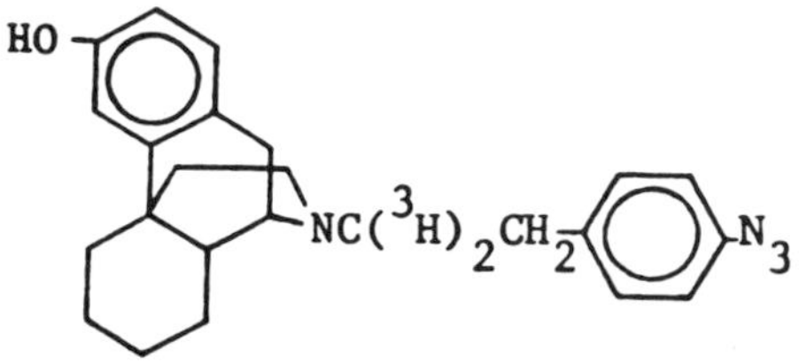

FIG. 1

molecules are constructed which react with the active site in the usual reversible manner, but which will form a covalent bond when irradiated with ultraviolet light.

A photoaffinity labeling derivative of levorphanol has been synthesized by Winter and Goldstein [19]. The formula of this compound, $[^3H]N-\beta-$(p-azidophenyl) ethylnorlevorphanol, is shown in Figure 1. This drug has potent opiate-like pharmacological activity in mice and in the isolated guinea pig ileum. Upon photolysis for 10 to 15 min in the presence of brain homogenate, using a Hanovia medium-pressure mercury arc lamp, radioactivity was irreversibly incorporated into the particulate matter of the homogenate. To date, no stereospecific blocking of this incorporation has been reported. However, compounds of this kind should be exceedingly useful once suitable conditions for their use have been worked out.

ACKNOWLEDGMENTS

The author's work was supported by grant DA-00017 from the National Institute on Drug Abuse. The author thanks his collaborators, Dr. J. M. Hiller, Ms. I. Edelman, and Ms. J. Groth and his students, Mr. N. Clendeninn, Mr. K. Stahl, and Dr. M. C. Walker for their valuable contributions to that portion of the work carried out in his laboratory.

REFERENCES

1. E. J. Simon, J. M. Hiller, and I. Edelman, Proc. Natl. Acad. Sci. U.S.A., 70:1947 (1973).

2. C. B. Pert and S. H. Snyder, Science, 197:1011 (1973).

3. L. Terenius, Acta Pharmacol. Toxicol., 32:317 (1973).

4. J. M. Hiller, J. Pearson, and E. J. Simon, Res. Commun. Chem. Pathol. Pharmacol., 6:1052 (1973).

5. L. I. Lowney, K. Schulz, P. J. Lowery, and A. Goldstein, Science, 183:749 (1974).

6. J. Cochin and J. W. Daly, Experientia, 18:294 (1961).

7. E. G. Gray and V. P. Whittaker, J. Anat., London, 96:79 (1962).

8. C. B. Pert, G. Pasternak, and S. H. Snyder, Science, 182:1359 (1973).

9. A. Goldstein, L. I. Lowney, and B. K. Pal, Proc. Natl. Acad. Sci. U.S.A., 68:1742 (1971).

10. W. Klee and M. Nirenberg, Proc. Natl. Acad. Sci. U.S.A., 71:3474 (1974).

11. O. H. Lowry, N. J. Rosebrough, A. L. Farr, and R. J. Randall, J. Biol. Chem., 193:265 (1951).

12. G. Weber, D. P. Borris, E. deRobertis, F. J. Barrantes, J. L. LaTorre, and M. DeCarlin, Mol. Pharmacol., 7:530 (1971).

13. H. H. Loh, T. M. Cho, Y. C. Wu, and E. L. Way, Life Sci., 14:2231 (1974).

14. E. J. Simon, J. M. Hiller, J. Groth, and I. Edelman, J. Pharmacol. Exptl. Therap., 192:531 (1975).

15. E. J. Simon, W. P. Dole, and J. M. Hiller, Proc. Natl. Acad. Sci. U.S.A., 69:1835 (1972).

16. P. Cuatrecasas, J. Biol. Chem., 245:3059 (1970).

17. J. C. Venter, J. E. Dixon, P. R. Maroko, and N. O. Kaplan, Proc. Natl. Acad. Sci. U.S.A., 69:1141 (1972).

18. A. Singh, E. R. Thornton, and F. H. Westheimer, J. Biol. Chem., 237:PC3006 (1962).

19. B. A. Winter and A. Goldstein, Mol. Pharmacol., 6:601 (1972).

Chapter 16

OXYTOCIN RECEPTORS IN THE MAMMARY GLAND AND UTERUS

Melvyn S. Soloff

Department of Biochemistry
Medical College of Ohio
Toledo, Ohio

I. INTRODUCTION   512

II. MATERIALS   512

    A. [^{3}H] Oxytocin   512
    B. Oxytocin Analogs   513

III. UPTAKE OF [^{3}H] OXYTOCIN BY TISSUES IN VITRO   514

    A. Mammary Tissue   514
    B. Uterus   515
    C. Limitations of Tissue Uptake Studies In Vitro   517

IV. AUTORADIOGRAPHIC LOCALIZATION OF OXYTOCIN
RECEPTORS   517

V. BINDING OF [^{3}H] OXYTOCIN TO SUBCELLULAR PARTICLES   518

    A. Preparation of 20,000-g Particles   518
    B. Binding Assay   519
    C. Enrichment of Oxytocin-Binding Activity by Sucrose
Density Gradient Centrifugation   522

VI. OXYTOCIN BINDING BY ISOLATED MAMMARY GLAND CELLS   523

    A. Dispersion of Mammary Cells   526

B. Binding Assay of Mammary Cells   526
C. Results   527

VII. OXYTOCIN BINDING TO OTHER MAMMALIAN TISSUES   528

ACKNOWLEDGMENTS   528

REFERENCES   529

I. INTRODUCTION

Oxytocin serves at least two major physiological roles in mammals. It causes ejection of milk from the lactating mammary gland and contraction of the uterus. Both responses involve target cells with contractile activity. Whereas mammary myoepithelial cells and uterine smooth muscle cells differ in embryonic origin, they share many similar properties with respect to their affinity for oxytocin. This report will review some of the methods involved in studies on the uptake of radioactivity from [³H]- oxytocin by tissue pieces in vitro, and the binding of hormone to isolated cells and broken cell preparations.

II. MATERIALS

A. [³H] Oxytocin

As is apparent from other chapters in this work, the preparation of radio-iodinated peptide hormones of high specific activity provided the impetus for the demonstration of a number of hormone receptors. However, radio-iodinated oxytocin, with the possible exception of affecting fat cell metabolism in pharmacological concentrations [1], is essentially inactive biologically [1, 2]. The studies reported here were made possible by the synthesis of ([³H] tyrosyl)oxytocin of specific activities ranging from 20 to 43 Ci/mmol.

The tritiated hormone was prepared by catalytic dehalogenation of [diiodotyrosyl] oxytocin with tritium [2, 3]. The details of the procedure are discussed by Jard et al. (this work, Chap. 22). The [³H] oxytocin used in our studies has been synthesized by the Commissariat a l'Energie Atomique (C.E.A.), Gif-sur-Yvette, France, and more recently by Schwarz-Mann, Orangeburg, New York. Full bioactivity of the [³H] oxytocin prepared by C.E.A. was claimed on the basis of the hydrosmotic test on frog bladder in vitro and by the avian blood depressor test (Jard et al. this work, Chap. 22).

Full bioactivity of the tritiated hormone was reported by Schwarz-Mann on the basis of the isolated rat uterus assay [4]. Biological activity appears to be essential for binding activity, because we have not obtained binding with [³H] oxytocin of high radiochemical purity but of low bioactivity.

The C. E. A. and Schwarz-Mann preparations of [³H] oxytocin were more than 90% pure as determined by thin layer chromatography on silica gel G, developed with the upper phase of the solvent system [5] butanol: acetic acid:water (4:1:5). [³H] Oxytocin has been stored in aliquots at -70°C for more than one year without any apparent change in chromatographic behavior or binding activity.

B.   Oxytocin Analogs

The demonstration of oxytocin receptors has been aided immeasurably by the availability of a number of hormonal analogs of a wide spectrum of biological activities (Fig. 1). Oxytocin, [deamino] oxytocin, [8-lysine]-vasopressin and deaminotocinol were gifts from Sandoz, Ltd., Basel. [8-Valine] oxytocin, [4-threonine] oxytocin, and [4-proline] oxytocin were synthesized by the solid phase method [6] and were kindly provided by Dr. Maurice Manning, Department of Biochemistry, Medical College of

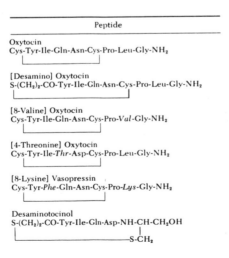

FIG. 1.   Oxytocin analogs employed in receptor studies.

Ohio at Toledo. The peptides range in oxytocic activities from those greater than oxytocin itself: ([deamino] oxytocin, [4-threonine] oxytocin), to those which are virtually inactive: ([4-proline] oxytocin, deaminotocinol).

The ability of each peptide to compete with [³H] oxytocin for either uptake by target tissues or for binding by isolated cells or broken cell preparations corresponded to its bioactivity [7-11]. Thus, oxytocin analogs have helped to define oxytocin-binding sites as receptors.

III. UPTAKE OF [³H] OXYTOCIN BY TISSUES IN VITRO

A. Mammary Tissue

Van Dongen and Hays [12] observed that pieces of mammary gland from the lactating rat respond to oxytocin in vitro by ejecting milk. This response, in fact, has served as the basis of an assay for oxytocin. The log of the time elapsed between immersion of the tissue into a solution containing oxytocin and the observation by microscope of the ejection of milk is proportional to the log of the concentration of oxytocin. The milk-ejecting activity of oxytocin by surviving segments of mammary tissue appears to be related to the tissue uptake of the radioactivity of [³H] oxytocin [7]. More radioactivity from [³H] oxytocin was taken up by mammary gland pieces than by pieces of abdominal muscle of comparable size. Furthermore, nonradioactive oxytocin and several synthetic analogs competed with [³H] oxytocin for uptake in the same rank order as their ability to cause milk ejection.

1. Preparation of Mammary Tissue

We have used lactating rats, between three and 11 days postpartum. At least eight pups were in each litter. The abdominal mammary gland or glands are dissected from the skin and placed into Tyrode's solution* at 20°C. The tissue is stripped of fascia and cut into cubes of 15 to 30 mg.

2. Incubation

Each tissue piece is incubated in a plastic test tube containing 1 ml of freshly prepared Tyrode's solution, pH 7.6, ~4 ng of [³H] oxytocin (~10^{-7} Ci), and either 1.2, 6, 30, 150, 750, or 3,750 ng of nonradioactive oxy-

---

*The composition of Tyrode's solution [13] in grams per liter is: NaCl, 8.0; KCl, 0.20; $CaCl_2$, 0.20; $MgCl_2$, 0.10; $NaHCO_3$, 1.00; NaH_2PO_4, 0.05; glucose, 1.00; adjust to pH 7.6 with 2 N HCl.

tocin or an oxytocin analog when ligand specificity is being measured. Incubation is carried out with shaking at 20°C in air. Under these conditions, the uptake of radioactivity is linear for at least 1 hr [7], although in our studies, incubation has been terminated after 20 min. An aliquot of 0.1 ml is taken from the incubation medium and transferred to 10 ml of dioxane-based scintillation solution for determination of radioactivity. The tissue piece is removed from the tube, blotted, weighed to the nearest 0.05 mg, wrapped in ashless filter paper, and compressed into a pellet with a pill press. The pellet is then combusted in a Packard Tritium Oxidizer to ^3H_2O, to which is added scintillation solution. Recovery of ^3H as ^3H_2O is > 97%. The efficiency of counting is determined by comparison of the channels ratio to that of a quenched series prepared with ^3H_2O.

3. Analysis of the Data

The data can be expressed either as dpm per mg of tissue (wet weight) or dpm per mg of tissue per dpm in the incubation medium per μl of medium. The relative potencies of oxytocin analogs in competing with [^3H] oxytocin for uptake are the same with either way of expression. As shown in Figure 2, a linear regression is obtained when uptake by rat uterus is plotted against the log concentration of nonradioactive oxytocin or its analogs (except [4-proline] oxytocin). These data are analyzed as parallel line assays according to Finney [14].

B. Uterus

Oxytocin causes uterine contraction both in vivo and in vitro [15]. As in the case with mammary pieces, surviving segments of rat uterus accumulated radioactivity from [^3H] oxytocin (Fig. 2) [8]. Oxytocin and several analogs competed with [^3H] oxytocin in proportion to their uterotonic activities.

1. Preparation of Uterine Tissue

Uterine horns are taken from rats (200-220 g) receiving 5 μg of diethylstilbestrol dipropionate in 0.2 ml of cotton seed oil subcutaneously for two days before being killed. The uterine horns are stripped of fat, slit longitudinally, and cut transversely into 10 to 15-mg segments.

Estrogen pretreatment is employed to increase the affinity and number of receptor sites for oxytocin [M. S. Soloff, Biochem. Biophys. Res. Commun., 65:205 (1975)]. These findings may explain why rat uteri are most sensitive to oxytocin when endogenous estrogen levels are high, as in proestrus [16, 17] or in estrus [18]. Follet and Bentley [19] have shown that

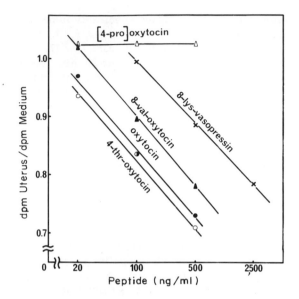

FIG. 2. Effect of oxytocin and analogs on the uptake of radioactivity from [³H] oxytocin by pieces of uterus. Incubation was carried for 1 hr at 20°C. The data are expressed as dpm per mg of fresh weight of tissue ÷ dpm per μl of medium. Each point is the mean of either three or six replicates. Reprinted from Ref. 8.

uterine sensitivity to oxytocin could be increased by more than 10-fold by treatment of rats with daily injections of stilbestrol for three days.

2. Uptake of Radioactivity from [³H] oxytocin

The uptake of radioactivity by uterine pieces is measured in the same way as with mammary pieces, except that the incubation period is 1 hr because the uterine uptake is less. The uptake of radioactivity from [³H] oxytocin by uterine and mammary pieces was compared to the uptake of [¹⁴C] inulin [7, 8] by including 2×10^{-7} Ci (48.4 μg) of [¹⁴C] inulin in the incubation medium (see Ref. 20). The tissue pieces were oxidized with a Packard Sample Oxidizer, Model 305, to yield ^3H_2O and $^{14}CO_2$. The ratio of ^3H to ^{14}C in mammary tissue after 20 min of incubation was 5.2 times greater than the ratio in the incubation medium [7] and the ratio in uterine pieces after 1 hr of incubation was 2.5 times greater than that in the medium [8].

C. Limitations of Tissue Uptake Studies In Vitro

The tissue uptake of radioactivity from [^{3}H] oxytocin was measured at 20 and 60 min, far exceeding the minute or two in which oxytocin exerts a biological response. Egan and Livingston [21] have looked at earlier times and have shown that mammary pieces concentrated radioactivity in 400 sec of incubation. However, the maximum contraction of mammary strips induced by oxytocin occurred by 100 sec. Because detectable binding did not precede activity, the uptake of oxytocin would not appear to be related to oxytocin-receptor interaction. However, there are reasons favoring the conclusion that uptake reflects oxytocin-receptor binding: (1) The ability of various oxytocin analogs to compete with [^{3}H] oxytocin is generally proportional to their bioactivity. (2) The concentration of radioactivity is target-organ specific. (3) The concentration of radioactivity in target organs is target-cell specific (see Sec. IV). (4) The selective uptake of radioactivity can be related to the binding of [^{3}H] oxytocin to discrete broken cell particulate fractions. (5) The ligand specificity of the particles corresponds to the uptake specificity of tissue pieces. (6) The apparent K_d for oxytocin binding to particulate fractions from rat mammary gland, rat uterus, and sow and human myometrium generally corresponds to the concentration of oxytocin required for a half-maximal contractile response. (7) Factors such as certain divalent cations and sulfhydryl reagents, which alter the binding of oxytocin to cell particles, alter the biological response commensurately.

To reconcile the temporal inconsistencies between uptake and bioactivity, we have suggested [7] that milk-ejecting activity is apparent when only a small fraction of the total receptor sites binds oxytocin. On the other hand, a larger number of sites must bind the hormone for enough radioactivity to be counted (which is the reason for the longer incubation periods).

Unlike experiments with broken cell preparations, the tissue incubation approach demonstrates hormone binding under conditions in which the biological response occurs. Thus, this approach has been very useful in the initial elucidation of presumptive oxytocin receptors. The tissue incubation method, however, is limited because of the inherent problems in obtaining uniform tissue pieces and the relatively high background from radioactivity which enters the tissue nonspecificity by diffusion.

IV. AUTORADIOGRAPHIC LOCALIZATION OF OXYTOCIN RECEPTORS

Cellular and subcellular binding sites for several hormones have been localized by autoradiography [22, 23]. [^{3}H] Oxytocin was incubated in vitro with pieces of oviduct and mammary gland and the tissues were examined by autoradiography [24]. Radioactivity was localized only in smooth muscle cells of the oviduct and in regions of mammary tissue where myoepithelial cells are found. In contrast, radioactivity was not concentrated in any region of skeletal muscle, a nontarget tissue for oxytocin. The localization of radioactivity in oviduct and mammary cells was absent when the tissues were incubated with [^{3}H] oxytocin and a 30-fold excess of unlabeled oxytocin. These findings provide evidence for the presence of specific, high-affinity receptors for oxytocin in target cells.

Tissue pieces, incubated with [^{3}H] oxytocin are removed from the incubation medium, blotted on filter paper, placed on tissue holders, and frozen in liquid propane at -180°C. Frozen sections, 2 or 4 μm, cut with a cryostatic microtome, are freeze-dried, and dry-mounted on desiccated photographic emulsion (Kodak NTB 3)-coated slides which are exposed at -15°C [25]. After photographic exposure for 10 to 16 months, the slides are photographically processed and stained with methylgreen pyronin.

V. BINDING OF [^{3}H] OXYTOCIN TO SUBCELLULAR PARTICLES

Radioactivity taken up by either mammary or uterine tissue in vitro was distributed among the particulate fractions sedimenting at 1,000 and 20,000 g for 10 min and 105,000 g for 1 hr [9, 10]. No oxytocin-binding activity appeared in the cytosol.

Further studies on both the mammary gland and uterus, for the most part, have involved the particulate fraction sedimenting between 1,000 and 20,000 g. This fraction was used because the binding activity expressed per milligram of protein was greater in the 20,000-g pellet than in the 1,000-g pellet. The 20,000-g particles were used instead of the 105,000-g particles because free and bound [^{3}H] oxytocin could be separated centrifugally in 10 min rather than 60 min.

A. Preparation of 20,000-g Particles

All operations are at 4°C. The tissue is homogenized in nine volumes of Tyrode's solution in an all-glass conical homogenizer. We also have homogenized samples of human myometrium with a VirTis homogenizer, followed by further blending in a Willems Polytron PT 10ST (Brinkmann Instruments) for 50 sec at the maximum setting [11].

The homogenate is centrifuged at 1,000 g for 10 min, and the resulting supernatant is centrifuged at 20,000 g for 10 min. The 20,000-g pellet is washed once in the original volume of Tyrode's solution and then resuspended in 1/2 volume. Suspensions have been stored up to six months at -70°C without any noticeable change in binding activity.

B. Binding Assay

The frozen material is thawed rapidly and centrifuged at 20,000 g for 10 min. The resulting pellet is washed twice with 50 mM tris-maleate buffer, pH 7.6, containing 5 mM $MnCl_2$ and 0.1% gelatin (hereafter referred to as tris buffer). The pellet is then homogenized in tris buffer to give 3 to 5 mg of protein per ml.

Each assay tube contains 0.6 to 1 mg of particulate protein, ~9,000 dpm of [^{3}H]oxytocin (usually ~150 ng), and for competition studies the appropriate amount of nonradioactive oxytocin or oxytocin analog in a total volume of 250 μl of tris buffer. Incubation is carried out usually for 1 hr at 20°C, and is terminated by centrifugation at 20,000 g for 10 min at 4°C. The supernatant is removed, and its content of radioactivity is determined by adding 100 μl to 10 ml of a dioxane-based scintillator for counting. The pellet is washed once with 1 ml of buffer and is heated with 0.1 ml of 2 N NaOH for ~30 min in a 60°C water bath. The mixture is transferred to a disk of Whatman No. 40 filter paper, 7-cm diam. The tube is rinsed twice with 0.1 ml of water and the rinses applied to the filter paper. The paper disk is dried in air and compressed with a pill press. The resulting pellet is combusted in a Packard Tritum oxidizer to ^3H_2O.

1. Effect of Incubation Time and Temperatures

The binding of [^{3}H]oxytocin to 20,000-g particles from rat mammary gland and sow myometrium is dependent upon time and temperature [9, 10]. For the myometrium, binding equilibrium is reached by 20 min at 37°C; at 20°C, equilibrium is reached by 40 min. However, about 2.5 times more [^{3}H]-oxytocin is bound at 20°C than at 37°C. The binding is low at 4°C and does not reach equilibrium by 80 min. Essentially the same results are obtained with mammary preparations [9]. For most assays, incubations have been carried out at 20°C for 1 hr.

2. The Effect of pH and Metal Ions on Binding Activity

The binding of [^{3}H]oxytocin by mammary particles is optimum at pH 7.6 [9], whereas the optimum for particles from sow uterus is in the range of pH 7.4 to 7.8 [10]. Mg^{2+} and Mn^{2+}, to an even greater degree, potentiate the action of oxytocin and its analogs on the isolated rat uterus [26]. Mg^{2+} also enhances oxytocin's activity on mammary strips in vitro [27]. Bentley [28] has proposed that the metal ions act by increasing the affinity of uterine receptors for oxytocin. Our findings [9, 10] support this hypothesis, because the binding of [^{3}H]oxytocin to particulate fractions from sow myometrium and rat mammary gland is enhanced by $Mn^{2+} = Co^{2+} > Mg^{2+} > Zn^{2+}$. The concentrations of Mn^{2+} giving maximal and half-maximal augmentation of binding are 5 and 0.4 mM, respectively. Binding is absent in 1 mM EDTA. Ca^{2+} has no effect upon binding at concentrations of 5 and 50 mM. Monovalent cations such as Na^+, K^+, and Li^+ do not affect binding at concentrations of 100 mM.

The metal ion appears to be required during incubation. Preincubation of mammary 20,000-g particles for 1 hr at 20°C in medium containing no Mg^{2+} did not reduce binding in a subsequent 1-hr incubation with 10 mM Mg^{2+} and [³H]oxytocin [9]. Similarly, bound [³H]oxytocin may be completely dissociated from the mammary particles with 1 mM EDTA. Binding can then be restored upon washing the particles free of EDTA and re-incubating with [³H]oxytocin in buffer containing Mg^{2+} or Mn^{2+}. This reversibility of binding may prove useful in stripping endogenous oxytocin from receptor sites and in the elution of receptor bound to oxytocin which is fixed to an insoluble matrix, for affinity chromatography.

The presence of Ca^{2+} in the medium bathing an isolated uterus is essential for oxytocin-induced uterine contraction [29-31]. The observation that Ca^{2+} does not appear to affect the binding of oxytocin implies that Ca^{2+} is involved in molecular events which take place after oxytocin-receptor interaction. Therefore, calcium binding to regulatory proteins such as troponin may be essential for oxytocin-induced contraction of myoepithelial cells and uterine smooth muscle cells, as in calcium-mediated cardiac and skeletal muscle contraction.

3. The Effect of Gelatin on Binding Activity

The incubation medium used for binding studies contained 0.1% (wt/vol) gelatin. In the absence of gelatin, more binding of [³H]oxytocin was observed with increasing amounts of [4-proline]oxytocin in the incubation medium (Fig. 3). Thus, the inert oxytocin analog [32] probably served as a carrier for [³H]oxytocin, protecting the hormone from nonspecific adsorption. The addition of 0.1% gelatin to the incubation medium as an inert carrier resulted in the absence of any effect of [4-proline]oxytocin on [³H]oxytocin binding, as would be expected from bioassay results (Fig. 3).

4. The Metabolism of Oxytocin by 20,000-g Particles

Oxytocin does not appear to be metabolized during incubation with mammary 20,000-g particles [9]. However, from 20 to 40% (five experiments) of the binding activity in the medium is lost when [³H]oxytocin is incubated with uterine 20,000-g particles [10]. The reduction in binding activity was assessed by incubating uterine particles in medium containing [³H]oxytocin which had been exposed for 1 hr to another sample of uterine particles

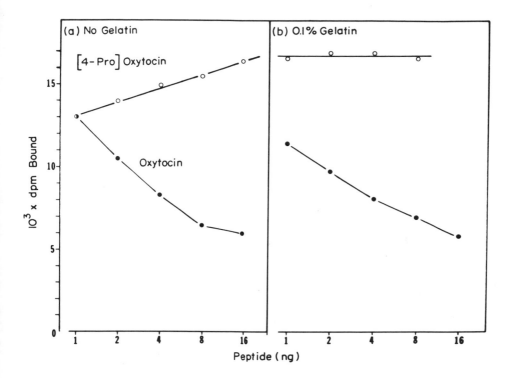

FIG. 3. The effect of gelatin on the binding of [³H] oxytocin to mammary 20,000-g particles. Each tube contained 1.2 mg of protein, 130,000 dpm of [³H] oxytocin, nonradioactive peptide in the amounts shown, and either no (a) or 0.1% (b) gelatin in a total volume of 550 µl. Incubation was carried out for 1 hr at 20°C.

[10]. The limited metabolism of oxytocin that occurs with crude uterine particles probably can be reduced by employing shorter incubation periods. The problems associated with the extensive metabolism of hormones such as glucagon by target-tissue preparations [33] do not appear with oxytocin targets.

5. Increased Sensitivity of the Oxytocin-Binding Assay

The sensitivity of the binding assay for [³H] oxytocin can be increased at least fourfold by incubating mammary 20,000-g particles with nonradio-active oxytocin standards for 1 hr, followed by addition of [³H] oxytocin and incubation for an additional 30 min (Fig. 4). The late addition of [¹³¹I] oxytocin likewise has been shown to increase the sensitivity of a

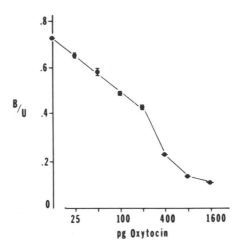

FIG. 4. Standard curve of oxytocin assay with increased sensitivity.
Each tube contained 2.8 mg of protein of the 20,000-g fraction from mammary gland in 200 μl of incubation medium plus nonradioactive oxytocin in
25 μl. The mixture was incubated for 1 hr at 20°C and 7,700 dpm (125 pg)
of [³H]oxytocin was then added. After an additional 30 min of incubation,
the particulate fraction was obtained by centrifugation and radioactivity
was determined on the resulting pellet (B) and supernatant (U) separately.
Each point is the mean ± S.E. of triplicates.

radioimmunoassay for oxytocin [34]. As shown in Figure 4, the assay
can be used to detect as little as 25 pg (~11 μunits, p < 0.02 vs no oxytocin).
This level of sensitivity in a radioligand assay should be sufficient to detect
oxytocin levels in 5 ml of plasma from dairy animals after stimulation by
mating (2-190 μunits/ml) [35], labor (120 μunits/ml), vaginal distention
(12 μunits/ml) [37], or suckling or hand milking (5-160 μunits/ml) [38].

C. Enrichment of Oxytocin-Binding Activity
by Sucrose Density Gradient Centrifugation

Oxytocin-binding activity in the 20,000- and 105,000-g particulate fractions
from rat mammary homogenates has been enriched 45 and 210%, respectively, by sucrose density gradient centrifugation. A greater degree of
purification of binding activity in homogenates of mammary tissue has not
yet been accomplished, probably because most of the particulate material
is from nontarget cells. It is necessary to isolate myoepithelial cells
before purifying oxytocin receptors in mammary tissue.

Sucrose gradient centrifugation also has been used to study the sub-cellular location of oxytocin receptors in mammary tissue. There was a general relationship between the distribution of binding activity and the activity of 5'-nucleotidase, a putative marker for mammary cell membranes (Tables 1 and 2). But, there was no relationship between binding activity and mitochondrial succinic dehydrogenase activity in the 20,000-$\underline{g}$ fraction (Table 1). The relationship between binding activity and 5'-nucleotidase activity was not precise, probably because of enzyme activity from nontarget cells.

The 20,000- and 105,000-$\underline{g}$ pellets obtained by differential centrifugation of a homogenate from the mammary gland of a lactating rat are each resuspended by homogenization in 50 mM tris-maleate buffer, pH 7.6, containing 5 mM $MnCl_2$, to give a concentration of 5 to 10 mg of particulate protein per ml. Aliquots, 0.5 ml each, of suspension are incubated with ~100,000 dpm of [^{3}H]oxytocin and either 25 ng of nonradioactive oxytocin or [4-proline]oxytocin for 1 hr at 20°C. The samples are then applied to the top of a freshly prepared discontinuous sucrose gradient of the following composition: 3 ml of 50% (wt/wt) sucrose and 3.5 ml each of 42%, 35%, 28%, and 10%. The tubes are centrifuged 1.5 hr at 14,000 rpm at 4°C in a Spinco SW-27 rotor. Thirty-five fractions of 0.5 ml each are taken with an Instrumentation Specialties Company Density Gradient Fractionator. The absorbance at 280 nm is measured with a flow cell of 5-mm path length. A 25-μl aliquot is taken from each fraction for determination of the sucrose concentration by refractometry. The remaining contents of each tube are transferred to pieces of filter paper, which are dried and combusted to yield ^3H_2O for counting. The specific binding of [^{3}H]oxytocin is expressed as the difference in dpm between the tubes containing 25 ng of [4-proline]oxytocin and those containing 25 ng of nonradioactive oxytocin. There were four discrete binding peaks, corresponding to four bands absorbing light at 280 nm. Each band was at or near the interface between discontinuities in the concentration of sucrose. For determination of the protein concentration in each peak, the appropriate fractions are pooled, diluted with tris buffer, mixed with an equal volume of 10% trichloroacetic acid, and centrifuged at 20,000 $\underline{g}$ for 15 min. The resulting pellets are dissolved in 1 N NaOH, and protein is measured according to the method of Lowry et al. [39] with bovine serum albumin as the standard. The activities of succinic dehydrogenase and 5'-nucleotidase for each peak are determined as described by Weaver and Boyle [40].

VI. OXYTOCIN BINDING BY ISOLATED MAMMARY GLAND CELLS

We have been exploring the possibility of isolating myoepithelial cells from dispersed mammary tissue. As pointed out in Sec. V, the isolation of oxytocin target cells would be very important for the eventual purification

TABLE 1. Sucrose Density Gradient Fractionation of Rat Mammary 20,000-g Particles

Peak	[^{3}H]Oxytocin bound (cpm)	Protein (μg)	cpm/μg	5'-Nucleotidase (nmol P$_i$/min per mg)	Succinic dehydrogenase (nmol/min per mg)
I					
10–28% interface	328	140	2.34	9.8	n.d.[a]
II					
28–35% interface	1,541	586	2.63	11.0	2.2
III					
35–42% interface	2,194	1,413	1.55	11.4	4.4
IV					
42–50% interface	732	485	1.51	3.3	8.7

[a]n.d.: Not detectable.

TABLE 2. Sucrose Density Gradient Fractionation of Rat Mammary 105,000-$\underline{g}$ Particles

Peak	[³H] Oxytocin bound (cpm)	Protein (μg)	cpm/μg	5'-Nucleotidase (nmol Pi/min per mg)	Succinic dehydrogenase (nmol/min per mg)
I 10–28% interface	3,921	549	7.14	35.2	n.d.[a]
II 28–35% interface	2,727	452	6.03	21.4	n.d.
III 35–42% interface	621	361	1.72	13.4	n.d
IV 42–50% interface	200	831	0.24	7.8	n.d

[a] n.d.: Not detectable.

of oxytocin receptors. These cells also would be required for studies on the biochemical events involved in oxytocin action.

A. Dispersion of Mammary Cells

The abdominal and inquinal mammary glands are removed from lactating rats on the third to tenth day postpartum. Generally, ~6 g of tissue are taken from each animal. The tissues are cut into pieces of ~2 mm diam while immersed in ice-cold Tyrode's solution, pH 7.6, containing 0.1% gelatin. The solution is changed several times, and the pieces are transferred to a Celstir spinner flask containing 5 ml of 0.1% collagenase (wt/vol; Sigma Type I) in Tyrode's solution (with 0.1% gelatin) per gram wet weight of mammary tissue. The suspension is incubated at 37°C with constant stirring. After 1 hr, dispersed cells are decanted from the side arm of the flask, and the dispersion procedure is repeated with the remaining tissue and a fresh solution of collagenase. The cells obtained after 1 and 2 hr of incubation are filtered through one layer of cheesecloth and centrifuged at 4°C in 50-ml conical tubes for 30 min at 125 $\underline{g}$. The supernatant is removed by aspiration, the cells are resuspended in 10 ml of medium, and recentrifuged. This washing procedure is repeated twice. The final cell pellet is resuspended in Tyrode's solution (with 0.1% gelatin) and 0.2 ml is taken for a cell count with a hemocytometer. Erythrocytes are not included in the count. Generally, the number of cells obtained after the second incubation is twice that from the first incubation. Cell viability, as determined by measuring the fraction of total cells excluding erythrosin B [41], is usually near 100%, and never less than 80%. The cells obtained from the two incubations are then pooled, and the appropriate dilution is made to give approximately 15×10^6 cells per ml of buffer.

B. Binding Assay of Mammary Cells

The cells are suspended uniformly by swirling with a vortex mixer. Two hundred microliters of suspension are dispensed into a series of centrifuge tubes containing 25 μl of [^{3}H] oxytocin (~12,000 dpm) and 25 μl of either buffer, nonradioactive oxytocin, or an oxytocin analog. The peptides are made up in Tyrode's solution (with gelatin). The tubes are incubated for 1 hr at 20°C. Incubation is terminated by centrifuging the tubes at 20,000 $\underline{g}$ for 10 min at 4°C. The supernatant is removed and the radioactivity in 100 μl is determined. The pellets are washed once with buffer and then dissolved in 100 μl of 1 N NaOH in a boiling water bath. Radioactivity is determined by combustion as described earlier.

C. Results

A Scatchard [42] analysis with the Rosenthal correction [43] of oxytocin binding to mammary cells indicated high- and low-affinity sites (Fig. 5). Oxytocin binding to the high-affinity sites had an apparent K_d of 1.8×10^{-9} M. This value is about twice that reported for broken cell preparations from mammary tissue [9], but the lower affinity is likely due to the suboptimal concentration of Mg^{2+} in Tyrode's solution. An apparent K_d of about 1.8×10^{-9} M also has been reported for oxytocin binding to broken cell preparations from the uterus of the rat [10], sow [10], and human [11]. The ligand specificity of isolated mammary cells for the oxytocin analogs [4-proline]oxytocin and [4-threonine]oxytocin, and for [8-lysine]vasopressin corresponded precisely to the specificity observed with the 20,000-g particulate fraction from rat mammary gland [9].

Because of a significant number of erythrocytes in the dispersed mammary cell population, the possibility of these cells binding oxytocin was examined. Erythrocytes were prepared from rat blood and treated in the manner described for the washing and assay of mammary cells. In support of the target cell specificity for oxytocin binding, erythrocytes bound only 3.5% of the [3H]oxytocin bound by an equal number of mammary cells. The amount of [3H]oxytocin bound by erythrocytes was not affected by the

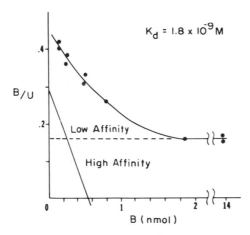

FIG. 5. Scatchard plot of the binding of [3H]oxytocin to isolated mammary cells. The points are the observed values. The broken line represents binding by low-affinity, high-capacity sites. The lower line represents the experimental curve corrected for low-affinity binding sites.

presence of an 100-fold excess of nonradioactive oxytocin. High-affinity binding sites were located, therefore, on oxytocin cells.

Trypsin has been used to disperse mammary cells [44, 45], but we, as others [48-52], prefer collagenase because 0.25% trypsin markedly reduced the viability of the isolated mammary cells.

VII. OXYTOCIN BINDING TO OTHER MAMMALIAN TISSUES

The tissues investigated for oxytocin-binding activity in our laboratory are listed in Table 3. Although the amount of oxytocin in the posterior pituitary of the male rat is comparable to that in the female, the role of oxytocin in the male is not clearly understood [53]. We have observed that oxytocin was not bound to male accessory sex tissues under the conditions in which the hormone was bound to mammary, oviduct, and uterus. The targets for oxytocin in the male, therefore, remain to be elucidated.

TABLE 3. Tissues Tested for Oxytocin Binding

Binding	No binding
Rat uterus	Rat ovary
oviduct	ventral prostrate
mammary (lactating)	seminal vesicles
Sow myometrium	vas deferens
Human myometrium	epididymis
	testes

ACKNOWLEDGMENTS

Theodore L. Swartz and Martha Morrison provided skilled technical assistance in all phases of the investigations. I thank Dr. Maurice Manning of this department and Sandoz, Ltd. for gifts of oxytocin and synthetic analogs. Thanks are also extended to Dr. Murray Saffran of this department for the initial support and helpful discussions. Supported by NIH contract 69-2193 and NIH grant HD-08406.

REFERENCES

1. E. E. Thompson, P. Freychet, and J. Roth, Endocrinology, 91:1199 (1972).

2. J. L. Morgat, L. T. Hung, R. Cardinaud, P. Fromageot, J. Bockaert, M. Imbert, and F. Morel, J. Labelled Compds., 6:276 (1970).

3. Y. Agishi and J. F. Dingman, Biochem. Biophys. Res. Commun., 18:92 (1965).

4. R. A. Munsick, Endocrinology, 66:451 (1960).

5. S. M. Partridge, Biochem. J., 42:238 (1948).

6. M. Manning, E. Coy, and W. H. Sawyer, Biochemistry, 9:3925 (1970).

7. M. S. Soloff, T. L. Swartz, and M. Saffran, Endocrinology, 91:213 (1972).

8. M. Soloff, T. Swartz, M. Morrison, and M. Saffran, Endocrinology, 92:104 (1973).

9. M. S. Soloff and T. L. Swartz, J. Biol. Chem., 248:6471 (1973).

10. M. S. Soloff and T. L. Swartz, J. Biol. Chem., 249:1376 (1974).

11. M. S. Soloff, T. L. Swartz, and A. H. Steinberg, J. Clin. Endocrinol. Metab., 38:1052 (1974).

12. C. G. Van Dongen and R. L. Hays, J. Animal Sci., 23:1229 (1964).

13. M. V. Tyrode, Arch. Intern. Pharmacodyn., 20:205 (1910).

14. D. H. Finney, Statistical Method in Biological Assay, 2nd ed., Griffin, London, 1964.

15. R. J. Fitzpatrick and P. J. Bentley, in Handbook of Experimental Pharmacology (B. Berde, ed.), Vol. 28, Springer-Verlag, New York, 1968, p. 190.

16. M. Flatters, Arch. Exptl. Pathol. Pharmakol., 221:171 (1954) (in German).

17. R. J. Fitzpatrick, in Oxytocin (R. Caldeyro-Barcia and H. Heller, eds.), Pergamon Press, Oxford, 1961, p. 358.

18. W. Y. Chan, M. O'Connell, and S. R. Pomeroy, Endocrinology, 72: 279 (1963).

19. B. K. Follet and P. J. Bentley, J. Endocrinol., 29:277 (1964).

20. J. Bockaert, S. Jard, F. Morel, and M. Montegut, Amer. J. Physiol., 219:1514 (1970).

21. S. M. Egan and A. Livingston, J. Endocrinol., 58:289 (1973).

22. M. Sar and W. E. Stumpf, Endocrinology, 94:1116 (1974).

23. A. R. Midgley, Jr., in Receptors for Reproductive Hormones, Advances in Experimental Medicine and Biology (B. W. O'Malley and A. R. Means, eds.), Vol. 36, Plenum, New York, 1973, p. 365.

24. M. S. Soloff, H. D. Rees, M. Sar, and W. E. Stumpf, Endocrinology, 96:1475 (1975).

25. W. E. Stumpf and M. Sar, in Hormones and Cyclic Nucleotides, Methods in Enzymology (B. W. O'Malley and J. G. Hardman, eds.), Academic Press, New York, 1975, p. 125.

26. P. J. Bentley, J. Endocrinol., 32:215 (1965).

27. A. V. Somlyo, C. Woo, and A. F. Somlyo, Amer. J. Physiol., 210:705 (1966).

28. P. J. Bentley, J. Endocrinol., 30:103 (1964).

29. H. Jung, in Oxytocin (R. Caldeyro-Barcia and H. Heller, eds.), Pergamon Press, Oxford, 1961, p. 87.

30. E. Berger and J. M. Marshall, Amer. J. Physiol., 201:931 (1961).

31. J. M. Marshall and A. I. Csapo, Endocrinology, 68:1026 (1961).

32. W. H. Sawyer, T. C. Wuu, J. W. M. Baxter, and M. Manning, Endocrinology, 85:385 (1969).

33. M. Rodbell, H. M. J. Krans, S. L. Pohl, and L. Birnbaumer, J. Biol. Chem., 246:1861 (1971).

34. T. Chard, M. L. Forsling, M. A. R. James, M. J. Kitau, and J. Landon, J. Endocrinol., 46:533 (1970).

35. A. S. McNeilly and S. J. Folley, J. Endocrinol., 48:ix (1970).

36. T. Chard, N. R. H. Boyd, M. L. Forsling, A. S. McNeilly, and J. Landon, J. Endocrinol., 48:223 (1970).

37. J. S. Roberts and L. Share, Endocrinology, 83:272 (1968).

38. A. S. McNeilly, J. Endocrinol., 52:177 (1972).

39. O. H. Lowry, N. J. Rosebrough, A. L. Farr, and R. J. Randall, J. Biol. Chem., 193:265 (1951).

40. R. A. Weaver and W. Boyle, Biochim. Biophys. Acta, 173:377 (1969).

41. J. H. Hanks, J. Cell. Comp. Physiol., 31:235 (1948).

42. G. Scatchard, Ann. N.Y. Acad. Sci., 51:660 (1949).

43. H. E. Rosenthal, Anal. Biochem., 20:525 (1967).

44. L. Kopelovich, S. Abraham, H. McGrath, and I. L. Chaikoff, Cancer Res., 26:1534 (1966).

45. F. Turba and N. Hilbert, Biochem. Z., 334:505 (1961).

46. E. Y. Lasfargues, Anat. Rec., 127:117 (1957).

47. K. E. Ebner, C. R. Hoover, E. C. Hageman, and B. L. Larson, Exptl. Cell. Res., 23:373 (1961).

48. T. D. D. Groves and B. L. Larson, Biochim. Biophys. Acta, 104: 462 (1965).

49. C. W. Daniel and K. B. DeOme, Science, 149:634 (1965).

50. D. R. Pitelka, P. R. Kerkof, H. T. Gagne, S. Smith, and S. Abraham, Exptl. Cell. Res., 57:43 (1969).

51. R. W. Turkington, Biochem. Biophys. Res. Commun., 41:1362 (1970).

52. J. M. Twarog and B. L. Larson, Exptl. Cell. Res., 28:350 (1972).

53. O. P. Sharma and R. L. Hayes, J. Reprod. Fertil., 35:359 (1973).

Chapter 17

PARATHYROID HORMONE RECEPTORS

James E. Zull
Craig C. Malbon*

Department of Biology
Case Western Reserve University
Cleveland, Ohio

I. INTRODUCTION   534

II. PURIFICATION OF PARATHYROID HORMONE   535

  A. Source of Material   535
  B. Carboxymethylcellulose Chromatography in Urea   536

III. PREPARATION OF RADIOACTIVE PARATHORMONE   538

  A. Acetamidination of PTH   539
  B. Iodination of PTH   546
  C. Comparison of Labeled PTH Preparations   548

IV. RECEPTOR PREPARATIONS   550

  A. Introduction   550
  B. Kidney Membrane Preparations   551
  C. Critique   556

*Current affiliation: Section of Physiological Chemistry, Division of Biological and Medical Sciences, Brown University, Providence, Rhode Island.

V. BINDING METHODOLOGY   556

     A. Introduction   556
     B. Binding Methods   556
     C. Critique   559

     ACKNOWLEDGMENTS   562

     REFERENCES   562

I. INTRODUCTION

The parathyroid hormone is a single chain of amino acids with a molecular weight of 9,500. Its principle function is to regulate the levels of calcium and phosphorous in the blood of higher organisms (above the amphibians) by acting on the kidney to increase reabsorption of calcium and decrease reabsorption of phosphate, and on the bone to mobilize calcium phosphate from the stored mineral. It is also possible that the parathyroid hormone acts on the kidney to activate the hydroxylation of 25-hydroxycholecalciferol (vitamin D) to 1,25-dihydroxycholecalciferol, which is the form of vitamin D active in stimulating calcium absorption in the intestine [1, 2]. Thus, directly or indirectly, PTH* regulates the flow of calcium between the cells of the organism and their environment at the three major sites for such flow: bone, kidney, and intestine. Therefore, the interaction of PTH with a receptor, or receptors in the kidney and bone, is a primary step in the fundamental process of calcium-phosphate homeostasis.

Despite its significance, investigation of PTH receptors has not progressed to the level of sophistication that has been achieved for many other peptide hormones. In fact, it is not possible to state unequivocally that a direct study of the "physiological" receptor for PTH has yet appeared in the literature. At least, if one accepts the requirement that demonstration of specific receptors should be possible at physiological concentrations of hormone, a question mark must still remain over all the published work related to direct studies of PTH receptors.

On the other hand, progress has been accelerating recently, and it is now possible to describe the basic methodology which one can use to study direct binding of PTH to putative "receptor" preparations. Thus, the primary emphasis in this chapter will be on the techniques for preparation of radioactive ligands, the methodology for preparation of various receptors,

---

*The abbreviations used are: PTH, parathyroid hormone; [³H] PTH, tritiated acetamidino parathyroid hormone; DTT, dithiothreitol; CMC, carboxymethylcellulose.

and the experimental approaches that have been utilized in direct binding studies of labeled PTH to such preparations.

II. PURIFICATION OF PARATHYROID HORMONE

One of the reasons for the slow progress in the field of PTH receptors has been the unavailability of pure hormone. Indeed, until 1971, all of the available techniques for preparation of PTH produced a product that was widely recognized to contain small but significant and variable amounts of unidentified contaminants, in addition to various forms of PTH itself; that is, isohormones. Thus, while the pioneering work of Rasmussen and Craig [3], and of Aurbach [4] appeared in 1960, and the utilization of carboxymethylcellulose (CMC) chromatography by both of these groups was introduced in 1965 for further purification of this hormone, it was not until the publication of Keutmann et al. [5] of a method utilizing CMC columns in 8 M urea that it was possible to obtain preparations of PTH which contained a single polypeptide chain. However, even the work of Keutmann et al. leaves many investigators without a ready source of highly purified PTH, since the procedures published by this group are large-scale, expensive, and involve a major input of laboratory function merely to prepare the hormone. While "purified" PTH is also available commercially, this material is prepared according to the earlier techniques of CMC chromatography in the absence of 8 M urea and the material available is always of questionable purity and activity. Therefore, we found it imperative to develop a procedure which would assure us of a ready supply of highly homogeneous parathyroid hormone in order to begin studies of the PTH receptor. We, therefore, modified the Keutmann method using commercially available hormone as starting material. This procedure makes it possible to purify significant amounts of PTH to a high state of homogeneity without a major input of time and expense. The following section describes this method, which has been a valuable component of our research on the PTH receptor.

A. Source of Material

The starting material for the following procedure has been either "purified PTH" or the "highly purified PTH" purchased from the Wilson Corporation (Chicago, Ill.). The former is purified according to the Potts and Aurbach method [49] up to the step involving CMC chromatography, and the latter has been further purified by inclusion of this step. It should be noted that these preparations are not reliable in their actual content of peptide material; "1-mg" lots of "highly purified hormone" contain as much as 40 to 50% salt. This has also been observed in other laboratories [6]. Such contamination also alters the biological potency of this material since it must then be expressed on a "mg-protein" basis and will thereby be elevated in some cases almost 100%.

Although the more crude preparations available commercially have not been utilized, in theory, the application of the procedures to be described could be applied to such preparations as well. It is also possible to directly purify crude TCA extracts of parathyroid glands by batch elution from CMC, producing a reasonably inexpensive material which subsequently can be further purified by the CMC technique [7].

B. Carboxymethylcellulose Chromatography in Urea

Prepare a small column of CMC (Whatman CM-52) in a Pasteur pipet (0.5 × 5 cm). Equilibrate the column with 0.01 M sodium acetate, 8 M urea, 1 mM DTT, at pH 4.9. Just prior to preparation of this solution, the urea is deionized as described by Keutmann et al. [5] on a Rexyn I-300 column (Fisher Scientific). Keutmann et al. measured the conductivity of all solutions to ensure the proper ionic strength, but solutions prepared in freshly deionized urea (within one day) always appear to give highly reproducible results. Ten milligrams of "purified PTH" is dissolved in 40 ml of the column buffer to reduce the ionic strength in the hormone solution to acceptable levels. The hormone is then applied to the column and the effluent collected in 0.8-ml fractions and measured for u.v. absorption. As the hormone passes onto the column, considerable u.v. absorbing material elutes (Fig. 1), and when all the sample has been applied, the column is washed with 4 to 5 ml of the starting buffer. A linear gradient of sodium acetate is then begun, utilizing 75 ml of starting buffer in the first reservoir and 75 ml of 0.1 M sodium acetate, 8 M urea, 1 mM DTT, pH 5.95, in the second reservoir. A shift in the base line may be observed as the gradient progresses, due to oxidation of DTT, which generates u.v. absorbing disulfides. It is likely that this oxidation is a common occurrence on CMC, and it may well explain the loss of biological activity which is sometimes associated with procedures utilizing small amounts of PTH on such columns.

The active hormone and its isohormones always elute at the region in the gradient where the salt concentration is between 0.06 and 0.08 M (pH ~5.3); and, as shown in Figure 1, two major forms of the hormone are usually observed in the Wilson preparations. However, the isohormone composition varies considerably and distributions quite similar to those reported by Keutmann et al. have been found in some Wilson preparations. This variable may depend on the source of the glands, and is perhaps related to the variety of animal which serves as the source of the material. The biological activity of both peaks I and II in Figure 1 has been fully confirmed both in the serum calcium and the urine phosphate assay for PTH [5, 8]. Keutmann reported that the two dominant

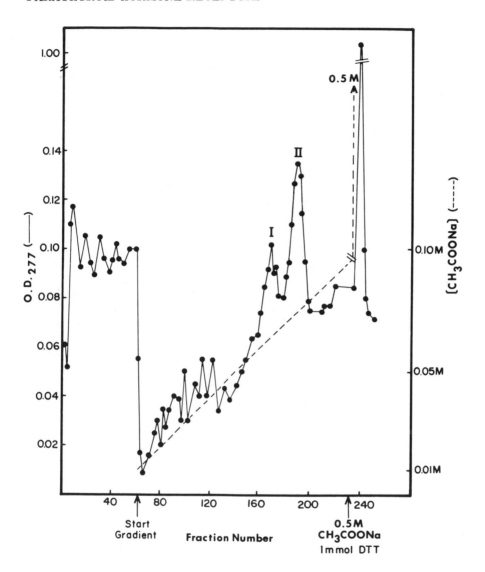

FIG. 1. Purification of PTH on CMC with 8 M urea.

isohormones differ by a single amino acid residue, and this observation is testimony to the high resolving power of the CMC–8 M urea column technique.

The eluted PTH can be separated from the urea by a second small CMC column. The hormone is diluted at least fourfold with 0.01 M sodium acetate buffer, pH 4.9, and then passed through a 0.5 × 1-cm CMC column equilibrated with the same buffer. The column is washed free of urea by passing the urea-free starting buffer through the column (1-2 times the diluted hormone volume), and the hormone is then quickly eluted with 0.5 M sodium acetate. All of the bound PTH elutes in 0.5 to 1.0 ml and is then ready for use.

The yield of highly purified PTH is ~2 mg (total of isohormones), and the procedure has become a routine two-day operation in our laboratory. The small columns have not been tested for capacity, but it seems likely that considerably more material could be applied without loss of resolution, because the hormone binds very tightly at the top of the column. Furthermore, very small amounts of PTH elute in the same position in the gradient as the larger amounts, so that the elution characteristics appear to be independent of the hormone concentration over a range of about 100 ng to 10 mg of starting material.

In order to utilize PTH for quantitative work as a tracer in receptor studies, it is essential to have an accurate measure of hormone concentration. Due to the relatively low u.v. absorbance of PTH and an absorption curve which is not linear with concentration, measurement of PTH concentration by u.v. was deemed inadequate. We have also found that the Lowry [9] method does not give reliable results because the concentration-absorbancy curves do not pass through the origin. Hormone concentration can best be determined by total nitrogen analysis [10, 11]. The method of amino terminal group analysis, utilized by Keutmann et al. [5], also appears satisfactory.

III. PREPARATION OF RADIOACTIVE PARATHORMONE

A major reason for the slow progress in PTH-receptor studies has been the difficulty of preparation of a valid radioactive tracer for active hormone. The technique of iodination, so dramatically useful for other peptides, proved to be destructive to the biological activity of PTH. Apparently, the oxidizing agents utilized for this procedure critically damage some important moiety in PTH, the most likely candidate being the methionine at position 8, which is readily oxidized and which must be in reduced form for retention of biological activity. Thus, a valid tracer for PTH was not prepared until 1972 [12].

The following section, therefore, describes in some detail the methods now available for labeling PTH and attempts to provide a comparison and evaluation of the materials which result from these preparations.

A. Acetamidination of PTH

All presently successful methods for labeling peptides at high specific activities are modification reactions introducing a foreign moiety which brings with it the radioactive atom. This point is sometimes forgotten—especially when iodination is used, perhaps because iodination introduces only one extra atom into the hormone molecules as they are generally labeled. All of the work on receptor binding of hormones has thus utilized a chemically modified form of the hormone.

The modification which we have found useful involves the reaction of the tritiated (T) ester of acetimidate with the free amino groups found at the N-terminal sites and at lysine residues in proteins. This reaction, Figure 2, was studied with proteins by Hunter and Ludwig [13] and by Wofsey and Singer [14]. The latter investigators studied the modification of rabbit antibodies to test the importance of amino groups in antibody-antigen interactions. Amidination had little effect on this particular interaction, and the conclusion at the time was that amino groups were not important in the binding reaction between the antibody and the antigens. However, it was also pointed out that modification of amino groups with acetimidate is a rather subtle structural change and leads to no resultant alteration in the electrostatic charge on the protein.

These points served as the beginning for our rationale in attempting to label PTH with tritium by acetamidination. In addition we made the following considerations: (1) Acetamidination of lysine residue produces a derivative which is sterically very similar to arginine (as shown in Fig. 3), and thus acetamidination of lysine is somewhat analogous to replacement with arginine, a well-known conservative amino acid replacement. (2) Amino and other charged groups are generally found on the molecular surface of proteins in their native configurations, so that modification of such a surface amino group in the subtle fashion characteristic of acetamidination might well result in no major alteration in conformation of PTH. (3) For the same reason, amino groups might be highly accessible for reaction, and the potential specific radioactivity obtainable in a peptide would be greater than that of the starting reagents in direct

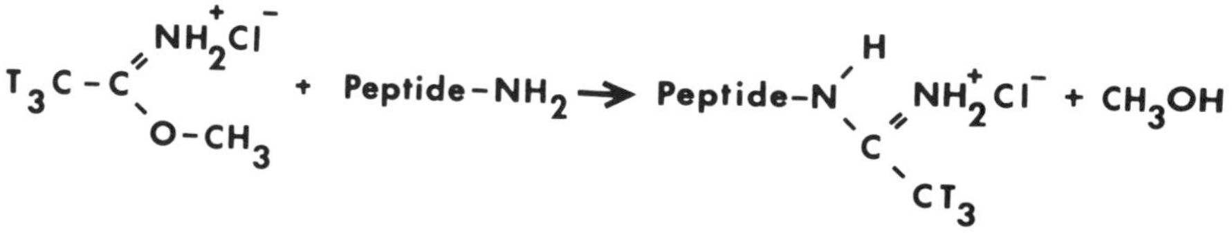

FIG. 2. Reaction of [^{3}H] acetimidate ester with amino groups.

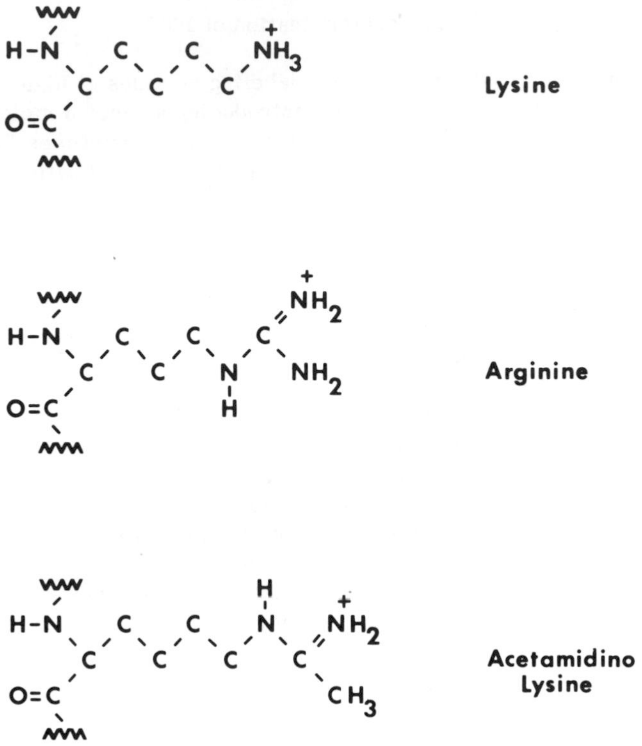

FIG. 3. Similarity in the chemical structures of lysine, arginine, and acetamidino-lysine.

proportion to the number of amino groups modified (with serum albumin, for example, this could result in a net amplification of ~50 in the specific activity of the protein over the starting imidate, a final activity of ~125 Ci/mmol with presently available methyl[^{3}H]acetimidate). (4) Tritium introduced in the methyl group of the reagent (see Fig. 2) should be virtually unexchangeable in aqueous solutions or biological fluids, so that a chemically stable derivative should be formed. As will be seen, all of these predictions appear to be accurate to some degree, and acetamidination has proven very useful for the preparation of a biologically active tracer for PTH.

1. Preparation of High Specific Gravity Methyl [^{3}H]Acetimidate

The most difficult and expensive aspect of tritiating with methyl acetimidate is the preparation of the labeling reagent. Once achieved, however, this material can be stored and utilized for years.

The procedure which we have evolved for this reaction is basically similar to that described by Hunter and Ludwig in 1959 [13], but scaled down and modified to handle very small amounts of reactants. The procedure described here is for the preparation of ~0.5 mmol of reagent, this small amount being dictated by the expense of the tritiated acetonitrile (custom synthesized by New England Nuclear). Hopefully, as demand increases, the cost will decrease.

One batch (0.5-0.6 mmol) of custom synthesized [3H]acetonitrile (specific acitivity 2-2.5 Ci/mmol) is used for the preparation of ~50 mg of methyl acetimidate. Dry HCl gas (bubbling through sulfuric acid) is channeled directly through polyethylene tubing into dry, synthetic grade methanol (equivalent amount to acetonitrile) in a serum-capped conical tube at -78°C. After a slight excess of HCl (excess over molar amount of methanol) has dissolved in the methanol (estimated by volume) the HCl inlet is disconnected, and the reaction vessel is warmed to room temperature and dried of all condensation. The HCl is then allowed to evaporate in a balance until an exact molar equivalent of HCl is retained in the methanol. The conical tube is then quickly returned to -78°C. The tritiated acetonitrile is added directly to the methanol-HCl mixture by syringe, taking care that none is lost on the sides of the reaction vessel. The acetonitrile freezes as a second phase on top of the methanolic-HCl. The reaction mixture is then allowed to stand overnight at 4°C, during which time the entire contents crystallize as methyl acetimidate. Nearly 100% yield can be achieved with experience. The product is washed several times with anhydrous ether and stirred vigorously, generating fine white crystals (mp 93-96°C). The ether is allowed to evaporate in a drying oven set at 50°C. The material (in ~1-mg lots) can then be transferred to small capillary tubes which are evacuated, sealed, and stored under liquid N_2.

It is critical to keep the entire system dry throughout the process, since the product is readily hydrolyzed and thus rendered useless. The exact 1:1:1 molar proportion for methanol, acetonitrile, and HCl is also important, since an excess of any reagent leads to the wrong products.

2. Labeling of PTH with Methyl [3H]Acetimidate

The procedure to be outlined is that which has evolved over a period of three years in our laboratory. The actual labeling of PTH, and peptides in general, is a simple task, remarkably devoid of side reactions or complications, involving virtually no special equipment, special reagents, or special training, and can be accomplished within one or two hours. Furthermore, the conditions described here are generally useful for proteins or peptides, since we have successfully labeled serum albumin, calcitonin, ACTH, insulin [15], and glucagon, as well as bungarotoxin with basically the same procedure. Of importance is the fact that these [3H]acetamidino

derivatives of ACTH, calcitonin, insulin, and bungarotoxin all retain biological activity. In fact, for PTH it is likely that some precautions are
necessary which can be abandoned with other peptides and proteins.

For PTH we begin by saturating all solutions with N_2. Normally,
250 to 700 μg of hormone are dissolved in 50 μl of 0.05 M borate buffer,
pH 9.0, containing 1% phenol as a free-radical scavenger and 0.5% β-
mercaptoethanol for protection against oxidation of methionine. For ex-
haustive amidination, 10 mg imidate is utilized per mg PTH (1,000-fold
molar excess). This large excess is required since the solution is 0.1 M
in phenol and 0.06 M in β-mercaptoethanol, both of which show some
reactivity toward the imidate. The methyl [^{3}H]acetimidate is neutralized
by dissolving it in an equivalent amount of base and transferred directly
to the hormone solution. The reaction is then allowed to proceed for 1 hr
at 0°C under N_2. (A precipitate occasionally forms when the reagents are
mixed but this does not appear to hinder the labeling in any fashion. It
can be eliminated by dilution with an equal volume of distilled water (100
μl), but this reduces the efficiency of reaction and may produce an incompletely labeled hormone product. The precipitate may represent phenol
which is salted out of solution since it seems to form a thin layer on top
of the reaction mixture.) The reaction is stopped by addition of 200 μl of
0.5 N HCl. The reaction mixture is transferred immediately to a 60 ×
0.9-cm column of Bio-Gel P-2 (50-100 mesh) equilibrated with 50 mM
acetic acid, adjusted to pH 2 with HCl. The column is run at room temperature and has a flow rate of about 1.3 ml/min. The labeled hormone
elutes in the void volume, ~15 ml, and thus is separated from the reaction mixture within 10 min. Separation is excellent, but slight contamination with small-molecular-weight components may remain due to the relatively immense amount of radioactivity in the second peak. Any contaminating, nonhormonal radioactive materials can be removed by a second
passage through Bio-Gel or by filtration on Amicon filters. It should be
mentioned that, since the imidate is much more radioactive than the hormone on a mg-N basis and since the procedure utilizes a large molar
excess of imidate, slight contamination of the hormone with imidate can
lead to significant errors in calculations of specific activity based on
nitrogen analysis.

3. Chemical Aspects of Acetamidination

The procedure deserves some further comment both in regard to the conditions utilized, and to the nature of the product formed under these conditions. Probably the most critical aspect of the reaction conditions is
the pH, since the reactive group in the hormone is actually the un-ionized
amino group(s). Thus, increasing pH leads to more rapid reaction rates,
but at the same time PTH-methionine becomes more susceptible to

oxidation catalyzed by base. In addition, the product and the reactant are both labile in base, and, therefore, it is important that the system be buffered. In practice, pH 8.5 to 9 appears most suitable for PTH. On the other hand, where the reactive groups are dominantly α-amino rather than ϵ-amino, as in insulin, lower pH conditions can be utilized, because of the lower pK of the α-amino group. This, of course, is an added flexibility of the procedure, since in theory one can label α-amino groups under pH conditions where little reaction with lysine amino groups takes place.

The extent and rate of reaction depends on the concentration of both reactants, hormone and imidate. For example, utilizing only 1 mg imidate under the conditions described reduces the extent of reaction of PTH in the 1-hr time period (utilizing smaller amounts of PTH gives similar results). Quantitative data on this question are not available since we have not had adequate amounts of PTH to conduct extensive chemical studies. However, under the conditions described, PTH is labeled to the maximum extent possible in 1 hr. Further reaction time does not improve the degree of reaction achieved, and addition of fresh imidate does not alter this parameter.

The maximum labeling with PTH is 70 to 80% of the theoretical value, that is, seven to eight amino groups per hormone molecule. Practically speaking, the tritiated acetamidino PTH labeled to the maximum extent possible has advantages. First, there can be no question of the presence of unlabeled hormone in such preparations, and, in fact, it is relatively certain that maximally labeled PTH consists of a homogeneous population of molecules [8]. In addition, the specific activity obtainable in the hormone product is seven to eight times that of the starting reagent.

Acetamidino-PTH and PTH chromatograph identically on Bio-Gel P-10 columns (run in 8 M urea), and electrophorese identically on polyacrylamide gels [8]. In addition, PTH labeled with eight acetamidino residues chromatographs identically to the parent isohormone on the CMC-urea column, which is a very high resolution system used in the purification of the hormone. The similarity of acetamidino PTH to native PTH on this particular column-type is impressive because such columns are designed to resolve materials of differing positive charge. Since acetamidination modifies positive sites on PTH, the coelution of tritiated acetamidino-PTH with the native hormone is indeed striking.

4. Biological Properties of Tritiated Acetamidino-PTH

Fully labeled, high specific activity acetamidino PTH is biologically active in four different assay systems tested to date: two in vivo and two in vitro assays. The most classic action of PTH, elevation of serum calcium in thyroparathyroidectomized rats [16-17], gives an identical dose-response curve for the native hormone and the fully acetamidinated derivative. The other assays utilized to test tritiated acetamidino-PTH were the elevation of urinary phosphate in thyroparathyroidectomized rats, the activation of kidney plasma membrane adenylate cyclase in vitro, and immunoassay utilizing a competitive-binding procedure. It is important to point out that in all the bioassays, the material actually assayed was the fully radioactive hormone derivative (not diluted with cold acetamidine groups). This same hormone was utilized in the in vitro binding and metabolism studies. This is an important point because of the possible radiation damage incurred in very highly labeled materials. Bioassays of labeled hormones diluted with native hormone, as has been done in some cases (see Table 1), may not give an accurate picture of the actual biological activity of the more intensely labeled preparation used for critical experiments at a later time.

Further support for the biological similarity of tritiated PTH and native hormone comes from the studies of Canterbury et al. on the metabolic breakdown products from this hormone produced in the liver [18]. Using immunoassay procedures, these workers were able to show that the products produced from breakdown of the tritiated acetamidino-PTH and the native PTH were the same, as measured by the two different assays (radioactivity and immunoassay). Further, the products generated were of a specific nature and clearly suggest the presence of a specific enzyme for PTH catabolism, which must recognize both intact PTH and acetamidino-PTH in vivo.

5. Stability of Tritiated Acetamidino-PTH

a. In Vitro

In general, the tritium is stable in the hormone for long periods of time. However, radioactivity can be lost under certain conditions. Repke and Zull [15] confirmed the base liability of acetamidino derivatives of insulin as a beginning for testing this question. From the data it was clear that acetamidino-labeled peptides should not be exposed to basic conditions for extended periods of time. At pH 10 for two weeks in the refrigerator (4°C), tritiated acetamidino-insulin loses, however, only ~20% of the radioactivity. Thus, the base lability should be recognized when one works with these materials, but it need not be a limiting factor under most conditions.

Under conditions of strong acid, e.g., those utilized for hydrolysis of the peptide bond, the acetamidino group is also hydrolyzed, so that it is not possible to do amino acid analysis of the labeled groups in PTH for direct determination of which residues are reactive.

Exposing the [³H]acetamidino-PTH to conditions required for reduction of oxidized methionine (heating with 0.1 M cysteine-HCl at 80°C for 2 hr at pH 2 [19]), leads to some loss of radioactivity from the hormone. The nature of this loss has not been fully determined, but it is possible that there is some cleavage at position 29 under these conditions since this bond is acid labile [20].

An additional precaution which should be included here regards the concentrating of large amounts of tritiated acetamidino-PTH into very small volumes. Attempts at concentrating 100 to 200 μg of highly tritiated hormone by CMC chromatography resulted in CMC-retention of large amounts of tightly bound radioactivity which could not be eluted by even very high salt concentrations. This is believed to stem from radiation damage developed as a consequence of such intense concentration of the hormone. Thus, it is not possible to label crude batches of PTH and purify the labeled hormone after the reaction, since large losses of radioactivity are incurred by this procedure.

Finally, a common problem found when utilizing low concentrations of labeled PTH is loss of material by adsorption to the storage vessels. This is best controlled by the investigator being aware of its likelihood and directly measuring the actual amounts of radioactivity dispensed in a particular experimental protocol. However, such nonspecific binding of PTH to glass, plastic, etc., can be considerably reduced by prerinsing containers with 1 M acid [21], and by inclusion of large amounts of serum albumin (e.g., 10% wt/vol) in the hormone solutions.

b. In Vivo

In regard to the in vivo stability of the label in PTH, the question is more difficult. No enzymes are known which remove the guanidino group of arginine while it is bound to intact protein molecules, and it seems unlikely that such enzymes, if they exist, would act on the acetamidino group. However, this point is difficult to test directly. Incubation of tritiated acetamidino-PTH with cell homogenates of many tissues generates significant amounts of TCA-soluble radioactivity. The major contributors to this process appear to be proteolytic enzymes which, of course, destroy PTH along with other peptides, nonspecifically. It has not yet been possible directly to test whether the acetamidino group is removed from PTH and perhaps transferred to another molecule of relatively high molecular weight. However, this possibility seems unlikely, since, at least in the liver, the products of metabolism are also identifiable by the antibodies directed against PTH [18].

c. Biological Activity

Parathyroid hormone is a reasonably stable protein. It can be stored in the purified state for long periods under the proper conditions, e.g., in the dry state, frozen, or in dilute acid solution at 4°C. However, any conditions which generate oxygen radicals or expose the hormone to molecular oxygen will lead to a loss of the biological activity of PTH. Such oxidation appears to occur primarily at the critical methionine at position 8 in the polypeptide chain.

Tritiated acetamidino-PTH stored under liquid nitrogen for longer than nine months was at least partially inactivated when rethawed for use. A possible explanation for this loss of activity is that radiation-generated free radicals are trapped at the low temperatures in such solutions, and therefore accumulate over the time of storage. Upon thawing, unstable radicals thus trapped could do extensive damage to the PTH. It was also noted that often the activity of the stored hormone could be partially or totally regained by reduction with cysteine or DTT. This observation, together with the knowledge that methionine oxidation in PTH is readily induced by treatment with hydrogen peroxide (oxygen radicals), appears to add support to the idea that oxidizing radicals may have contributed to the loss of activity seen upon storage at liquid N_2 temperature.

Storing [^{3}H] PTH in 50 mM acetic acid at 4°C has been the most successful means of maintaining biological activity over long periods of time. Solutions as dilute as 1 ng/μl can be successfully kept in this fashion for three to four months without significant loss in their capacity to bind to receptor membranes in vitro or to be displaced by cold PTH. Of course, direct bioassay of such dilute solutions by presently accepted assays is not possible, but the retention of specific binding properties is suggestive of retention of biological activity. When stored frozen, the tritiated hormone should be quickly frozen to avoid concentrating effects and then stored not at extremely low temperatures, but preferably at -10 to -20°C.

B. Iodination of PTH

For many, if not most, proteins, the method of choice for producing a highly labeled derivative is iodination with ^{131}I or ^{125}I. Although these isotopes both have relatively short half-lives (8 and 60 days, respectively), the high specific activities obtainable compensate for this drawback to a great degree.

Because the classic methods of iodination produce a biologically inactive PTH derivative, alternative methods for iodination have been sought. Two methods are now reported in the literature: iodination by the electrolytic technique of Pennisi and Rosa [22], utilized by Sammon et al. [23], and iodination by the lactoperoxidase method of Marchalonis [24], utilized for PTH by Sutcliffe et al. [25]. Since both of these preparations have been utilized for receptor studies, the basics of the methodology will be described here, and a comparison made with tritiated acetamidino-PTH.

1. Electrolytic Iodination

Of the two iodinated PTH preparations, that described by Sammon et al. [23] is best characterized and will be discussed first. The technique utilized by these investigators makes use of the fact that I^- can be oxidized to I_2, but not to further oxidation products, e.g., IO_3^-, by controlled electrolysis. The technique is well-described by Sammon et al. [23] and basically involves careful control of the electrolysis voltage at < 800 V. The technique is flexible in that varying amounts of hormone can be iodinated at any one time, and the procedure for labeling the hormone takes less than one-half hour. Equimolar amounts of ^{125}I and PTH are mixed at pH 7.4 and the electrolysis begun. At the end of the reaction period, when residual current at 780 V drops below 5 μA, β-mercaptoethanol is added to scavenge trace amounts of iodine, and carrier albumin is then added at a final concentration of 25 mg/ml. Free iodide and iodate are separated from the reaction mixture by passage through a small Dowex column (Ag1-X4).

Chemical studies have shown that the PTH product labeled with iodine by the electrolytic technique consists predominantly of tyrosine-labeled hormone, and that histidines are not labeled to any significant degree in PTH, although histidine itself is readily iodinated [21]. This point is relevant to the labeling studies with imidate, which reveal the unreactivity of certain lysine residues in PTH. The fact that hormone histidines (positions 9, 14, 32, and 63) are also inaccessible adds more information to our accumulating knowledge about the structure of this hormone in solution. Iodination of the smaller amino terminal fragment, 1-34 PTH, which is biologically active, leads to a radioactive product, so that some histidine residues must be accessible in the smaller fragment.

Electrolytically labeled PTH was assayed by Sammon et al. [23] in three bioassay systems: the in vitro kidney mitochondria assay described by Rasmussen et al. [26]; calcium mobilization from cultured bone rudiments described by Raisz and Niemann [27]; and the in vivo serum calcium bioassay of Munson et al. [16], as modified by Amer [28]. DiBella et al. [29] also assayed electrolytically iodinated PTH in the adenylate cyclase system [30]. In all cases, iodinated hormone generated responses very similar to those found for the control hormone. However, it is important to note that the specific activity of the hormone utilized for the bioassay work of Sammon et al. was not reported, and the iodinated hormone assay reported by DiBella et al. was performed with $[^{127}I]$iodo-PTH. It is therefore difficult to assess the effects, if any, of radiation damage to the hormone, especially the higher specific activity preparations which are necessary for physiological experiments with PTH either in vivo or in vitro.

Iodinated PTH was homogeneous by the criteria of ultracentrifugal sedimentation, chromato-electrophoresis, and polyacrylamide gel electrophoresis in 7% gels. However, there is some contamination (at least 20%) of the radioactive preparations with noniodinated PTH. In addition, the iodinated PTH loses some radioactivity upon storage and freezing [21].

Electrolytically iodinated PTH and the 1-34 PTH amino terminal fragment have been utilized for receptor studies with kidney membranes, and apparently significant specific binding has been demonstrated [29]. Thus, the material has already been of use for receptor studies, and undoubtedly will be even more useful as it becomes better characterized.

2. Lactoperoxidase Catalyzed Iodination

Sutcliffe et al. [25] described iodination of PTH by the method of Marchalonis [24]; subsequently, Heath and Aurbach also utilized this technique [30]. In both cases, the conditions were very similar, involving the incubation of microgram amounts (~ 1-10) of hormone with 0.1 M H_2O_2 in the presence of lactoperoxidase, at pH 7.4 for 10 min, in a total volume of 50 μl at 37°C. The procedure apparently generates an active iodinated PTH, although no details are yet available on many of the important characteristics of these preparations. Difficulties in determining hormone concentrations made exact knowledge of specific activities impossible and assumptions of recoveries necessary. In addition, labeled hormone diluted with [127]I was utilized in bioassays (adenylate cyclase), so that no assessment of the occurrence or extent of radiation damage to the more highly labeled preparations utilized for receptor studies could be made (Table 1). At present, no information is available on the sites of labeling, the extent of reaction, the stability of the labeled hormone, or other important features; and, in addition, these preparations undoubtedly contain significant amounts of unlabeled hormone. Nonetheless, this material has been used successfully for receptor studies with chick plasma membranes [31] and with beef membranes, and clearly is a very useful preparation.

C. Comparison of Labeled PTH Preparations

The salient features of the radioactive hormone preparations described above are summarized in Table 1. Each preparation has advantages and disadvantages; the tritiated hormone being somewhat limited by the presently available specific activities, and the iodinated by complications such as instability of the label, contamination with cold hormone, and lack of information on the biological activity of high specific activity hormone.

The practical limit in specific activity presently imposed on the tritiated PTH is ~ 2.5 Ci/mmol of free amino group, or ~ 20 Ci/mmol of

centrifuge equipped with a SW-41 rotor. Two major bands of turbidity and a pellet are resolved by this step. Obtain the uppermost band (38% sucrose) by aspiration with a Pasteur pipet. Dilute with three volumes of TE buffer and centrifuge at 4,500 rpm for 15 min on the Sorvall RC2-B. Resuspend the pellet, "highly purified" membranes, in the desired volume of STE buffer.

c. Results

Renal plasma membranes (38% band) prepared from undissected rat kidney by this method display a number of interesting features. A 4.4-fold reduction in the specific activity of glucose-6-phosphatase indicates that this method can effectively eliminate much of the microsomal contamination in these membranes. A similar decrease in specific activity of two brush border enzyme markers 5'-nucleotidase [43] and alkaline phosphatase [44] further indicate that this preparation is, perhaps, derived from the serosal surface of the kidney tubule cell. Additional evidence suggesting the antiluminal surface as the origin of these membranes is provided by the 2.7-fold increase in Na^+-K^+-ATPase enzyme activity and the 15- and 24-fold increase over homogenate in NaF-stimulated and PTH-sensitive adenylate cyclase activity, respectively. Thus, utilizing this methodology, it is possible to obtain a hormone-responsive renal plasma membrane preparation which displays a high specific activity, PTH-sensitive adenylate cyclase.

3. Application of Marx Method to Bovine Kidney

Our interest in probing the PTH receptor in bovine tissue prompted us to investigate the applicability of this protocol to the preparation of bovine renal cortical plasma membranes. Through experimentation and modification of this technique, the following procedure was developed [45].

a. Procedure

Bovine kidneys provided immediately after slaughter are packed in ice and transported to the laboratory within 20 min. Cortical sections are excised, weighed, and diluted with one volume of STE buffer. The tissue is then homogenized in a Sorvall Omnimixer fitted with an ice-jacketed 250-ml cannister. Homogenize at maximum rpm for 5 to 10 sec. Dilute the homogenate 1:1 with STE buffer and rehomogenize in an ice-jacketed large-capacity Potter-Elvejhem homogenizer. After 15 full strokes, the homogenate is processed to the point of PPM as described (Sec. IV. B. 2). This PPM is then layered over 11.0 ml continuous, linear, 32 to 45% sucrose density gradients. Extension of the gradient range significantly sharpens band delineation. Centrifuge at 4°C at 40,000 rpm for 90 min in a Beckman L-65 ultracentrifuge equipped with an SW-41 rotor. This procedure produces three bands of turbidity and a pellet. The uppermost layer, at the sample/gradient interphase is lipid in nature and is discarded. The two remaining bands and pellet are extracted and processed as previously described.

b. Results

Biochemical analysis of these fractions indicated that the lighter band of material (36% sucrose: density = 1.1717) was enriched in Na^+-K^+-ATPase activity and in both NaF-stimulated and PTH-sensitive adenylate cyclase activity. Previously reported preparations of plasma membranes from kidney display only a 2- to 24-fold increase in NaF-stimulated and PTH-sensitive adenylate cyclase activity when compared with crude homogenate. Our procedure revealed an 8- to 10-fold increase in the specific activity of PTH-sensitive adenylate cyclase over the partially purified membranes and a 37-fold increase in specific activity when compared to the homogenate. A similar increase in Na^+-K^+-ATPase activity was demonstrated in this preparation. Only moderate reductions in the specific activities of glucose-6-phosphatase and 5'-nucleotidase were achieved by this process. This reduction in the later brush border enzyme marker is in contrast to a small increase in the specific activity of another putative brush border enzyme marker, alkaline phosphatase. Mitochondrial contamination as assayed by succinic dehydrogenase activity appears to undergo a moderate increase in specific activity.

c. Large-Scale Bovine Kidney Plasma Membrane Preparation

We have recently developed a large-scale modification of this procedure which can increase the product yield threefold. Large 33.0-ml gradients, prepared in Beckman cellulose nitrate tubes (No. 302237) are overlaid with 5.5 ml of the partially purified membranes. These tubes are then centrifuged in a Beckman L-65 ultracentrifuge equipped with a SW-27 6-bucket rotor. The centrifugation is performed at 4°C at 27,000 rpm for 90 min. Utilizing this protocol, 150 grams of kidney tissue may be processed by a single ultracentrifugational run.

4. Method of Sutcliffe et al. [25]

a. Reagents

STC buffer: 0.25 M; 50 mM tris, pH 7.4; 5 mM $CaCl_2$

b. Procedure

Beef kidneys obtained from slaughter are packed in ice and processed at 0°C. After decapsulation, the kidneys are sectioned into 3-cm pieces and the cortex carefully excised from the medulla. These cortical sections

are then minced and homogenized in a Sorvall Omnimixer equipped with a
500-ml container. Calibration of the speed and time of homogenization is
correlated with visual examination of the homogenate under phase contrast
microscopy by using a green filter. Once the optimum conditions for preparation of plasma membranes has been determined, dilute the prepared
homogenate to 1,000 ml with STC buffer and filter through four layers of
surgical gauze. Centrifuge filtrate at 700 g for 15 min in a refrigerated
Sorvall centrifuge equipped with an SS-34 rotor. Collect the top, creamy
layer and resuspend in STC buffer by two full strokes of a loose-fitting
Dounce homogenizer. Repeat this centrifugation and resuspension three
more times until the creamy material appears homogeneous. Mix 1.5
ml of this fraction with 11.0 ml of d 1.25 sucrose solution. Place 2.0
ml of this mixture in 5.0-ml Beckman cellulose tubes (No. 305050) and
overlay with 1.0-ml portions of d 1.20, d 1.18, and d 1.16 sucrose solutions. Centrifuge in a Beckman preparative ultracentrifuge equipped with
a SW 50.1 rotor at 32,000 g for 60 min. Aspirate the d 1.18/d 1.16 interphase band, dilute with 50 mM tris-HCl buffer, pH 7.4, and centrifuge at
27,000 g for 30 min in a Sorvall SS-34 rotor to remove sucrose.

c. Results

Biochemical analysis of the d 1.18/d 1.16 interphase material revealed an
enrichment in 5'-nucleotidase activity and a reduction in β-glucuronidase
and glucose-6-phosphatase activity. Mitochondrial contamination, as
assayed by glutamate dehydrogenase activity, displayed little reduction
throughout this procedure. PTH-sensitive adenylate cyclase activity was
increased fourfold over the crude homogenate.

5. Method of Martin et al. [46]

a. Reagents

0.25 M sucrose solution

TD Buffer: 50 mM tris, pH 7.4; 10% dimethyl-sulfoxide (vol/vol)

b. Procedure

Following the procedure of Marcus and Aurbach [32], kidneys of two-to-
four-week old white Leghorn chicks are excised, placed in chilled 0.25 M
sucrose solution, and the outer cortex carefully dissected from the medulla.
Five hundred milligrams of cortical tissue is diluted with 4.0 ml of TD
buffer and homogenized in a P and E homogenizer. Centrifuge at 2,000 g
for 10 min. Discard supernatant and resuspend pellet in 4.0 ml of TD
buffer as before and recentrifuge at 2,000 g for 10 min. Resuspend final
pellet in desired volume of TD buffer.

This procedure produces a crude chick membranous preparation possessing an adenylate cyclase which responds to very low concentrations of PTH. Its sensitivity to PTH is 10 to 20 times greater than that of similar preparations obtained from rat kidney cortex [46]. In addition, the metabolic degradation of PTH by the chick kidney membranes is much less than that observed for rat membranes.

C. Critique

The various advantages of these procedures for PTH-receptor preparation warrant a brief discussion. Adenylate cyclase sensitivity to PTH is greatest in the chick preparation of Martin et al., followed, in general, by the rat, and, finally, bovine preparations. The highest specific activity of PTH-sensitive adenylate cyclase is obtained, however, in rat plasma membranes prepared by Marx et al. [42]. The highest specific activity PTH-sensitive adenylate cyclase demonstrated from bovine source is obtained by method of Fitzpatrick, as used by DiBella et al. [29]. Data on the extent of mitochondrial and microsomal contamination in this bovine fraction is, however, lacking. The greatest increase in specific activity of PTH-sensitive adenylate cyclase and Na^+-K^+-ATPase activity is achieved by the method of Malbon et al. [45].

For the highly purified plasma membrane preparations, the Fitzpatrick procedures provide the shortest preparation time and reasonable yields, whereas the procedure of Marx et al. [42] and Malbon et al. [45] require time-consuming gradient making and yield less product. Although best described as a very crude membrane preparation highly contaminated with many other cellular constituents, the chick system of Martin et al. [46] displays the highest degree of sensitivity to PTH. The simplicity and brevity of the procedure for preparing this membrane fraction may in part explain this increased sensitivity.

The metabolic destruction of PTH, as measured by generation of TCA-soluble fragments, appears highest in rat membrane preparation in general, while the beef preparations and the chick membranes are much less destructive of the hormone.

V. BINDING METHODOLOGY

A. Introduction

Utilizing the labeled hormone and membrane preparations described in Sec. IV, specific binding of PTH can be demonstrated. The methodology developed and successfully utilized in other hormone investigations have been adapted to achieve this end, and these methods and summaries of the results derived from their application are described in the following sections.

B. Binding Methods

1. Microcentrifugation Assay of Rodbell et al. [47]

a. Procedure

Small, 10×15-mm, glass test tubes are used as the incubation vessels. A 20 mM tris-HCl buffer, pH 7.6, containing 1 mM EDTA, 2.5% albumin buffer, and the desired amount of labeled hormone serves as the incubation medium. At zero time, membranes previously suspended in a solution of 20 mM tris-HCl, pH 7.6, 2.5% albumin are added to the incubation medium containing the hormone, to a final volume of 125 μl. After the desired incubation time, 25-μl or 50-μl aliquots from the incubation medium are layered onto 300 μl of 20 mM tris-HCl, pH 7.6, and 2.5% albumin contained in plastic microcentrifuge tubes. Centrifuge in Beckman microfuge for 5 min in a cold (5°C) room. Aspirate supernatant carefully and wash the surface of the pellet with 300 μl of a 10% sucrose solution without disturbing the pellet. Aspirate this wash solution and cut off the tip of the microfuge tube containing the pellet with a razor blade. Transfer the tip to scintillation vial for counting purposes.

b. Results

Utilizing this technique with minor modifications, DiBella et al. [29] have demonstrated and preliminarily characterized a specific binding process between electrolytically iodinated PTH of ^{125}I-labeled bovine PTH ([^{125}I]- bPTH (I-84)) and the ^{125}I-labeled synthetic NH_2-terminal 1-34 biologically active fragment of PTH ([^{125}I]bPTH (1-34)). Half-maximal inhibition of this binding by the unlabeled bPTH (1-34) peptide occurred at a concentration of 500 nM for [^{125}I]bPTH (1-84) and at a concentration of 750 nM for the [^{125}I]bPTH (1-34). Similar studies utilizing various other hormones and the biologically inactive, H_2O_2-oxidized forms of bPTH (1-84) and bPTH (1-34) as competitors displayed no significant inhibition. Kinetic studies indicated that maximal binding was achieved within 15 min.

We have utilized the same methodology with some modifications [45]. Ninety micrograms of membrane protein (purified beef cortex membrane) are incubated with 5 to 10 ng [^{3}H]PTH in a total volume of 80 μl. Incubation buffer consists of 50 mM imidazole-HCl, pH 7.5; 1 mM EDTA; and 6.25% bovine serum albumin. Preincubation with cold PTH or other competing peptides were conducted for 5 min prior to addition of the tritiated hormone, and centrifugation was done after an additional 5 min of incubation. The pellets obtained were rinsed once with 10% sucrose.

The average percentage of binding obtained in the absence of competitor under these conditions with 5 ng tritiated hormone is 15-20%. The amount of labeled hormone bound to membranes increased in proportion to membrane concentration. Binding is not inhibited by concentrations of insulin, ACTH, glucagon, or vasopressin in excess of 1 μM. Of the bound radioactivity, ~50% is displaceable by cold PTH at 100 nM concentration. Generally, it is not possible to displace more than 60% of the bound radioactivity with cold PTH. Specific binding is heat-sensitive and is destroyed by treatment of the membranes with trypsin.

Using a similar methodology, Martin et al. have reported similar binding studies using crude chick kidney membrane and bovine PTH labeled with ^{125}I by the lactoperoxidase method [46]. [^{125}I]bPTH binding to these membranes displayed a high degree of sensitivity to competition by unlabeled bPTH, half-maximal inhibition of binding occurring at 51 nM concentrations of PTH.

2. Microcentrifugation Method of Sutcliffe et al. [25]

a. Description

Spinco microfuge tubes (400 μl) serve as the incubation vessels. One hundred-microliter aliquots of buffer (50 mM tris-HCl, pH 7.4; 3% BSA) containing 100 to 200 μg of membrane preparation are incubated with labeled PTH for 20 to 30 min at 30°C. Competition studies are performed by first preincubating the membranes with unlabeled PTH, followed by incubations with the labeled PTH, maintaining a final volume of 125 μl. At the end of the incubation period, centrifuge the tubes at 12,000 g for 1.0 min in a Spinco microcentrifuge. Carefully aspirate the resultant supernatant from the microfuge tube and clip off the pellet-containing tip. Assay the tip for radioactivity.

b. Results

The binding of ^{125}I-labeled PTH (prepared both by chloramine-T and enzymatic iodination) to bovine kidney plasma membranes was examined by Sutcliffe et al. following this method. Enzymatically iodinated PTH displayed a specific, displaceable binding which could be competitively inhibited by cold PTH. [^{125}I] PTH prepared by the chloramine-T method displayed no such binding. The binding of the lactoperoxidase iodinated PTH was abolished upon heating the membranes at 60°C for 1 hr prior to incubations and appeared to be inhibited by Ca^{2+} concentrations from 1 to 5 mM (5 mM reducing binding by 58%). Of interest in this system was the reported inhibition of [^{125}I] PTH binding by microgram quantities of insulin.

3. Gel Filtration Assay of Malbon and Zull [48]

a. Method

Gel filtration provides a means of selectively separating membranes from unbound hormone. The membranes behave as large molecules and pass through the columns in the void volume, while the unbound PTH is retarded. The following procedure is typical of that used for this method: 300 to 1,000 μg membrane protein are diluted with incubation buffer consisting of 0.25 M sucrose, 70 mM imidazole, 1 mM EDTA, pH 7.9, to a final volume of 200 to 500 μl in polyethylene vials. Incubations are for 5 min at 0°C with 10 ng tritiated PTH, with or without 5 min preincubations with competing peptides. At the end of the incubation period, the entire sample is applied to a 30 × 0.9-cm column (Pharmacia) packed with Bio-Gel P-30, (50-100 mesh) and chromatographed at 3°C in the incubation buffer. One-milliliter fractions are collected and assayed for protein and total radioactivity. Membrane-bound and free hormone are well-separated. Calculations of total bound and free hormone can be made.

b. Results

Early studies performed with rat kidney plasma membranes revealed the ability of these membranes (300 μg) to bind ~40% of the 10-ng quantities of [3H] PTH with which they were incubated. Seventy percent of this binding was displaceable by preincubating the membranes with 200 nM unlabeled PTH. Similar preincubations with insulin, ACTH, and glucagon, however, failed to inhibit this binding. The H_2O_2-oxidized form of [3H] PTH displayed no significant binding to these membranes [48].

Plasma membranes prepared from bovine renal cortex display a capacity to bind approximately 20% of the 10-ng quantities of [3H] PTH when incubated with 1,000 μg of membrane material. Seventy percent inhibition of this binding was observed with 320 nM concentrations of unlabeled PTH. Other peptides demonstrated no consistently significant inhibition of binding by [3H] PTH [45].

C. Critique

All of the methodology described must be considered as general operational guidelines and not as the only, or even the best, methods for measuring putative PTH receptors. Considerable refinement and improvement will be required in all the presently used procedures before it can be certain that a physiologically important process is being measured, i.e., a process sensitive to physiological concentrations of PTH (10-100 pM), since even the most sensitive system to date shows displacement of labeled PTH only at concentrations of unlabeled hormone above 10 nM.

With this in mind, the following comments can be made about the general considerations which presently appear important in the measurement of PTH binding to putative receptors in vitro:

1. Incubation Time

Short times are usually adequate to achieve maximal binding, and total binding generally decreases beyond 5-min incubation in most of the systems described. The time course of specific binding has not been reported.

2. Temperature

Temperature seems to have little effect on binding of PTH in the systems described. Incubations at 0°C have been used in some cases to reduce metabolism of the hormone, but this does not significantly alter the binding seen at 37°C.

3. Concentrations of Membranes

Binding increases with membrane concentration, the increase being proportional to the membrane concentration within a limited range. The use of very small amounts of membrane (10–20 μg protein) improves the assay method of Sutcliffe et al. [25] (Sec. V. B. 2), since trapping of unbound hormone is reduced. However, this reduces the bound radioactivity to quite low levels with the tritiated PTH. Much larger amounts of membrane can be utilized by the column method of Malbon and Zull [48]. In no case has it yet been possible to demonstrate total binding of added hormone, but in the column method, up to 40% of the hormone is bound.

4. pH

Heath and Aurbach [30] report that specific binding of PTH to membranes is maximal at pH 6.0. Zull et al. [45] also report increased displacement of bound PTH from purified beef kidney membranes at pH 6.0. However, the specificity of binding is greatest at 7.5, since at pH 6.0, displacement of tritiated hormone can be demonstrated with ACTH, insulin, and glucagon, as well as cold PTH.

5. Incubation Medium

Very little detail is available on components of the incubation medium which are necessary or particularly enhance specific binding of PTH to receptor membranes. Sutcliffe et al. reported that calcium inhibits

binding at 5 mM concentration [25], but Heath and Aurbach were unable
to demonstrate any effects of Ca^{2+} on PTH binding [30]. Most systems
contain high amounts of serum albumin to reduce nonspecific binding, and
DiBella et al. [29] and Malbon et al. [45] use extremely high BSA concentrations (6.25%).

6. Treatment of Receptor Membranes

PTH receptor membranes have been stored for up to six months in liquid
N_2 with retention of their specific binding properties. However, a decrease in binding is seen with age, and one freeze-thaw cycle eliminates
specific binding. We believe that the PTH receptor may be sensitive to
mechanical factors. The greatest sensitivity and total binding in our laboratory has always been achieved with the column method of assay, which
is much gentler than the centrifugation methods. In this regard, it is
also of interest that the best results to date using the centrifuge methodology have been obtained with membranes which, although very crude, have
not been subjected to mechanical stress of extensive fractionation.

7. Manipulations

The assays described all involve manipulations which are difficult to carry
out in rapid sequence on multiple samples. In our experience, the transfers required with the Rodbell technique [47] make kinetic experiments
very difficult, especially if one conducts sextuplicate sampling as we
routinely do. The column method is inadequate for kinetic experiments
since it requires at least 15 min for separation of bound and unbound hormone, and it is not an equilibrium method.

8. Quantitative Aspects

No truly quantitative measures of PTH binding have been reported. Most
published work give data which is expressed as percentages. Lack of accurate information on specific activities makes calculations of binding
capacities of the membranes impossible with iodinated PTH preparations.
Our data suggest that a minimal binding figure of 100 fmol/mg of purified
beef membranes for the capacity of specific binding, but this estimate is
subject to modification according to the experimental conditions and other
variables described above. None of the methods or systems described
appears adequate for good quantitative work at the present time.

ACKNOWLEDGMENTS

The authors are indebted to Mrs. Jacinta Chuang for her expert technical assistance, and to Mrs. Evelyn Jordan and Veralynne Bosko for assistance in the preparation of the manuscript. This work was supported by grants AM-14496-01 and DEC-2587 from NIH and P3B2813 from the NSF. J.E.Z. is supported by Career Development Award AM-70031 from NIH, and C.E.M. is a recipient of a Case Western Reserve Graduate Alumni Research Award.

REFERENCES

1. H. Rasmussen, M. Wong, D. Bikle, and D. B. P. Goodman, J. Clin. Invest., 51:2502 (1972).

2. I. T. Boyle, L. Miravet, R. W. Gray, M. F. Holick, and H. F. DeLuca, Endocrinology, 90:605 (1972).

3. H. Rasmussen and L. C. Craig, J. Amer. Chem. Soc., 81:5003 (1959).

4. G. D. Aurbach, J. Biol. Chem., 234:3179 (1959).

5. H. T. Keutmann, G. D. Aurbach, B. F. Dawson, H. D. Niall, L. J. Deftos, and J. T. Potts, Jr., Biochemistry, 10:2779 (1971).

6. D. Cohn and W. Neuman, personal communication 1974.

7. J. D. Sallis, personal communication 1974.

8. J. E. Zull and J. Chuang, J. Biol. Chem., 250:1668 (1975).

9. O. H. Lowry, N. J. Rosebrough, A. L. Farr, and R. J. Randall, J. Biol. Chem., 193:265 (1951).

10. S. Jacobs, Nature, 183:262 (1959).

11. S. Jacobs, Analyst, 85:257 (1960).

12. J. E. Zull and D. W. Repke, J. Biol. Chem., 247:2183 (1972).

13. M. J. Hunter and M. L. Ludwig, J. Am. Chem. Soc., 84:3491 (1962).

14. L. Wofsey and S. J. Singer, Biochemistry, 2:104 (1963).

15. D. W. Repke and J. E. Zull, J. Biol. Chem., 247:2189 (1972).

16. P. L. Munson, A. D. Kenny, and O. A. Iseri, Federation Proc., Federation Am. Soc. Exptl. Biol., 12:249, (Abstract) (1953).

17. A. Causton, B. Chorlton, and G. A. Rose, J. Endocrinol., 33:1 (1965).

18. J. M. Canterbury, L. A. Bricker, G. S. Levey, P. L. Kozlovskis, E. Ruiz, J. E. Zull, and E. Reiss, J. Clin. Invest., 55:1245 (1975).

19. A. Tashjian, D. Ontjes, and P. Munson, Biochemistry, 3:1175 (1964).

20. H. T. Keutmann, B. F. Dawson, G. D. Aurbach, and J. T. Potts, Jr., Biochemistry, 11:1973 (1972).

21. W. F. Neuman, M. W. Neuman, P. J. Sammon, W. Simon, and K. Lane, Calcified Tissue Res., in press.

22. F. Pennisi and V. Rosa, J. Nucl. Biol. Med., 13:64 (1969).

23. P. J. Sammon, J. S. Brand, W. F. Neuman, and L. G. Raisz, Endocrinology, 92:1596 (1973).

24. J. J. Marchalonis, Biochem. J., 113:299 (1969).

25. H. S. Sutcliffe, T. J. Martin, J. A. Eisman, and R. Pilczyk, Biochem. J., 134:913 (1973).

26. H. Rasmussen, H. Shirasu, E. Ogata, and C. Hawker, J. Biol. Chem., 242:4669 (1967).

27. L. G. Raisz and I. Niemann, Endocrinology, 85:446 (1969).

28. M. S. Amer, Endocrinology, 82:166 (1968).

29. F. DiBella, T. P. Dousa, S. S. Miller, and C. D. Arnaud, Proc. Natl. Acad. Sci. U.S.A., 71:723 (1974).

30. D. Heath and G. D. Aurbach, in Calcium Regulating Hormones: Proceedings of the Fifth International Parathyroid Conference, Oxford, England, Excerpta Medica (Talmadge, Owen, and Parsons, eds.), Amsterdam, 1975, pp. 159-162.

31. T. J. Martin, J. M. Moseley, J. A. Eisman, S. J. Livesey, and G. W. Treagear, ibid., pp. 177-179.

32. R. Marcus and G. D. Aurbach, Endocrinology, 85:801 (1969).

33. W. Peck, J. G. Carpenter, and R. I. Schuster, in Calcium Regulating Hormones: Proceedings of the Fifth International Parathyroid Conference, op. cit., pp. 204-212.

34. D. M. Smith, G. G. Johnston, and A. R. Severson, Calcified Tissue Res., 11:56 (1973).

35. R. Dziak and J. S. Brand, J. Cell Physiol., 84:85 (1974).

36. G. Nichols and P. Rodgers, Calcified Tissue Res., 9:81 (1972).

37. R. Rabkin, A. H. Rubenstein, and J. A. Colwell, Am. J. Physiol., 223:1093 (1972).

38. G. Sayers, personal communication 1974.

39. J. E. Zull and D. W. Repke, J. Biol. Chem., 247:2195 (1972).

40. M. A. Kerr and A. J. Kenny, Biochem. J., 137:477 (1974).

41. D. F. Fitzpatrick, G. R. Davenport, L. Forte, and E. J. Landon, J. Biol. Chem., 244:3561 (1969).

42. S. J. Marx, S. A. Fedak, and G. D. Aurbach, J. Biol. Chem., 247:6913 (1972).

43. R. F. Wilfong and D. M. Neville, Jr., J. Biol. Chem., 245:6106 (1970).

44. H. Glossman and D. M. Neville, Jr., Fed. Eur. Biochem. Soc. Lett., 19:340 (1972).

45. J. E. Zull, C. C. Malbon, and J. Chuang, J. Biol. Chem., in press (1976).

46. T. J. Martin, N. Vakakis, J. A. Eisman, S. J. Livesey, and G. W. Tregear, J. Endocrinol., in press.

47. M. Rodbell, H. M. Krans, S. L. Pohl, and L. Birnbaumer, J. Biol. Chem., 246:1861 (1971).

48. C. C. Malbon and J. E. Zull, Biochem. Biophys. Res. Commun., 56:952 (1974).

49. G. D. Aurbach and J. T. Potts, Jr., Endocrinology, 75:290 (1964).

Chapter 18

PROLACTIN RECEPTORS

Robert P. C. Shiu*
Henry G. Friesen

Department of Physiology
Faculty of Medicine
University of Manitoba
Winnipeg, Manitoba, Canada

I. INTRODUCTION   566

II. STUDIES ON PROLACTIN RECEPTORS USING A
    PARTICULATE CELL MEMBRANE PREPARATION   567

    A. Tissue Source   567
    B. Preparation of Prolactin-Binding Subcellular Particles   567
    C. Preparation of Labeled Hormones   568
    D. Procedures for Testing Prolactin-Binding Activity   569
    E. Distribution of Prolactin Receptor Activity in Subcellular
       Fractions Obtained from Mammary Gland Homogenate   570
    F. Some Properties of the Prolactin Receptor   572
    G. Other Physiological Studies on the Prolactin Receptor   575
    H. Radioreceptor Assay for Prolactin and Other Lactogens   575
    I. Some Characteristics of the Radioreceptor Assay   577

*Current affiliation: Canadian Centennial Fellow at the National Institutes
of Health, Bethesda, Maryland.

III. STUDIES ON THE SOLUBLE PROLACTIN RECEPTORS   579

    A. Solubilization of Membrane Proteins   580
    B. Protein Determination   580
    C. Detection of Receptor Activity   581
    D. The Problem of [^{125}I] Prolactin with Detergent   583
    E. Preparation of Affinity Adsorbent   587
    F. Purification of Prolactin Receptors by Affinity
        Chromatography   588
    G. Analysis of Prolactin Receptor by Disk Gel
        Electrophoresis and Gel Isoelectric Focusing   592

IV. CONCLUDING REMARKS   592

    ACKNOWLEDGMENTS   595

    REFERENCES   596

I. INTRODUCTION

A detailed discussion on the development of the concept that the interaction of a peptide hormone with its receptor on target cell membranes is the initial step of hormone action now seems unnecessary. This problem has been adequately dealt with in a number of excellent articles [1, 2]. In this chapter, we propose to review very briefly the evidence upon which the concept of a prolactin receptor is based. This discussion may be particularly useful to those readers who are not working in this general area and also appeal to those who might not be too well-acquainted with the pituitary hormone, prolactin.

It is generally accepted that in mammals one of the principal target tissues for prolactin is the mammary gland. The direct effects and mechanism of action of prolactin on mammary growth, differentiation, and function have been examined extensively [3]. Turkington [4] reported that prolactin covalently linked to Sepharose is biologically active on mouse mammary epithelial cells, and he suggested that prolactin initiates its effect by an action on the cell membrane, because it is presumed that the Sepharose-prolactin complexes do not enter the cells. Falconer [5] and Birkinshaw and Falconer [6] have demonstrated that [^{125}I] ovine prolactin binds to rabbit mammary tissue in vitro and in vivo. Using autoradiographic studies, these investigators were able to show that [^{125}I] prolactin which is associated with epithelial cells is localized on the surface adjacent to capillaries. We and others have demonstrated that [^{125}I] prolactin binds to membrane preparations isolated from mammary glands and other organs of the rabbit, rat, and mouse [7-12]. It has also been reported that, in animals, prolactin-binding activity varies with prevailing physiological conditions, as well as under different pathological states [11, 13-18]. All these findings suggest an important role of the receptor in mediating the action of prolactin.

In this chapter, we intend to outline the methods used in our laboratory to study the biochemistry and physiology of the prolactin receptor and, when appropriate, to compare our methods with those employed by other investigators.

II. STUDIES ON PROLACTIN RECEPTORS USING A PARTICULATE CELL MEMBRANE PREPARATION

A. Tissue Source

Initially, midpregnant New Zealand white rabbits were injected intramuscularly with 10 mg of human placental lactogen and 5 mg of hydrocortisone daily for four days to achieve maximum stimulation of mammary glands [19], and the glands dissected from these hormone-primed rabbits were used for the preparation of receptor particles. However, subsequently it became apparent that mammary tissues obtained from pregnant rabbits one or two days prior to parturition or rabbits in early lactation (one or two days) possess similar prolactin-binding characteristics. Therefore, we have stopped using rabbits prepared by the former procedure. Immediately after a lethal dose of nembutal, mammary glands were dissected from the rabbit, stripped clean of muscle, and then processed immediately or stored at -20°C. Although no systematic study has been carried out to check the effect of storage of tissue upon receptor activity, our experience suggests that under these storage conditions a period as long as three months does not lead to any significant change in receptor activity.

B. Preparation of Prolactin-Binding Subcellular Particles

Mammary tissue was washed thoroughly in ice-cold 0.3 M sucrose solution to get rid of as much milk as possible and the tissue cut into smaller fragments before homogenization in five volumes of sucrose solution. Homogenization was carried out at 0-4°C for 5 min using a VirTis homogenizer with the dial set at "medium." Homogenization using a Polytron homogenizer (Brinkmann), type PT 10, at full speed for 1 min is also satisfactory. The homogenate was filtered twice, first through four layers and then eight layers of cheesecloth. The filtrate was centrifuged at 1,500 g for 20 min at 4°C. "Partially purified" plasma membranes were isolated from this pellet using the procedure of Neville [20] as modified by Meldolesi et al. [21]. To obtain a crude membrane fraction which binds prolactin, the supernatant was centrifuged at 15,000 g for 20 min, and the "mitochondrial"

pellet was discarded because it contained no receptor activity [8]. The
postmitochondrial particles (total microsomal fraction) were obtained
after centrifuging the supernatant at 100,000 g for 60 min in a Beckman
Ultra-centrifuge, model L2-65B. The total microsomal pellet, which
contains most of the broken cell membranes, also contains 76% of the
total prolactin-binding activity [8]. Unless otherwise noted, this crude
membrane preparation was used in all of the studies. The microsomal
pellet was resuspended in 0.025 M tris-HCl buffer, pH 7.6, containing
10 mM $MgCl_2$, because at this concentration the salt was found to pro-
mote binding of prolactin [8]. The volume of buffer added was such that
0.1 ml of the suspension contained 200 to 400 μg of protein as determined
by the procedure of Lowry et al. [22]. For this determination, particles
were solubilized by boiling in 1.0 N NaOH for 30 min. Upon storage at
-20°C, the prolactin-binding activity of the suspended particles was stable
for as long as six months. Membranes obtained from one rabbit normally
provide sufficient material for a few thousand determinations.

C. Preparation of Labeled Hormones

Human and ovine prolactin (hPRL and oPRL) and human growth hormone
(hGH) were iodinated at room temperature using a procedure similar to
that of Thorell and Johansson [23]. The typical iodination procedure involves the following: To a disposable (12×75 mm) tube the following
reagents are added in order: 1 mCi of carrier-free $Na^{125}I$ (25 μl in 0.5
M sodium phosphate buffer, pH 7.2); 5 μg of hormone (10-25 μl in 0.1 M
NH_4HCO_3, pH 8.2); 25 μl of 0.05 M sodium phosphate buffer, pH 7.2; 5 μg
of lactoperoxidase (5 μl in the phosphate buffer); and 5 μl of H_2O_2 (30%
solution diluted with distilled water, 1:15,000). The reaction is allowed
to proceed for 1 min with gentle tapping of the tube. The reaction is
stopped by addition of 0.05 M phosphate buffer to a final volume of 1 ml.
To remove unreacted iodide and damaged hormone, the mixture was immediately fractionated on a Sephadex G-100 column (1.5 $\times$ 50 cm) previously
equilibrated with tris-HCl buffer, 0.025 M, pH 7.6. Generally, three
radioactive peaks were observed. The radioactive material that was eluted
in the void volume represented damaged and aggregated hormone. This
material was discarded because it did not bind to receptors when subsequently tested. The radioactive material that was eluted from the column
at a position where the native hormone appears was used for all binding
studies. This material generally shows superior binding to receptors and
normally 70 to 90% can be precipitated by excess antibodies. The third
radioactive peak represented free iodide.

  The specific radioactivity of the labeled hormone was determined as
follows: After the reaction had been stopped, 5 μl of the iodination mixture
was taken out and diluted with tris-HCl buffer, 0.025 M, pH 7.6, contain-

ing 0.1% (wt/vol) bovine serum albumin such that 1 ml of the diluted mixture gives $\sim$50,000 cpm. Duplicate samples were used as a routine. Subsequently, 2 ml of cold 10% (wt/vol) trichloroacetic acid was added. The tubes were mixed and allowed to stand at 4°C for 1 hr before centrifugation at 750 g for 10 min. The radioactivity that was precipitated by trichloroacetic acid was assumed to represent labeled hormone. The percentage of radioactivity incorporated into the hormone was thus obtained. By knowing the counting efficiency (70%) and the exact amount of Na^{125}I used, the specific radioactivity of the iodinated hormone can be calculated. The specific radioactivity of [^{125}I]prolactin or [^{125}I]human growth hormone using the lactoperoxidase methods was generally between 60 and 120 μCi/μg.

For purposes of comparison, iodinated hormones were also prepared by the method of Hunter and Greenwood [24] using chloramine-T as the oxidizing agent. The iodinated hormones were further purified using the method already described.

The integrity of the radio-iodinated hormones prepared by both procedures merits a comment. We consistently observe that the [^{125}I]prolactin prepared by the enzymatic method exhibits better binding to receptors when subsequently tested as compared with that prepared by the Hunter and Greenwood procedure. Higher specific binding and lower nonspecific binding are generally observed for the former preparation although, immunologically, iodinated hormones prepared by the two procedures behave similarly. We have not assessed the biological activity of the [^{125}I]prolactin. Frantz and Turkington [25], however, reported that 60% of the biological activity is retained for [^{125}I]prolactin prepared by the lactoperoxidase method, compared with 0.7% for the labeled hormone prepared by the chloramine-T procedure. However, others have reported for many other hormones that, if the iodination is carefully controlled, a satisfactorily labeled hormone preparation can also be obtained using chloramine-T (see Ref. 1). Further, some investigators even utilized ion-exchange chromatography to purify iodinated prolactin and obtained satisfactory results [25].

D. Procedures for Testing Prolactin-Binding Activity

The partially purified or crude membrane particulate suspension prepared as described was thawed and kept on ice until it was dispersed with a glass homogenizer immediately before use. Prolonged standing after the suspension had been thawed, or repeated freezing and thawing, was generally avoided, although the membrane fractions could be frozen and thawed as many as three times without any major effect on receptor activity. The particulate suspension (0.1 ml containing 200 to 400 μg of protein) was incubated with 1 to 1.2 $\times$ 10^5 cpm of [^{125}I] PRL (ovine or human) in a final volume of 0.5 ml in a 12 $\times$ 75-mm disposable tube. The buffer employed for all dilutions and additions was 0.025 M tris-HCl, pH 7.6, containing 10 mM $MgCl_2$ and 0.1% (wt/vol) bovine serum albumin. Incubations were carried out at room temperature (23°C) for 6 to 12 hr [8]. At the end of the incubation period, 3 ml of ice-cold buffer was added, and the contents of each tube were filtered through a Millipore membrane (type EGWP 02500, pore size $0.2\,\mu$, or EHWP 02500, pore size $0.45\,\mu$ for faster flow rate) under suction. The membrane was washed twice with 5 ml of the same cold buffer. The filtering procedure normally required less than a minute. The filter membrane was then counted in a plastic tube in a LKB (Wallac) gamma counter.

Membrane particles stored frozen in the absence of sucrose or glycerol, but in the presence of $CaCl_2$ or $MgCl_2$, tend to form irreversible aggregates which sediment at a relatively low speed of centrifugation. Hence, the alternative method of separating bound and free hormone by centrifugation in a IEC PR-6000 centrifuge at 750 g was employed. At the end of the incubation period, the contents of each tube were diluted with 3 ml of ice-cold buffer and immediately centrifuged for 30 min at 4°C. The supernatant was decanted carefully, and the mouth of the tube was blotted on absorbent papers. The tube was then counted in the same manner.

Determinations of binding were carried out in duplicate as a routine. In experiments where only specific binding of [125 I] prolactin was required, for each determination another set of duplicate tubes was set up in the presence of excess (0.5-1 µg) of unlabeled prolactin (26 IU/mg). In the absence of unlabeled prolactin, 10 to 20% of the labeled hormone added to the medium was bound, whereas in the presence of unlabeled hormone, 80% less binding was observed. The difference between the two represents specific binding of [125 I] prolactin. The binding of [125 I] prolactin observed in the presence of excess unlabeled hormone was assumed to represent nonspecific binding to proteins, tube, or Millipore filter.

It is worthwhile mentioning that the two methods (membrane filtration and centrifugation) of separating bound and free hormone produce essentially identical results. Centrifugation is preferable because large number of samples can be handled easily and the costs of tubes is much less than that of filter disks.

E. Distribution of Prolactin Receptor Activity in Subcellular Fractions
Obtained from Mammary Gland Homogenate

Results summarized in Table 1 show that the partially "purified" plasma membranes have the highest specific prolactin-binding activity. The same preparation has the highest activity of 5'-nucleotidase. The majority of the prolactin-binding activity, however, is recovered in the post-

TABLE 1. Distribution of [^{125}I] Prolactin–Binding Activity in Subcellular Particles Isolated from the Homogenate of Rabbit Mammary Gland[a]

Subcellular particles	Specific binding of [^{125}I]oPRL per mg protein (cpm)	Percent total binding capacity	5'–Nucleotidase (munit/mg protein)	Specific binding of [^{125}I]oPRL per munit of enzyme activity (cpm)
Partially purified membranes	31,350	3	7.3	4,295
Microsomal particles	22,950	76	5.5	4,172
Nuclear pellet	9,240	21	–	–

[a]Isolation of subcellular particles is described in the text and 5'–nucleotidase activity was assayed as described [8]. One unit of enzyme activity is defined as the activity that liberates 1 μmol of P_i from AMP per minute. Modified from Ref. 8, by courtesy of The Biochemical Journal.

mitochondrial particles. We attribute this to the rather vigorous homogenization employed to disrupt the mammary tissue, resulting in the frag-
mentation of cell membranes. Especially in sucrose solutions, the latter
remain in the supernatant at 15,000 g centrifugation. That the prolactin-
binding activity in this fraction is due to the binding of hormone to cell
membrane fragments is supported by several bits of evidence. This fraction contains substantial 5'-nucleotidase activity. When the prolactin-
binding activity is expressed in terms of unit enzyme activity, the value
is identical to that for the partially purified membranes. After refrac-
tionation of the postmitochondrial particles by centrifugation on a discontinuous sucrose gradient between 0.3 M and 1.58 M sucrose (the same
procedure used to obtain partially purified membranes from the 1,500-g
pellet), the material recovered in the interface contains 5'-nucleotidase
activity as well as prolactin-binding activity. The ribosomal pellet contains little binding activity. These observations suggest that fragments
of plasma membrane in the microsomal pellet are responsible for the
binding of prolactin, and not the ribosomes or other contaminating subcellular particles found in the same fractions. The binding activity in the
"nuclear" pellet is probably due to intact epithelial cells, as the latter
were observed by light microscopy. The mitochondrial pellet (15,000 g)
contains essentially no binding activity.

To strengthen our view, we have injected [^{125}I] ovine prolactin into a
pregnant rabbit. The animal was sacrificed one hour later and the mammary glands were dissected and subjected to the homogenization and centrifugation steps described in Sec. II. B. About 65% of the trichloroacetic
acid-precipitable radioactivity in the glands was found to be associated
with the microsomal particles (unpublished observation), a value similar
to that obtained when receptor activity was compared (that is, 76%). Since
the autoradiographic studies by Birkinshaw and Falconer [6] demonstrated
that no [^{125}I] prolactin, when injected in vivo, appeared inside the cell, but
was associated with the cell surface, we conclude that the prolactin-binding
activity which we observed in the microsomal particles is the result of
binding of prolactin to plasma cell membranes. This method of preparing
prolactin-binding subcellular particles has been used routinely for all of
the studies on prolactin receptor in our laboratory, mainly because of
simplicity and high recovery of prolactin-binding activity (in contrast to
the situation where purified membrane preparations are used).

F. Some Properties of the Prolactin Receptor

Using the procedures outlined, we have demonstrated that the prolactin
receptors in rabbit mammary gland bind all lactogenic hormones. Figure
1 shows that human prolactin as well as prolactin obtained from several
species inhibits the binding of [^{125}I] hPRL to the receptors in proportion

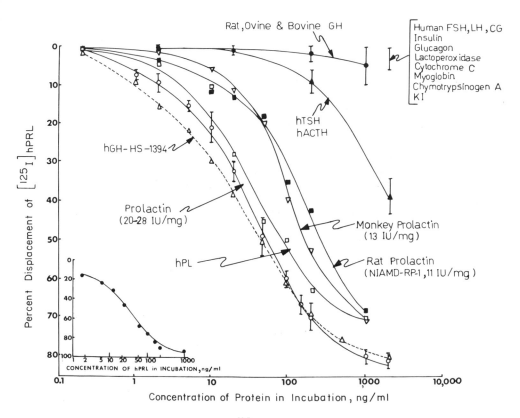

FIG. 1. Specificity of binding of [^{125}I]hPRL to membrane fractions isolated from the rabbit mammary gland. Membrane particles were incubated with about 10^5 cpm of [^{125}I]hPRL in the presence of increasing concentrations of unlabeled hormones or proteins. Binding of [^{125}I]hPRL was determined according to the procedures described in the text. The amount of [^{125}I]hPRL bound at each concentration of unlabeled hormone was compared to control incubations in which no unlabeled hormone was present, and results were expressed as percent displacement of [^{125}I]hPRL. Vertical bars in the prolactin displacement curve indicate the range observed when six different preparations of bovine, ovine, and human prolactin within biological potency from 20 to 30 IU/mg were tested (see Ref. 7 for more details; reprinted from Ref. 7 by courtesy of Science). Inset curve represents displacement by unlabeled hPRL of [^{125}I]hPRL to partially purified plasma membrane fraction. Reprinted from Ref. 8 by courtesy of The Biochemical Journal.

to the known biological potency of the prolactin preparation [7]. Human
growth hormone (hGH) and placental lactogen (hPL), which in the rabbit
have lactogenic potency similar to prolactin [3, 26, 27], also inhibit the
binding of [^{125}I]hPRL, although different preparations of placental lactogen
obtained from different sources vary somewhat in their capacity to displace
labeled prolactin; values of 30 to 70% as potent as purified prolactin have
been encountered. Several growth hormones from nonprimates which are
not lactogenic by conventional bioassays for prolactin activity also fail to
compete with prolactin for binding sites. Several polypeptide hormones
did not inhibit the binding of [^{125}I]prolactin. The slight displacement
caused by high concentrations of human thyroid stimulating hormone (hTSH)
and adrenocorticotropic hormone (hACTH) was due to a 2 to 3% contamination of these preparations by hGH, as shown by radioimmunoassay for hGH.
Identical binding characteristics of prolactin were observed when partially
purified plasma membranes prepared from the 1,500-g pellet were used
in the study in place of the crude membrane fraction (inset, Fig. 1). It
has also been demonstrated (not shown in the Figure) that, when [^{125}I]hGH
was used as the labeled hormone, purified prolactin could inhibit the binding of [^{125}I]hGH to the receptor to the same extent as purified hGH. Similarly, [^{125}I]ovine prolactin can also be used in these studies instead of
[^{125}I]human prolactin. The hormone specificity exhibited by prolactin-
binding structure(s) further strengthens the notion that the prolactin-binding
structures we detected are indeed biologically significant receptors. The
similar biological effect produced in the rabbit by lactogens, namely, prolactin, human growth hormone (but not growth hormones from nonprimates),
and placental lactogens has been well-established [3]. It appears from
our study that all these hormones act on the rabbit mammary gland through
the same set of receptors.

We have also examined a few other properties of the prolactin receptor using the crude membrane particles, and the findings are summarized
as follows (for details, see Ref. 8):

1. Receptor activity is associated with subcellular particles which also
   possess 5'-nucleotidase activity.

2. Receptor activity is sensitive to trypsin and phospholipase C digestion.

3. No apparent hormone-degrading activity is found to associate with
   receptor.

4. Binding of prolactin to receptor is dependent on time, temperature,
   pH, and ionic environment.

5. Binding of prolactin to receptor is unaffected by many compounds, e.g.,
   steroids, cyclic and noncyclic nucleotides, gluthathione, creatine phosphate, thyrotropin-releasing hormone, and 2-bromo-α-ergocryptine
   (CB 154).

6. Binding of prolactin to receptor is reversible and of high affinity, $K_a = 3 \times 10^9 \ M^{-1}$.

7. Prolactin receptor activity is not confined to mammary gland but is also found in liver, adrenal, kidney, ovary, testis, and prostate glands.

These properties are very similar to those reported for other hormone receptors where studies were carried out using tissues, intact cells, and highly purified plasma membrane preparations (see Ref. 1). Further, some of these properties of prolactin binding are reproducible in experiments using tissue slices [28].

G. Other Physiological Studies on the Prolactin Receptor

Employing these techniques to monitor prolactin receptor activity, we and others have been able to make several interesting observations regarding the physiological changes which influence and control prolactin receptors. Since this work deals mainly with methods in receptor research, a detailed description of these findings is not warranted. However, a brief summary of these observations may be appreciated because they demonstrate the wide applicability of the methods we have outlined.

We have been able to show that prolactin receptor activity is a dynamic phenomenon, because great variations in prolactin binding are found among different species, organs, stages of development, and sex of animals [10, 11]. The prolactin receptor activity is influenced by hormones which could be of pituitary origin [13, 15, 29], female and male sex steroid hormones [13, 16]. We predict that many additional factors may, in the future, be found to exert a regulatory role on prolactin receptors. Most of these factors are known to affect the physiology of prolactin as well. Further, certain metabolic inhibitors (e.g., cycloheximide) can greatly alter prolactin receptor activity in the rat [15], suggesting the continuous synthesis and turnover of the receptor. Further, we and others [17, 18] have shown that prolactin receptor may be one factor that determines prolactin responsiveness of a carcinogen-induced mammary carcinoma in rats. Hence, we have a situation in which the prolactin receptor is dynamically controlled by a variety of factors and the net result of these vectors determines the biological effect of prolactin. It is interesting to note that insulin receptor activity has been shown to vary with many physiological and pathological conditions as well [1, 2].

H. Radioreceptor Assay for Prolactin and Other Lactogens

We have previously reported a radioreceptor assay (RRA) for the determination of prolactin and other lactogenic hormones [7] using the prolactin receptor preparation. The RRA is useful because it serves as a complementary assay system to radioimmunoassays and bioassays for prolactin. However, its greatest asset is that it has enabled us to identify and quantitate many new placental lactogens which, in the past, could only be detected by difficult and insensitive bioassays [7, 30, 31]. Using the RRA to monitor these hormones, we and others have been able to purify placental lactogens from sheep [32, 33] and rat [34], and several others are likely to be purified in the near future. These achievements would not have been possible in the past because there were no suitable assay systems to monitor these hormones. We foresee that the RRA will have an even wider application, particularly in the area of research on placental hormones and functions. It may be advantageous to those who are interested in this area of research to recapitulate the methods employed in RRA, with emphasis on some of the details which were not described previously.

The preparation of a crude membrane particulate receptor fraction and [^{125}I] prolactin has been described earlier.

1. Procedures for Assaying Samples Other Than Sera

Assay tubes were set up in the following manner: Each tube contains 0.2 ml tris-HCl buffer, 0.025 M, pH 7.6, containing 10 mM $MgCl_2$ and 0.1% (wt/vol) bovine serum albumin (this buffer is also used for all dilutions and additions); 0.1 ml of the sample or prolactin standard; 0.1 ml of receptor suspension (containing ~300 μg protein); and 0.1 ml of [^{125}I] prolactin (ovine or human) which contains ~10^5 cpm (0.5–1 ng of hormone). The final volume in the assay tube is always 0.5 ml. Duplicate tubes were set up for each sample or standard as a routine. The unknown samples were frequently prepared in buffers other than the diluting buffer mentioned; the pH of the unknown solution was always adjusted to the desired value by neutralization or further dilution using the diluting buffer. The assay tubes were incubated at 23°C (room temperature) for at least 6 hr. However, it is very convenient to incubate the reaction mixture overnight. The termination of incubation, the separation of bound and free hormone, and the counting of the bound radioactive hormone have been described earlier. A standard or displacement curve is obtained by plotting the radioactivity bound versus the concentration of the standard prolactin solutions. The standard prolactin used, under most circumstances, is ovine prolactin (N.I.H., 26 IU/mg). The concentration of prolactin in an unknown sample can then be determined from the standard curve.

2. Procedures for Assaying Serum Samples

Sera were found to exert nonspecific interference on the binding of [^{125}I]-prolactin to receptors. To compensate for this "serum effect," serum obtained from hypophysectomized rats or surgically hypophysectomized patients was included in the prolactin standards. Occasionally, normal male serum which contains low levels of immunoassayable prolactin and growth hormone (if normal male human serum was used) was also used. Assay tubes containing prolactin standards were set up as follows: 0.25 ml of dilution buffer, 0.025 ml of control serum, 0.025 ml of prolactin standard solution, 0.1 ml of receptor suspension and tracer prolactin, respectively. The assay tubes containing the unknown serum samples were set up in the following manner: 0.275 ml of dilution buffer, 0.025 ml of unknown serum sample, and 0.1 ml of receptor suspension and tracer prolactin, respectively. The incubation conditions and further manipulations for the determination of binding of $[^{125}I]$ prolactin were identical to that described (see Sec. II. D).

I. Some Characteristics of the Radioreceptor Assay

The specificity of the RRA has been adequately described earlier. Briefly, the assay is not species specific, hence prolactin from many species can be measured. Moreover, the assay is not specific for prolactin, but human growth hormone (but not growth hormones from nonprimate species) and placental lactogen can also be detected. Several dilutions of pituitary extracts from a number of species (e.g., rabbit, mouse, rat, guinea pig, turkey, and humans) all inhibit the binding of $[^{125}I]$ prolactin to receptors in a parallel manner compared with standard prolactin. Extracts of placenta from a number of species (e.g., humans, guinea pig, rat, mouse, hamster, sheep, and goat) behave in the same manner. This is due to their content of placental lactogen.

A typical standard curve is identical to that presented in Figure 2 (closed circles) when prolactin of 26 IU/mg was used as the standard. The minimum amount of prolactin which is detected is ~0.5 ng. Using a sample volume of 0.1 ml, a sample concentration of 5 ng/ml could readily be detected. The usable range of the assay for "nonserum" samples is normally from 5 ng/ml to 300 ng/ml. In general, the RRA is quite satisfactory for measuring prolactin and other lactogens in tissue extracts, column fractions, pure and crude preparations of these hormones with fairly good precision. The coefficient of variation for within- and between-assays is generally 5 to 15%.

On assaying serum samples, however, it was observed that serum depresses the binding of $[^{125}I]$ prolactin to receptors. If a standard curve obtained in the absence of serum was used to read the prolactin values for the unknown serum samples, incorrect values would be obtained. The extent of the "serum effect" was, therefore, examined. It was observed that the interference increases with increased amounts of serum in the incubation mixture. This effect is not entirely due to the high concentration

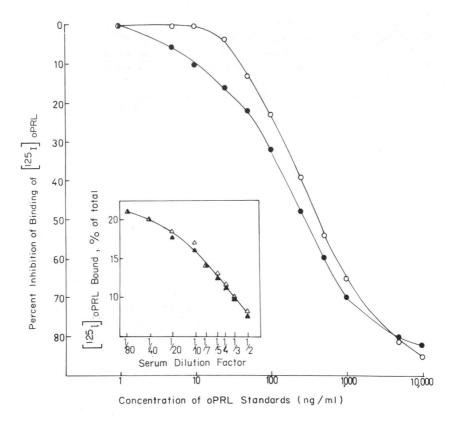

FIG. 2. Standard curves of radioreceptor assay for prolactin: (●), for "nonserum" assays; (○), for serum assays (see text for details).

of protein in the serum, because the serum effect could still be observed even when the concentration of bovine serum albumin in the incubation medium was increased to 10% (wt/vol). Therefore, control serum (see Sec. II. H) was added to the prolactin standards to compensate for the serum effect. To obtain a fairly good binding-displacement curve, only 0.025 ml sample was used. A larger sample volume would depress the initial binding too much, while decreasing the sample volume would decrease the lower limit of detection of prolactin. The effect of sera obtained from different species varies somewhat. Indeed, the effect of different batches of sera obtained from the same species can be variable. In the case of rat serum, it is not uncommon to find that the serum effect becomes more pronounced upon prolonged storage. We have no explanation for all these observations at present. It is, therefore, advisable to test a batch of control serum before it is used and to avoid prolonged storage. Furthermore, when unknown serum samples from one species are to be measured, control serum obtained from the same species should be added to the prolactin standards.

Figure 2 compares the standard curves of the RRA for measuring serum and nonserum samples. Due to the fact that the sample size of the prolactin standards used in the assay for sera was 0.025 ml, the sensitivity of the assay became 20 to 30 ng.ml, compared to a threshold of 5 ng/ml when 0.1 ml of "nonserum" samples were assayed. The inset in Figure 2 shows the result obtained when a serum sample from a patient, that contained 1,080 ng/ml of prolactin (determined by radioimmunoassay), was serially diluted and tested in the receptor assay; it inhibited the binding of $[^{125}I]$oPRL in a manner parallel to that observed in a similarly diluted hypophysectomized rat serum to which standard ovine prolactin was added to a concentration of 1,000 ng/ml. This shows that it is possible to introduce control serum into the prolactin standards for the measurement of prolactin in serum samples.

Experience in this laboratory shows that the within-assay coefficient of variation for the RRA for serum samples ranged from 6 to 20% and the between-assay coefficient of variation was 14 to 45% depending on the actual values to be determined. The corresponding values for the radioimmunoassay of human prolactin in serum were 5 to 10% and 10 to 20%, respectively [35]. Similar values were reported for the radioimmunoassay for gonadotropins [36]. Therefore, the variability of the radioreceptor assay is at least two orders of magnitude greater than that of radioimmunoassays.

The radioreceptor assay, despite its shortcomings, provides another useful tool for quantitation of prolactin preparations in many species. More importantly, it provides a convenient method for studies on new placental lactogens which are secreted during pregnancy in many species.

III. STUDIES ON THE SOLUBLE PROLACTIN RECEPTORS

Most of the studies on peptide hormone receptors in the past have employed intact cells or particulate membrane suspensions. This approach undoubtedly suffers from a number of disadvantages. These include high nonspecific binding, hormone degrading activity, heterogeneity of particulate membranes, and technical difficulties in controlling receptor concentration. For these reasons, it is desirable to use soluble receptor preparations for more accurate work. Further, in order to obtain a better understanding of the interaction between hormone and receptor, the availability of purified receptors is highly desirable. In this chapter, we shall outline the procedures used in our laboratory for the studies on the soluble prolactin receptor and our attempts to purify it [9].

A. Solubilization of Membrane Proteins

The starting material was the crude membrane fraction (100,000-g pellet) obtained by differential centrifugation of the tissue homogenate of the rabbit mammary gland as outlined earlier. The particles were resuspended in tris-HCl buffer, 0.025 M, pH 7.6, to give a protein concentration of 4 to 10 mg/ml. The nonionic detergent Triton X-100 was added to give a final concentration of 1% (vol/vol), and the suspension was stirred at room temperature for 30 min. At the end of stirring, the mixture was centrifuged at 4°C for 2 hr at 200,000 g. A layer of finely dispersed lipid-like material was frequently observed at the top of the tube after centrifugation. This lipid-like material was carefully removed by aspiration. The supernatant or extract contained the soluble receptors for prolactin as well as other solubilized proteins. The extract was divided into aliquots and stored at -20°C until further use. The receptor activity is stable for several months under these storage conditions, and repetitive thawing and freezing do not seem to affect the activity of the receptor.

Between 30 and 65% of the total protein in the particulate membrane fraction is solubilized with 1% Triton X-100 under the conditions employed. The efficiency of solubilization of proteins seems to be inversely proportional to the concentration of proteins in the original particulate suspension in the range from 4 to 10 mg/ml. The effect of Triton concentration on solubilization has not been examined. Furthermore, it was not uncommon that the total binding capacity of the solubilized receptor activity exceeded that found in the particulate fraction from which the soluble receptors were extracted. Values as high as three times the activity in the original material were encountered. Cuatrecasas [37] reported a similar finding for the solubilization of insulin receptors. We have not extensively examined the possibility of using other detergents. However, a few preliminary experiments suggested that other nonionic detergents, such as NP-40 and Lubrol-PX, did not offer much advantage over Triton X-100. The ionic detergent, sodium deoxycholate did not appear suitable for this system. It should be emphasized that some of these detergents have been used successfully by other investigators for the solubilization of other hormone receptor (see other chapters in this work).

B. Protein Determination

Since soluble proteins in the presence of Triton X-100 could not be estimated by absorbance at 280 nm, the procedure of Lowry et al. [22] was employed. However, it is worth noting that when protein solutions that contained high concentration ($\geq$ 1%) of Triton X-100 were used in the Lowry test, white precipitates formed. The precipitates could be removed easily by centrifugation at 750 g for 5 min after the color had fully developed. The formation of the precipitates did not affect the accuracy of the protein determination. For some affinity chromatography experiments, which will be outlined later, a more sensitive method using fluorescamine for determination of protein was employed [38]. Triton X-100 does not interfere in this assay procedure.

C. Detection of Receptor Activity

Two methods were used to detect receptor activity, namely, the use of column chromatography to detect the hormone-receptor complexes, and the use of polyethylene glycol (PEG) to precipitate the complexes as outlined by Cuatrecasas [37]. These procedures are as follows.

1. Gel Filtration Chromatography

A 0.1-ml aliquot of a soluble receptor preparation containing 50 to 150 μg of protein was incubated for 6 hr or overnight at room temperature with about 5×10^4 cpm (~ 0.5 ng) of $[^{125}I]$hGH (reasons for the use of this labeled hormone instead of $[^{125}I]$oPRL are discussed later) in a total volume of 0.5 ml. The buffer used for this incubation as well as all other incubations was 0.025 M tris-HCl, pH 7.6, containing 0.1% bovine serum albumin and 10 mmol $MgCl_2$. At the end of the incubation period, 0.5 ml of cold buffer (containing 0.1% detergent) was added, and the mixture was fractionated at 4°C on a column of Sephadex G-100 (1 × 38 cm) previously equilibrated with tris-HCl buffer containing 0.1% Triton X-100. The same buffer was used for elution. Flow rate was 10 ml/hr, and 1-ml fractions were collected. The volume of each fraction was constant, being monitored by a drop-counter. Subsequently the radioactivity in each fraction was determined. The result of such an experiment is shown in Figure 3 (closed circles). Almost 75% of the radioactivity is associated with a large-molecular-weight species which emerged at the void volume. This represents the hormone-receptor complex. When a parallel incubation in the presence of excess unlabeled hormone was filtered in the same manner, almost 90% of the radioactivity was displaced from the receptor to a position about twice the void volume where free or unbound labeled hormone appears (open circles).

2. Precipitation of Hormone-Receptor Complex by Polyethylene Glycol (PEG)

It is obvious that the gel filtration technique could not be used for routine assay of large number of samples containing receptor. Thus, a simple and convenient assay method similar to that of Cuatrecasas [37], which employed PEG to precipitate hormone-receptor complexes was used: 25

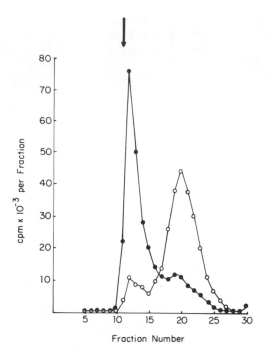

FIG. 3. Detection of soluble prolactin receptors by gel filtration on
Sephadex G-100. Arrow indicates void volume of the column (see text
for details).

to 200 μl (depending on the concentration of receptor protein in samples
to be measured) of sample was added to a disposable tube containing 3 to
5×10^4 cpm of either $[^{125}I]hGH$ or $[^{125}I]oPRL$. The former tracer was
used when the final Triton X-100 concentration in the assay mixture was
$> 0.01\%$ and, conversely, the $[^{125}I]oPRL$ was used for Triton X-100 $< 0.01\%$.
A detailed explanation for the choice of tracers is found in Sec. III. D.
Unlabeled oPRL (0.5-1 μg; in control tubes only) and an appropriate volume of incubation buffer necessary to bring the final incubation mixture to
0.5 ml was added. Incubation at room temperature was allowed to proceed for 6 hr, or more conveniently, overnight (~15 hours). At the end
of the incubation period, 0.5 ml of cold 0.1 M sodium phosphate buffer
(pH 7.5) containing 0.1% (wt/vol) rabbit or bovine γ-globulin (fraction II)
was added to each tube, followed by 1 ml of cold 25% (wt/vol) PEG 6000
dissolved in the same phosphate buffer. The final concentration of PEG
was 12.5%. The tubes were mixed vigorously. The hormone-receptor
complexes which precipitated were separated from other soluble proteins
by one of the following two methods. The contents of each tube were

filtered under reduced pressure on cellulose acetate Millipore filter (type EHWP 02500, pore size 0.45 μ) and the filter was washed by two 5-ml portions of cold phosphate buffer containing 12.5% PEG. The filter was then transferred to another tube and was counted. This filtering method suffers from the obvious disadvantage that it is time-consuming and expensive if large numbers of samples are being assayed. Therefore, another procedure which involved centrifugation was used. After the hormone-receptor complexes had been precipitated by PEG, the tubes were centrifuged at 3,000 g at 4°C for 30 min in a IEC PR-6000 centrifuge which can handle 168 tubes per run. The supernatant from each tube was drained off and the mouth of the tube was blotted by absorbent paper, and the tube was counted.

Under these conditions, 40 to 70% of the added labeled hormone was bound (depending on the amount of receptor and labeled hormone present) in the absence of unlabeled hormone in the incubation mixture. In control tubes in which excess cold hormone was added, 2 to 10% of the added labeled hormone was precipitated. This represents nonspecific binding to receptors, filter, or tube, or nonspecific precipitation by PEG. The difference in binding observed under these two situations represents specific binding. The results obtained by the filtering or centrifugation techniques were almost identical. The nonspecific binding observed with the latter technique is generally higher by 2 to 4%, but the specific binding observed was the same.

The effect of PEG concentration on the precipitation of hormone-receptor complexes has been examined using the techniques outlined. Figure 4 shows that 12% PEG is sufficient to cause total precipitation of hormone-receptor complexes. Nonspecific binding remains relatively constant at concentrations of PEG from 11 to 17%. Only 4 to 5% of the nonspecific binding observed was due to nonspecific precipitation of the [^{125}I]hGH. Therefore, 12.5% of PEG is used for assays for receptor activity.

D. The Problem of [^{125}I] Prolactin with Detergent

Initial attempts to demonstrate specific binding of [^{125}I]prolactin to extracts of membranes in the presence of detergent were without success. When [^{125}I]oPRL was fractionated on Sephadex G-100 in the presence of detergent, the hormone appeared close to the void volume (Fig. 5a), whereas in the absence of detergent, [^{125}I]oPRL eluted at a position about twice the void volume where purified prolactin is normally found. [^{125}I]hGH, on the other hand, has the same elution volume in the presence and absence of Triton X-100 (Fig. 5b). The formation of the large-molecular-weight species of [^{125}I]oPRL would have prevented the detection of the receptor-[^{125}I]oPRL complex as this would also eluted near the void volume of the column.

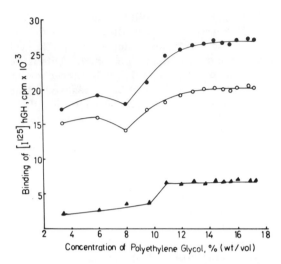

FIG. 4. Effect of polyethylene glycol concentration on the precipitation of hormone-receptor complexes (see text for details): (●), total binding; (○), specific binding; (▲), nonspecific binding. Reprinted from Ref. 9, by courtesy of J. Biol. Chem.

Another experiment was set up to examine if this "large" prolactin could be precipitated by PEG, and if so, what is the effect of detergent concentration on this phenomenon. Figure 6 shows that ~25% of the total [125I]oPRL added to the incubation can be precipitated by 12.5% PEG at a detergent concentration of only 0.04%; and up to 45% of the tracer hormone is precipitated in the presence of 0.2% of Triton X-100. [125I]hPRL behaved in the same manner in the presence of detergent (not shown in the Figure). The precipitation of this amount of large [125I]prolactin under normal assay conditions would totally mask the hormone-receptor complex, which is also precipitated by the same concentration of PEG. Moreover, the large prolactin is not adsorbed to dextran-coated charcoal. On the other hand, growth hormone is not affected by detergent concentrations as great as 0.3% in the final incubation mixture. The large [125I]-oPRL seems to be "resolubilized" (though it will still not bind to charcoal) at detergent concentrations > 0.3%. The concentration of Triton X-100 in the assays performed throughout this study is always < 0.1%. Even at detergent concentrations between 0.02 and 0.1%, [125I]hGH is preferred because the nonspecific precipitation is still considerable in the case of [125I]oPRL. It must be emphasized that the use of either labeled hormone is possible only because the prolactin receptor from the rabbit mammary gland fails to discriminate between prolactin and human growth hormone (see Fig. 1).

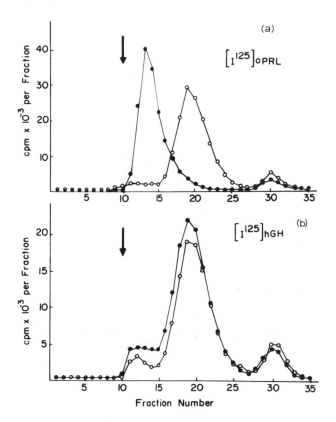

FIG. 5. Effect of Triton X-100 on the elution pattern on Sephadex G-100 column of $[^{125}I]$oPRL (a) and $[^{125}I]$hGH (b) (see text for details). Arrow indicates void volume of column: (●), in presence and (○), in absence of detergent. Reprinted from Ref. 9, by courtesy of J. Biol. Chem.

When the large $[^{125}I]$oPRL was subsequently analyzed on a Sepharose 6B column in the presence of detergent, it had an apparent molecular weight of ~80,000. Unlabeled prolactin is affected by the detergent to the same extent as $[^{125}I]$prolactin. However, the large prolactin does not seem to be a denatured aggregate of the hormone, because the large pro-lactin still quantitatively inhibits the binding of $[^{125}I]$hGH. For example, when a known amount of purified oPRL treated with detergent is fractionated on a Sepharose 6B column in the presence of detergent and the fractions assayed for prolactin by the radioreceptor assay (see Sec. II. H and II. I), the prolactin could be detected in the region corresponding to a molecular weight of ~80,000. When the same experiment was performed for hGH, the hormone was recovered in a region corresponding to a molecular

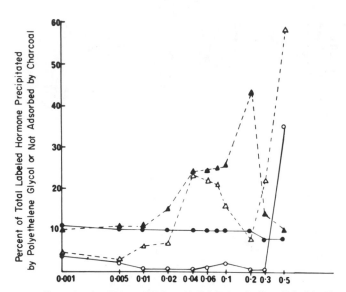

FIG. 6. Effect of Triton X-100 on the precipitation by polyethylene glycol and the adsorption by charcoal of $[^{125}I]$oPRL and $[^{125}I]$hGH. About 36,000 cpm of $[^{125}I]$hGH or 45,000 cpm of $[^{125}I]$oPRL was incubated in the presence of varying concentrations of Triton X-100. At the end of the incubation, to one set of tubes for each hormone was added PEG to a final concentration of 12.5% and the precipitates from each tube were centrifuged and counted. To the other set of tubes for each hormone was added 1 ml of Dextran-coated charcoal (12.5 mg) per tube. After mixing and standing for 10 min, the tubes were centrifuged and the radioactivity in the charcoal pellet was counted. Results are expressed as percent of total $[^{125}I]$hormone added per tube precipitated by PEG and not adsorbed by charcoal. For $[^{125}I]$hGH: (●), precipitated by PEG and (○), not adsorbed by charcoal. For $[^{125}I]$oPRL: (▲), precipitated by PEG and (△), not adsorbed by charcoal. Reprinted from Ref. 9, by courtesy of J. Biol. Chem.

weight of ~20,000. The experiments suggest that the large prolactin formed in the presence of detergent still retains its ability to bind to receptor. It is of interest to note that glucagon appears to undergo similar changes in the presence of Triton X-100 [39].

We have also examined whether detergent affects binding of prolactin to receptor, using various concentrations of detergent in the medium. The method of Holloway [40] utilizing Bio-Beads SM-2 (Bio-Rad Lab.) proved to be an efficient way of selectively removing Triton X-100 without apparent loss of protein from the solution. A three-hour treatment period with Bio-Beads resulted in the removal of 90% of detergent. On the other hand, a 48-hour dialysis with several changes of buffer resulted in the removal of only 10% of detergent. Using these two procedures, receptor solutions with varying concentration of Triton X-100 could be obtained. When these solutions were tested for hormone binding, it was found that the detergent did not affect binding of [^{125}I] hGH to receptor. However, when [^{125}I] oPRL was used in the presence of 0.11% Triton X-100, 27% of the total [^{125}I] oPRL added was precipitated nonspecifically by PEG, apparently due to the formation of the large [^{125}I] oPRL which is precipitated. When the Triton X-100 concentration was lowered to 0.01%, very much less [^{125}I] oPRL was nonspecifically precipitated and specific binding of hormone became evident. Thus, the detergent does not affect binding of hormone to receptor as such, but it does enhance the precipitation of [^{125}I] prolactin such that specific binding is often masked.

These procedures provided us with some very convenient techniques such that we have been able to examine some properties of the soluble prolactin receptor. These properties are summarized as follows (see Ref. 9):

1. The soluble receptor retains its specificity of binding hormones such that all lactogenic hormones bind to the receptor.

2. The soluble receptor retains most of the characteristics in binding hormone, e.g., the dependence of binding on time and temperature exhibited by the soluble receptor is similar to that found with the particulate receptor.

3. The affinity of the soluble receptor for prolactin is about five times that of its particulate counterpart; the affinity constant as determined by Scatchard analysis [41] for the former is 11 to 16×10^9 M^{-1}, whereas that for the latter is 2 to 3×10^9 M^{-1}.

4. The molecular weight of the soluble receptor as determined by gel filtration on Sepharose 6B is ~220,000.

With the availability of a convenient assay procedure for the soluble prolactin receptor, we proceeded to purify the receptor molecules employing affinity chromatography.

E. Preparation of Affinity Adsorbent

Purified human growth hormone (N.I.H., 1 mg) was coupled in 0.1 M NaHCO$_3$, pH 8.5, to 1 g dry weight of N-hydroxysuccinimide ester of 3,3'-diaminodipropylaminosuccinyl agarose (Affi-Gel 10) according to the instructions supplied by the manufacturer (Bio-Rad Lab.). Upon swelling, 1 g of dry agarose yielded 10 to 15 ml packed gel. The coupled gel was saturated with either bovine serum albumin or glycine and washed according to Cuatrecasas [42]. The latter involves repetitive washing in 8 M urea, 6 M guanidine hydrochloride, and 0.1 M NaHCO$_3$, pH 8.5. To estimate the coupling efficiency of the hormone, a known quantity of [^{125}I] hGH was added to the hGH before coupling. The radioactivity that remained bound to the agarose beads after extensive washing was taken to represent covalently bound hormone. About 80% of the growth hormone was coupled under these conditions. It is worth mentioning that we employed hGH instead of prolactin in preparing the affinity adsorbent to avoid further complications due to the presence of detergent.

F. Purification of Prolactin Receptors by Affinity Chromatography

Initial attempts to purify receptors from Triton X-100 extracts of membrane particles using conditions similar to that for immunoadsorbent purification of proteins met with failure. It was soon learned that the reagents used for elution of the receptors from the affinity column were inappropriate. The receptor activity was found to be very labile when exposed to many dissociating agents. They either failed to dissociate the receptor from the hormone (e.g., 6 M urea and 4 M NaCl) or more often, they completely destroyed receptor activity upon even very brief exposure (e.g., 4 M sodium thiocyanate, 4 M guanidine hydrochloride, and 1 M acetic acid). Attempts to use lower concentrations of these reagents at lower temperatures were also unsuccessful. Magnesium chloride at 2.5 to 5 M, however, not only effectively dissociates the receptor from the hormone, but also preserves the activity of the receptor; other salts have not been tested.

Figure 7 shows a typical profile for the purification of prolactin receptors by affinity chromatography. In this experiment, 7.5 ml of crude receptor extract in Triton X-100 was diluted with an equal volume of tris-HCl buffer, 0.025 M, pH 7.6, containing 10 mM MgCl$_2$. The solution was allowed to run through 5 ml of packed hGH-coupled Affi-Gel 10 in a 2 × 18-cm column at room temperature. The flow rate was 15 ml/hr. Eluate was collected in 1-ml fractions. At least 20 bed volumes of 0.1 M borate buffer, pH 7.6, containing 0.1% Triton X-100 were used to wash the column until no protein and no receptor activity were eluted. Washing was always carried out at 4°C to minimize dissociation. Elution was achieved with one bed volume of 5.0 M MgCl$_2$ (warming is necessary to prepare this solution) in the same buffer, followed by several bed volumes of buffer. Fractions of 2 ml each were collected during elution. The first 10 fractions were dialyzed (in separate dialyzing tubing) against at least 200 volumes of borate buffer overnight at 4°C. Due to the influx of buffer into the dialysis tubing as a result of the high osmotic pressure created by the initial high salt concentration, the content of each tubing was diluted

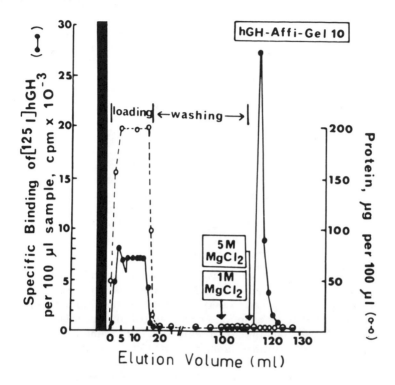

FIG. 7. Purification of prolactin receptors by affinity chromatography
(see text for details). Reprinted from Ref. 9, by courtesy of J. Biol.
Chem.

after dialysis. The volume of each fraction after dialysis was always
noted for subsequent calculations of recovery. Normally, 50 to 100 μl
of the fractions (including original extract, unadsorbed fractions, washings, and eluted fractions) were assayed for receptor activity and protein
content. The protein concentration of the eluted fractions was always too
low to be detected by any conventional method. About 75% of the total
receptor activity was retained by the adsorbent and, of this, 30% could
be eluted from the absorbent by 5 M $MgCl_2$. No activity was eluted with
1 M $MgCl_2$. When bovine serum albumin–coupled Affi-Gel 10 was used
as the adsorbent, no receptor activity was retained [9], demonstrating
that the receptors were specifically adsorbed by the agarose derivative
coupled with hGH.

Three attempts have been made to purify receptors by using hGH
coupled to cyanogen bromide–activated Sepharose 4B [43]. No receptor
activity was retained by the adsorbent in two experiments, but in one,

considerable receptor activity was adsorbed (~40%) but only 3% was recovered upon elution. The same batch of hGH-Sepharose adsorbent was
effective in adsorbing and selectively purifying antibodies to hGH from
rabbit antiserum to hGH. The fact that hGH-coupled Affi-Gel 10, but not
the hGH-coupled Sepharose 4B, was used successfully further demonstrated
that an "arm" or "spacer" separating the matrix backbone and the coupled
ligand is essential for the purification of large macromolecules such as
hormone receptors. The spacer presumably minimizes steric effects by
offering freedom of movement for the coupled ligand, and this facilitates
the binding of receptor to hormone. The application of such agarose
derivatives for the purification of many types of macromolecules, the
insulin receptor being one of these, has been documented [44]. Moreover,
the presence of bovine serum albumin in the buffer system did not lead to
an increase in yield of receptor activity. It was also found that the presence of at least 0.01% Triton X-100 in the buffer systems is essential to
achieve good yield of receptor by this technique.

Due to the high binding capacity of the adsorbent (hGH-Affi-Gel 10),
it was possible to use the adsorbent for the purification of receptors on a
much larger scale compared to that described earlier. However, it is
worth mentioning that we have also observed that different batches of
hGH-Affi-Gel 10 vary somewhat in their capacity to bind receptor. Triton
X-100 extracts of membranes isolated from 100 g of fresh mammary tissue could pass through a 5-ml adsorbent at one time without saturating
the binding sites on the adsorbent. However, partial saturation seems to
take place such that less receptor activity was retained near the end of a
large-scale run. In this case, fractions which contained substantial receptor activity were recycled after the adsorbent has been eluted with 5 M
MgCl$_2$. We routinely employed three to four such affinity columns when
Triton X-100 extracts derived from more than 300 g of fresh tissue were
used. In this type of large-scale experiment, the reservoir that contained
the membrane extract was kept at 4°C, while the affinity columns were
kept at room temperature. Sufficient space above the packed adsorbent
was ensured to allow the extract to achieve room temperature. As a pre-
cautionary measure, sodium azide was routinely added to the extract to a
final concentration of 3 mM to eliminate bacterial growth. The eluate
was channeled back into a reservoir kept at 4°C. The purified receptors
thus obtained were concentrated by UM-10 membrane in an Amicon cell.

Table 2 summarizes the data on the purification of prolactin receptors
when 100 g of tissue was used. By combining differential centrifugation,
detergent extraction, and affinity chromatography, the prolactin receptor
was purified ~1,500-fold. The effectiveness of affinity chromatography
is borne out by the fact that 200-fold purification could be achieved in a
single step. The final yield (determined by comparing the total capacity
to bind prolactin) was 7%, and the yield was ~15% when compared to the

TABLE 2. Summary of the Purification of Prolactin Receptors[a]

Sample	Total yield of protein (mg)	Prolactin-binding capacity (pmol/mg protein)	Fold-purification	Total prolactin-binding capacity recovered	
				pmol	percent
Homogenate	11,000	0.025	1	275	100
Crude membrane fraction	1,220	0.147	6	179	65
Triton X-100 extract	800	0.2	8	160	58
Partially purified receptor	0.5	38.0	1,500	19	7

[a]One hundred grams of fresh mammary gland (wet weight) was used as starting material. Modified from Ref. 9, by courtesy of The Journal of Biological Chemistry.

crude extract applied to the affinity column. It is not clear at present
what factors contribute to the low recovery of receptors eluted from the
affinity adsorbent, although events such as incomplete elution and denaturation of receptor may be responsible. If denaturation did take place,
then we have underestimated the purity of the final product.

We also examined the possibility of using other biochemical techniques
to purify the receptor. Gel filtration chromatography on Sepharose 6B of
the membrane extract met with little success, because the receptor activity eluted from the column in the same fractions as the majority of proteins. Precipitation of receptors by changing pH was also unsuccessful,
because the receptors and bulk of proteins were precipitated at a similar
pH. The use of ion-exchange chromatography was also unsuccessful.
Chromatography on diethylaminoethyl cellulose (DEAE cellulose) at pH
7.6 resulted in a twofold purification, but only 20% of the receptor activity
was recovered. Carboxymethyl cellulose (CM cellulose) chromatography
at pH 7.6 and 5.5 was tried. In the first instance, receptors were not
adsorbed by the adsorbent, but over 95% of the toal proteins were also not
adsorbed. At pH 5.5, 60% of the receptors were adsorbed but only a twofold purification was achieved. In addition, the use of hydroxyapatite
resulted in little success. These methods undoubtedly do not offer much
help in the purification of the prolactin receptors. No further conventional
methods were therefore tried.

G. Analysis of Prolactin Receptor by Disk Gel Electrophoresis and Gel Isoelectric Focusing

On subjecting the receptor, purified by affinity chromatography, to electrophoresis at pH 8.9 in 7.5% (wt/vol) polyacrylamide gel according to
Davis [45], more than one band of stained protein was observed (Fig. 8).
On assaying the receptor activity in gel segments obtained from a duplicate gel, the peak activity occurred at R_f 0.12, which also corresponds
to the R_f of 1 (or possibly 2) of the major protein bands. Upon analysis
of the same material on thin layer polyacrylamide gel (6%, wt/vol) isoelectric focusing in a LKB Multiphor apparatus according to the instructions supplied by the manufacturer, the isoelectric point of the receptor
activity appeared to be between pH 6 and 7 (Fig. 9). Again, heterogeneity
of the preparation is evident. These analyses demonstrated that we have
achieved only partial purification of the prolactin-binding molecule.

IV. CONCLUDING REMARKS

In this chapter, we have outlined the procedures used in our laboratory
to study a cell membrane structure found in rabbit mammary glands,

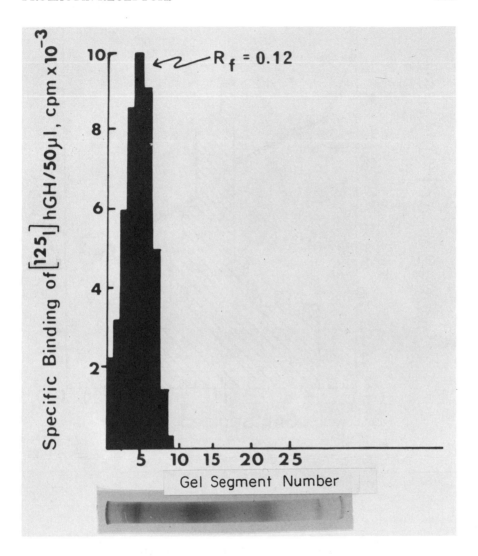

FIG. 8. Disk gel electrophoresis of partially purified prolactin receptor protein by affinity chromatography (see text for details). Reprinted from Ref. 9, by courtesy of J. Biol. Chem.

which specifically binds prolactin and other lactogenic hormones. By employing these procedures, we and others have been able to demonstrate that the prolactin-binding activity is dynamically controlled by a variety of physiological and pathological factors. Although all these findings

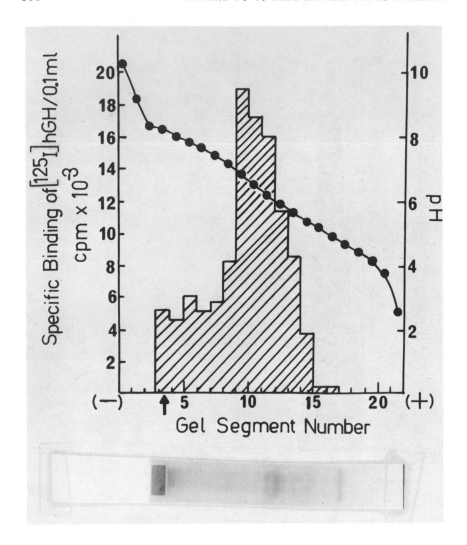

FIG. 9. Thin layer gel isoelectric focusing of partially purified prolactin receptor protein by affinity chromatography (see text for details).

suggest that the binding of prolactin to a target tissue is probably a physiologically significant phenomenon, conclusive evidence to show that this prolactin-binding structure is the true receptor is lacking. This is by no means unique to the binding of prolactin. Indeed, no one has yet successfully demonstrated that a peptide hormone-binding site is the physio-logically significant receptor. To achieve this is by no means simple, in view of the fact that so little is known about the mechanism of actions of peptide hormones. Even for hormones that activate adenylate cyclase, interpretation of experiments correlating hormone binding and activation of the enzyme activity or other intracellular metabolic events has been difficult [2, 46-51]. It is perhaps more difficult to establish a true recep-tor concept for prolactin, in view of the fact that it is doubtful that prolactin activates adenylate cyclase [52, 53] or any membrane-bound enzyme. In this context, the term "receptor" is used for operational purposes, and until the hormone-binding structure is proven to be a "receptor," we feel that the word "receptor" should be used with caution.

Despite the lack of conclusive evidence that the prolactin-binding site is a true receptor, our data do demonstrate a good correlation between hormone binding and the biological activity of the test preparations. This, taken together with the dynamic changes of the prolactin-binding activity under different physiological, pathological, and hormonal influences, sug-gests very strongly that the prolactin-binding activity is probably physio-logically significant. One may anticipate that the availability of a highly purified receptor preparation may greatly facilitate studies on the elucida-tion of the role of receptor in the mediation of hormone action. With this idea in mind, we have devised a procedure to purify the prolactin receptor. Although the receptor preparation we have obtained is by no means homo-geneous, it may be adequate for immunization purposes. The availability of antibodies to the receptor may offer an approach in defining the functional role of receptors and also in facilitating the quantitation of receptors.

Another spin-off of our studies on the prolactin receptor has been the development of the radioreceptor assay for prolactin-like hormones. Due to the fact that peptide hormones biologically related to prolactin bind to the same set of receptors in the rabbit mammary gland, we have been able to obtain some novel data on the identification, quantitation, and purification of new placental lactogenic peptides from a number of species. Hence, the studies on the prolactin receptor may not only help to elucidate the mechanism of action of this hormone, but also open up a new area of research in reproductive physiology.

ACKNOWLEDGMENTS

This work was supported by grants from the Medical Research Council of Canada and the United States Public Health Service (NICHD and NCI). R. P. C. S. is a recipient of a fellowship from the University of Manitoba.

REFERENCES

1. J. Roth, Metabolism, 22:1059 (1973).

2. P. Cuatrecasas, Ann. Rev. Biochem., 43:169 (1974).

3. A. T. Cowie and J. S. Tindal, Physiology of Lactation, Edward Arnold Publishers, London, 1971.

4. R. W. Turkington, Biochem. Biophys. Res. Commun., 41:1362 (1970).

5. I. R. Falconer, Biochem. J., 126:8 (1972).

6. M. Birkinshaw and I. R. Falconer, J. Endocrinol., 55:323 (1972).

7. R. P. C. Shiu, P. A. Kelly, and H. G. Friesen, Science, 180:968 (1973).

8. R. P. C. Shiu and H. G. Friesen, Biochem. J., 140:301 (1974).

9. R. P. C. Shiu and H. G. Friesen, J. Biol. Chem., 249:7902 (1975).

10. B. I. Posner, P. A. Kelly, R. P. C. Shiu, and H. G. Friesen, Endocrinology, 95:521 (1974).

11. P. A. Kelly, B. I. Posner, T. Tsushima, and H. G. Friesen, Endocrinology, 95:532 (1974).

12. R. W. Turkington, G. C. Majunder, N. Kadohama, J. H. MacIndoe, and W. L. Frantz, Recent Progr. Hormone Res., 29:417 (1973).

13. B. I. Posner, P. A. Kelly, and H. G. Friesen, Proc. Natl. Acad. Sci. U.S.A., 71:2407 (1974).

14. P. A. Kelly, B. I. Posner, T. Tsushima, R. P. C. Shiu, and H. G. Friesen, in Advances in Human Growth Hormone Research (S. Raiti, ed.), N.I.H., U.S. Government Printing Office, Washington, D.C., 1974, pp. 567-584.

15. P. A. Kelly, B. I. Posner, and H. G. Friesen, Endocrinology, 97: 1408 (1975).

16. C. Aragona and H. G. Friesen, Endocrinology, 97:677 (1975).

17. P. A. Kelly, C. Bradley, R. P. C. Shiu, J. Meites, and H. G. Friesen, Proc. Soc. Exptl. Biol. Med., 146:816 (1974).

18. R. W. Turkington, Cancer Res., 34:758 (1974).

19. H. G. Friesen, Endocrinology, 79:212 (1966).

20. D. M. Neville, Biochim. Biophys. Acta, 154:540 (1968).

21. J. Meldolesi, J. D. Jamieson, and G. E. Palade, J. Cell Biol., 49: 109 (1971).

22. O. H. Lowry, N. J. Rosebrough, A. L. Farr, and R. J. Randall, J. Biol. Chem., 193:265 (1951).

23. J. I. Thorell and B. G. Johansson, Biochim. Biophys. Acta, 251:363 (1971).

24. W. M. Hunter and F. C. Greenwood, Nature (London), 194:495 (1962).

25. W. L. Frantz and R. W. Turkington, Endocrinology, 91:1545 (1972).

26. I. A. Forsyth, S. J. Folley, and A. Chadwick, J. Endocrinol., 31: 115 (1965).

27. I. A. Forsyth and S. J. Folley, in Ovo-Implantation, Human Gonad-otropins and Prolactin (P. O. Hubinot, F. Leroy, C. Robyn, and P. Leleux, eds.), Karger, Basel and New York, 1970, pp. 226-278.

28. H. Moenkemeyer and H. G. Friesen, to be presented at the Can. Soc. Clin. Res., Jan. 1975 (Abstract).

29. B. I. Posner, P. A. Kelly, and H. G. Friesen, submitted for publication 1974.

30. P. A. Kelly, T. Tsushima, R. P. C. Shiu, and H. G. Friesen, submitted for publication 1974.

31. P. A. Kelly, R. P. C. Shiu, H. G. Friesen, and H. A. Robertson, 55th Annual Meeting of the Endocrine Society, p. A-233, Abstract 370, 1973.

32. J. S. D. Chan, H. A. Robertson, and H. G. Friesen, Endocrinology, 98:65 (1976).

33. R. E. Fellows, T. Hurley, W. Maurer, and B. S. Handwerger, 56th Annual Meeting of the Endocrine Society, p. A-113, Abstracts 116 and 117, 1974.

34. M. C. Robertson and H. G. Friesen, Endocrinology, 97:621 (1975).

35. P. Hwang, Ph.D. Thesis, McGill University, Montreal, Quebec, Canada, 1973.

36. D. Rodbard, P. L. Rayford, J. A. Cooper, and G. T. Ross, J. Clin. Endocrinol. Metab., 28:1412 (1968).

37. P. Cuatrecasas, Proc. Natl. Acad. Sci. U.S.A., 69:318 (1972).

38. S. Udenfriend, S. Stein, P. Bohlen, W. Dairman, W. Leimgruber, and M. Weigele, Science, 178:871 (1972).

39. M. Blecher, N. A. Giorgio, and C. B. Johnson, in The Role of Membranes in Metabolic Regulation (M. A. Mehlman and R. W. Hanson, eds.), Academic Press, New York, 1972, pp. 367-383.

40. P. W. Holloway, Anal. Biochem., 53:304 (1973).

41. G. Scatchard, Ann. N.Y. Acad. Sci., 51:660 (1964).

42. P. Cuatrecasas, Proc. Natl. Acad. Sci. U.S.A., 63:450 (1969).

43. P. Cuatrecasas, M. Wilchek, and C. B. Anfinsen, Proc. Natl. Acad. Sci. U.S.A., 61:636 (1968).

44. P. Cuatrecasas and C. B. Anfinsen, Ann. Rev. Biochem., 40:259 (1971).

45. B. J. Davis, Ann. N.Y. Acad. Sci., 121:404 (1964).

46. T. Kono and F. W. Barham, J. Biol. Chem., 246:6210 (1971).

47. L. Birnbaumer and S. L. Pohl, J. Biol. Chem., 248:2056 (1973).

48. J. Gliemann and S. Gammeltoft, 4th International Congress on Endocrinology, Excerpta Medica, Amsterdam, International Congress Series No. 256, 1972, p. 198 (Abstract).

49. G. Sayers, R. J. Beall, and S. Seelig, Science, 175:1131 (1972).

50. M. L. Dufau, T. Tsuruhara, K. Watanabe, and K. J. Catt, 4th International Congress on Endocrinology, Excerpta Medica, Amsterdam, International Congress Series No. 256, 1972, p. 199 (Abstract).

51. D. Rodbard, in Receptors for Reproductive Hormones (B. W. O'Malley and A. R. Means, eds.), Plenum, New York, 1973, p. 342.

52. G. C. Majumder and R. W. Turkington, J. Biol. Chem., 246:5545 (1971).

53. M. Sapag-Hagar and A. L. Greenbaum, Eur. J. Biochem., 47:303 (1974).

Chapter 19

PROSTAGLANDIN RECEPTORS IN ADIPOSE TISSUE

John L. Humes
Helen G. Oien
Frederick A. Kuehl, Jr.

Department of Inflammation and Arthritis
Merck Institute for Therapeutic Research
Rahway, New Jersey

I. INTRODUCTION   600

II. PREPARATION OF LIPOCYTES   600

III. BINDING TO INTACT LIPOCYTES   601

IV. BINDING TO THE RECEPTOR PREPARATION   601

V. RECEPTOR PREPARATION FOR PG QUANTITATION   606

VI. PROPERTIES OF THE PGE RECEPTOR PREPARATION   608

    A. Adenylate Cyclase   608
    B. Membrane ATPase   609
    C. cAMP Phosphodiesterase   609
    D. Effect of Compounds on the Binding of PGE_1 609

VII. APPLICATION OF THE BINDING REACTION   609

    REFERENCES   613

I. INTRODUCTION

The prostaglandins (PGs) comprise a family of 20-carbon fatty acids which have been implicated in the regulation of a vast array of physiological, pharmacological, and pathological events. Since their discovery in 1930 [1], these substances have been detected in virtually all animal cells, fluids, and secretions examined, as well as in cells of some lower organisms [2].

The existence of a receptor unique to prostaglandins was implied by the biological specificity of these compounds and by the inhibitory action of antagonists containing similar structural features. Evidence that such a receptor is localized or fixed in the plasma membrane of divers mammalian cell types was inferred from the many studies in intact cells and tissues which showed that PGs, especially those of the E-series, increase cAMP levels, and that this effect was blocked by these antagonists [3-5]. In the limited number of cell types, which when homogenized responded to PGs, the effect upon cAMP levels was demonstrated to be due to stimulation of the enzyme adenylate cyclase. Thus, it is evident that in most instances prostaglandins are capable of mimicking the action of hormones in stimulating second-messenger cAMP formation. On the other hand there are a few instances, notably the fat cell, toad bladder, and Purkinje cell, wherein prostaglandins oppose hormonally induced increases in cAMP. It is on the first of these, the fat cell, that we wish to focus our attention in this chapter.

Adipocytes prepared from rat epididymal fat pads by the method of Rodbell [6] represent a homogeneous cell population. They have been shown to be uniquely sensitive to a vast array of hormonal stimulators (ACTH, epinephrine, glucagon, etc.), all of which induce lipolysis by increasing the cAMP levels. Prostaglandins, in particular those of the E-series, have been found effective at extremely low levels in blocking this rise in cAMP and the subsequent lipolytic response [3, 7]. Thus, although the inhibitory action of PGs on cAMP represents the exception rather than the rule in this instance, it seemed possible, nevertheless, that the initial interaction of the E-prostaglandins with their binding site in adipocytes might be representative of that which occurs in all tissues. Subsequent binding studies in bovine corpus luteum membranes [8] and in bovine thyroid membranes [9], tissues in which PGE_1 stimulates cAMP synthesis, support this belief.

II. PREPARATION OF LIPOCYTES

$[5,6-^3H]$ Prostaglandin E_1 (specific activity 83 Ci/mmol) was purchased from New England Nuclear Corporation and used in these studies without further purification. Epididymal fat was obtained from male Holtzman

rats (220–300 g) maintained on Purina chow and water <u>ad libitum</u> until
sacrificed by decapitation. Bacterial collagenase (CLS) was purchased
from Worthington Biochemical Corporation.

Initial efforts to demonstrate the binding of PGE_1 were performed with
a suspension of intact lipocytes. However, these early experiments, utilizing cell suspensions prepared in a manner essentially analogous to the
method described by Rodbell [6], were unsuccessful. We subsequently
found that by employing Krebs–Ringer solutions devoid of the prescribed
bovine serum albumin throughout the entire procedures of collagenase
digestion, isolation, and incubation would yield cell suspensions that were
capable of binding $[^3H]\,PGE_1$. The reason(s) for the inhibitory effect of
exogenous albumin on the binding of PGE_1 to the lipocyte were not investigated. However, recent reports that prostaglandins have a finite affinity
for serum and plasma proteins [10, 11] posed the possibility that bovine
serum albumin in the quantities employed might compete with the lipocyte-
binding site with the consequent loss of $[^3H]\,PGE_1$ uptake by the receptor.
A study of metal ions revealed that various salts of the Krebs–Ringer solution ($MgSO_4$, KCl, $CaCl_2$) were not necessary either in the preparation of
lipocyte suspensions or for the binding of radioactive PGE_1. Thus, lipocyte suspensions were prepared by modification of the Rodbell procedure
[12] utilizing tris-saline buffer, pH 7.5, [0.01 M tris-HCl; 0.15 M NaCl].
Two grams of epididymal fat pads were digested with 20 mg of collagenase
for 60 min at 37°C in 5 ml of buffer. After disruption of the tissue by
gentle stirring, the lipocytes were washed with two successive 5-ml aliquots of buffer. The cellular fraction was suspended in buffer to achieve
a final volume of 3 ml and filtered through two layers of cheesecloth.

III. BINDING TO INTACT LIPOCYTES

Aliquots of the cell suspension (maintained in suspension by gentle agitation),
0.1 ml containing 100 to 200 μg protein, were added to 0.05 ml tris-saline
buffer containing 0.1 μCi (0.4 ng) $[^3H]\,PGE_1$. In appropriate tubes, 0.4
ng and 0.8 ng PGE_1 were included along with the tritiated PGE_1. The incubation and work-up procedures were carried out as described in Sec.
IV. Evidence of binding is shown graphically in Figure 1. These studies,
limited in scope, demonstrating the binding to intact lipocytes were not
explored further.

IV. BINDING TO THE RECEPTOR PREPARATION

Five milliliters of the lipocyte suspension prepared as described for the
binding studies in intact cells were homogenized with eight strokes in a
size D Duall glass-to-glass, motor driven homogenizer (Knotes Glass Co.).

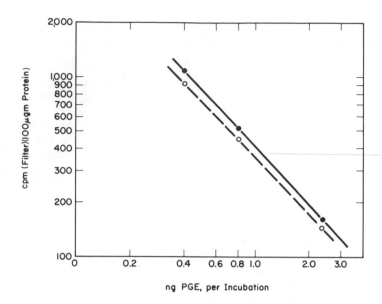

FIG. 1.   The binding of [³H] PGE₁ to intact lipocytes -O---O- and to the
receptor preparation —●—●— .

This homogenate was centrifuged for 5 min at 1,000 g and 25°C. The pelleted materials and aqueous infranatant phase were aspirated from beneath
the lipid cake and its clear oily supernatant phase. The clear, floating
oil phase was removed by aspiration, and the lipid cake was resuspended
in 3 ml of the tris-saline buffer. This suspension was again centrifuged
and separated as previously described. The excess adhering oil was removed by carefully wiping the sides of the tube with lens paper. The lipid
cake was finally resuspended in 1 ml of buffer, and 0.1-ml aliquots of this
suspension were used for the binding experiments.

Each incubation mixture contained 0.1 ml of the binding preparation
(80-200 μg protein), 0.05 ml buffer containing 0.1 μCi [5, 6-³H] PGE₁ (0.4
ng), and prostaglandin or test substance in 10 μl of methyl alcohol or dimethylsulfoxide. The tubes were incubated with shaking at 37°C for 60
min unless otherwise indicated.

In our initial work, the bound PGE₁ was separated from the nonbound
material by filtration through HAWP 0.45-mμ Millipore filters. However,
these filtration procedures proved laborious and time-consuming, since
the high lipid content of the binding preparation had a tendency to occlude
the filters. Hence, a simplified filtration system was devised consisting
of a glass wool plug compressed to a length of 1 cm in a 14.6-cm disposable
Pasteur pipet. Separation of the bound PGE₁ was achieved by applying the

incubates, diluted with 1 ml of buffer, to these columns. The columns were then washed with two successive 0.5-ml portions of buffer; the residual buffer was expelled by air pressure exerted with a rubber bulb. The segment of the columns containing the glass wool plug, ~2.5 cm, was severed from the column with a glass-cutting file. The radioactivity associated with the glass wool filter, corresponding to the amount of [^{3}H] PGE$_1$ bound to the binding preparation, was determined by expelling the plug and glass segment into a toluene/ethanol (70:30 vol/vol) counting solution.

The amount of radioactivity bound to the heat-denatured receptor preparation (5 min, 100°C) was used as a measure of the nonspecific binding. Similar values were obtained when a vast excess of PGE$_1$ (5,000–10,000 ng) was added. These values were subtracted from all observed readings.

As shown in Figure 2, the association of [^{3}H] PGE$_1$ with the lipocyte receptor preparation maximized within 15 min of incubation at 37°C; however, most assays were performed for 60 min to ensure complete equilibration. The binding of PGE$_1$ to the receptor preparation demonstrated strict temperature dependence, with the maximum amount of binding occurring at 37°C and a marked decline at higher or lower temperatures (Fig. 3).

The displacement of 0.4 ng [^{3}H] PGE$_1$ by unlabeled PGE$_1$ is shown in Figure 4. In this protocol, the unlabeled PGE$_1$ was premixed with [^{3}H] PGE$_1$

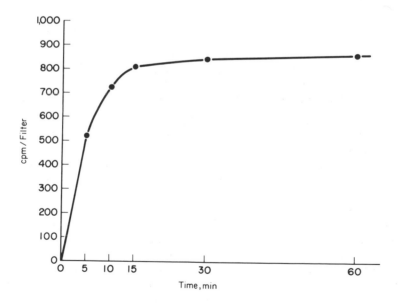

FIG. 2. The rate of association of [^{3}H] PGE$_1$ to the receptor preparation.

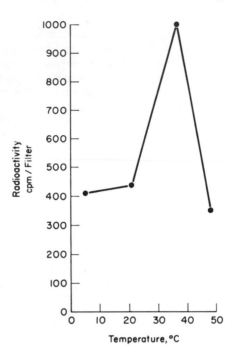

FIG. 3. The effect of temperature on the association of [³H] PGE₁ to the
receptor preparation.

and incubated for 60 min. However, the binding of PGE₁ to this preparation appears to be essentially nonreversible, as the addition of unlabeled
material to the incubation after equilibrium has been established results
in only a small displacement of the bound [³H] PGE₁.

Essentially all of the bound [³H] PGE₁ could be extracted from the
glass wool filter, chromatographed, and identified as unchanged PGE₁,
as shown in Figure 5. The glass wool filters from two identical incubates
were combined, added to 2 ml water, and extracted with three successive
2-ml portions of n-hexane to remove neutral lipids. The aqueous phase
was then acidified to pH 3.8 with 0.3 M citric acid and extracted with
three successive 2-ml aliquots of ethyl acetate. The combined organic
phase was backwashed with three repetitive 2-ml aliquots of water. The
ethyl acetate phase was reduced to dryness under a stream of nitrogen at
40°C. The residue was dissolved in a small amount of ethyl acetate,
chromatographed on a 1 × 14-cm lane of silica gel G and developed with
Andersen's F VI development solvent [13]. The radioactivity in various
areas of the chromatogram was determined by counting 1-cm portions of
the gel in ethanol/toluene (30:70) counting solution.

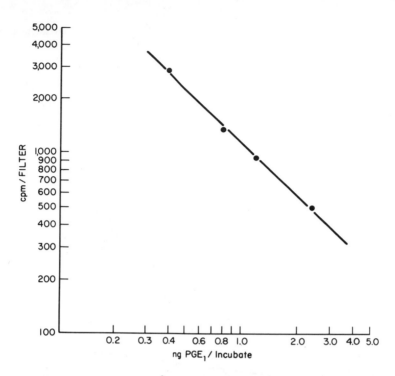

FIG. 4. The displacement of [³H] PGE₁ by PGE₁. Reproduced from Ref. 21, with the permission of the copyright owner.

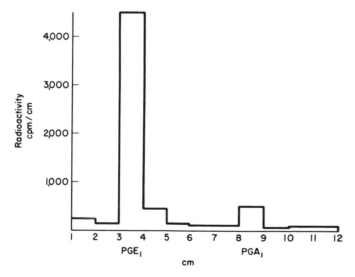

FIG. 5. Thin layer chromatogram of the ethyl acetate-extracted bound [³H] PGE₁.

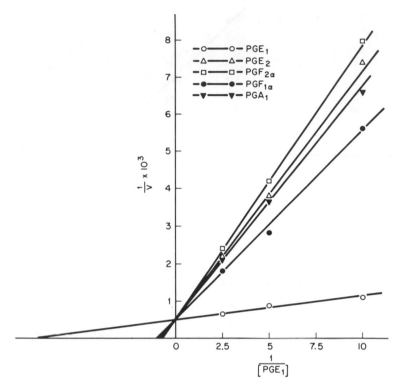

FIG. 6. Competitive interaction of various prostaglandins (PGE_2, 1 ng; $PGF_{1\alpha}$, $PGF_{2\alpha}$ and PGA_1, 100 ng). [Reproduced from Ref. 21 with the permission of the copyright owner.]

Association constants for the various classes of PGs were obtained by classical Lineweaver-Burk kinetic analysis. Binding constants for PGE_1 and PGE_2 were ~3 nM, whereas the corresponding values for $PGF_{1\alpha}$, $PGF_{2\alpha}$, and PGA_1 were 300 nM. The receptor preparation exhibited a maximum saturation value of 0.57 pmol/mg protein (Fig. 6).

V. RECEPTOR PREPARATION FOR PG QUANTITATION

At the inception of this work, radioimmunoassay methods for PGs were in the early developmental stages; thus, limited studies were undertaken to establish the feasibility of using the lipocyte receptor preparation for the quantitation of tissue levels of PGs. As previously discussed, the association of [³H] PGE_1 with the receptor preparation was essentially nonreversible since the addition of unlabeled PGE_1 to the incubation mixture, after equilibrium had been achieved, resulted in negligible displace-

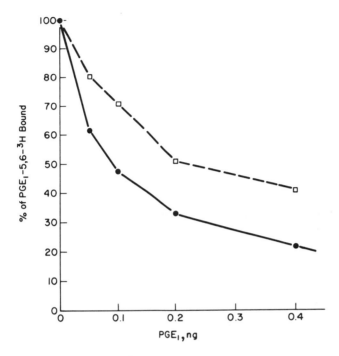

FIG. 7. The association of [^{3}H] PGE with no preincubation -□---□- and after 30 min preincubation —●——●— to the receptor preparation.

ment of the bound [^{3}H] PGE$_1$. Thus, if an equilibrium were established between the receptor preparation and unlabeled PGE$_1$ prior to incubation with [^{3}H] PGE$_1$, the sensitivity of the method was improved. As demonstrated in Figure 7, a 50% displacement of [^{3}H] PGE$_1$ was achieved by 0.1 ng PGE$_1$ when the receptor preparation was preincubated for 30 min with unlabeled PGE$_1$, followed by a subsequent 60 min incubation with 0.1 μCi [^{3}H] PGE$_1$. However, if both the PGE$_1$ and [^{3}H] PGE$_1$ were simultaneously incubated for 60 min with the binding preparation, approximately four times more PGE$_1$ was required to achieve an equal displacement. Thus, with the preincubation technique it was possible to achieve an assay with sensitivity comparable to radioimmunoassays. Unfortunately, despite the sensitivity and specificity of the method, the lability of the receptor preparation proved to be a more insurmountable obstacle. The receptor preparation completely lost the ability to bind [^{3}H] PGE$_1$ when subjected to freezing; indeed, diminished binding activity was observed when the preparation was cooled to 4°C for 60 min. Various attempts to store the lipocytes or receptor preparation in nonionic solvents (dimethyl sulfoxide, glycerol, sucrose) were unsuccessful. Ultimately, the instability of the receptor preparation, plus gradual improvements in radioimmunoassays forced the conclusion that this method was not suitable for routine assay purposes.

VI. PROPERTIES OF THE PGE RECEPTOR PREPARATION

The interfacial material between the aqueous infranatant and oil phases of the centrifuged lipocyte homogenate, designated the PGE receptor preparation, contained the majority of the total adenylate cyclase activity, a membrane-associated enzyme. Thus, the receptor preparation was considered to be derived from the lipocyte membrane. The pelleted fraction, most certainly containing nuclear components and large membrane fragments, was devoid of PGE-binding activity and contained only a small fraction of the total adenylate cyclase activity. In addition, these activities were not detected in the aqueous infranatant or floating oil phases. The report by Gorman and Miller [14] that fat cell ghosts possessed similar binding characteristics confirms our original contention that the PGE receptor and other associated enzymes were removed from other membrane fragments by the homogenization conditions. The binding preparation representing 1/1,000 the weight of the total fat cell suspension and 1/10 of the protein clearly has lipophilic properties, which undoubtedly account for its separation from other proteins during centrifugation. Since the receptor preparation is sensitive to chymotrypsin, it is reasonable to suggest that the material is a lipoprotein. The instability of the preparation, combined with the inability to store the fraction, mediated against further fractionation.

In an attempt to determine the relationship between PGE binding and the well-recognized ability of the PGs to inhibit hormonally induced increases in intracellular cAMP in the intact fat cell, studies were undertaken to explore the effects of PGEs and various lipolytic agents on cAMP-related enzymes in the binding preparation.

A. Adenylate Cyclase

The conversion of $[^{14}C]$ATP to radioactive cAMP was measured by incubating 0.01 M tris-HCl, pH 7.5; 0.15 M NaCl (7.5 μmol); ATP (0.225 μmol); $[^{14}C]$ATP (2 μCi); theophylline (1.05 μmol); pyruvate kinase (4.6 IU); PEP-Na (0.75 μmol); MgCl$_2$ (0.75 μmol); cAMP (0.135 μmol); and water to a final volume of 0.05 ml with 0.1 ml of the binding fraction for 20 min at 37°C. Using a modification of the Krishna method for measuring the product [15], a 0.03% basal conversion was observed. Fluoride ion (0.01 M), and epinephrine (1 $\times$ 10^{-4} M), increased the conversion rates to 0.18 and 0.07%, respectively. The addition of PGE$_1$ or PGE$_2$ to these incubates had no effect, either stimulatory or inhibitory, on the basal or hormonally stimulated rates. PGEs were also ineffectual when AMP-PNP (0.03 μmol plus AMP-PN ^{32}P, 1 μCi) was used as a substrate.

B. Membrane ATPase

Ion-dependent ATPase was evaluated by employing the incubation conditions of Stanbury et al. [16], adding 0.5 μCi [^{14}C] ATP to a final volume of 0.05 ml. The binding preparation (0.1 ml) was added, and the samples were incubated for 10 min at 37°C. No significant difference between metabolism to ADP plus AMP for control samples (22%) and those to which PGE$_1$ (1 μg or 10 μg) was added (19% for both) was observed.

C. cAMP Phosphodiesterase

This enzyme, responsible for degrading cAMP, was measured by incubating [^{3}H] cAMP (0.05 ml containing 0.5 μCi), cAMP (0.05 ml containing 1 $\times$ 10^{-6} mmol or 1 $\times$ 10^{-4} mmol) and 0.05 ml of 0.2 M tris-HCl, pH 7.5; 0.01 M MgSO$_4$ with 0.1 ml of the binding preparation for 10 min at 37°C. Both a low (2 $\times$ 10^{-6} M) and a high (1 $\times$ 10^{-4} M) Km enzyme were found in the binding fraction; PGE$_1$ at levels of 0.5 to 2.0 μg had no significant effect on the system. In a representative experiment containing 108 μg protein per 0.1 ml binding fraction, 21% metabolism occurred in a control sample after 10 min, compared to 23.5% at 1.0 μg PGE$_1$.

D. Effect of Compounds on the Binding of PGE$_1$

When the binding reaction was run in the manner described, epinephrine at levels capable of stimulating cAMP formation (1 $\times$ 10^{-6}-1 $\times$ 10^{-3} M) had no effect on the interaction of PGE$_1$ with its receptor. The same was also found to be true when GTP (1 $\times$ 10^{-6}-1 $\times$ 10^{-4} M), ACTH (2 $\times$ 10^{-7}-2 $\times$ 10^{-4} M), and glucagon (1 $\times$ 10^{-7}-1 $\times$ 10^{-4} M) were added to the reaction mixture.

VII. APPLICATION OF THE BINDING REACTION

Arachidonic acid, the substrate for PGE$_2$ biosynthesis, demonstrated a weak affinity for the PG receptor preparation. However at identical concentrations, other fatty acids as well as progesterone and testosterone did not influence the binding of [^{3}H] PGE$_1$ (Fig. 8). The inclusion of indomethacin, a potent PG synthetase inhibitor which does not influence PGE binding, did not alter the ability of arachidonic acid to displace [^{3}H] PGE$_1$. These observations suggest that arachidonic acid per se may exert an intrinsic, albeit weak, affinity for this PGE receptor; however, possible contamination by a small amount of PGE$_2$ cannot be excluded.

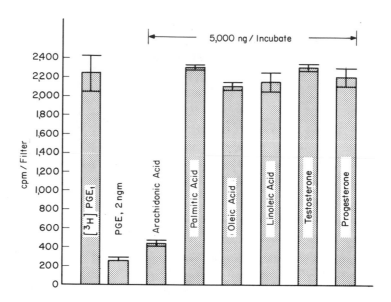

FIG. 8. The effect of various lipids on PGE₁ binding. Reproduced from Ref. 21, with the permission of the copyright owner.

The effects of various known PG antagonists on the binding of [³H] PGE₁ to the receptor preparation is shown in Figure 9. It can be seen that 7-oxa-13-prostynoic acid [I(d)] elicited a weak displacement; however, 10 to 20 times greater activity was derived with the 15-hydroxyl analog, 7-oxa-15-hydroxy-13-prostynoic acid [I(g)]. The latter compound, but not the former, stimulated the synthesis of cAMP in isolated mouse ovaries [17]. Polyphloretin phosphate (PPP), which has been reported to antagonize PGE₂-induced elevation of intraoccular pressure [18], and 1-acetyl-2-(8-chloro-10,11-dihydrodibenz[b,f]-[1,4]oxazepine-10-carbonyl)hydrazine [SC 19220] were inactive. It has been reported that PPP antagonizes the action of PGE₁ by interfering with processes subsequent to PGE₁-induced stimulation of cAMP formation [19].

The ability of various PGs of the E-series to displace [³H] PGE₁ from the receptor preparation was compared with the ability of 1 μg/ml of these compounds to stimulate cAMP synthesis in the mouse ovary [17]. As shown in Table 1, the antipode of PGE₁ [+ PGE₁] does not interact with the receptor preparation, nor does it inhibit the binding of PGE₁, since the racemic mixture [± PGE₁] elicits one-half the activity of the natural isomer [- PGE₁]. A free carboxyl group does not appear to be requisite for binding, since the methyl ester of PGE₁ exhibits approximately the

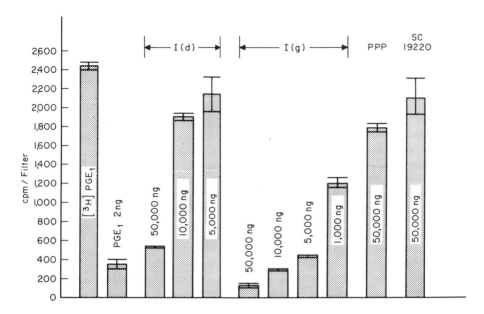

FIG. 9. The effect of various prostaglandin antagonists on PGE_1 binding. Reproduced from Ref. 21, with the permission of the copyright owner.

same displacement value as the free acid. However, it is not possible to exclude the possibility that hydrolysis of the ester could have occurred during the incubations. The insertion of the 5, 6-double bond (PGE_2) imparts little effect to the binding characteristics, whereas the reduction of the 13, 14-double bond [13, 14-dihydro PGE_1] results in a 10-fold reduction in binding affinity. The obligatory requirement of the 15-hydroxyl function in the (S)-configuration is clearly demonstrated, since 15-keto-PGE_1 is essentially inactive, and the binding of 15-(R)-hydroxy-($\pm$)-PGE_1 is diminished by a factor of 10 when compared with 15-(S)-hydroxy-($\pm$)-PGE_1. As would be expected, an important cellular PG metabolite, 13, 14-dihydro-15-keto-PGE_1 exhibited negligible activity.

It is evident that there is a high degree of structural specificity associated with the binding interaction, and in general this correlates well with the biological activities of these prostaglandins. The additional correlation between binding to the lipocyte receptor and the ability to increase cAMP levels in the mouse ovary in vitro is consistent with a PGE-cAMP interrelationship. This binding reaction also proved useful for detecting PGE-like activity in a series of linear fatty acids which showed biological activity in a number of test systems [20].

TABLE 1. A Comparison of the Ability of Various PGEs to Bind to the Receptor Preparation and to Stimulate cAMP Synthesis[a]

Compound	Structure	PG binding, relative activity	cAMP accumulation mouse ovaries
(−)-PGE$_1$		1.0	1.0
(+)-PGE$_1$		0.01	0
(±)-PGE$_1$		0.5	0.7
15-epi (±)-PGE$_1$		0.04	0.7
PGE$_1$ methyl ester		0.8	0.8
PGE$_2$		0.7	0.8
13,14-Dihydro-PGE$_1$		0.2	1.0
15-keto-PGE$_1$		0.01	0.08
13,14-Dihydro-15-keto-PGE$_1$		0.004	0.14

[a]For comparative purposes, a value of unity is assigned for the binding of PGE$_1$ to the lipocyte receptor and the ability to stimulate cAMP formation in the mouse ovary. Relative potencies of other prostaglandins are based on this figure. In actual fact, the binding constant of PGE$_1$ is 10^{-9} M and, at 1 μg/ml, a stimulation of ~40-fold is observed in cAMP formation in the mouse ovary.

REFERENCES

1. R. Kurzrok and C. C. Lieb, Proc. Soc. Exptl. Biol. Med., 28:268 (1930).

2. E. J. Christ and D. A. vanDorp, in Advances in the Biosciences (S. Bergström, ed.), Vol. 9, Pergamon Press, Oxford, 1973, pp. 35-38.

3. R. W. Butcher and C. E. Baird, J. Biol. Chem., 243:1713 (1968).

4. F. A. Kuehl, Jr., V. J. Cirillo, E. A. Ham, and J. L. Humes, in Advances in the Biosciences (S. Bergström, ed.), Vol. 9, Pergamon Press, Oxford, 1973, pp. 155-172.

5. F. A. Kuehl, Jr., J. L. Humes, V. J. Cirillo, and E. A. Ham, in Advances in Cyclic Nucleotide Research (P. Greengard, R. Paoletti, and G. A. Robison, eds.), Vol. 1, Raven Press, New York, 1972, pp. 493-502.

6. M. Rodbell, J. Biol. Chem., 239:375 (1964).

7. J. L. Humes, L. R. Mandel, and F. A. Kuehl, Jr., in Prostaglandin Symposium of the Worcester Foundation for Experimental Biology (P. W. Ramwell and J. E. Shaw, eds.), Interscience, New York, 1967, pp. 79-91.

8. C. V. Rao, J. Biol. Chem., 249:7203 (1974).

9. W. V. Moore and J. Wolff, J. Biol. Chem., 248:5705 (1973).

10. A. A. Attallah and G. C. Schussler, Prostaglandins, 4:479 (1973).

11. A. Raz, Biochem. J., 130:631 (1972).

12. F. A. Kuehl, Jr. and J. L. Humes, Proc. Natl. Acad. Sci. U.S.A., 69:480 (1972).

13. N. H. Andersen, J. Lipid Res., 10:316 (1969).

14. R. R. Gorman and O. V. Miller, Biochim. Biophys. Acta, 332:358 (1974).

15. G. Krishna, B. Weiss, and B. B. Brodie, J. Pharmacol. Exptl. Therap., 163:379 (1968).

16. J. B. Stanbury, J. V. Wicker, and M. A. Lafferty, J. Memb. Biol., 1:495 (1969).

17. F. A. Kuehl, Jr., J. L. Humes, J. Tarnoff, V. J. Cirillo, and E. A. Ham, Science, 169:883 (1970).

18. R. A. Bethel and K. E. Eakins, Federation Proc., 30:626 (1971).

19. F. A. Kuehl, Jr., J. L. Humes, L. R. Mandel, V. J. Cirillo, M. E. Zanetti, and E. A. Ham, Biochem. Biophys. Res. Commun., 44:1464 (1971).

20. J. B. Bicking, R. L. Smith, and E. J. Cragoe, personal communication.

21. Proc. Natl. Acad. Sci. U.S.A., 69:480 (1972).

Chapter 20

PROSTAGLANDIN E RECEPTORS IN CORPORA LUTEA

Ch. Venkateswara Rao

Departments of Obstetrics-Gynecology and Biochemistry
University of Louisville
School of Medicine
Louisville, Kentucky

I. INTRODUCTION 616

II. PREPARATION OF CELL MEMBRANES 616

III. BINDING ASSAY FOR [3H] PROSTAGLANDIN E_1 617

    A. Incubations 617
    B. Separation of Bound and Free [3H] PGE_1 619

IV. THIN LAYER CHROMATOGRAPHY OF [3H] PROSTAGLANDIN
    E_1 620

V. BINDING CONDITIONS 622

    A. Membrane Protein and Concentration of [3H] PGE_1 622
    B. Time, Temperature, and pH 622

VI. BINDING CONSTANTS FOR [3H] PGE_1-MEMBRANE
    INTERACTION 626

VII. SPECIFICITY OF PGE RECEPTORS 631

VIII. MACROMOLECULAR NATURE OF PGE RECEPTORS 632

IX.   EFFECT OF CHEMICAL MODIFICATION OF MEMBRANE
      PROTEINS ON [^{3}H] PGE$_1$ BINDING   635

      ACKNOWLEDGMENTS   636

      REFERENCES   637

I. INTRODUCTION

Prostaglandins (PGs) are a family of substances with a wide variety of
biological effects and are perhaps ubiquitous in their tissue distribution.
PGs, especially PGE$_1$ and PGE$_2$, mimic a variety of peptide hormones by
virtue of their ability to modulate adenylate cyclase activity [1-4]. PGEs
activate adenylate cyclase in a wide variety of tissues [5], except fat cells,
where they inhibit this enzyme activity [1]. These observations led to the
belief that PGEs may serve as mediators in the stimulation of adenylate
cyclase by peptide hormones [3, 5, 7]. It was also implied from these
observations that there would be receptors for PGEs (include only PGE$_1$
and PGE$_2$) in outer cell membranes. A variety of recent experimental
data did not support the possiblity of PGEs serving an intermediary role
in peptide hormone stimulation of adenylate cyclase [8-13]. It was only
recently that the presence of PGE receptors in the cell membrane fraction
of corpus luteum [9, 14], thyroid [11], fat [15], and liver cells [16] was
confirmed. Several studies have also demonstrated PGE-binding sites in
tissue slices [17-20], homogenates [21], and mitochondrial [22], microsomal [23-25] and cytosol [26-28] fractions of various tissues. While the
cell membrane binding of PGEs seems to be related to the modulation of
adenylate cyclase, the biological significance of intracellular binding of
PGEs remains essentially unknown. Since PGEs are quite different from
other hormones and agents which are known to bind to cell membranes, it
is of considerable interest to study the properties of PGEs binding to membranes. In view of the fact that human choriogonadotropin (hCG) and
PGEs evoke similar biological responses in bovine corpus luteum [8], it
was interesting to examine if they bound to a single receptor site, as had
been speculated earlier [3]. Therefore, we set out to study the properties
of PGE receptors and the methodological approaches and rationale used
in these studies are presented in detail in this chapter.

II. PREPARATION OF CELL MEMBRANES

Bovine corpora lutea are collected in a slaughterhouse from cattle with a
foetus crown-to-rump length of up to 20 cm. Recent studies in our laboratory have shown, however, that the corpora lutea obtained from cows with

foetus lengths of up to 98 cm contain PGE receptors and, therefore, they apparently can also be used for preparation of the cell membrane fraction [29]. Immediately after collection, the corpora lutea are placed in cold homogenizing buffer of the following composition: 0.01 M tris-HCl, pH 7.0, containing 0.25 M sucrose, 0.001 M $CaCl_2$, 0.001 M dithiothreitol (DTT) and 0.1% gelatin. This composition was found to be necessary for optimal recovery of PGE receptors. Gelatin in the homogenizing buffer does not bind [^{3}H] PGE_1 or interfere with its binding to membranes.

The corpora lutea are brought to the laboratory within 2 hr of collection and dissected free from surrounding ovarian tissue, minced, and homogenized in a glass-teflon homogenizer with 10 strokes in homogenizing buffer at 4°C. The homogenates are filtered through four layers of cheesecloth, and the filtrate is then centrifuged at 2,000 g for 20 min at 4°C. The method described by Campbell et al. [30] is used with minor modifications to isolate the cell membrane fraction from 2,000-g pellets of the homogenate. This isolation procedure is illustrated in Figure 1. As can be seen from this figure, the procedure does not require the use of an ultracentrifuge, and the time required for the entire procedure is relatively short. Thus, one can use this procedure, after careful validation, to make membrane preparations when only a low-speed, refrigerated centrifuge is available in the laboratory and when time taken for the entire procedure needs to be short.

Campbell et al. [30] reported that the renal cell membranes isolated using this procedure contained high Na^+-K^+-ATPase and adenylate cyclase activities. The phase contrast microscopic examinations of membrane preparations revealed an abundance of membrane fragments, with no unbroken cells and very few nuclei. These membrane preparations also contained a very high [^{125}I] hCG-binding capacity (fmol bound per mg protein). The cell membranes are stored in aliquots at -20°C with little or no loss of [^{3}H] PGE_1-binding activity for at least three to four weeks.

Aliquots of membrane fractions are suspended in a known volume of 0.1 N NaOH containing 0.1% sodium dodecyl sulphate and heated for 5 to 10 min in boiling water. Aliquots of this solution are then taken for protein determination by the method of Lowry et al. [31], using bovine serum albumin as the standard. The net protein in the membrane fractions is obtained by subtracting the protein content due to gelatin in an aliquot of homogenizing buffer.

III. BINDING ASSAY FOR [^{3}H] PROSTAGLANDIN E_1

A. Incubations

[^{3}H] PGE_1 (110 Ci/mmol) was purchased from New England Nuclear Corporation and used within three months. Unlabeled PGs were generously donated by Dr. John Pike of the Upjohn Company. Both [^{3}H] PGE_1 and

618   Ch. VENKATESWARA RAO

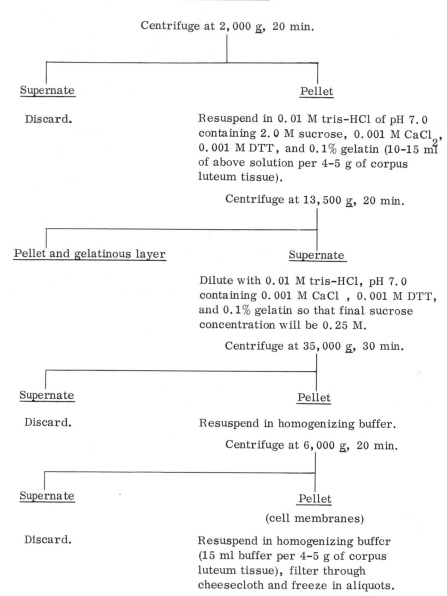

FIG. 1. Schematic presentation of the preparation of cell membrane
fraction.

unlabeled PGs are not purified further before use. Various lines of our data suggested that any role impurities in [^{3}H] PGE$_1$ play in binding would be quite insignificant (see Sec. VII). The labeled and unlabeled PGs solutions are made in redistilled ethanol and stored under nitrogen at -20°C between uses.

[^{3}H] PGE$_1$ and unlabeled PGs (wherever indicated) in redistilled ethanol are pipetted into 12 × 75-mm disposable glass tubes. The ethanol is blown dry under a stream of nitrogen, and the residue is dissolved in 0.1 ml of 0.01 M tris-HCl buffer of pH 7.0. In a few preliminary experiments, we found that [^{3}H] PGE$_1$ could be added directly to the membranes in small amounts of ethanol, up to a final volume/volume concentration of 10% (this method should be validated whenever [^{3}H] PGE$_1$ and membrane fractions are incubated with additional reagents), and a [^{3}H] PGE$_1$ solution can be made in 0.01 M tris-HCl, pH 7.0, and stored in the cold for use on a short-term basis. Membrane fractions containing known amounts of protein are added, and the samples incubated in a Dubnoff metabolic shaker for 1 hr at 38°C unless stated otherwise. Almost all of the incubations are conducted with the same amount of [^{3}H] PGE$_1$ (~0.1 μCi). However, the final concentration of [^{3}H] PGE$_1$ is different in some experiments because of different incubation volumes (incubation volumes in most experiments are 0.2 ml). The final composition of incubation buffer generally is: 0.01 M tris-HCl, pH 7.0; 0.125 M sucrose; 0.5 mM CaCl$_2$; 0.5 mM DTT; and 0.05% gelatin.

Nonspecific binding is assessed in each experiment by incubating aliquots of the membrane fraction with [^{3}H] PGE$_1$ and unlabeled PGE$_1$ (10^{-6} M to 10^{-5} M). The cpm remaining in these pellets are subtracted from the total binding to obtain specific binding. The cpm in nonspecific binding tubes are approximately the same as the cpm retained in the absence of membrane fractions (blanks), suggesting that nonspecific binding is insignificant in these membrane fractions. Moore and Wolff [11] have compared a [^{14}C] glucose blank with conventional nonspecific binding (PGE$_1$ + [^{3}H] PGE$_1$) and found it to be close, and subsequently used a [^{14}C] glucose blank for the determination of nonspecific binding. However, it is quite important, and generally safer, to determine nonspecific binding in the presence of excess unlabeled PGE$_1$ with each experiment.

B. Separation of Bound and Free [^{3}H] PGE$_1$

Following incubation, bound and free [^{3}H] PGE$_1$ can be separated by either centrifugation or by Millipore filtration. In the centrifugation method, 1.0 ml of cold homogenizing buffer is added to each tube following incubation. The tubes are then centrifuged at 6,000 g for 20 min. The supernates are aspirated and the pellets washed with 1.0 ml of the incubation buffer. The washed pellets are then scraped, with Pasteur pipets, and transferred quantitatively into scintillation vials using 5 × 2-ml aliquots of scintillation fluid.

In the Millipore filtration method, 1.0 ml of cold 0.01 M tris-HCl buffer of pH 7.0 is added to each tube at the end of the incubation period. The tubes are centrifuged at 6,000 $\underline{g}$ for 20 min, and the supernates are aspirated. The pellets are resuspended in 1.0 ml of 0.01 M tris-HCl buffer and poured onto Millipore filters positioned on a Millipore manifold under vacuum. We found that quite a few lots of EHWP filters bind excess free [^{3}H] PGE$_1$. To reduce this binding to the filters, the centrifugation step prior to Millipore filtration was introduced. The tubes are then rinsed once with 1.0 ml of tris-HCl buffer and filtered. Finally, each filter is washed with 10.0 ml of 0.01 M tris-HCl buffer. The use of homogenizing buffer for these purposes was found to be undesirable because of occasional clogging of the filter pores. The filters are then cut into halves and placed into scintillation vials containing 10.0 ml of scintillation fluid and counted in a Packard scintillation counter with an average counting efficiency of 18.8%. The scintillation fluid consisted of toluene:Triton X-100:Packard's Perma-fluor (25 x) in the ratio of 16.0:8.3:1.0 (vol/vol). There is good agreement between centrifugation and Millipore filtration methods in assessing [^{3}H] PGE$_1$ binding except, apparently, at high concentrations of added [^{3}H] PGE$_1$.

Some of the methods that have been used for the separation of bound and free [^{3}H] PGE$_1$ are: gel column chromatography [24, 25], filtration on glass wool columns [21], discontinuous sucrose gradient centrifugation [11], and adsorption of free by activated charcoal [25, 27, 28]. Although gel column chromatography has been used for binding studies with particulate membrane preparations [24], it is not generally suitable for this purpose. All these methods, including the centrifugation procedure, are cumbersome and time-consuming. It is our experience that the Millipore filtration method is a rapid and convenient means of separating bound and free [^{3}H] PGE$_1$.

The methods described so far are applicable to all the experiments to be described. The other methodological details vary with each experiment and will be described in appropriate places in the text.

IV.   THIN LAYER CHROMATOGRAPHY OF [^{3}H] PROSTAGLANDIN E$_1$

Following incubation of membrane fractions with 4.5×10^{-9} M [^{3}H] PGE$_1$ for 1 hr at 38°C, the bound and free [^{3}H] PGE$_1$ are separated by centrifugation. The bound and free [^{3}H] PGE$_1$ fractions are then extracted separately three times with 10.0 ml of ethyl acetate acidified with 2 M citric acid. The pooled ethyl acetate extracts are dried under a stream of nitrogen, and the residues are dissolved in 1.0 ml of redistilled ethanol. Aliquots of these solutions are directly spotted on Eastman Kodak thin layer silica gel chromatography sheets, with or without silver nitrate impregnation.

Aliquots of unincubated [^{3}H] PGE$_1$ are also spotted on both edges of the same thin layer sheets. The silver nitrate–impregnated sheet is developed in a solvent system consisting of ethyl acetate:methanol:water, 8:2:5 (vol/vol), as described by Green and Samuelsson [32]. The second thin layer sheet is developed in ethyl acetate:methanol:water, 8:5:2 (vol/vol). After development of the thin layer sheets, they are air dried and 1.3–cm strips are cut from the origin to the solvent front and placed in a vial containing 10.0 ml of scintillation fluid and counted. The extracts of membrane–bound and free [^{3}H] PGE$_1$ moved identically with those of unincubated [^{3}H] PGE$_1$ in the two different chromatographic runs and solvent systems (Fig. 2). The R$_f$ value (0.60) for [^{3}H] PGE$_1$ on silver nitrate–impregnated thin layer sheets is in close agreement with Green and Samuelsson [32], whereas in the second solvent system, the R$_f$ value for [^{3}H] PGE$_1$ is higher (0.86), which may be due to a decreased polar phase. These solvent systems have been shown to separate PGEs from other PGs as well as to separate different PGEs [32]. These data suggest that no significant metabolic conversion of receptor-bound and free [^{3}H] PGE$_1$ occurs under the present incubation conditions.

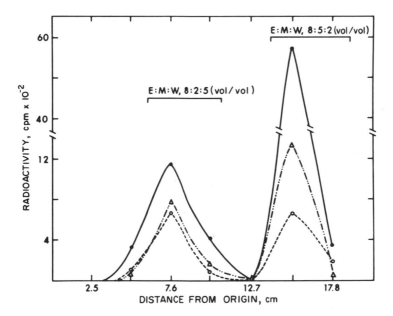

FIG. 2. Thin layer chromatography of unincubated (solid line), membrane-bound (broken line and open circles), and free (broken line and triangles) [^{3}H] PGE$_1$. The solvent front for the first set of curves (from left) was 12.7 cm from the origin, whereas for the second set of curves it was 17.8 cm.

V. BINDING CONDITIONS

A. Membrane Protein and Concentration of [³H] PGE₁

When the same amounts of membrane protein (734 μg) are incubated with increasing amounts of [^{3}H] PGE$_1$, the specific binding of [^{3}H] PGE$_1$ steadily increases (Fig. 3a). Both the centrifugation and Millipore filtration methods were used for the separation of bound and free [^{3}H] PGE$_1$. There is a close agreement between these two methods in assessing specific binding of [^{3}H] PGE$_1$ if the concentration of added [^{3}H] PGE$_1$ does not exceed 5.0×10^{-9} M.

When increasing amounts of membrane protein are incubated with the same amount of [^{3}H] PGE$_1$ (3.0×10^{-9} M), the specific binding of [^{3}H] PGE$_1$ again steadily increases (Fig. 3b). Half-maximal specific binding of [^{3}H]-PGE$_1$ occurs with ~ 500 μg of membrane protein.

B. Time, Temperature, and pH

The time and temperature effects on the specific binding of [^{3}H] PGE$_1$ are studied by incubating fixed amounts of membrane protein and [^{3}H] PGE$_1$. The specific binding of [^{3}H] PGE$_1$ is dependent on both duration and temperature of incubation (Fig. 4a). Although the maximum binding occurs at 38°C after 1 hr of incubation, half-maximal binding occurs after ~ 10 min of incubation, suggesting that the binding of [^{3}H] PGE$_1$ is extremely rapid in nature. A slightly different time course for [^{3}H] PGE$_1$ binding is observed when Millipore filtration, instead of the centrifugation method, is used for the separation of bound and free ligand [33]. The difference appears to be largely due to filtration problems that arise for samples incubated for short periods of time at 38°C or incubated at lower temperatures.

Procedures such as several-fold dilution of the incubation mixture or the addition of excess unlabeled hormone following initial attainment of binding equilibrium are used to study the phenomenon of dissociation of bound hormone. We use the following technique to study this dissociation process. Tubes containing fixed amounts of membrane protein and [^{3}H]-PGE$_1$ are preincubated at 38°C to reach equilibrium. Following preincubation, bound and free [^{3}H] PGE$_1$ are separated by centrifugation, and the pellets are resuspended in 1.0 ml of 0.01 M tris-HCl, pH 7.0, and incubated again at indicated temperatures and times (Fig. 4b). This procedure is particularly useful when the binding is not readily reversible in nature. At 38°C, [^{3}H] PGE$_1$ dissociates rapidly from the membrane complex, reaching 20% of the initial value after 4 hr of incubation. The dissociation of [^{3}H] PGE$_1$ from the membranes is insignificant at 0 and 22°C compared to 38°C.

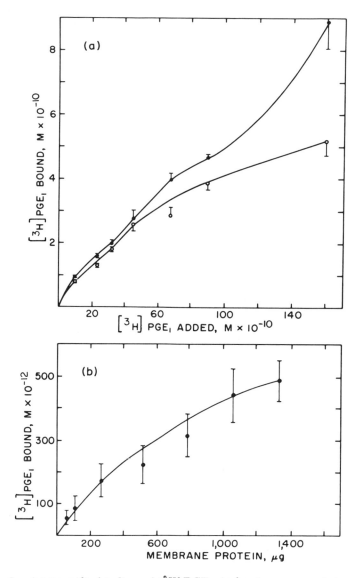

FIG. 3. (a) Specific binding of [³H] PGE₁ to bovine corpus luteum cell membranes as a function of increasing concentrations of [³H] PGE₁ added. Bound and free [³H] PGE₁ were separated by centrifugation (closed circles) and by Millipore filtration (open circles). Each observation in Figures 3 to 8 represents the mean with its standard error. (Reprinted from Ref. 36 by permission of the American Society of Biological Chemists.) (b) Specific binding of [³H] PGE₁ to bovine corpus luteum cell membranes with increasing amounts of membrane protein added.

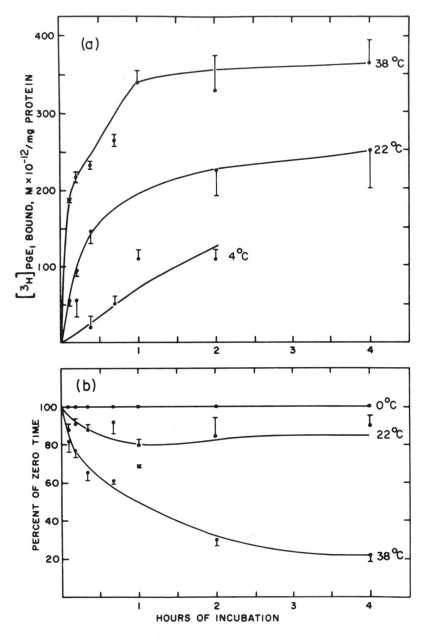

FIG. 4. (a) Time and temperature dependence of specific binding of
[³H] PGE₁ to bovine corpus luteum cell membranes (Reprinted from Ref.
36 by permission of the American Society of Biological Chemists.) (b)
The effects of time and temperature on the dissociation of [³H] PGE₁ from
bovine corpus luteum cell membrane complex. (Reprinted from Ref. 36
by permission of the American Society of Biological Chemists.)

In order to study the effect of pH on binding, the tubes containing fixed amounts of membrane protein and [^{3}H] PGE$_1$ are incubated in 0.1 M sodium acetate (pH 4.0, 5.0, and 6.2), 0.1 M sodium phosphate (pH 7.0 and 8.0), and 0.1 M sodium bicarbonate (pH 9.0 and 10.0) buffers. One needs to take into account the possibility that buffer salts may have an effect on binding independent of their pH effects. Adjusting the pH of 50 mM tris-HCl to values which will give final desired pH is an alternate method which can be used. The maximum specific binding occurs at pH 6.2, which was in constrast to the occurrence of maximum nonspecific binding, which occurs at pH 4.0 or lower (Fig. 5). The binding is entirely nonspecific below pH 4.0 and above pH 10.0. In spite of the observation on maximum specific binding at pH 6.2, all the incubations are conducted at pH 7.0.

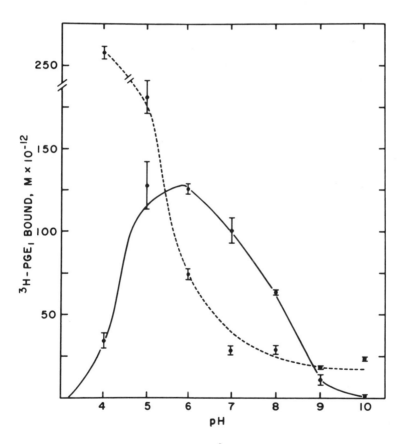

FIG. 5. Effect of pH on the binding of [^{3}H] PGE$_1$ to bovine corpus luteum cell membranes. Solid line: specific binding; broken line: nonspecific binding. (Reprinted from Ref. 36 by permission of the American Society of Biological Chemists.)

VI. BINDING CONSTANTS FOR [³H] PGE₁-MEMBRANE INTERACTION

Scatchard plot analysis [34] is widely used to interpret [³H] PGE₁-
binding data. It should be realized that Scatchard analysis was originally derived for soluble macromolecules containing independent low-
affinity binding sites for small-molecular-weight ligands. Therefore,
it is imperative to bear in mind that this analysis may not strictly
hold true for small ligands binding to insoluble membrane fragments,
at least in some instances. Lineweaver-Burk plots are used by some
investigators to analyze [³H] PGE₁-binding data [21, 35]. If the receptor system is heterogeneous, the Lineweaver-Burk plots may not readily indicate the presence of second low-affinity binding sites. This is
evident in the case of fat cells, where [³H] PGE₁ binding is reported
to be homogeneous [21] using Lineweaver-Burk plot analysis and heterogeneous [15] by analyzing the data by Scatchard plot analysis. We
feel that both methods are useful and should be considered in analysis
of [³H] PGE₁ data. However, when a single ligand is used, Scatchard
analysis may be more useful, but when different unlabeled ligands are
used with a same labeled ligand, the Lineweaver-Burk plots will provide more information.

We used Scatchard plot analysis to interpret the binding data presented
in Figure 3(a) (Fig. 6). It is evident from this figure that PGE₁ receptors
in bovine corpus luteum cell membranes are heterogeneous with respect
to affinity for [³H] PGE₁. These two orders of binding sites are high affinity-low capacity and low affinity-high capacity. The dissociation constants
(K_d) and number of binding sites of high- and low-affinity sites obtained
by centrifugation and by Millipore filtration methods are in good agreement
with each other. The apparent affinity constant ($1/K_d$) of high-affinity
binding sites is 7.7 times higher, and the number of these receptors 5.4
times lower, than the similar values for low-affinity binding sites (see
Millipore filtration data in Table 1).

Free energy changes of +12.6 and +11.4 kcal/mol (thermodynamic
property of [³H] PGE₁-receptor interaction) are calculated from the equilibrium dissociation constants of high- and low-affinity binding sites,
respectively, using the equation, $\Delta F = -RT \ln K_d$. These free energy
changes are consistent with the view that, although binding is strong, it
is not covalent in nature.

The equilibrium studies revealed the presence of two compartments
of binding sites having different dissociation constants. It is quite likely
that these two compartments of binding sites correspond to the kinetic
compartments of binding. Since the PGE receptors in these membrane
preparations are heterogeneous, the exact kinetic constants cannot be

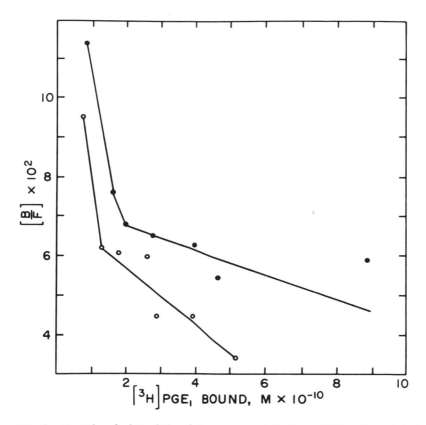

FIG. 6. Scatchard plot of the data presented in Fig. 3(a). (Reprinted from Ref. 36 by permission of the American Society of Biological Chemists.)

simply obtained, as association and dissociation may not follow simple second- and first-order kinetics, respectively, in view of participation of both sites in the binding reaction. Since it is impossible to resolve the overall association and dissociation into two components which could be ascribed to the high- and low-affinity binding sites, a simple assumption is made in these calculations; the overall association represents the sum of two separate second-order rates and the overall dissociation represents the sum of two first-order rates.

The rate constants are calculated from the initial binding velocities [Fig. 4 (a) and (b)] and estimated binding capacities of the membranes (Fig. 6). These constants, along with the apparent K_ds obtained from

TABLE 1.   Equilibrium Constants for [^{3}H] PGE$_1$-Bovine Corpus Luteum
Cell Membrane Interaction at 38°C

Method	K_{d_1}	K_{d_2}	N$_1$	N$_2$
			fmol/mg protein	
Millipore filtration	1.3×10^{-9} M	1.0×10^{-8} M	54.5	193.5
Centrifugation	1.6×10^{-9} M	2.3×10^{-8} M	70.8	468.7

the ratio of rate constants at 22 and 38°C, are in good agreement with each
other (Table 2). However, the values for the apparent K_ds obtained from
the kinetic data are closer to the K_d of low-affinity binding sites than to
the K_d of high-affinity binding sites, which may be due to the greater contribution of low-affinity binding sites to the rapid dissociating component.

Whatever the affinities of [^{3}H] PGE$_1$-receptor interaction, they should
be in agreement with in vivo concentrations of PGEs in order to be mean-
ingful in a physiological sense. Unfortunately, such a comparison could
not be made at this time because PGEs levels, in many instances, remain
virtually unknown. Therefore, it appears that correlation between affinities and in vitro concentrations of PGEs required for half maximal stimulation of adenylate cyclase in the same tissue would be the best alternative
(Table 3).

Although these comparisons may not be best served, because the data
was obtained under different conditions and sometimes taken from two
different species, it does however, point out tremendous differences between affinities of PGE binding and concentrations of PGEs needed for half
maximal stimulation of adenylate cyclase. Such discrepancies are occasionally observed in the case of other hormone receptors as well [44, 45].
Although the exact reason for such discrepancies is not known, it is quite
likely that tissue fractionation procedures may alter the affinity of the
receptor and/or decrease the efficiency of coupling of events, i.e., hormone-receptor interaction with activation of adenylate cyclase.

In spite of the lack of exact correspondence between these two parameters in bovine corpus luteum cell membranes, we still feel that PGE
binding represents a biologically significant receptor interaction, because
the specificity of the binding and relative affinities of other PGs to this
receptor correlate extremely well with their ability to stimulate adenylate
cyclase activity and progesterone synthesis [8].

TABLE 2. Kinetic and Equilibrium Constants for [^{3}H] PGE$_1$–Bovine Corpus Luteum Cell Membrane Interaction[a]

Temperature	Association rate, K_1 (M^{-1} sec^{-1})	Dissociation rate, K_{-1} (sec^{-1})	Dissociation constant, K_{-1}/K_1	Dissociation constants from equilibrium data
22°C	8.6×10^4	2.4×10^{-3}	2.8×10^{-8} M	–
38°C	1.9×10^5	2.8×10^{-3}	1.5×10^{-8} M	1.3×10^{-9} M and 1.0×10^{-8} M

[a]Reprinted from Ref. 36, by permission of the American Society of Biological Chemists.

TABLE 3. Comparisons of Affinity Constants with Concentrations of
PGEs Needed for Half Maximal Stimulation of Adenylate
Cyclase[a]

Tissue	Apparent $K_d s$[b] (M)	Ref.	Concentrations of PGEs (M)	Ref.
Corpus luteum	1.3×10^{-9} and 1.0×10^{-8}	[36]	2.3×10^{-7}	[8]
Uterus	1.7×10^{-10} and 1.3×10^{-8}	[27]	1.0×10^{-6}	[38]
Adrenal	1.5×10^{-8}	[35]	4.0×10^{-8}	[35]
Thyroid	6.3×10^{-11} and 6.3×10^{-9}	[11]	2.0×10^{-6}	[39]
Liver	1.0×10^{-9} and 2.5×10^{-8}	[16]	2.4×10^{-5}	[40]
Thymocytes	7.0×10^{-11} and 2.0×10^{-9}	[41]	2.8×10^{-6}	[42]

[a]PGEs stimulate adenylate cyclase in all the tissues except fat cells,
where they inhibit this enzyme activity.

[b]Two values for K_ds indicate heterogeneity in receptors.

The role of low-affinity PGE sites in biochemical effects in corpus
luteum remains unknown, but it is seen that this constant (10^{-8} M) is close
to the concentrations of PGEs needed for half-maximal stimulation of
adenylate cyclase (10^{-7} M). Recently we also observed that various steroids
modulate [^{3}H] PGE$_1$ binding involving only the appearance of new or disappearance of existing low-affinity sites [33].

The detailed discussion above provides some insight into the methods
of analysis of [^{3}H] PGE$_1$-binding data and interpretation of binding constants
in terms of physiological meaning.

VII. SPECIFICITY OF PGE RECEPTORS

The binding of $[^3H]$ PGE_1 is not readily displaceable but can be inhibited if the competing substances are present in the incubation media prior to the addition of membranes. Therefore, the specificity of $[^3H]$ PGE_1 binding can be best studied by mixing a fixed amount of $[^3H]$ PGE_1 with varying amounts of unlabeled PGs or other test compounds prior to incubation with membranes. The presence of unlabeled PGE_1 and E_2 in the incubates results in a dose-dependent inhibition of $[^3H]$ PGE_1 binding, with complete inhibition occurring at 1.4×10^{-7} M (Fig. 7). A 100-fold greater concentration of other unlabeled PGs (PGA_1, A_2, B_1, $F_{1\alpha}$, and $F_{2\alpha}$) are needed to inhibit 80 to 100% of $[^3H]$ PGE_1 binding. hCG, which binds to gonadotropin receptors [46], has no effect on $[^3H]$ PGE_1 binding in the same membrane preparations. These data only suggest that hCG and other PGs do not bind to PGE receptors, but leaves the possibility open that they may bind to sites of their own. This is evident in the case of hCG, which has specific receptors in these membranes [46]. Binding of labeled PGs other than $PGF_{2\alpha}$ has not been tested yet in our laboratory.

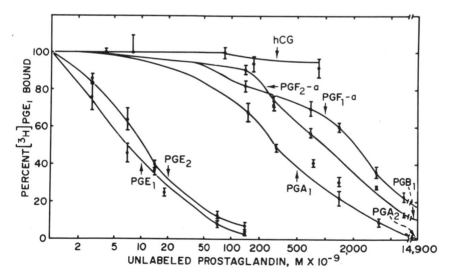

FIG. 7. The specificity of $[^3H]$ PGE_1 binding to bovine corpus luteum cell membranes. The cpm bound in the control tubes were taken as 100%. (Reprinted from Ref. 36 by permission of the American Society of Biological Chemists.)

The small amounts of impurities in [^{3}H] PGE$_1$ play, if any, an insignificant role in [^{3}H] PGE$_1$ binding to the membranes. This conclusion is deduced from the following observations: (1) Impurities are generally expected to contribute to nonspecific binding, which is found to be negligible in our studies. (2) The impurities in [^{3}H] PGE$_1$ could very well be other PGs, whose affinities for PGE receptors are too weak to interfere with [^{3}H] PGE$_1$ binding.

VIII. MACROMOLECULAR NATURE OF PGE RECEPTORS

To investigate the macromolecular nature of the PGE receptors, aliquots of membrane protein (3.4 mg) are preincubated at pH 7.0 with several enzymes for 30 min at 38°C. Following preincubation, the tubes are centrifuged at 6,000 g for 20 min. The supernates are aspirated and the pellets washed twice with 0.01 M tris-HCl, pH 7.0. Finally, the pellets are resuspended in a known volume of homogenizing buffer, and aliquots are used for testing the specific binding of [^{3}H] PGE$_1$. Membranes for controls are preincubated without enzymes and are subjected to centrifugation similar to the treated membranes. The appropriate controls would be the ones described above because the preincubation of membranes without ligand itself can cause significant reductions in the specific binding. Since the enzymes apparently have no effects on the ligand, enzymes can be added during the incubation with ligand, or at least the centrifugation step to remove the enzymes following preincubation can be eliminated. The reason for our protocol is that the effect of enzyme treatment on [^{3}H] PGE$_1$ and [^{125}I] hCG binding was simultaneously studied.

The enzymes used in this experiment had the following activities: pronase, 120 PUK/mg; chymotrypsinogen A, 0.19% intrinsic chymotrypsin; soybean trypsin inhibitor; trypsinogen, 1 x crystallized; trypsin, 189 units/mg; neuraminidase (V. cholerae), 500 units/ml; DNase, 2689 units/ mg; RNase, 100 units/mg; lipase, 270 units/mg; phospholipase A, 7.7 units/mg; phospholipase C (Cl. perfringens), 2 units/mg; phospholipase C (Cl. welchii), 4-5 units/mg; and phospholipase D, 22 units/mg. The following amounts of enzymes were used in preincubation of membranes. Enzyme:membrane protein ratio was 1:3.4 for pronase, trypsin, trypsinogen, chymotrypsinogen, RNase, DNase, lipase, phospholipase C (Cl. perfringens), phospholipase C (Cl. welchii), and phospholipase D. Phospholipase A was added at the ratio of 1:11.2 enzyme to membrane protein. Soybean trypsin inhibitor:trypsin (2:1) was added. Neuraminidase was added at 4.40 IU/mg membrane protein.

We studied enzyme effects at a single dose and under conditions favorable for retention of binding rather than for maximal activity of the enzymes. It is quite important to realize that it is better to have enzymes functioning at lower levels than to have losses of binding not related to enzyme effects. Therefore, in a strict sense, the enzyme effects are not quantitative, and so the results must be interpreted cautiously. In many instances, the enzyme effects are thought to be due to the modification of the receptor itself. Although this interpretation may hold true in some instances, it may not be true in others. The latter instance may arise from the fact that these enzymes are capable of attacking a variety of other membrane components whose structure and function may be essential for the binding function of the receptor. In spite of these limitations, it is better to get some idea on the macromolecular nature of the receptors in the membranes, realizing that the final confirmation of these results will have to come from similar studies on physico-chemically pure receptors.

Trypsin reduces $[^3H] PGE_1$ binding by 40%, and its effect is completely inhibited by the addition of soybean trypsin inhibitor (Table 4). Pronase, trypsinogen, chymotrypsinogen, RNase, and DNase have no effect on $[^3H] PGE_1$ binding. Removal of membrane lipids and phospholipids by lipase and phospholipases A and C results in a 67 to 100% loss of $[^3H] PGE_1$ binding. Phospholipase D and neuraminidase have no significant effect on $[^3H] PGE_1$ binding. The fact that treatment of membranes with phospholipase D (removes only the phospholipid base) has no effect on PGE_1 binding, whereas treatment with phospholipase C (removes polar head chain) greatly reduces $[^3H] PGE_1$ binding suggests that exterior hydrophilic groups of phospholipids are involved in the binding interaction of the receptors. Phospholipase A treatment of membranes completely abolishes receptor binding of $[^3H] PGE_1$, which may be due to the disruption of membrane conformation following β-ester bond cleavage by this enzyme and/or inhibition of binding by the detergent effects of lysophospholipids. The decreased binding following phospholipase A and C treatment may have been due to the requirement of phospholipids at the binding site and/or conformational changes of the receptors resulting in a decreased affinity rather than a loss of binding sites.

Incubation of membranes with proteolytic enzymes results in losses of specific binding of both $[^3H] PGE_1$ and $[^{125}I] hCG$. However, the extent of loss of $[^{125}I] hCG$ binding is much greater than the loss of $[^3H] PGE_1$ binding (Table 5). This greater loss of $[^{125}I] hCG$ binding compared to $[^3H] PGE_1$ binding suggests that either hCG receptors are present in a more hydrophilic environment compared to PGE receptors (more hydrophobic) in the cell membrane structure, or that these enzyme may be left behind in the tubes following the washing procedure and cause a breakdown of $[^{125}I] hCG$ in the final incubation. To resolve these possibilities, membranes were preincubated with trypsin and washed as described earlier. The membrane fraction was then divided into two aliquots and one of the

TABLE 4.   Effect of Enzyme Treatment on the Specific Binding of
           [³H] PGE_1 to Bovine Corpus Luteum Cell Membranes

Enzyme treatment	[³H] PGE_1 bound $(10^{-10} \times M)$
None	1.5 ± 0.0
Pronase	1.2 ± 0.0
Trypsin	0.9 ± 0.0
Trypsin plus soybean trypsin inhibitor	1.5 ± 0.1
Trypsinogen	1.2 ± 0.0
Chymotrypsinogen	1.4 ± 0.0
RNase	1.3 ± 0.0
DNase	1.5 ± 0.0
Neuraminidase (V. cholerae)	1.3 ± 0.0
Phospholipase D	1.2 ± 0.1
Lipase	0.1 ± 0.0
Phospholipase A	0.0 ± 0.0
Phospholipase C (Cl. perfringens)	0.4 ± 0.0
Phospholipase C (Cl. welchii)	0.5 ± 0.0

TABLE 5.   Effect of Enzyme Treatment of Bovine Corpus Luteum Cell
           Membranes on the Specific Binding of [³H] PGE_1 and [¹²⁵I] hCG

Enzyme treatment	[³H] PGE_1	[¹²⁵I] hCG
	(% bound)	
Control	100.0	
Pronase	80.0 ± 0.0	0.0 ± 0.0
Trypsin	60.0 ± 0.0	5.9 ± 0.0
Trypsin plus soybean trypsin inhibitor	100.0 ± 6.7	101.0 ± 1.0

aliquots was reincubated at 38°C for 30 min with 1.0 mg of soybean trypsin inhibitor and washed. Membranes incubated with and without soybean trypsin inhibitor were then tested for [^{125}I] hCG binding. Identical results were obtained with both groups of membranes, suggesting that no active form of trypsin was left in the tubes following the washings. Besides differences in the physical location of these receptors, they also exhibit differences with regard to their binding constants and responses to various reagents [47, 48].

IX. EFFECT OF CHEMICAL MODIFICATION OF

MEMBRANE PROTEINS ON [^{3}H] PGE$_1$ BINDING

In order to determine the possible involvement of specific functional groups in binding interaction, membranes are preincubated with several protein modifying reagents for 45 min at 22°C. Following preincubation, the tubes are centrifuged at 6,000 g for 20 min. The supernates are aspirated and the pellets washed twice with 0.01 M tris-HCl, pH 7.0. Finally, the pellets are resuspended in a known volume of homogenizing buffer and aliquots are used for testing the specific binding of [^{3}H] PGE$_1$. We have not tested the possibility of adding these reagents directly during final incubation. Membranes for controls are incubated without protein-modifying reagents and subjected to centrifugation similar to treated membranes. Tetranitromethane (TNM), dinitrofluorobenzene (DNFB), and acetic anhydride are added in ethanol, giving a final ethanol concentration of 10% in the incubation media. The corresponding controls also contain the same concentration of ethanol.

The same considerations, as outlined in the discussion of enzyme treatment (Sec. VIII) with regard to effects and interpretations of results also apply to these experiments. Furthermore, it must be realized that these reagents may not be absolutely specific for the indicated functional groups and the decrease of [^{3}H] PGE$_1$ binding may be secondary to the changes in other membrane proteins. Despite these possibilities, we, and several other investigators, have successfully used these reagents in structure-function studies of membrane receptors. But these results can only be confirmed following the conducting of similar experiments on solubilized and purified receptors.

The treatment of membranes with various sulfhydryl group-modifying reagents either had no effect or significantly increased [^{3}H] PGE$_1$ binding, which may be due to a decreased aggregation of membranes resulting in an increased binding following alkylation of −SH groups (Table 6). The binding of [^{3}H] PGE$_1$ is significantly reduced following the treatment of membranes with TNM, DNFB, and acetic anhydride. Tyrosyl residues are known to be modified following treatment with TNM, DNFB, and acetic

TABLE 6. Effect of Treatment of Bovine Corpus Luteum Cell Membranes with Protein Modifying Reagents on the Specific Binding of $[^3H]$ PGE$_1$

Reagent	$[^3H]$ PGE$_1$ bound $(10^{-10}$ M)
None	3.1 ± 0.0
1 mM p-Chloromercuribenzoate	3.0 ± 0.2
1 mM p-Chloromercuribenzoate plus 10 mM dithiothreitol	4.3 ± 0.2
10 mM Iodoacetamide	5.0 ± 0.2
10 mM Mercaptoethanol	5.2 ± 0.2
10 mM N-Ethylmaleimide	4.4 ± 0.3
13 mM Tetranitromethane	1.0 ± 0.0
10 mM Dinitrofluorobenzene	0.1 ± 0.0
100 mM Acetic anhydride	0.4 ± 0.1
Urea: 1 M	2.3 ± 0.1
2 M	2.4 ± 0.0
5 M	0.2 ± 0.0

anhydride; however, TNM is highly specific for this residue and tryptophan [49, 50], whereas the latter two react with other groups as well (histidyl and free amino groups). The greatly reduced $[^3H]$ PGE$_1$ binding following the treatment of membranes with TNM, DNFB, and acetic anhydride, therefore, allows us to suggest that tyrosyl residues are needed for binding interaction, but the possibility of involvement of other residues cannot be excluded. Urea, in concentrations of 1.0 M or above, markedly decreased $[^3H]$ PGE$_1$ binding, which may be due to denaturation of the receptors.

ACKNOWLEDGMENTS

The excellent technical assistance of Mr. Fred Carman, Jr. is gratefully acknowledged. This work was supported by grants M73.57 and M74.50 from the Population Council, New York, New York.

REFERENCES

1. R. W. Butcher and C. E. Baird, J. Biol. Chem., 243:1713 (1968).

2. J. D. Flack, R. Jessup, and P. W. Ramwell, Science, 163:691 (1969).

3. F. A. Kuehl, Jr., J. L. Humes, J. Tarnoff, V. J. Cirillo, and E. A. Ham, Science, 169:883 (1970).

4. J. Field, A. Dekker, U. Zor, and T. Kaneko, Ann. N.Y. Acad. Sci., 180:278 (1971).

5. G. A. Robinson, R. W. Butcher, and E. W. Sutherland, Cyclic AMP, Academic Press, New York, 1971, pp. 384-388.

6. G. Burke, Am. J. Physiol., 218:1445 (1970).

7. T. Saruta and N. M. Kaplan, J. Clin. Invest., 51:2246 (1972).

8. J. M. Marsh, Ann. N.Y. Acad. Sci., 180:416 (1970).

9. Ch. V. Rao, Prostaglandins, 4:567 (1973).

10. G. Burke, L. L. Chang, and M. Szabo, Science, 180:872 (1973).

11. W. V. Moore and J. Wolff, J. Biol. Chem., 248:5705 (1973).

12. E. G. Loten and J. G. T. Sneyd, Endocrinology, 93:1315 (1973).

13. U. Zor, S. Bauminger, S. A. Lamprecht, Y. Koch, P. Chobsieng, and H. R. Lindner, Prostaglandins, 4:499 (1973).

14. Ch. V. Rao, Proceedings of Symposium on Advances in Chemistry, Biology and Immunology of Gonadotropins, Bangalore, India, October, 1973.

15. R. R. Gorman and O. V. Miller, Biochim. Biophys. Acta, 323:560 (1973).

16. M. Smigel and S. Fleischer, Biochim. Biophys. Acta, 332:358 (1974).

17. A. E. Wakeling, K. T. Kirton, and L. J. Wyngarden, Prostaglandins, 4:1 (1973).

18. A. E. Wakeling and C. H. Spilman, Prostaglandins, 4:405 (1973).

19. M. S. Soloff, M. J. Morrison, and T. L. Swartz, Prostaglandins, 4:853 (1973).

20. O. V. Miller and W. E. Magee, Advan. Biosci., 9:83 (1973).

21. F. A. Kuehl, Jr. and J. L. Humes, Proc. Natl. Acad. Sci., U.S.A., 69:480 (1972).

22. E. Carafoli and F. Crovetti, <u>Arch. Biochem. Biophys.</u>, <u>154</u>:40 (1973).

23. Ch. V. Rao, in <u>Recent Progress in Reproductive Endocrinology</u> (P. G. Grosignani and V. H. T. James, eds.), Academic Press, London, 1974, pp. 509-521.

24. W. S. Powell, S. Hammerstrom, and B. Samuelsson, <u>Eur. J. Biochem.</u>, <u>41</u>:103 (1974).

25. A. E. Wakeling and L. J. Wyngarden, <u>Prostaglandins</u>, <u>5</u>:291 (1974).

26. G. Litwack, R. Filler, S. Rosenfield, and N. Lichtash, <u>Biochem. Biophys. Res. Commun.</u>, <u>55</u>:977 (1973).

27. F. A. Kimball and L. J. Wyngarden, <u>Prostaglandins</u>, <u>9</u>:413 (1975).

28. F. A. Kimball, K. T. Kirton, C. H. Spillman, and L. J. Wyngarden, <u>Biol. Reprod.</u>, <u>13</u>:482 (1975).

29. Ch. V. Rao, <u>Fert. Ster.</u>, <u>26</u>:1185 (1975).

30. B. J. Campbell, G. Woodward, and V. Borberg, <u>J. Biol. Chem.</u>, <u>247</u>:6167 (1972).

31. O. H. Lowry, N. J. Rosebrough, A. L. Farr, and R. J. Randall, <u>J. Biol. Chem.</u>, <u>193</u>:265 (1951).

32. K. Green and B. Samuelsson, <u>J. Lipid Res.</u>, <u>5</u>:117 (1964).

33. Ch. V. Rao, <u>Prostaglandins</u>, <u>9</u>:569 (1975).

34. G. Scatchard, <u>Ann. N.Y. Acad. Sci.</u>, <u>51</u>:660 (1949).

35. A. Dazord, A. M. Morera, J. Bertrand, and J. M. Saez, <u>Endocrinology</u>, <u>95</u>:352 (1974).

36. Ch. V. Rao, <u>J. Biol. Chem.</u>, <u>249</u>:7203 (1974).

37. A. E. Wakeling and L. J. Wyngarden, <u>Endocrinology</u>, <u>95</u>:55 (1974).

38. M. F. Vesin and S. Harbon, <u>Mol. Pharmacol.</u>, <u>10</u>:457 (1974).

39. J. Wolff and A. B. Jones, <u>J. Biol. Chem.</u>, <u>246</u>:3939 (1971).

40. T. V. Zenser, F. R. DeRubertis, and R. T. Curnow, <u>Endocrinology</u>, <u>94</u>:1404 (1974).

41. B. P. Schaumburg, <u>Biochim. Biophys. Acta</u>, <u>326</u>:127 (1973).

42. D. J. Franks, J. P. MacManus, and J. F. Whitfield, <u>Biochem. Biophys. Res. Commun.</u>, <u>44</u>:1177 (1971).

43. J. N. Fain, S. Psychoyos, A. J. Czernik, S. Frost, and W. D. Cash, Endocrinology, 93:632 (1973).

44. H. Glossman, A. J. Baukal, and K. J. Catt, J. Biol. Chem., 249: 825 (1974).

45. W. V. Moore and J. Wolff, J. Biol. Chem., 249:6255 (1974).

46. Ch. V. Rao, J. Biol. Chem., 249:2864 (1974).

47. Ch. V. Rao, Prostaglandins, 6:313 (1974).

48. Ch. V. Rao, Prostaglandins, 6:533 (1974).

49. M. Sokolovsky, J. R. Riordan, and B. L. Vallee, Biochemistry, 5:3582 (1966).

50. P. Cuatrecasas, S. Fuchs, and C. B. Anfinsen, J. Biol. Chem., 243:4787 (1968).

Chapter 21

THYROTROPIN RECEPTORS

Serge Lissitzky
Guy Fayet
Bernard Verrier

Laboratoire de Biochimie Médicale et Unité 38
de l'Institut National de la Santé
et de la Recherche Médicale
Faculté de Médecine
Marseille, France

I.   INTRODUCTION   642

II. RADIOLABELED THYROTROPIN   642

     A. Nature and Properties of Thyrotropin   643
     B. Preparation and Purification of Labeled Thyrotropins 643

III. RECEPTOR PREPARATIONS   651

     A. Intact Thyroid Cells   651
     B. Plasma Membranes   652
     C. Crude Particulate Preparations   655

IV. BINDING ASSAYS   656

     A. Intact Cells   656
     B. Plasma Membranes and Crude Particulate Fractions   657
     C. Comments   658

V. QUANTITATIVE ASPECTS OF TSH-RECEPTOR INTERACTION   658

    A. Intact Thyroid Cells and Their Derived Plasma Membranes   658
    B. Plasma Membranes and Crude Particulate Fractions
        Isolated from Thyroid Gland Homogenates   661
    C. Correlation of Binding and Physiological Effects   661
    D. Factors Affecting Thyrotropin Binding and Adenylate
        Cyclase Activity   662

    REFERENCES   663

I. INTRODUCTION

The physiological thyroid stimulator, thyroid-stimulating hormone (TSH) or thyrotropin, is secreted by the thyreotroph cells of the adenohypophysis. It is a glycoprotein which acts on the thyroid gland by stimulating the biosynthesis and secretion of the thyroid hormones and the growth of the follicular cells.

The first suggestion that TSH interacts with its target tissue at a superficial cell site was made on the basis of experiments showing a persistent effect of TSH on $1-{}^{14}C$ glucose oxidation in thyroid slices exposed to the hormone and washed thoroughly in hormone-free medium [1]. This effect could also be reversed by a short exposure of the tissue to anti-TSH antibodies. Since antibodies are not supposed to enter the cell, such experiments suggested that, at the time it was acting, the hormone was still in equilibrium with the medium, i.e., on the surface of the cell.

Additional support to this idea was given by experiments showing that plasma membranes purified from bovine thyroid glands contained a TSH-responsive adenylate cyclase [2, 3]. At the present time, there is no doubt that most of the effects of TSH are mediated by intracellular cAMP. Evidence that the Sutherland model of many polypeptide hormone actions apply to TSH and the thyroid has been extensively reviewed [4].

The first step in TSH action, i.e., the reversible binding of the hormone to specific receptor sites located on the outer side of the follicular cell plasma membrane, has been demonstrated using intact cells [5, 6] or purified plasma membranes [6-8]. Binding of TSH to intact thyroid tissue [9] or a crude particulate fraction of thyroid homogenate [10] has also been studied.

II. RADIOLABELED THYROTROPIN

Studies on the interaction of hormones with receptors need the availability of radioactively labeled hormones of high specific radioactivity with preserved biological potency. Over the past few years, radioiodination with ^{125}I or ^{131}I has proved the most useful method to reach this objective.

A. Nature and Properties of Thyrotropin

Thyrotropin is one of the glycoprotein hormones secreted by the anterior pituitary of vertebrates. The extensive studies of Pierce and co-workers (see Ref. 11) have revealed that the native bovine molecule is formed of two dissimilar, noncovalently associated subunits designated α and β. The linear sequences of TSH-α and TSH-β are known. Both contain intrachain disulfide bonds and heteropolysaccharide side chains (two in TSH-α and one in TSH-β). Five tyrosine residues are present in the α-subunit and 11 in the β-subunit.

Based on amino acid sequences and carbohydrate composition, the molecular weights of bovine TSH, TSH-α, and TSH-β are 28,300, 13,600 and 14,700, respectively. It is now well established that the linear sequences of the α-subunits of TSH, luteinizing hormone, and human chorionic gonadotropin are identical, or nearly so. In contrast, the β-subunits are hormone specific. This was shown by recombination experiments of isolated subunits. Biological activity of recombinants is always specified by the origin of the β-subunit. Immunochemical studies are in accord with chemical and biological data. Both α- and β-subunits are by themselves biologically inactive.

The physico-chemical properties and the amino acid sequence of the subunits of porcine TSH are closely related to that of the bovine hormone [12, 13].

B. Preparation and Purification of Labeled Thyrotropins

1. Lactoperoxidase-Catalyzed Iodination [14]

a. Method

Iodination of TSH or its subunits with ^{125}I was performed by a modification of the procedure described by Thorell and Johansson [15]. Highly purified porcine TSH (37 IU/mg in the McKenzie bioassay) was used. The following solutions in 0.5 M aceto-acetate pH 5.6 are prepared:

Solution A: porcine TSH, 1 mg/ml.

Solution B: carrier-free ^{125}I as NaI (1 mCi/10 μl) without reducing agent (Radiochemical Center, Amersham, England).

Solution C: lactoperoxidase (A_{412}/A_{280} = 0.65, Calbiochem, Los Angeles, USA), 1 mg/ml.

Solution D: hydrogen peroxide (Merck, Darmstadt, West Germany), 10 ng/ml.

In a 10×75 nm glass tube the following are added consecutively: 30 μl solution A, 30 μl solution B, 5 μl solution C and 10 μl solution D. *

When the amount of TSH to be iodinated is reduced to 5 μg use 5 μl solution A, 35 μl buffer, 10 μl solution B, and 10 μl of a 1:10 dilution of solution C and 10 μl solution D.

After one minute contact with occasional hand shaking, 0.4 ml of 0.5 M aceto-acetate buffer pH 5.6 containing 0.05% KI and 0.25% bovine serum albumin is added to stop the reaction. Ten μl of the mixture is withdrawn and diluted 1:1000 for paper electrophoretic control of the degree of iodination. All these steps are performed at room temperature.

The remainder of the iodination mixture was initially purified by 2 consecutive gel chromatographic runs on Sephadex G–50 and G–200 [14]. It was later shown that purification of ^{125}I-labeled TSH could be performed in a single gel filtration step on a 1.5×80-cm column of Sephadex G–100 (fine) equilibrated with 0.1 M tris-Cl pH 7.0 containing 1% bovine serum albumin. Immediately after the 1-min period of reaction, the iodination mixture is deposited on the column and elution with the same buffer is carried out at 4°C at a flow rate of 5 ml/hr. Fractions of 1 ml are collected. The labeled hormone is eluted as a retarded symmetrical peak well separated from a small amount of material in the void volume and from unreacted labeled iodide. Radioactivity of the fractions are estimated in a well-type scintillation spectrometer with modified geometry and the top fractions of the labeled TSH peak representing about 50% of its total radioactivity are pooled and used for binding experiments. In our hands such preparations of ^{125}I-labeled TSH can be stored at 0°C or in liquid nitrogen for up to 15 days without loss of biological activity.

b. Iodination Characteristics

Using this procedure, specific radioactivities of 60 to 100 μCi/μg were obtained. The iodination yield, i.e., the percent of radioactive iodine incorporated into the hormone, is usually 50 to 80%, but it depends on

---

*In ten consecutive labeling experiments, we have recently shown that H_2O_2 addition was not necessary due to the presence of peroxides in the preparations of ^{125}I obtained from the supplier.

the quality of the ^{125}I provided by the supplier [16]. Occasionally, due to "bad" [125]I, it fell to 10% or less.

Chromatoelectrophoresis on paper [17] of the top peak fractions showed that 94 to 96% of the labeled material remained at origin.

Concentration of [^{125}I] TSH is calculated taking into account the radioactivity losses on the iodination tube and the pipet used for the transfer of the iodination mixture to the column. These losses do not exceed 5 to 7% of the total radioactivity of ^{125}I added, and were assumed to represent iodinated TSH. Repeated controls showed that negligible amounts of radioactivity were retained by the components of the columns or by the gel.

c. Chemical and Immunochemical Characterization

The ^{125}I-labeled TSH preparations obtained by the lactoperoxidase method of iodination described were fairly homogeneous on the basis of the following criteria: (1) 94 to 96% of radioactivity remains at origin in chromatoelectrophoresis; (2) rechromatography on Sephadex G-200 gives a single and symmetrical peak; (3) polyacrylamide gel electrophoresis in 0.1% sodium dodecylsulfate in tris-glycine, pH 8.5, and 10% gels showed ~95% of the radioactivity applied to the gel migrating as a narrow peak; no material of smaller molecular weight was detected, indicating that the preparations do not contain TSH subunits.

After enzymic digestion and ion-exchange chromatography [18], the labeled TSH preparations (1.5 to 2 iodine atoms per mole) were shown to contain ~80% monoiodotyrosine, 12% diiodotyrosine, and the remainder of the radioactivity as undigested material.

Addition of homospecific antibody in excess failed to precipitate all the radioactivity in the double antibody assay. Using 10 preparations of iodine, content 1.5 to 2 iodine atoms per mole TSH, 74.3 ± 2.2% (mean ± SEM) was immunoprecipitable. This is likely due to the loss of antigenic properties in relation to iodination. Indeed, an inverse relationship between iodine content and immunoreactivity has been observed [14].

d. Biological Activity

A radioiodinated hormone suitable for receptor-binding studies should retain the biological activity of the native hormone. In the case of ^{125}I-labeled TSH, this was tested taking advantage of the property of the hormone of stimulating the reassociation into follicles of isolated thyroid cells maintained in vitro in conditions of culture.

Isolated thyroid cells obtained by trypsinization of porcine glands form, in culture, a monolayer typical of other epithelial cells. Addition of TSH at the onset of culturing stimulates cell aggregation and the re-organization of the aggregates into three-dimensional follicles [19, 20]. In contrast to unstimulated cells, which are unable to concentrate iodide after two to three days of culture, TSH-induced reorganized cells actively take up iodide from the medium, iodinate thyroglobulin, and synthesize thyroid hormones [21]. The capacity of isolated cells to reorganize into follicles and to concentrate iodide is directly related to TSH concentration. This property of the hormone was used to estimate the biological potency of ^{125}I-labeled TSH preparations [22].

Freshly isolated porcine thyroid cells (see Sec. III. A. 1) in complete Eagle medium at a concentration of 3×10^6 cells per ml are seeded in 35-mm, plastic petri dishes (1 ml per dish). Fifty microliters of TSH dissolved in the same medium are added, to give a final concentration of 100 pg to 10 ng/ml. Controls are supplemented with hormone-free medium. After four days of incubation at 35°C in 95% air-5% CO_2, 50 μl of $Na^{127}I$ (50 nM final concentration) in complete medium and traced with 2 μCi carrier-free $Na^{125}I$ are added to each dish. Incubation at 35°C in air-CO_2 is continued for 6 hr, at the end of which the dishes are placed on crushed ice. The incubation medium is carefully removed with a Pasteur pipet and the cell layer is washed three times with 0.14 M NaCl.

The cells are detached from the support by the addition of 1 ml 0.1 N NaOH. After 15 min of mild rotatory shaking at room temperature, the cell suspension is transferred into a counting tube. The procedure is repeated once and the radioactivity of the pooled solutions is estimated.

A typical dose-response curve is shown in Figure 1. The semilog-arithmic plot of TSH concentration versus iodine uptake is linear between 0.25 and 5 ng/ml, i.e., 9 and 180 pM on the basis of a molecular weight of 28,000 for pTSH. The response of cells versus TSH concentration is saturable and its amplitude is high, since the value of the maximum re-sponse is about 20 to 30-fold that of the control without hormone. The reproducibility of the method is good: In eleven experiments using differ-ent cell batches, half-maximal stimulation was obtained for pTSH concen-trations between 0.9 and 1.4 ng/ml (32 to 50 pM).

The biological potency of [125I] TSH preparations was compared to that of the very TSH solution used for radioiodination. As shown in Figure 2, an almost identical response is obtained for both native and modified pTSH iodinated with 1.7 iodine atoms per mole.

Although, for unknown reasons, the curve of [125I] TSH sometimes crossed that of native pTSH, identical maximum responses were always obtained for the same concentration of both forms of the hormone. La-beled TSH containing 1.2 to 1.9 iodine atoms per mole was undistinguish-able from native TSH within experimental errors.

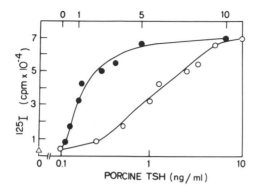

FIG. 1. Relation between Na^{125}I uptake by intact porcine thyroid cells and porcine TSH concentration. Amount of Na^{125}I added per dish, 2 μCi: ●, algebraic scale (upper abcissa); O, logarithmic scale (lower abcissa); △, control value (no TSH).

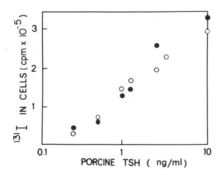

FIG. 2. Comparison of Na^{131}I uptake by porcine thyroid cells, and porcine ^{125}I-labeled TSH (●) or native procine TSH (O) concentration. ^{125}I-labeled TSH: 97.9 μCi/μg.

    Another in vitro bioassay was used to estimate the biological activity of radioiodinated TSH preparations [23]. It is based on the property of TSH to stimulate iodide efflux from the follicular cells.

    Freshly isolated porcine thyroid cells are cultured in complete Eagle medium in 75-cm^2, plastic Falcon flasks in the presence of 0.4 mM dibutyryl cAMP. Each flask is seeded with 20 ml of cell suspension at the concentration of 3×10^6 cells per ml. After two days incubation at 35°C in 95% air–5% CO_2, the medium is withdrawn, the cell layer is washed with 10 ml of spinner salt (SS) solution (see Sec. III. A. 1) and the cells are

postincubated for 10 min in the presence of 10 ml of Mg^{2+}-free SS solution
containing 3 mM EGTA. Cells partially detach from the support. They
are collected by gentle scraping with a rubber policeman and transferred
into a conical tube. The cells are washed three times by suspension and
centrifuged at 200 g and 2°C for 8 min. The final cell pellet is resuspended
in Earle's salt solution buffered with 20 mM HEPES at pH 7.0 and cell
concentration is adjusted to 20×10^6 cells per ml.

Loading of cells with radioactive iodide was performed as follows. In
1×7-cm, polyethylene tubes are introduced 0.1 ml of cell suspension and
0.25 ml Earle-HEPES buffer. The tubes are preincubated for 3 min at
35°C with shaking at maximum speed of the shaker (Gallenkamp IH 350,
London, England); 0.1 ml of 5 μM $Na^{127}I$ containing 1 μCi of carrier-free
$Na^{131}I$ in the same buffer is then rapidly added. After 30 min postincuba-
tion at 35°C with shaking, 50 μl of the TSH solution in 0.1 M phosphate
buffer, pH 7.2, containing 0.1% BSA is added. The tube is rapidly mixed
by hand, incubated for exactly 5 min at the same temperature in the shaking device and 3.5 ml of precooled (0°C) Earle-HEPES buffer containing
1 μM $Na^{127}I$ are rapidly added. The tubes are centrifuged at 1,500 g and
2°C for a total period of 1 min between start and stop of the rotor. The
supernatant is aspirated and discarded, the cell pellet is washed once with
4 ml of the same medium, and the radioactivity of the cell pellet is measured.

As shown in Figure 3, intracellular iodide is rapidly chased from the
cells by TSH. The response is linear between 0 and 5 min. For 5-min action, a direct relation is observed between TSH concentration and rate of
efflux for TSH concentrations comprised between 57 pM and 28 nM (Fig. 4).

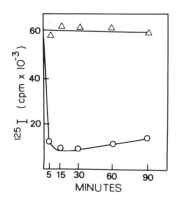

FIG. 3.   Effect of porcine TSH on iodide efflux in porcine thyroid cells.
Cells were preincubated for 30 min with 1 μM $Na^{127}I$ containing 1 μCi
carrier-free $Na^{125}I$.   o, porcine TSH 0.5 μg/ml; $\triangle$, controls without TSH.

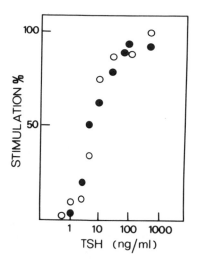

FIG. 4. Stimulation of iodide efflux from porcine thyroid cells by increasing concentrations of native porcine TSH (O) or ^{125}I-labeled porcine TSH (●) (93.5 μCi/μg).

The same figure compares the activity of a radioiodinated TSH preparation with that of the native TSH from which it derives. Within experimental errors, no difference is visible.

This method of TSH biological potency estimation is less sensitive than that based on iodide uptake and organification by cultured thyroid cells. On the other hand, it is less time-consuming and easier to work out.

e. Comments

Radioiodination using lactoperoxidase and hydrogen peroxide has been successfully applied to obtain $[^{125}I]$ TSH of high specific radioactivity with preserved biological potency. The preparations used for binding to receptors contained 1.5 to 2 iodine atoms per mole. The amount of noniodinated TSH remaining in these preparations has not been directly determined. However, it is likely that it does represent only a small percentage of the material submitted to iodination. Indeed, $[^{125}I]$ TSH preparations containing 1 to 4.8 iodine atoms per mole showed an almost identical distribution of the radioactivity in monoiodotyrosine (~80%) and in diiodotyrosine (~12%) residues, indicating that new reactive tyrosine residues are iodinated when increasing iodide is added.

2. Chemical Radioiodination

The classical chloramine-T method [24] of iodide oxidation has also been applied to the radioiodination of bovine TSH [10]. Radioiodination of 5 μg bTSH (25 IU/mg) was performed using 1 to 2 mCi of Na^{125}I. The iodination mixture was applied to a column (0.5 × 3 cm) of dry cellulose powder. Unreacted [^{125}I] iodide and damaged material were eluted in 10 ml of phosphate buffered saline (PBS: 140 mM NaCl, 2 mM phosphate buffer, pH 7.4). Adsorbed [^{125}I] TSH was eluted in 10 ml 5% BSA in PBS and immediately filtered on a 2.5 × 50-cm column of Sephadex G-100 (superfine) in PBS, containing 0.02% BSA. The peak emerging at 1.8-times the void volume was taken, adequately diluted, and stored at -30°C for up to six weeks.

Before use, the labeled hormone preparation was thawed and purified by rechromatography on Sephadex G-100 or by receptor adsorption. The latter procedure consists of the incubation of the [^{125}I] TSH preparation with a crude particulate fraction (800-10,000 g) obtained from a guinea pig thyroid homogenate (see Sec. III. C). After centrifugation and washing with PBS, the [^{125}I] TSH bound to particles is released by incubation with 2 M NaSCN. The mixture is then treated with polyethylene glycol (10% final concentration) and centrifuged to precipitate the particles. The supernatant is filtered on a column of Sephadex G-100 (superfine) in the conditions previously described, and the ^{125}I-labeled TSH is recovered as a peak at 1.8-times the void volume.

As specified by the authors, [^{125}I] TSH obtained by receptor adsorption purification shows full immunoreactivity and better binding properties to fresh particles than the labeled hormone purified by Sephadex filtration. However, the material must be used immediately or stored for no more than five days at -30°C. Its specific radioactivity was not specified.

3. Tritiated Thyrotropin

Tritiated bovine TSH has been prepared by a modification [25] of the method of Morell et al. [26], which involves oxidation of the terminal galactose of the heteropolysaccharide side chains of glycoproteins by the specific enzyme, galactose oxidase, followed by reduction with tritiated borohydride. Such ^{3}H-labeled TSH preparations have a specific radioactivity of 0.006 to 0.024 Ci/mmol for a theoretical specific activity with one [^{3}H] molecule of 29 Ci/mmol, indicating that only a small fraction of hormone molecules is actually labeled. Tritiated bovine TSH preparations were reported to have a biological activity of 80 to 85% that of the native hormone, but it is difficult to determine if the biological activity is due to the labeled hormone or to residual unlabeled molecules. Storage of the tritiated hormone is done as a lyophilized powder at -70°C over silica gel. Under these conditions, its biological half-life is 2.5 weeks.

III. RECEPTOR PREPARATIONS

Up to the present time, three types of preparations have been used for
TSH receptor studies: intact porcine thyroid cells [5, 6], purified plasma
membranes from cultured porcine thyroid cells [6] or from bovine thyroid
glands [7, 8], and a crude particulate fraction from guinea pig thyroid
homogenates [10].

A. Intact Thyroid Cells

1. Isolation and Culture

Porcine thyroid glands are collected at the local abattoir from adult animals (100-120 kg) and transported to the laboratory at 0°C in sterile modified spinner salt solution [27] (SS solution, containing in mg/l: $NaH_2 PO_4 \cdot$
H_2O, 1,400; NaCl, 6,800; KCl, 400; $MgSO_4 \cdot 7 H_2O$, 200; $NaHCO_3$, 1,300;
glucose, 1,000; phenol red, 10). Processing of the glands is usually done
within one hour after collection. All subsequent operations are performed
under sterile conditions. The glands (100 to 150 g) are carefully trimmed
free of fat and connective tissue and reduced to small fragments with scis-
sors. The minced tissue is introduced into a Fourneau glass flask, and
300 ml of a solution of crude trypsin (Institut Pasteur, Paris) at 0.25%
(wt/vol) in SS solution at pH 7.0 is added. The mixture is then gently
agitated under magnetic stirring. After 15 min, the supernatant containing the released cells is centrifuged at 200 $\underline{g}$ for 7 min, and the cell pellet
is washed once with SS solution at pH 6.8 and 0°C. The washed cells are
stored in crushed ice. This cycle of operations is repeated 12 to 16 times.
The cell pellets are suspended in 100 ml SS solution, pH 6.8, and filtered
through a stainless steel sieve to remove tissue debris and collagen fibers.
The first two batches of cells, which are much contaminated with red
blood cells, are discarded.

Cell viability is estimated in a hemocytometer by the absence of diffusion of erythrosin (0.1% final concentration) into the cells after 1 min
contact. After recentrifugation, the cells are suspended in Eagle minimum
essential medium [27] supplemented with penicillin (200 units/ml), streptomycin sulfate (50 μg/ml) and 20% (vol/vol) calf serum (complete Eagle
medium). Before addition of cells, the pH was 6.8 to 7.0 in order to obtain a pH of 7.2 to 7.4 after temperature equilibrium. Cell concentration
is adjusted to 3×10^6 viable cells per ml. This method has allowed the
routine isolation of 1.5 to 2×10^9 viable cells from ~ 150 g porcine thyroid
glands.

Tong [28] has described a continuous flow trypsinization procedure to
prepare isolated cells from bovine glands.

The freshly isolated thyroid cells may be used for metabolic investigations after standing for several hours at 0 to 2°C. However, this does

not allow the cells to fully recover from trypsinization. For this purpose, maintenance of cells in cell culture conditions proved very useful.

Falcon plastic bottles of 25 or 75 cm^2 are seeded with 5 or 20 ml of cell suspension, respectively (3×10^6 viable cells per ml in complete Eagle medium) and incubated at 35°C in humidified 95% air-5% CO_2. After 12 hr, the medium is changed, and fresh medium is added so that cells which did not adhere to the plastic bottom wall during this time period are discarded. Other medium changes are routinely performed every three or four days.

2. Properties of Cultured Thyroid Cells

Freshly isolated thyroid cell preparations are composed mostly of isolated cells round in shape and variable amounts of clumps of a few cells, representing fragments of the follicular epithelium or small aggregates of isolated cells. In the first hours of culturing, the cells adhere to the plastic support, and strands of cytoplasm spread from the cells and ensure adherence to the support. By the third day of culture, the cells form an uniform monolayer typical of cells of epithelial origin. Addition of porcine or bovine TSH at the onset of culturing induces an aggregation of isolated cells, followed by a rearrangement into histiotypic follicular structures. The three-dimensional organization of the newly formed structures has been established by electron microscopy after fixation in situ [20]. Rearranged cells show the typical structural and ultrastructural features of gland follicles. This morphogenetic effect of TSH is mediated by cAMP [21, 29]. Dibutyryl cAMP (0.4 mM) is routinely used to induce thyroid cell reassociation into follicles in the absence of TSH. Such cells have free TSH receptor sites, in contrast to TSH-stimulated cells.

After three days of culture, TSH- or dibutyryl cAMP-reassociated cells show the typical specific metabolic properties of gland follicles. They actively concentrate iodide, iodinate thyroglobulin, and synthesize and release thyroid hormones into the medium [21]. In contrast, cells in monolayer have lost these properties. However, both unstimulated and stimulated cells continue to synthesize thyroglobulin at the same rate. In the conditions of culture used, follicular structures maintain activity for seven days and for about 15 days if hydrocortisone (2.3 μM) is added together with the stimulator at the onset of culturing.

B. Plasma Membranes

1. Purification from Cultured Thyroid Cells [6]

Suspensions of porcine cells cultured for four days in the presence of 0.4 mM dibutyryl cAMP are obtained by the following procedure. The culture medium is discarded and the cell layer is washed twice with 5 ml Earle's salt solution without calcium (medium 1, containing in mg/ml: NaCl, 6,800; KCl, 400; $NaH_2PO_4 \cdot H_2O$, 140; $MgSO_4 \cdot 7 H_2O$, 200; $NaHCO_3$, 2,200). The cells are collected by gentle scraping with a rubber policeman in the presence of 10 ml medium per 75-cm^2 bottle. Every three bottles are washed with 20 ml medium 1 and the washing added to the cell suspension to give a final volume of 50 ml. After centrifugation at 200 g for 6 min at 4°C, the cell pellet is washed twice with medium 1 containing 0.5 mM $CaCl_2$ [30]. A final washing is performed in the homogenization solution (1 mM $NaHCO_3$ and 0.5 mM $CaCl_2$; medium 2). This procedure makes it possible to obtain unbroken cells as shown by light microscopy.

Highly purified plasma membranes are prepared from these cells by the technique of Neville [31] described for rat liver, as used by Emmelot et al. [32] and modified by Ray [30].

All steps are performed at 0 to 4°C in siliconized glass material. The preparation is described for 6×10^8 cells. The wet cell pellet is weighed and a volume of medium 2 equal to 2.5 times the cell weight plus 0.5 ml is added [33]. Cell disruption is performed in a loose-fitting Dounce homogenizer with enough strokes (usually ~10) to obtain 99% broken cells as shown by microscopic examination. The homogenate is diluted 100-fold with medium 2 and centrifuged at 1,500 g for 30 min at 4°C. Pellets are suspended in the same volume of medium 2 by two strokes of the Dounce homogenizer. Microscopic examination showed absence of intact cells. The homogenate is diluted 50-fold with medium 2 and centrifuged for 15 min at 1,250 g and 4°C. The supernatant is discarded, and the pooled pellets are gently resuspended in 7.6 ml of medium 2 and enriched with 60% (wt/wt) sucrose solution in the same medium to obtain a final concentration of 48% sucrose (d = 1.218 g/ml). Eight milliliters of the sucrose enriched suspension are introduced in 38.5-ml tubes (4 tubes in all) and overlaid by sucrose solutions of 45% (d = 1.202 g/ml, 10 ml), 41% (d = 1.181 g/ml, 10 ml), 37% (d = 1.161 g/ml, 6 ml), and 26% (d = 1.107 g/ml, 4 ml) in medium 2. Centrifugation is performed in a Spinco model L2-50 ultracentrifuge in rotor SW 27 at 24,000 rpm for 2 hr at 1°C. Plasma membranes from four tubes are harvested by aspiration with a Pasteur pipet from the 26% to 37% and the 37% to 41% interfaces, diluted to a final volume of 30 ml with medium 2, and centrifuged at 4°C for 30 min at 10,000 g. About 80% of membranes are collected at the 37-41% interface. The final plasma membrane pellet is suspended in 1 ml medium 2 and 0.1-ml aliquots are stored in liquid nitrogen. The yield is ~2 mg membrane protein per 6×10^8 cells. Before use, membrane preparations must be quickly thawed, diluted tenfold with medium 2, and centrifuged for 30 min at 10,000 g and 4°C.

2. Purification from Bovine Thyroid Glands

Mammalian thyroid glands consist of follicles formed of a closed monolayer of epithelial cells encompassing an amorphous mass essentially made

of thyroglobulin. They also contain parafollicular cells secreting calcitonin and unrelated to thyroid hormone synthesis. The follicles are em-
bedded in connective tissue, which gives a rough consistency to the gland.
This renders the thyroid gland difficult to homogenize, and special care
must be taken in this critical step of the purification of plasma membranes
to preserve hormonal responsiveness.

Two procedures of thyroid plasma membrane preparation from bovine
glands have been proposed [2, 3]. Both use slices of ~1-mm thickness
obtained with a Stadie–Riggs microtome. One has been described in detail
[34] and involves the following steps: homogenization of slices in a loose-
fitting Dounce homogenizer in 1 mM $NaHCO_3$, pH 7.5, filtration of the
homogenate on cheesecloth, and centrifugation at 1,800 g, resulting in a
pellet which contains most of the plasma membranes and nuclei.

After washing once in the same conditions, the pellet is suspended in
the medium and mixed with 63% sucrose solution to provide a final concentration of 48% sucrose. The membrane suspension in sucrose is then
centrifuged in a discontinuous gradient composed of 45, 41, and 37% sucrose solutions. Plasma membranes are obtained at the interface between
the layers of 37% and 41% sucrose solutions. The yield of plasma membrane protein is 0.32 to 0.50 mg/g of protein of the original homogenate.

The other procedure [3] uses a motor-driven Polytron homogenizer
to disrupt the slices. The homogenate in 250 mM sucrose, 1 mM Mg-
EGTA, 1 mM dithiothreitol, and 3 mM tris-Cl buffer, pH 7.4, is filtered
on cotton gauze and centrifuged at 1,000 g. With this homogenization procedure, plasma membranes are contained in the supernatant. They are
sedimented at 37,000 g_{av}, resuspended in the medium, and recentrifuged
at 11,000 rpm (14,500 g_{av}) for 10 min. The upper portion of the pellet is
floated off and the procedure is repeated once. The two top portions are
then submitted to centrifugation in discontinuous gradients of 45, 40, 37,
and 30% sucrose, in medium. The fractions sedimenting at the 37% and
40% boundaries contain the TSH-responsive plasma membranes. The yield
in the 37% fraction, which showed the highest specific activity of plasma
membrane marker enzymes, is 0.1 to 0.2 mg membrane protein per gram
protein in the 1,000-g supernatant. A similar technique has been reported
by other investigators [7].

3. Properties of Plasma Membranes

Assessment of the purity of purified thyroid plasma membranes has been
performed by electron microscopy and marker enzyme activity measurements. Vesicular and linear structures are visible, both showing the
typical triple-layer ultrastructure at high magnification. Membranes in
the form of sheets are often arranged in pairs, joined by cell junctions of

different kinds including desmosomes. In the best preparations, no recognizable organelles are visible except rare ribosome-coated vesicles [6].

In all types of preparations, the activities of enzymes considered to be present in plasma membranes (adenylate cyclase, 5'-nucleotidase, $\underline{p}$-nitrophenylphosphatase, and Na^+- K^+-dependent ATPase) copurify with the membranes. Membranal adenylate cyclase can be stimulated by TSH and fluoride ions. Relative to the whole homogenate, the specific activity of TSH-stimulated adenylate cyclase is 40 to 80 times higher in membranes purified from glands [2, 3] and about 20 times higher in membranes from porcine cells [6]. Fluoride-stimulated adenylate cyclase activity also accumulates in the membrane preparations and is two to five times greater than the TSH-stimulated activity.

Contamination of the membrane preparations by mitochondria and microsomes has been followed by determination of cytochrome-C oxidase or succinate dehydrogenase, and NADPH-cytochrom-C reductase or NADH oxidase, respectively. Often the best preparations contain 3 to 10% contamination by mitochondrial and microsomal protein. A high molar ratio of cholesterol/phospholipid has been described as a general characteristic of plasma membranes from various tissues. The ratio in bovine thyroid plasma membranes is 0.79, as compared to 0.32 in total membranes, indicating that its estimation can be used as a criterion of thyroid plasma membrane purification [34].

C. Crude Particulate Preparations

Guinea pig thyroid particulate fractions have been used to study [^{125}I] TSH binding [10].

Hyperplastic thyroid tissue is obtained by maintaining guinea pigs for 3 to 12 months on a diet of lucerne and 0.1% propylthiouracil in drinking water. To suppress endogenous TSH, the goitrigen was withdrawn two to three days before death, or the animals were injected intraperitoneally with 50 μg L-thyroxine 24 hr before sacrifice. This treatment results in glands about 10 times larger than normal, with no change in their TSH-binding properties. Normal glands can also be used.

After slicing and mincing with a razor blade, the tissue is homogenized by hand in 10 volumes of 10 mM tris-Cl, pH 7.4, with 10 strokes of a tight-fitting, all-glass homogenizer with a rotary action. The homogenate is then filtered through a thin cotton cloth and centrifuged for 10 min at 800 $\underline{g}$. The supernatant is collected and spun at 10,000 g for 20 min. After pipetting off the supernatant, the pellet is resuspended in the homogenization medium supplemented with BSA (1 mg/ml). All operations are performed at 4°C. The crude particulate fraction can be stored at -30°C for one week with no loss of TSH-binding activity. Similar preparations were also obtained from guinea pig [35] and human [36] thyroid glands.

Basal and TSH-stimulated adenylate cyclase activities are present in the particulate preparations.

IV. BINDING ASSAYS

A. Intact Cells

Cultured thyroid cells are detached as described in Sec. III. B. 1 and suspended in cold Eagle minimum essential medium buffered with 20 mM N-2-hydroxyethylpiperazine-N'-2-ethane sulfonate (HEPES) at pH 7.4, containing 20% calf serum (HEPES-medium E). Cell concentration is adjusted to 4 to 8×10^6 cells per ml. Cells (0.25 ml) are distributed in 1×7-cm polyethylene tubes and stored in crushed ice. Preincubation and incubation are carried out in a shaking incubator (Gallenkamp London, England) set at maximum speed. After a 3-min period preincubation at 35°C for temperature equilibration, 0.25 ml of prewarmed (35°C) solution of ^{125}I-labeled TSH in HEPES-medium E is rapidly added, and incubation at 35°C is started for the required time. To prevent the possible uptake of traces of $[^{125}I]$ iodide that might have contaminated the hormonal preparations, potassium iodide (10 nM) is added in the labeled thyrotropin solution. At the end of incubation, separation of cell-bound from free $[^{125}I]$-thyrotropin is performed by the quick addition of 3.5 ml of cold HEPES-medium E and centrifugation at 1,500 g and 0°C for a total period of 1 min between start and stop of the rotor. The supernatant is aspirated and the cell pellet is washed once with 4 ml of the same medium. In these conditions, 100% of cells are recovered.

The radioactivity of the cell pellet is estimated in a well-type scintillation spectrometer for enough time to lower the counting error to < 2%. In each series of experiments, controls of labeled thyrotropin adsorption on tube walls are performed by omitting cells. Adsorption never exceeded 0.1% of total radioactivity added. Specific binding is obtained by subtracting, from the total radioactivity bound, the amount which is not displaced by the addition to the assay mixture of an excess of native TSH (1 μM).

The release of labeled TSH bound to cells can be studied as follows. Cells are incubated in the presence of labeled hormone for enough time to reach equilibrium of binding. The cells are then centrifuged and washed once at 0°C as already described. The cell pellet is quickly resuspended by vortexing in HEPES-medium E and incubated at the desired temperature in the shaking conditions used for binding and in the presence or absence of excess native TSH. At various time intervals, 3.5 ml cold medium is added, tubes are centrifuged, and the radioactivity of the cell pellet is determined.

B. Plasma Membranes and Crude Particulate Fractions

Measurements of labeled TSH binding to plasma membranes may be performed in several medium conditions. When correlation between binding and adenylate cyclase activity is to be studied, the medium adequate for assay of the latter must be used.

Since monovalent and divalent cations modify hormone binding properties, optimal results are obtained using 50 mM tris-Cl, pH 7.4, containing 1 mM EGTA and 1% crystalline bovine serum albumin. Standard assays contain 15 to 25 μg membrane protein and [^{125}I] TSH in a final volume of 0.150 ml. Membranes and additives are suspended in the same medium. Assays of binding in the conditions of adenylate cyclase activity measurement are performed in 50 mM tris-Cl, pH 7.4; 4 mM MgCl$_2$; 2 mM ATP; 10 mM theophylline; 10 nM creatine; 20 μg creatine kinase; 0.1% crystalline bovine serum albumin; and 1 mM EGTA [3] (final volume, 60 μl).

In our hands, separation of membrane-bound from free labeled TSH by membrane filtration methods was inadequate because of excessive adsorption of the labeled hormone on the filter. Separation of membrane-bound TSH was carried out by centrifugation according to the procedure of Rodbell et al. [37]. Incubation is performed in 0.4-ml polyethylene tubes (Eppendorf, West Germany) under shaking. Prewarmed [^{125}I] TSH is added to the membrane solution which has been preincubated for 3 min at the selected temperature. The reaction is stopped by the addition of 250 μl cold medium, and tubes are centrifuged at 10,000 $\underline{g}$ for 3 min at 0°C in a microcentrifuge (Hettich, Tuttlingen, West Germany). After aspiration of the supernatant, the pellet is carefully washed, rinsed with 300 μl of medium containing 20% sucrose, and the washing solution is aspirated. The bottom of the tube is cut ~2 mm above the pellet and radioactivity is measured. Alternatively, the incubation mixture can be layered on a 20% sucrose incubation medium before centrifugation.

In the case of [^{125}I] TSH binding to crude particulate fractions [10], complete precipitation of bound hormone has been ensured by addition of polyethylene glycol (PEG; mol wt 4,000) in the presence of bovine γ-globulin (BGG). The standard incubation mixture in plastic tubes contains: 50 μl of labeled hormone in PBS, containing 1 mg BSA/ml; 20 μl native TSH or other agents in 10 mM tris-Cl, pH 7.4; with 1 mg BSA/ml and 50 μl of the particulate fraction in the latter medium. After incubation, the tube is transferred to an ice bath and 500 μl 0.32% BGG and 620 μl of 20% PEG in 1 M NaCl at 4°C are added.

After 10 min centrifugation at 10,000 $\underline{g}$, the supernatant is aspirated and the radioactivity of the precipitate is measured. According to the authors, polyethylene glycol and bovine γ-globulin addition ensures complete sedimentation of bound radioactivity and compactness of the pellet.

Nonspecific precipitation of $[^{125}I]$ TSH due these agents is 7 to 11% under standard conditions. The presence of high concentration of NaCl (0.56 M final) in the medium causes some dissociation of receptor-TSH complexes. However, the authors observed that saturation curves and Scatchard plots for labeled TSH binding obtained by PEG precipitation showed dose relationships and slopes essentially identical to those obtained by centrifugation of the undiluted incubation mixture.

C. Comments

For most purposes, methods using centrifugation to separate free hormone from that bound to receptor are more appropriate for the following reasons: (1) with a microcentrifuge, small volumes of incubation can be handled with no loss due to transferring; (2) the use of plastic tubes and discontinuous gradients decreases nonspecific binding to low levels; (3) if force and duration of centrifugation are appropriate, cells or membranes are completely precipitated; (4) many samples can be centrifuged simultaneously.

Filtration on artificial membranes has been used in many studies of hormone binding to receptors. In the case of TSH, despite previous soaking of filters in concentrated protein solution, significant adsorption of the labeled hormone to filters precluded their utilization. Selection of an appropriate type of filter with a very low adsorption capacity for labeled TSH will be rewarding, since membrane filtration provides a more rapid separation of bound from free hormone and, therefore, decreases the risks of changes in the distribution of the two forms of the hormone due to the separation procedure. Vacuum filtration through oxoid filters presoaked with bovine serum albumin has been proposed [7].

V. QUANTITATIVE ASPECTS OF TSH-RECEPTOR INTERACTION

Direct measurement of TSH interaction with superficial sites of its target tissue was recently studied using different systems.

A. Intact Thyroid Cells and Their Derived Plasma Membranes [5, 6]

The advantages of using intact thyroid cells to study TSH-receptor interaction have recently been reviewed [38]. After three days of maintenance in culture conditions, porcine thyroid cells stimulated by TSH or by dibutyryl cAMP show the morphological and metabolic properties of gland follicles. They are viable and offer exposed plasma membranes to the serum-like medium in which they are cultured. Especially, they permit a comparison of the properties of receptors in intact living cells and in their derived purified plasma membranes. Although this system closely resembles by its qualitative metabolic properties the thyroid follicular cell in vivo, there is no definitive evidence that quantitative values, such as the number of TSH receptor sites on the cell membrane, obtained in vitro with intact cells are representative of the situation in vivo.

Binding of ^{125}I-labeled pTSH to intact porcine thyroid cells is a saturable process with respect to hormone concentration, is directly proportional to cell concentration, and is temperature-dependent, with binding decreasing from 37 to 0°C. Thyrotropin binding is highly specific. All the polypeptide hormones tested so far, including the other pituitary glycoprotein hormones LH and FSH, are unable to affect the binding of labeled TSH to cells. Binding is inhibited by a short pretreatment with trypsin, indicating the presence of the receptors at the external surface of the cells.

Kinetic studies showed that [^{125}I] TSH association to cells or derived plasma membranes is a time-dependent process. At 0.35 nM labeled hormone, half-maximum binding occurred in ~3 min at 35°C. Scatchard plots of the specific uptake of labeled TSH by cells as a function of hormone concentration showed a single class of high-affinity, noninteracting sites, with an apparent equilibrium-association constant of 1.9 nM^{-1}. Calculated from the number of [^{125}I] TSH molecules bound at saturation, on the assumption that sites and hormone are univalent, the number of TSH receptor sites was 500 to 1000 per cell. This number is relatively small when compared to other hormone receptors (~10,000 [39] and 2,000 [40] for insulin in rat adipose and human peripheral mononuclear cells, respectively). Whether it represents the actual situation in vivo is unknown. It is perhaps interesting to consider that TSH receptor sites are probably only located on the basal plasma membrane of the follicular cell in the gland.

In contrast to association, [^{125}I] TSH release from cells or membranes is not single-order. In the presence of excess native hormone in the medium to inhibit rebinding, 60% of the bound labeled hormone is released rapidly with a half-life of 3 min, while the remainder dissociates with a half-life of 30 min.

Assuming a simple reversible bimolecular reaction for hormone-receptor interaction, association- and dissociation-rate constants have been calculated for the specific binding of [^{125}I] TSH to intact cells and their derived plasma membranes. As shown in Table 1, a very good agreement was found between values for both types of receptor preparations. In both systems, the values of the equilibrium-association constants derived from the ratio of the rate constants or from equilibrium data were very similar. However, K_a was three times higher for cells than from their derived plasma membranes. This difference may be explained by the different temperature at which the experiments were performed (35°C for cells, 27°C for membranes) or by the different composition of the media

TABLE 1.   Rate and Equilibrium Constants of Thyrotropin Binding to
Specific Binding Sites of Intact Thyroid Cells and Their
Derived Plasma Membranes[a]

Binding tested in	k_a (nM^{-1}/min^{-1})	k_d (min^{-1})	k_a/k_d (nM^{-1})	K_a (from equilibrium data) (nM^{-1})
Intact cells	0.56	0.36	1.50	1.90
Plasma membranes	0.11	0.25	0.44	0.58

[a] Measurements made at 35°C for intact cells and at 27°C for plasma
membranes.

used to study hormone binding (complete Eagle medium for cells, tris-Cl
containing EGTA for membranes). It may also simply reflect the better
functional integrity of receptor sites in intact living cells than in fragmented,
isolated plasma membranes.

Binding of labeled TSH to intact cell-derived plasma membrane has an
optimum at pH 6. Concentration of sites calculated from Scatchard plots
was 0.13 to 0.22 pmol/mg membrane protein.

In contrast to association which revealed a linear relation between
bound/free and bound hormone, suggesting the presence of a single class
of binding sites, dissociation of ^{125}I-labeled TSH from intact cells or their
derived plasma membranes showed two kinetic components. The experiments were performed in the same medium and temperature conditions.
Since the results cannot be explained by negative cooperativity of binding
sites [41], it is possible that secondary rearrangement of the primary
receptor-hormone complex might lead to another conformational species
dissociating at a slower rate than the primary complex. The physiological
significance of this observation is unknown.

Since TSH is made of two different, noncovalently associated subunits,
the role each subunit may play in binding at the receptor site is of biological importance. Highly purified porcine ^{125}I-labeled TSH subunits did
not bind to intact porcine thyroid cells; in addition, unlabeled pTSH-β, pLH,
or its subunits could not compete with the binding of ^{125}I-labeled porcine
TSH [42]. Small effects were observed with TSH-α, which were likely
due to slight contamination with native TSH, as shown by the in vivo mouse
bioassay and the capacity of the hormone to stimulate thyroid cell reorga-
nization into follicles in vitro. It was concluded that binding to receptor

sites required a subunit conformation such as that realized by their association in the native hormone. Other results [43] showed that bTSH-β
and bLH-α slightly inhibited the binding of [^{3}H] TSH to bovine plasma membranes and were able to activate some parameters of thyroid function in
vitro (4-8% of the response to native TSH), whereas TSH-α was almost
inactive. These discrepancies with our results [42] might be explained
by contamination of subunit preparations with the intact hormone, despite
efforts made to minimize it.

B. Plasma Membranes and Crude Particulate Fractions Isolated from Thyroid Gland Homogenates

Experiments on labeled TSH binding at equilibrium to bovine plasma membranes [7, 8] or a guinea pig particulate fraction of thyroid homogenate [10]
also showed a single class of high-affinity sites with K_a comprised between
0.26 and 1.8 nM^{-1}. In contrast with other results, a low-affinity site of
$K_a = 0.7 \mu M^{-1}$ was found in addition to the high-affinity site for bovine
plasma membranes [8]. In all these systems, optimum pH of binding was
in the acidic region (~ 5.5-6.0).

In the crude particulate system, capacity of binding using bovine ^{125}I-
labeled TSH was higher by a factor of 3 to 10 in guinea pig than in other
mammalian (ox, sheep, rat, mouse) thyroids [10]. Since thyrotropins are
known to have some species specificity, these results cannot be safely
related to receptor density.

C. Correlation of Binding and Physiological Effects

To be an integral part of hormone action, binding of a hormone to receptor
sites of target cells must be quantitatively related to some biological effect.
It is known that TSH action is mediated by cAMP via the activation of plasma membrane adenylate cyclase. Thyrotropin activation of adenylate
cyclase is a very rapid phenomenon, occurring in the minute following its
addition to intact cells [38], and is likely the earliest event following hormone binding.

Using plasma membranes derived from intact cells and time conditions
of equilibrium binding of TSH, the semilogarithmic plot of TSH concentration was shown to correlate sigmoidally with the percent of maximum
adenylate cyclase activation. Half-maximum stimulation was obtained
for a TSH concentration of 1.8 nM, which is identical to the K_d value of
1.78 nM determined for [^{125}I] TSH binding to membranes in conditions of
assay of adenylate cyclase [6]. In the crude particulate system from
guinea pig thyroid, the dose-response curve for stimulation of adenylate
cyclase by TSH also closely corresponded to that for saturation of binding

[10]. A correlation has also been observed between binding of labeled TSH (K_a = 0.5 nM) to intact porcine thyroid cells and a very rapid effect of TSH, the stimulation of iodide efflux from the cells. Hormone concentration for half-stimulation was 0.3 nM [23].

These observations strongly suggest that TSH binding to plasma membranes represents a physiologically significant event.

The equilibrium constants observed in in vitro systems are comparable but somewhat low compared to physiological concentrations of circulating TSH in vivo. For instance, resting TSH plasma levels in pig plasma as shown by radioimmunoassay using antibodies specific to porcine TSH are 0.025 to 0.1 nM (G. Hennen, personal communication), i.e., 17 to 70 times lower than the K_d (1.7 nM) of binding to intact porcine cells in vitro. It may be that the value of the K_d measured in vitro is higher than that existing in vivo or that a few percent occupancy of receptor sites in vivo would be enough to ensure the regulation of thyroid metabolism in the normal animal. That the procedure of preparation of isolated cells or acellular fractions alters the affinity constant for TSH is uncertain.

D. Factors Affecting Thyrotropin Binding and Adenylate Cyclase Activity

Binding of labeled TSH to plasma membranes derived from cultured thyroid cells is inhibited by univalent and divalent cations. At concentrations above 50 mM and up to 200 mM, Na^+, K^+, and Li^+ caused an 80% inhibition of binding or more, but showed little effect at 5 mM [38]. Calcium and magnesium ions reduced the binding by 50% at 1 and 2 mM, respectively. Similar observations have been made using plasma membranes purified from bovine glands [7, 8] and crude particles from guinea pig thyroid [10]. The inhibitory effect of Ca^{2+} on binding was shown to result from an alteration of the number of binding sites and not of the affinity for TSH [8].

The relations between the TSH receptor and the effector system (adenylate cyclase) are still unknown. Some indirect arguments have been given favoring the idea that the receptor and the enzyme may be different entities [8]. For instance, GTP and ITP, which enhance cyclase activity in plasma membranes in the range 0.1 μM to 0.1 mM, have no effect on labeled TSH binding at the same concentrations. This situation is at variance with that found for the glucagon-liver receptor [37, 44] and the angiotensin-adrenal receptor [45] interactions in which GTP stimulates the rate of dissociation of the hormones from their receptor and decreases the apparent Km for hormone action [44]. On the other hand, some agents such as phospholipase A inhibit cyclase but enhance binding.

An interesting property of the TSH receptor concerns its ability to recognize the long-acting thyroid stimulator (LATS). This immunoglobulin G is found in the serum of many patients with thyrotoxicosis. Evidence has accumulated that LATS is able to reproduce most of the metabolic effects elicited by TSH upon the thyroid, and especially activation of adenylate cyclase. Recent experiments showed that LATS-containing sera inhibited receptor binding of ^{125}I-labeled TSH in intact thyroid cells [46] and in particulate fractions of guinea pig [47] or human [36] thyroid homogenates. In the case of the free systems, IgG prepared from LATS-sera gave similar results.

The interaction between IgG containing LATS and the receptor resulted in a decrease of sites available for TSH and not in a decreased affinity [47]; these results suggest that TSH and LATS bind to the same receptor site.

REFERENCES*

1. I. Pastan, J. Roth, and V. Macchia, Proc. Natl. Acad. Sci. U.S.A., 56:1802 (1966).

2. K. Yamashita and J. B. Field, Biochem. Biophys. Res. Commun., 40:171 (1970).

3. J. Wolff and A. B. Jones, J. Biol. Chem., 246:3939 (1971).

4. J. Dumont, Vitamins Hormones, 29:287 (1971).

5. S. Lissitzky, G. Fayet, B. Verrier, G. Hennen, and P. Jaquet, FEBS Lett., 29:20 (1973).

6. B. Verrier, G. Fayet, and S. Lissitzky, Eur. J. Biochem., 42:355 (1974).

7. S. M. Amir, T. F. Carraway, Jr., L. D. Kohn, and R. Winand, J. Biol. Chem., 248:4092 (1973).

8. W. V. Moore and J. Wolff, J. Biol. Chem., 249:6255 (1974).

9. S. W. Manley, J. R. Bourke, and R. W. Hawker, J. Endocrinol., 55:555 (1972).

10. S. W. Manley, J. R. Bourke, and R. W. Hawker, J. Endocrinol., 61:419 (1974).

11. J. G. Pierce, T. H. Liao, and R. B. Carlsen, in Hormonal Proteins and Peptides (C. H. Li, ed.), Academic Press, New York and London, Vol. 1, 1973, pp. 17-57.

12. J. Closset and G. Hennen, Eur. J. Biochem., 46:595 (1974).

13. J. Closset and G. Hennen, personal communication.

14. P. Jaquet, G. Hennen, and S. Lissitzky, Biochimie, 56:769 (1974).

*Reference review completed up to November, 1974.

15. J. I. Thorell and B. G. Johansson, Biochim. Biophys. Acta, 251:363 (1971).

16. G. S. David, Science, 184:138 (1974).

17. S. A. Berson and R. S. Yalow, Ann. N.Y. Acad. Sci., 35:36 (1958).

18. M. Rolland, R. Aquaron, and S. Lissitzky, Anal. Biochem., 33:307 (1970).

19. G. Fayet, H. Pacheco, and R. Tixier, Bull. Soc. Chim. Biol., 52:299 (1970).

20. G. Fayet, M. Michel-Béchet, and S. Lissitzky, Eur. J. Biochem., 24:100 (1971).

21. S. Lissitzky, G. Fayet, A. Giraud, B. Verrier, and J. Torresani, Eur. J. Biochem., 24:88 (1971).

22. R. Planells, G. Fayet, S. Lissitzky, G. Hennen, and J. Closset, FEBS Lett., 53:87 (1975).

23. G. Fayet and S. Housepian, Mol. Cell. Endocr., submitted.

24. F. C. Greenwood, W. M. Hunter, and J. S. Glover, Biochem. J., 89:114 (1963).

25. R. J. Winand and L. D. Kohn, J. Biol. Chem., 245:967 (1970).

26. A. G. Morell, C. J. A. Van der Hamer, I. H. Schemberg, and G. Ashwell, J. Biol. Chem., 241:3745 (1966).

27. H. Eagle, Science, 130:432 (1969).

28. W. Tong, in Methods in Investigative and Diagnostic Endocrinology (J. E. Rall and I. J. Kopin, eds.), Part 1, North-Holland, Amsterdam and London, 1972, pp. 63-81.

29. G. Fayet and S. Lissitzky, FEBS Lett., 11:185 (1971).

30. T. K. Ray, Biochim. Biophys. Acta, 196:1 (1970).

31. D. H. Neville, Jr., J. Biophys. Biochim. Cytol., 8:413 (1960).

32. P. Emmelot, C. J. Bos, E. L. Benedetti, and P. H. Rümke, Biochim. Biophys. Acta, 90:126 (1964).

33. A. Solyom, C. J. Lauter, and E. G. Trams, Biochim. Biophys. Acta, 274:631 (1972).

34. K. Yamashita and J. B. Field, in Methods in Enzymology (S. Fleischer and L. Packer, eds.), Vol. 31, Academic Press, New York and London, 1974, p. 144.

35. B. R. Smith and R. Hall, FEBS Lett., 42:301 (1974).

36. B. R. Smith and R. Hall, Lancet: 427 (1974).

37. M. Rodbell, H. M. J. Krans, S. L. Pohl, and L. Birnbaumer, J. Biol. Chem., 246:18 (1971).

38. S. Lissitzky, G. Fayet, and B. Verrier, Advances in Cyclic Nucleotide Research, Vol. 5, 1975, pp. 133-152.

39. P. Cuatrecasas, Proc. Natl. Acad. Sci. U.S.A., 68:1264 (1971).

40. J. R. Gavin, III, P. Gorden, J. Roth, J. A. Archer, and D. N. Buell, J. Biol. Chem., 248:2202 (1973).

41. P. de Meyts, J. Roth, D. H. Neville, Jr., J. R. Gavin, III, and M. A. Lesniak, Biochem. Biophys. Res. Commun., 55:154 (1973).

42. S. Lissitzky, G. Fayet, B. Verrier, J. Closset, and G. Hennen, FEBS Lett., 48:275 (1974).

43. J. Wolff, R. J. Winand, and L. S. Kohn, Proc. Natl. Acad. Sci. U.S.A., 71:3460 (1974).

44. M. Rodbell, M. C. Lin, and Y. Salomon, J. Biol. Chem., 249:59 (1974).

45. H. Glossman, A. Bankal, and K. J. Catt, J. Biol. Chem., 249:664 (1974).

46. G. Fayet, B. Verrier, A. Giraud, S. Lissitzky, A. Pinchera, J. H. Romaldini, and G. Fenzi, FEBS Lett., 32:299 (1973).

47. S. W. Manley, J. R. Bourke, and R. W. Hawker, J. Endocrinol., 61:437 (1974).

Chapter 22

VASOPRESSIN RECEPTORS

Serge Jard
Joël Bockaert
Christian Roy
Rabary Rajerison

Laboratoire de Physiologie Cellulaire
Collège de France
Paris, France

I. INTRODUCTION   668

II. PREPARATION OF LABELED NEUROHYPOPHYSEAL
    PEPTIDES   669

    A. Review of Methods   669
    B. Iodine-Tritium Substitution Technique   669
    C. Characteristics of the Final Product   672

III. CHARACTERIZATION OF OXYTOCIN RECEPTOR(S) ON
     INTACT EPITHELIAL CELLS   675

    A. Methodological Problems   675
    B. Preparation of Isolated Frog Skin Epithelium   678
    C. Measurement of [^{3}H] Oxytocin Uptake by Frog Skin
       Epithelium   679
    D. Characteristics of Hormone Uptake: Relationship to
       Physiological Response   679

IV. CHARACTERIZATION OF THE VASOPRESSIN RECEPTOR
    IN MEMBRANE FRACTIONS   681

    A. Methodological Problems   681
    B. Preparation of a Hormone-Responsive Subcellular System 682
    C. Adenylate Cyclase Assay   684
    D. Hormone Binding Assay   685
    E. Characterization of Vasopressin-Binding Sites on Pig
       Renal Medulla Membranes   686
    F. Identification of Vasopressin-Binding Sites with
       Physiological Receptors   689

 V. SOLUBILIZATION OF MEMBRANE VASOPRESSIN
    RECEPTORS   693

    A. Methodological Problems   693
    B. Solubilization Procedure   693
    C. Binding Assay for Vasopressin with Soluble Sites   695
    D. Characterization of Soluble Vasopressin Receptors   696

    ACKNOWLEDGMENTS   700

    REFERENCES   701

I. INTRODUCTION

This chapter will be confined to a description of the main techniques used
to characterize vasopressin receptors in epithelial-responsive cells, i.e.,
amphibian skin and bladder epithelial cells and tubular cells from the terminal part of the mammalian nephron. It has been clearly established on
these structures that cAMP is the second messenger of hormonal action
[1-4]. The primary effect of hormone is specific activation of membrane-
bound adenylate cyclase [5-13]. These findings justify the search for a
vasopressin receptor either at the surface of responsive cells or at the
level of subcellular fractions which are obtained from these cells and contain hormone-sensitive adenylate cyclase. A hormonal receptor may be
primarily defined as a molecule which binds the hormone so as to produce
a hormone-receptor complex capable of triggering a chain of events leading to the expression of a physiological effect. Thus, characterization of
a hormonal receptor is based on the demonstration of a series of correlations between binding and hormonal effects (i.e., physiological effects and
adenylate cyclase activation depending on whether the receptor is studied
on intact or broken cell preparations). The four main correlations usually
considered are time- and dose-dependency, reversibility, and the structural requirements for binding and response. As for the other hormone-responsive systems so far studied [14], the epithelial target cells

for vasopressin contain only a few hormonal receptors. Detection of these receptors depends on the possibility of preparing a radioactive hormonal molecule exhibiting both high affinity for the receptor and high specific radioactivity.

II. PREPARATION OF LABELED NEUROHYPOPHYSEAL PEPTIDES

A. Review of Methods

In order to be suitable both for detection of specific binding sites and for quantitative analysis of binding-response relationships, the labeled hormone must possess high specific radioactivity (higher than several Ci/mmol) and intact biological properties. The latter prerequisite is of special importance in the case of antidiuretic hormone, since it has been shown that even minor changes in the structure of the vasopressin molecule can strikingly affect the relationships between receptor occupancy and adenylate cyclase activation [15-17].

External labeling with radioactive iodine has been successfully applied to oxytocin and vasopressin and has resulted in the synthesis of radioactive molecules of high specific radioactivity. However, iodination of these small peptidic molecules significantly reduced their biological activities. [Monoiodotyrosine]^2-oxytocin had only 10 to 40% of the activity of oxytocin in stimulating adenylate cyclase in toad bladder epithelium homogenates, and 75 to 80% of oxytocin activity in stimulating glucose oxidation by isolated fat cells [18]. In the rat, purified preparations of iodinated lysine- and arginine-vasopressin were found to have < 1% of the antidiuretic activity of the native molecules [19, 20].

Tritiated neurohypophysial peptides were prepared by the three following methods: tritium hydrogen exchange, using either the original technique [21, 22] or a modified [20] Wilzbach technique [23]; total synthesis [21, 24, 25]; and catalytic substitution of ^{3}H for I in the iodinated peptides [26-30]. The iodine-tritium substitution technique was the method found most effective for producing highly labeled oxytocin and vasopressin. A detailed description of the method is given in the next section.

B. Iodine-Tritium Substitution Technique

1. Iodination and Purification of Iodo-oxytocin and Iodo-vasopressin

Oxytocin and vasopressin contain a tyrosine and a cystine residue, the latter closing a 20-membered ring. Using the conventional iodine-iodate mixture for iodinating oxytocin, it was shown [29] that the resulting compounds contained more than two I atoms per molecule. This indicated that halogenation was not limited to the aromatic tyrosine ring but attacked the disulfide bridge, thus altering the entire hormonal structure. Attack of the disulfide bridge was due to the presence in the incubation mixture of I_2, from which the halogenation species I^+ is formed in minute amounts. The use of ICl at neutral pH as an I^+ generating reagent prevents significant destruction of the S–S bond.

The following procedure was used by Morgat et al. [29] for oxytocin iodination and by Pradelles et al. [27] for vasopressin iodination: the starting material consisted of highly purified synthetic oxytocin or vasopressin dissolved in phosphate buffer 0.1 M, pH 6.0 (2-5 μmol of peptide per ml). ICl together with a tracer amount of ^{125}ICl in 0.25 ml anhydrous methanol was slowly added under continuous stirring to 2 ml of the peptide solution. The amount of ICl usually added is 2.5 to 4 times the stochiometric amount in relation to the hormone. Iodination was allowed to proceed at 5°C for a few minutes, and a slight excess of thiosulfate was then added to the mixture to stop the reaction and destroy unreacted iodine. Quantitative evaluation of iodine incorporation into the peptide may be checked by paper electrophoresis, which permits separation of free mineral from bound iodine. An aliquot of the reaction mixture was placed on Whatman paper No. 1 impregnated with 7×10^{-2} M pyridine-acetic acid buffer, pH 6.5, and submitted to electrophoresis (12 V/cm for 1 hr). An average of two iodine atoms were found to have been incorporated per peptide molecule.

Removal of inorganic salts and purification of the iodinated peptide may be obtained by filtration through a Bio-gel P-2 column. A small peak of u.v.-absorbing material was eluted with 1 mM acetic acid; 1% acetic acid was then added and a second peak of peptide recovered. It represented ~80% of the total product and was found to be diiodinated peptide free of any significant amount of impurity.

2. Tritiation

Dehalogenation of iodo-oxytocin and/or iodo-vasopressin can be carried out using palladium black dispersed on alumina or calcium carbonate as a catalyst. Palladium black is known to catalyze an exchange between the hydrogen of water and either molecular hydrogen or tritium. However, the velocity of the exchange between water hydrogen and tritium gas is very slow compared to the velocity of the dehalogenation process itself [29-31]. It is thus possible to carry out the iodine-tritium exchange using iodopeptide in aqueous solution. For oxytocin, the tritiation technique is described in detail by Morgat et al. [29]. It was applied with only a few minor modifications to the preparation of tritiated vasopressin by Pradelles et al. [27]. These authors concentrated the iodopeptide solution into a small volume (0.5 to 1 ml) which they placed in the tritiation vessel (Fig. 1),

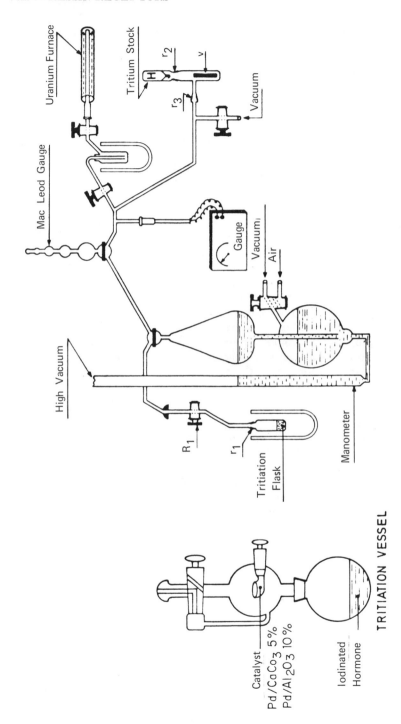

FIG. 1. Diagram of the tritium gas handling apparatus and tritiation vessel. Modified from Ref. 29, pp. 28 and 283.

and the catalyst was placed in the tritiation vessel cup. The peptide solution was frozen in liquid nitrogen and pure tritium allowed to enter the flask in order to flush the catalyst. The tritium gas was eliminated. Then 5 to 10 Ci of ^{3}H gas were again introduced into the flask by means of a Toeppler pump (Fig. 1), and the cup was inverted in order to drop the catalyst into the frozen peptide solution. After the mixture had been brought to room temperature, the reaction proceeded under stirring for 20 min.

After elimination of the tritium gas, the catalyst was removed from the peptide solution by filtration on Millipore membranes (MITEX). The ionizable ^{3}H atoms in the solution were eliminated by successive dilution-concentration steps using large amounts of distilled water.

Elimination of salts and partial purification of the tritiated peptides may be obtained by filtration on a Bio-gel P-2 column as described for iodopeptide separation.

3. Tritiated Oxytocin and Vasopressin Purification

Whereas conventional techniques were found effective for [^{3}H] oxytocin purification [29], the affinity chromatography technique proposed by Cohen et al. [32], which combines the advantages of high specificity and simplicity, seems the most convenient method for the present purposes. The adsorbant is a conjugate of bovine neurophysins covalently bound to Agarose gel, prepared according to the general coupling technique of Axen and Ernback [33] and Cuatrecasas [34].

The following technique was used by Pradelles et al. [27] to purify [^{3}H] vasopressin. Five milliliters of affinity adsorbant were placed on a column, intensively washed, and equilibrated with 0.1 M acetate buffer, pH 5.7, the optimal pH for binding vasopressin to neurophysins [32]. The tritiated material, dissolved in a minimum volume of acetate buffer, was layered at the top of the column. Elution of the column with acetate buffer led to recovery of two peaks containing both ^{3}H and ^{125}I radioactivities (Fig. 2). When no significant amount of radioactivity was measured in the column effluent, the acetate buffer was replaced by formic acid, 0.1 N, pH 2.5, in order to dissociate the tritiated vasopressin from the Sepharose-bound neurophysins. As shown in Figure 2, a single peak of ^{3}H radioactivity was eluted without any measurable contamination by ^{125}I radioactivity.

C. Characteristics of the Final Product

1. Radiochemical Purity and Specific Radioactivity

Radiochemical purity of the tritiated product may be checked by thin layer chromatography. Five-microliter aliquots of the labeled material were

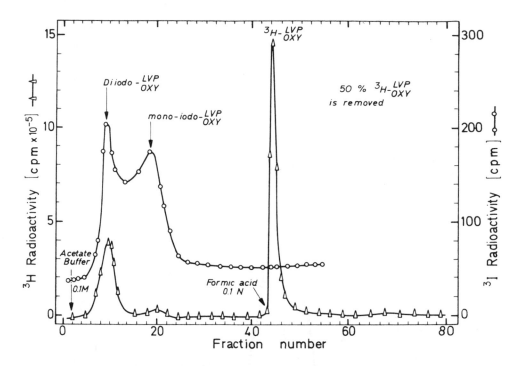

FIG. 2. Affinity chromatography of the tritiated oxytocin and vasopressin preparations on a neurophysin-Sepharose conjugate. The figure gives the elution profiles of ^{3}H and ^{125}I radioactivities. Experimental conditions are described in the text. ^{3}H radioactivity was measured on a 5-μl aliquot of each fraction. ^{125}I radioactivity was measured on the total fraction volume (1 ml). Modified from Ref. 27 p. 190.

spotted on cellulose (oxytocin) or silica (vasopressin) plates, together with an excess of the corresponding unlabeled peptide. The chromatograms (see Fig. 3) were developed in solvent systems composed of n-butanol:acetic acid: water (4:1:5, vol/vol) for oxytocin, and n-butanol:pyridine:acetic acid:water (15:10:3:6, vol/vol) for vasopressin. The chromatogram was then divided into successive strips and the peptide extracted from the cellulose powder by 0.5 ml acetic acid (5%). After centrifugation, the radioactivity and biological activity in the supernatants were measured. There was no trace of labeled impurity on either the tritiated oxytocin or the vasopressin preparations. Labeled and unlabeled molecules exhibited identical behavior. To determine specific radioactivity, the peptide content of the final purified material was measured by Lowry's method [35] using unlabeled synthetic hormone as a standard (volume of the reaction mixture 750 μl, peptide content 1 to 4 μg).

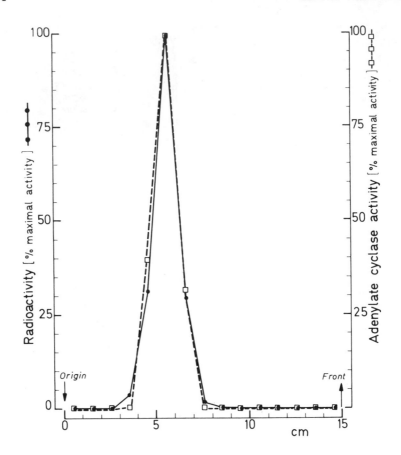

FIG. 3. Radiochromatogram of purified [³H] vasopressin. A tracer amount
of the neurophysin–Sepharose column eluate was spotted together with unlabeled vasopressin (10 IU) on a cellulose plate. Experimental details are
given in the text. The figure gives the elution profiles of radioactivity and
biological activity of the unlabeled vasopressin. The latter was measured
by activation of pig kidney adenylate cyclase. Reproduced from Ref. 27,
p. 190, by courtesy of the North-Holland Publishing Company, Amsterdam.

2. Biological Assays

The biological potencies of the tritiated molecules were determined using
conventional bioassay procedures and the adenylate cyclase activation test.
The synthetic oxytocin and vasopressin preparations used for tritiation
serve as reference compounds. For a complete description of the biological assays for neurohypophysial peptides, see, for instance, Ref. 36.

The adenylate cyclase activation test is described in Sec. IV. C. It was observed that denaturation of the labeled hormone occurring after long storage periods (and sometimes during preparation) does not affect different biological activities equally. It is thus necessary to compare the behavior of labeled and unlabeled hormones by means of different bioassay procedures. Finally, the integrity of the biological properties of the tritiated peptide can be tested on the membrane binding assay (see Sec. IV) by measuring the modifications of radioactivity binding after known dilutions of the labeled molecule with the unlabeled hormone.

When stored in liquid nitrogen, [^{3}H] oxytocin and [^{3}H] vasopressin dissolved in 0.1 M formic acid (200 μCi/ml) were found stable for up to six months. Thereafter, a rapid and pronounced drop in biological activity was usually observed, especially as regards the ability of the hormone to activate membrane adenylate cyclase.

3. Characteristics of the Tritiated Oxytocin and Vasopressin

Table 1 summarizes the main characteristics of different batches of [^{3}H] oxytocin and [^{3}H] vasopressin prepared by various methods including the one already described. It clearly shows that catalytic dehalogenation of iodinated peptide in the presence of tritium gas can lead to high specific radioactivities (20 to 50% of the maximal theoretical value) and is compatible with the maintenance of high biological potency.

III. CHARACTERIZATION OF OXYTOCIN RECEPTOR(S)
ON INTACT EPITHELIAL CELLS

A. Methodological Problems

In order to characterize a hormonal receptor on intact cells, the biological material used must permit: (1) simultaneous measurements of labeled hormone binding and physiological response, and (2) estimation of possible penetration and metabolism of the hormonal molecule within the intracellular compartment.

Of the epithelial structures responsive to neurohypophysial peptides, the amphibian skin and bladder appear to constitute the most suitable material, since they permit simple in vitro measurement of the biological response, i.e., increased osmotic water permeability and active sodium transport stimulation. However, amphibian skin and bladder are histologically heterogeneous [37, 38]. They contain several types of epithelial cells supported by connective tissue. Isolated epithelial cells may be obtained from the amphibian bladder by using a calcium-free medium and

TABLE 1. Characteristics of Different Preparations of Tritiated Oxytocin and Vasopressin

Technique used and hormone labeled	Specific radioactivity (Ci/mM)	Biological activity (IU/mg)
Wilzbach Technique		
Arginine-vasopressin [20][a]	0.4	400: rat vasopressor
Oxytocin [21]	0.012	330 (73%)[b]: avian depressor
Total Synthesis		
Oxytocin [21]	0.13	500: avian depressor
Oxytocin [24]	2.9[c]	
Lysine-vasopressin [24]	1.8[c]	
[³H] I Substitution		
Oxytocin [26]	0.23	550 (12%): avian depressor
Lysine-vasopressin [28]	0.36	Active on toad bladder water permeability at concentration < 1 μM
Oxytocin [44]	24	440 (98%): avian depressor 450 (100%): frog natriferic

[29]	37	450 (100%): frog bladder adenylate cyclase
		300 (67%): avian depressor
		376 (84%): frog hydro-osmotic
Lysine-vasopressin [27]	10	228 ± 20 (80%): rat vasopressor
		269 (95%): pig kidney adenylate cyclase

[a]Reference for synthesis.

[b]Percent activity as compared to the starting material.

[c]Calculated from the biological activity of the labeled peptide assuming a potency of 490 IU/mg (rat uterus) for oxytocin and 175 IU/mg (rat vasopressor) for lysine-vasopressin.

collagenase treatment [39]. However, no simple method is yet available for assessing the responsiveness of these cells to neurohypophysial peptides. The frog bladder epithelial layer can be separated from the supporting connective tissue [40]. This preparation permits precise determination of the response to neurohypophysial peptides [40], but it remains difficult to obtain enough material for hormone-binding studies. So far, the isolated frog skin epithelium, obtainable in large quantities, is the most suitable material despite its greater histological heterogeneity.

When using intact tissues to characterize a membrane receptor, the radioactivity retained by the structure exposed to the labeled hormone may correspond to one or more of the following: (1) hormone bound to physiological receptors, (2) hormone adsorbed on nonspecific sites, (3) radioactivity trapped in intercellular spaces, and (4) radioactivity resulting from possible penetration and metabolism of the labeled hormone within the intracellular compartment. It is, thus, necessary to estimate the relative importance of these components in the total uptake of radioactivity by the tissue.

B. Preparation of Isolated Frog Skin Epithelium

The method used [41] was derived from that described by Aceves and Erlij [42]. The epithelium was separated from the underlying corium by the combined action of hydrostatic pressure and collagenase treatment. About 40 cm^2 of ventral skin of the frog (Rana esculenta) was fixed over a glass pipe (diam, 5 cm), internal side downwards. The pipe was filled with Ringer solution (Na$^+$, 112 mM; K$^+$, 3.2 mM; Ca^{2+}, 1 mM; Cl$^-$, 119 mM; HCO$_3^-$, 2.5 mM; pH 8.1) containing 3 mM glucose and 40 units/ml of collagenase type I derived from Clostridium histolyticum. It was immersed in aerated Ringer solution for 90 min at 35°C; 15 cm H$_2$O hydrostatic pressure was applied to the skin's internal surface. At the end of the incubation period, the skin was removed from the pipe and rinsed in fresh Ringer solution. Complete separation of the epithelium was ensured by gently moving the smooth edge of a glass slide along the external surface of the skin. It is thus possible to obtain a continuous sheet of ∼15 cm^2 of epithelium from which four to six circular pieces can be punched out.

Each piece of epithelium was spread over a nylon mesh, mucosal surface downwards, and mounted horizontally between two cylindrical lucite chambers filled with Ringer solution. The transepithelial potential difference was continuously monitored through calomel electrodes. The increase in potential difference following the addition of hormone to the serosal chamber was shown to be a good index of active sodium transport stimulation. Electron microscopy studies revealed that splitting occurred between the plasma membrane of the stratum germinativum cells and the underlying basement membrane. Furthermore, no morphological alteration of intracellular organelles was detected [43]. This separation procedure preserves most of the transport and permeability characteristics of intact skin, as well as its responsiveness to neurohypophysial peptides, cAMP and theophylline [41].

Taking into account the variable radioactivity uptake and biological response observed from one preparation to another, each experiment was performed using epithelium pieces originating from the same frog skin. Furthermore, the use of symmetrical fragments made it possible to eliminate differences due to their position along the longitudinal axis.

C. Measurement of [³H] Oxytocin Uptake by Frog Skin Epithelium

Total radioactivity uptake was measured after incubating the preparation in the presence of [³H] oxytocin added to the Ringer solution bathing the internal surface of the epithelium. The volume of the extracellular spaces was determined by the use of [¹⁴C] inulin. It was assumed that the hormone concentration in the extracellular spaces was identical to that in the incubation medium. The determination of extracellular volume was used to calculate the fraction of total uptake corresponding to free extracellular hormone. It was shown that part of the total radioactivity uptake corresponded to the incorporation of [³H] tyrosine into newly synthesized proteins. Whether the free [³H] tyrosine originates from the presence of trace amounts (< 0.1%) in the labeled hormone preparation or from hormone hydrolysis within the tissue, its incorporation into proteins may be blocked either by the presence of unlabeled tyrosine or by protein synthesis inhibitors [44]. All experiments were performed under conditions allowing complete inhibition of [³H] tyrosine incorporation (tyrosine, 1 mM; and puromycin, 200 µg/ml, or cycloheximide, 20 µg/ml).

After incubation of the epithelium in the presence of [³H] oxytocin, the scrosal medium was removed and the chamber rinsed three times with Ringer solution within 30 sec. This rapid washing procedure allowed almost complete elimination of the [¹⁴C] inulin and extracellular [³H] oxytocin, while leaving intracellular or bound ³H radioactivity unchanged. The epithelium pieces were gently blotted on filter paper, weighed, solubilized, and their radioactivity counted.

The possibility that the "nonextracellular" radioactivity, i.e., the difference between the total and extracellular radioactivities, might correspond to hormonal binding on physiological receptor sites was examined.

D. Characteristics of Hormone Uptake:
Relationship to Physiological Response

Due to the presence of several intermediary steps between hormone-receptor interaction and the response measured, only qualitative criteria

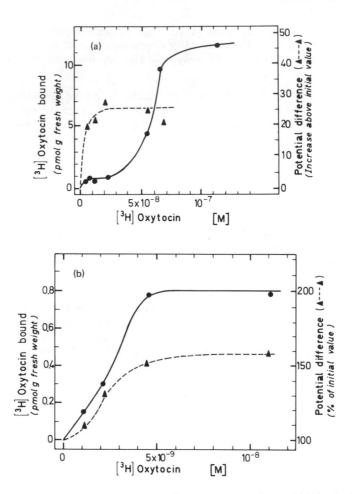

FIG. 4. Dose-dependency of the radioactivity uptake and biological response of isolated frog skin epithelium. Pieces of epithelium were incubated for 20 min in the presence of the [³H] oxytocin concentrations indicated. Note the existence of a first saturation plateau in the submaximum concentration range (b) and the existence of a second plateau for supramaximum [³H] oxytocin concentrations (a). Modified from Ref. 44, pp. 235 and 236.

could be used to identify the uptake process with the process of hormonal binding to specific receptors. Four main criteria should be considered: (1) the fact that radioactivity uptake must either precede or be concomitant with the onset of the response; (2) gradual saturation of the uptake process and of the dose-dependent response must be observable in the same hormonal concentration range unless spare receptors [45] are present; (3) reversal of the uptake must parallel reversal of the biological response; and (4) identical structural requirements for uptake and biological activities (agonistic or antagonistic properties) must be demonstrable.

[³H] oxytocin uptake by the frog skin epithelium partially satisfied these criteria. Measurements of [³H] oxytocin uptake as a function of the concentration of labeled hormone in the medium showed the existence of two sets of sites [44, 46, and Fig. 4(a)]. These sets had different binding capacities and different affinities for oxytocin and its analogs. Sites with a low binding capacity (1 to 2 pmol/g fresh weight; ~1,000 sites per cell) were saturable within the range of hormonal concentrations for which dose-dependent stimulation of active Na^+-transport was observed (apparent K_m value: 2.5 nM; Fig. 4b). The time course of binding to these sites was faster than that of the biological response. Binding to these sites was partially reversible once the labeled hormone had been eliminated from the medium. A significant amount of radioactivity was still present in the tissue, despite complete reversal of biological response. This fraction (~40% of the total uptake) was released when dithiothreitol (10 mM) was added to the incubation medium during the rinsing period; it might correspond to covalent binding of the hormone to the structure and be unrelated to the biological effect. This interpretation is supported by the observation that [0-methyl tyrosine] ^{2}-carba-1-oxytocin, an oxytocin competitor lacking the disulfide bond [47], only inhibited the total uptake by 60%. The observation that [8-arginine]-oxytocin and [8-lysine]-vasopressin was able to inhibit [³H] oxytocin binding to high-affinity sites corresponded to what might be expected in view of the relative biological potencies of these analogs. It may be concluded that at least part of the [³H] oxytocin uptake at low hormonal concentrations corresponded to the attachment of the hormone to the receptors involved in oxytocin-stimulated active Na^+ transport.

The second set of sites is characterized by a lower affinity (apparent K_m value ~50 nM) and a higher binding capacity (~30 pmol/g fresh weight). Binding to these low-affinity sites was highly cooperative. Furthermore, it was not possible to correlate this component of [³H] oxytocin uptake to any known physiological effect of this hormone on the frog skin.

IV. CHARACTERIZATION OF THE VASOPRESSIN
RECEPTOR IN MEMBRANE FRACTIONS

A. Methodological Problems

The hormone-induced increase in the adenylate cyclase activity present in plasma membranes prepared from neurohypophysial peptide target cells is the earliest known consequence of hormone-receptor interaction. To permit characterization of the hormonal receptor at the membrane level, the procedure used for membrane preparation must (1) preserve the responsiveness of adenylate cyclase to the hormone, as well as its high sensitivity and specificity towards structurally related molecules; (2) eliminate most of the enzymic activities which might alter the hormonal molecule's biological activity; (3) reduce nonspecific adsorption of the hormone; (4) produce sufficient material remaining stable during storage; and (5) ensure that the plasma membranes are free of other subcellular particles.

B. Preparation of a Hormone-Responsive Subcellular System

Pig kidney medulla (40 g) was rapidly dissected at $0°C$ and immediately homogenized in 400 ml of a medium containing 250 mM sucrose; 5 mM tris-HCl, pH 8.0; 3 mM $MgCl_2$; and 1 mM EDTA tris, pH 8.0, using a tight, glass Potter-Elvehjem. Homogenization in an isotonic medium was found to be a crucial condition for preserving adenylate cyclase responsiveness to antidiuretic hormone. After filtration on glass wool, a low-speed sediment was collected by centrifugation at 300 g for 10 min. The pellet was dispersed in 800 ml of the same homogenization medium, without the sucrose, and submitted to continuous stirring for 10 min at room temperature. The 300-g pellet was washed four times using the same medium. These successive washings in a medium containing EDTA led to progressive elimination of the components responsible for hormone inactivation and for nonspecific [3H] vasopressin binding (see Table 2). Furthermore, an increase was observed in the ratio of vasopressin-stimulated adenylate cyclase activity to basal activity. In relation to the starting homogenate, the specific activity of the vasopressin-stimulated adenylate cyclase increased six- to sevenfold. However, the final pellet was contaminated by mitochondrial enzymatic activities; the specific activity of succinate cytochrome-C reductase dropped by 87% during the successive washings of the 300-g pellet. Centrifugation, 60,000 g, of the 300-g pellet for 60 min in a nonlinear sucrose gradient (densities were 1.16, 1.18, 1.20, and 1.30) resolved the pellet into three bands, each containing adenylate cyclase activity. In none of these bands was the specific activity of vasopressin-sensitive adenylate cyclase enhanced. The use of Emmelot et al's. method [48] resulted in satisfactory purification of renal medulla plasma membranes, as indicated by the increase in basal adenylate cyclase and Na^+-K^+ ATPase specific activities; however, the activation by vasopressin dropped during purification [9]. As reported by Campbell et al. [10], application of Fitzpatrick et al's. technique [49] purified the plasma membranes of pig kidney medulla but failed to eliminate enzymatic activities responsible for vasopressin degradation. Finally, the washed 300-g pellet seemed the best preparation for preserving hormonal responsiveness and eliminating hormonal-inactivating substances. Furthermore, this preparation remained stable for at least one month when stored in liquid nitrogen.

TABLE 2. Evolution of Adenylate Cyclase Activity and [³H] Vasopressin Binding During Membrane Preparation

Fractions	Adenylate cyclase activity			[³H] Vasopressin binding	
	Specific activity (pmoles cAMP per 10 min per mg protein)		Activation ratio LVP/basal	Specific binding (pmoles [³H] LVP bound per mg protein)	Nonspecific binding (% of specific binding)
	Basal	LVP			
Homogenate: total	36	85	2.46	0.040	93.5
Homogenate: 300-g pellet	64	186	2.90	0.140	123.0
Homogenate: 300-g supernatant	32	53	1.64	0.021	229.0
Lysate pellet	75	298	3.98	0.152	32.7
Final enzyme	88	420	4.77	0.138	19.5

C. Adenylate Cyclase Assay

When studying the modulation of adenylate cyclase activity, it should be remembered that the action of the effector tested may be time-dependent. For instance, it was shown that 15-min preincubations of pig kidney membranes at 30°C in the presence of vasopressin were necessary for correct estimation of dose-dependent adenylate cyclase activation [9].

An assay method should, therefore, be used which permits determination of instantaneous enzyme velocity, rather than the more classical method based on measuring cAMP accumulation for the whole period during which the effector is in contact with the enzyme. This is possible by preincubating the enzyme in the presence of the regulatory agent before adding the substrate necessary for the adenylate cyclase reaction. When assaying adenylate cyclase activity by the conversion of labeled ATP having high specific radioactivity, tracer amounts of the radioactive precursor can be added to the incubation medium at the end of the preincubation period without affecting the other incubation conditions.

The experimental conditions chosen for determining the dose-response relationship for vasopressin were the following: the preincubation medium (95 μl) contained 100 mM tris-HCl, pH 8.0; 0.25 mM ATP (disodium salt); 1 mM cAMP; 1 to 10 mM $MgCl_2$; 1 mg/ml creatine kinase; 20 mM phosphocreatine; 150 to 250 μg of membrane proteins; and various amounts of hormone. At the end of the 15-min preincubation period, 10 μl of solution containing 1 μCi [α-^{32}P]ATP (1-2 Ci/mmol) were added, and incubation was allowed to proceed for 5 min.

An ATP-regenerating system was necessary to maintain a constant ATP concentration and to allow correct determination of ATP-specific radioactivity during the final stage of incubation. Moreover, the regenerating system prevented accumulation of ATP metabolites which interfere with adenylate cyclase activity [13]. Varying the Mg^{2+} concentration permits the modulation of adenylate cyclase activation by vasopressin. Finally, the large amount of cAMP present during incubation prevented hydrolysis by phosphodiesterases of the minute amounts of cAMP formed.

The reaction was stopped by cooling and diluting the [α-^{32}P]ATP in an excess of unlabeled ATP. This was done by adding to each sample 150 μl of a cold solution composed of 50 mM tris-HCl, pH 7.6; 5 mM cAMP; 3.3 mM ATP; and 5×10^{-3} μCi cyclic[^{3}H]AMP. cAMP was separated by filtration on dry aluminum oxide columns as proposed by Ramachandran and Lee [50]. Calculation of the separation procedure yield was based on the amount of cyclic[^{3}H]AMP recovered. Eluted ^{32}P radioactivity was corrected for a blank value measured on samples to which the "stopping" solution was added before the enzyme. Adenylate cyclase activity was expressed in picomoles of cAMP formed per 5 minutes and per milligram of protein.

Control experiments validating this separation procedure were described
by Bockaert et al. [13].

D. Hormone Binding Assay

The choice of an experimental method for separating bound hormone from
free hormone must take into account the kinetic parameters of the hormone-
receptor interaction, and especially the velocity of the hormone-receptor
dissociation reaction. In the case of [³H] vasopressin binding to pig kidney
membranes, the half-life of the hormone-receptor complex (20-35 min at
30°C) is long enough to allow the use of a centrifugation technique [51] or
a Millipore filtration technique. The latter, which is quicker, was the
more appropriate for kinetic studies.

  Tritiated vasopressin-binding assay [9] was performed under incubation conditions identical to those used for adenylate cyclase assay, except
that the ATP-regenerating system was omitted. The characteristics of
the hormone-receptor interaction remained unchanged under these conditions. After incubation in the presence of [³H] vasopressin, 2 ml of solution A kept at 4°C, and containing 100 mM tris-HCl, pH 8.0, and 10 mM
$MgCl_2$, were added to each test tube. The samples were then filtered
through Millipore filters (EAWP, 0.45 μ) prewashed with 5 ml of a cold
solution B containing 0.1% bovine serum albumin, 10 mM tris-HCl, pH
8.0, and 1 mM $MgCl_2$. The filters were then washed three times at 4°C
with 10 ml of the same solution. They were dried and their radioactivity
counted. The time between the end of incubation and the end of filtration
did not exceed 30 sec. For each experimental condition, both specific
and nonspecific binding were determined in duplicate. Nonspecific binding
is defined as the amount of radioactivity recovered on the Millipore filter
when the membranes were incubated in the presence of [³H] vasopressin
plus an excess (10^{-5} M) of unlabeled hormone. It corresponds to nonspecific adsorption of the labeled hormone on the membranes and retention
of free hormone on the filter. The latter component (blank value) was
measured by direct filtration of a sample incubated without membranes.
Specific binding was calculated as the difference between total and nonspecific binding. Nonspecific adsorption of [³H] vasopressin on membranes
increased linearly with the labeled peptide concentration in the incubation
medium. The blank value was linear with [³H] vasopressin concentration
from 5×10^{-9} M to 4×10^{-8} M and increased sharply thereafter. For the
highest [³H] vasopressin concentrations, the blank value's share in total
binding was important enough to prevent accurate determination of specific
binding. Thus, in order to measure specific binding at the highest hormonal concentrations, the [³H] vasopressin was diluted with increasing
amounts of unlabeled hormone. When [³H] vasopressin was used at a concentration of 2.5×10^{-8} M, the blank value represented $\sim 1\%$ of the total

binding, and nonspecific adsorption ~5%. Previous control experiments had shown that the specific component of total binding was not reduced by rinsing the Millipore filters [9].

E. Characterization of Vasopressin-Binding Sites
on Pig Renal Medulla Membranes

The binding of lysine-vasopressin to pig renal medulla membranes is both time-dependent and reversible (Fig. 5a). The rate of hormone-receptor complex formation decreased when the temperature was lowered (Q_{10} about

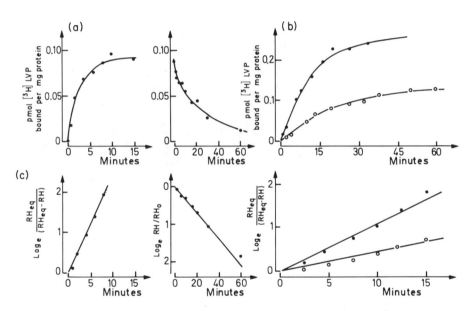

FIG. 5. Time courses of the association and dissociation of [³H] vasopressin with renal plasma membrane receptors. Effects of hormonal concentration and temperature on the association time course. The experiment illustrated in (a) was performed at 30°C in the presence of 10^{-8} M [³H]-vasopressin ([³H] LVP). To test the reversibility of binding, the membranes were first preincubated at 30°C for 15 min in the presence of [³H] LVP (10^{-8} M). The hormonal concentration was then lowered to 5×10^{-10} M by dilution with solution A (see Sec. IV. D). Residual binding was measured after dilution as a function of time. The experiment illustrated in (b) was performed at 15°C using two different [³H] LVP concentrations: 2×10^{-8} M (●) and 5×10^{-9} M (○). The semilogarithmic plots of the association and dissociation curves are shown in (c). Modified from Ref. 9, pp. 5926 and 5927.

six between 15 and 30°C). The time needed to reach equilibrium value
increased when the initial hormonal concentration in the incubation medium
was lowered. The two observations indicate that hormone-receptor interaction itself is the rate-limiting step for the observed binding time course,
rather than diffusion or uptake of the hormone within closed membrane
vesicles. The dissociation curve may be adequately described by a mono-
exponential process (Fig. 5c). This observation may be taken as evidence
for the homogeneity of the binding site population. Under the conditions
that prevailed for the experiment described in Figure 5, the amount of
hormone bound to the membrane was negligible in comparison with the
total amount present in the incubation medium, so that the concentration
of free hormone only dropped by 2.5% and, thus, may be considered as a
constant. This may account for the observation that the association process conforms to first-order reaction kinetics (Fig. 5c).

Assuming that we are dealing with reversible binding of vasopressin
molecules to a homogeneous population of independent binding sites,

$$R + H \underset{k_{-1}}{\overset{k_1}{\rightleftharpoons}} RH$$

R and RH being the free and bound receptors, and H the free hormone,
the rate constants k_1 and k_{-1} for the formation and dissociation of the
hormone-receptor complex may be deduced from the association and dissociation curves. If the concentration of free hormone ([H]) is considered
as a constant, the time course of RH formation is rendered by:

$$\log_e \frac{[RHeq]}{[RHeq] - [RH]} = (k_1 [H] + k_{-1}) t$$

in which [RHeq] is the concentration of hormone-receptor complex at
equilibrium. The corresponding equation for dissociation is:

$$\log_e \frac{[RH]}{[RH_o]} = -k_{-1} t$$

in which [RH$_o$] is the concentration of hormone-receptor complex when
eliminating the free hormone from the incubation medium.

It should be emphasized that the rate constants calculated can only be
considered as "apparent values" since, as will be indicated, the binding
process is slightly cooperative. To determine dose-dependent binding at
equilibrium, it is important to note that at very low hormonal concentrations the half-time for the formation of hormone-receptor complex tends
towards the finite value of $0.69/k_{-1}$.

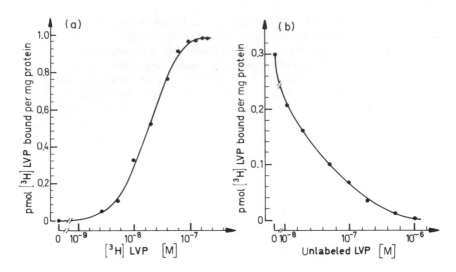

FIG. 6. Dose-dependency of [³H] vasopressin binding to pig kidney membranes. The experiment illustrated in (a) shows gradual saturation of
binding sites by increasing concentrations of [³H] vasopressin ([³H] LVP).
All values were corrected for nonspecific binding. For hormonal concentrations exceeding 4×10^{-8} M, the saturation curve was established using
known specific radioactivity dilutions of the labeled hormone. The experiment illustrated in (b) shows the effect of increasing concentrations of
unlabeled LVP on the binding of the constant amount of labeled hormone
(10^{-8} M). Modified from Ref. 15, p. 3152.

The dose-binding curve at equilibrium (Fig. 6a) indicates that the maximal binding capacity of pig renal medulla membranes was close to 1.0
pmol/mg protein and the apparent Km value (hormonal concentration leading to 50% receptor occupancy) was 2×10^{-8} M. The Hill coefficient of
the binding curve (n = 1.42) is not compatible with great heterogeneity of
the receptor site population with respect to its affinity for the hormonal
molecule.

The limited capacity of the vasopressin-binding sites is further illustrated by the competition experiment shown in Figure 6 (b). Unlabeled
vasopressin inhibited [³H] vasopressin binding in a dose-dependent manner.
Inhibition was maximal at 10^{-6} M unlabeled vasopressin and remained unchanged up to a concentration of 5×10^{-5} M. It was thus not possible to
demonstrate the limited capacity of the nonspecific component. The inhibition curve illustrates another method for determining the apparent Km
of vasopressin for its receptors. The apparent Km for unlabeled vasopressin is rendered by the following equation:

$$(Km)_{LVP} = [LVP]_{50} \times \frac{(Km)\ [^3H]\ LVP}{(Km)\ [^3H]\ LVP + \left[[^3H]\ LVP \right]}$$

in which $(Km)_{LVP}$ and $(Km)\ [^3H]\ LVP$ are the apparent Km values for the unlabeled and labeled hormone, respectively, and $[LVP]_{50}$ is the concentration of unlabeled hormone leading to 50% inhibition of radioactivity binding. Here again, the formula is only valid for a noncooperative binding process. However, when a sufficiently high concentration of $[^3H]$vasopressin is used (0.5 to 2 apparent Km), as was the case for this experiment, the calculated (Km) LVP of 2.3×10^{-8} M was close to the apparent affinity deduced from the $[^3H]$vasopressin dose-binding curve (2×10^{-8} M). Such competition experiments can be used to determine the apparent affinity of unlabeled vasopressin analogs, provided it is first demonstrated that they are able to interact with the entire population of vasopressin-binding sites.

F. Identification of Vasopressin-Binding Sites with Physiological Receptors

Identification of the vasopressin-binding sites with the physiological receptors involved in adenylate cyclase activation was based on the demonstration of close correlations between the binding and activation processes with respect to time- and dose-dependency and to specificity towards structurally modified hormonal molecules.

Using an inframaximal vasopressin concentration, it was demonstrated that hormone binding and enzyme activation followed identical time courses (Fig. 7). This observation suggests that the hormone-binding sites detected are involved in adenylate cyclase activation. It also indicates that the enzyme response is a function of receptor occupancy rather than of the frequency of hormone-receptor interactions (rate theory). This experiment made it clear that correct comparison of the dose-dependencies for binding and enzyme activation could only be derived from determinations of both these activities under equilibrium conditions. Under these conditions, the hormonal binding and adenylate cyclase-activiation curves were not superimposable (Fig. 8a), despite the fact that vasopressin concentrations leading to maximum binding and maximum adenylate cyclase activation were identical. At a vasopressin concentration of 10^{-10} M leading to occupation of < 0.5% of the binding sites, ~40% of the maximum adenylate cyclase activation was obtained.

Using a series of 32 structural analogs of neurohypophysial hormones, it was demonstrated that all the active peptides were able to inhibit $[^3H]$-vasopressin binding [15, 16]. As exemplified by Figure 9, maximum inhibition was identical to that induced by unlabeled vasopressin. For all the active analogs (full and partial agonists), the hormonal concentration needed to obtain maximum enzyme activation was identical to that ensuring

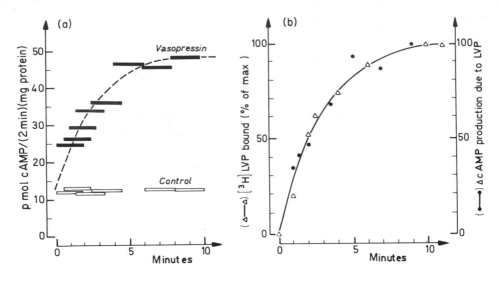

FIG. 7. Time course of adenylate cyclase activation by vasopressin.
Enzyme (2.9 mg protein in 0.8 ml) and two standard adenylate cyclase
assay incubation media without $[\alpha^{32}\text{-P}]$ATP (0.7 ml) were individually
pre-equilibrated at 30°C. One of the incubation media contained vasopressin so that its final concentration, when mixed with enzyme, was 10^{-8} M
(▬). The other incubation medium did not contain vasopressin and was
used for control measurements (▭). After thermal equilibration, the
enzyme and standard incubation media were mixed and continuously stirred
at 30°C. Duplicate aliquot samples (0.15 ml each) were taken at various
times and immediately assayed at 30°C in test tubes containing 0.02 ml of
$[\alpha^{32}\text{-P}]$ATP (1.5 μCi total activity). Labeled cAMP formation was measured for 2 min. To maintain filtration conditions through the aluminum
oxide column unchanged, the volume of the solution added to stop the reaction (5 mM ATP; 3.3 mM cAMP; 5.0×10^{-3} μCi cyclic$[^3\text{H}]$AMP; 50 mM
tris-HCl, pH 7.4) was reduced from 0.15 ml to 0.1 ml. The blank value
did not exceed 12% of the lowest adenylate cyclase activity measured in
this experiment. The entire experiment was performed twice. Values
are the mean of three experimental determinations. The adenylate cyclase
activities measured are plotted as a function of time after mixing enzyme
with the incubation media (a). Abscissae of the two ends of the horizontal
bars indicate the beginning and the end of the final incubation in the presence of $[\alpha^{32}\text{-P}]$ATP. In (b), the percentage of adenylate cyclase activation
was plotted as a function of time, 100% activation corresponding to the
maximum stimulatory effect obtained at 10^{-8} M vasopressin [see (a)].
Position of the experimental values (●) on the abscissae corresponds to
half the final incubation time. The time course of $[^3\text{H}]$vasopressin (10^{-8} M)
binding (△) at 30°C is shown on the same figure; 100% binding corresponded
to the equilibrium value at 10^{-8} M which in this experiment was equal to
0.093 pmol of $[^3\text{H}]$vasopressin per mg of protein. Reproduced from Ref. 9,
p. 5928, by courtesy of the American Society of Biological Chemists, Inc.

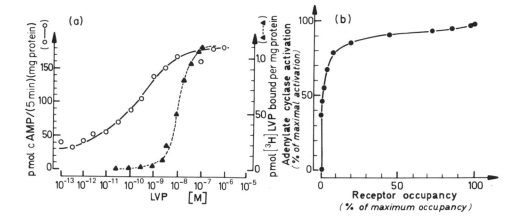

FIG. 8. Relationship between receptor occupancy and adenylate cyclase activation. (a): Dose-dependent adenylate cyclase activation and vasopressin (LVP) binding were determined on the same membrane preparation under equilibrium conditions. Mg^{2+} concentration in the incubation medium was 10 mM. (b): Fractional receptor saturation was determined for each vasopressin concentration used to establish the binding curve. The resulting adenylate cyclase activation was deduced from the dose-response curve. Modified from Ref. 17, p. 45.

saturation of the vasopressin receptor sites. Several analogs such as N-carbamoyl-[o-methyltyrosine]^2- and N-pivaloyl-[o-methyltyrosine]^2-oxytocin, which are competitors of [^{3}H] vasopressin for binding but are in themselves inactive, were found to inhibit adenylate cyclase stimulation induced by active peptides in a competitive manner [16]. These striking similarities between the structural requirements for binding and interaction with adenylate cyclase activity may be considered as strong evidence in favor of identifying the binding sites detected with the physiological vasopressin receptors. For the entire series of active analogs tested, an almost continuous transition was observed between analogs with low affinity for the binding sites, for which the dose-binding and dose-response curves were almost superimposable, and highly potent analogs, for which greater adenylate cyclase activation was observed at a low level of receptor occupancy. For these latter analogs, the dose-dependent adenylate cyclase activation curves exhibited marked apparent negative cooperativity (Hill coefficient as low as 0.30 for vasopressin). These results were taken as evidence for the existence of a nonlinear relationship between receptor occupancy and adenylate cyclase response (see Fig. 8b). The nonlinearity of the coupling function depends on the chemical structure of the active peptide used.

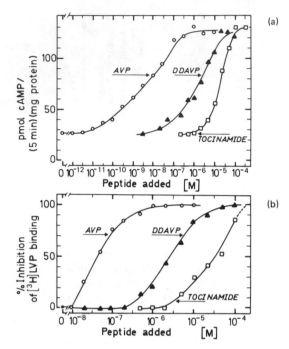

FIG. 9. Specificity of adenylate cyclase activation and hormonal binding
on pig kidney plasma membranes. Adenylate cyclase activities and specific [³H] vasopressin binding (10^{-8} M) were measured in the presence of
the indicated amounts of either [Arg⁸] vasopressin (AVP), deamino[D-Arg⁸]-
vasopressin (DDAVP) or tocinamide and under identical experimental
conditions. (a): Dose-response curves for adenylate cyclase activation.
The apparent Km values and Hill coefficient for adenylate cyclase activation were, respectively, 3×10^{-9} M and 0.45 for AVP, 2×10^{-6} M and
0.77 for DDAVP, and 2×10^{-5} M and 1.13 for tocinamide. (b): Inhibition
of [³H] vasopressin binding expressed as a percentage of the maximal inhibition induced by vasopressin (10^{-5} M) is plotted as a function of the
unlabeled peptide concentration in the incubation medium. Apparent Km
values for binding, determined as indicated in Sec. IV. E were, respec-
tively, 2.8×10^{-8} M, 1.8×10^{-6} M, and 1.4×10^{-5} M for AVP, DDAVP,
and tocinamide. Note that the nature of the enzyme activation receptor
occupancy relationship depends on the structure of the active peptide
tested. It is typically nonlinear for AVP (compare with vasopressin, Fig.
8). It is almost linear for tocinamide. Modified from Ref. 17, p. 39.

V. SOLUBILIZATION OF MEMBRANE VASOPRESSIN RECEPTORS

A. Methodological Problems

The only formal criteria for identifying a hormonal receptor is its ability to induce a biological response after interaction with the hormonal molecule. The extraction of receptors from their environment can modify hormone-receptor interaction and/or events following this interaction. After solubilization of both vasopressin receptors and membrane-bound adenylate cyclase, the enzyme was no longer stimulable by the hormone [52]. Under these conditions, the identification of soluble vasopressin receptors, disconnected from any biological activity, could only be based on careful comparison of their properties with those of the membrane-bound receptors. In addition, the possibility must be considered that the properties of the solubilized molecules might be modified by removing them from their normal environment and/or interference with the hormonal binding of components present in the solubilization medium, e.g., detergent, solubilized phospholipids and/or proteins. Taking into account all these possible modifications of receptors and of hormone-receptor interaction, an additional prerequisite is total solubilization of the membrane-bound hormonal receptors. In any case, the final proof that the soluble binding molecule is the physiological receptor would be the reconstitution of a hormone-regulated system from its isolated components.

Several criteria can be used to determine the best solubilization conditions: total extraction of the binding molecules, nondenaturation, and maintenance of the main characteristics of hormone-receptor interaction. Finally, the solubilization procedure should not unmask a large number of nonspecific binding sites or hormone-inactivating systems.

The validity of the criteria usually applied when defining a component as soluble, i.e., nonsedimentation after high speed centrifugation and/or filtration through a Millipore filter must be checked by determination of the Svedberg coefficient.

B. Solubilization Procedure

Our experimental approach [52] was based on the use of the nonionic detergent Triton X-100, which had already proved a very effective solubilizer (see, for instance, Refs. 53-55). Most membraneous enzymes retain their activity in its presence. Studies by Helenius and Söderlund [56] on the solubilization by Triton X-100 of the Semliki Forest virus membrane indicated that the binding of Triton X-100 started below the critical micellar concentration (CMC = 150 μg/ml). When the detergent concentration was higher than the CMC, the membrane dissociated into micelles composed of proteins, lipids, and detergent. Delipidation of these micelles occurred for a Triton X-100 concentration on the order of 0.016%. When examining the effect of Triton X-100 on membrane, two important factors must be considered: the detergent concentration and the protein/detergent ratio.

1. Solubilization of Vasopressin Receptors and Adenylate Cyclase

Pig kidney plasma membranes (5 to 7 mg protein per ml) were mixed in a centrifuge tube with an equal volume of a medium containing 200 mM tris-HCL, pH 8.0; 20 mM $MgCl_2$ and 1% (vol/vol) Triton X-100 (total volume: 2 ml). Each sample was incubated for 3 to 6 hr at 4°C under continuous stirring. Each tube was then centrifuged for 70 min at 4°C in a Beckman centrifuge (rotor 50-Ti, 50,000 rpm, 226,000 g at the bottom of the tube, 190,000 g at the meniscus). After centrifugation, the brake was switched off at 10,000 rpm to avoid vibration. Two distinct phases were observable in the 226,000-g supernatant. The upper phase (0.6 ml) was slightly opalescent. The lower phase was much more lipid. The boundary between the two phases was very unstable. Even when the phases were hardly distinguishable, they were collected separately. Visualization of this phenomenon depends largely on protein concentration. In all cases, the phases exhibited different properties (Sec. V.D). In most of our experiments, the lower phase was used as a source of soluble receptors.

Incubation at 4°C before centrifugation was found necessary to solubilize a maximum and a reproducible amount of receptors. When incubation was carried out at 30°C for 30 min, the solubilization yield obtained was equal to that measured after 30 min at 4°C. We therefore concluded that temperature did not affect the kinetics of receptor extraction. When the protein concentration in the solubilization medium rose above 5 mg/ml, the receptor solubilization yield dropped noticeably.

Adenylate cyclase activity was solubilized together with vasopressin receptors. However, the maximum solubilization yield for adenylate cyclase activity was obtained within half an hour, indicating that the detergent exerted a differential effect on the solubilization of vasopressin receptors and of adenylate cyclase.

2. Solubilization of the Vasopressin-Receptor Complex

Membranes (3.3 to 4.6 mg/ml) were incubated in a medium identical to that described for measuring hormone binding on membrane fractions (see Sec. IV.D). For nonspecific binding determinations, 10^{-5} M unlabeled vasopressin was added. Incubation was carried out at 30°C for 20 min to allow binding to reach equilibrium. After incubation, samples were cooled at 4°C in order to slow down the dissociation process considerably. The solubilization medium was then added so as to obtain the same solubilization conditions as those described above for the unoccupied receptor (see Sec. IV. B. 1). All further steps were the same as those used for the free receptor.

C. Binding Assay for Vasopressin with Soluble Sites

The same incubation medium was used as that described for hormone binding to membrane fractions (see Sec. IV. D), except that detergent was present in the soluble fraction (final concentration 0.3 to 0.5%, total volume 105 μl). Incubation was carried out for 20 min at 30°C. The bound and free hormone were separated by gel filtration. One hundred-microliter aliquots of each sample were layered at the top of P_{30} Bio-gel columns (Bio-Rad, 100-200 mesh; 9.5 × 0.6 cm). The columns were pre-equilibrated with 100 mM tris-HCl, pH 8.0; 10 mM $MgCl_2$; and Triton X-100 at a concentration equal to that of the sample to be filtered. The presence of Triton X-100 in the elution medium avoided possible precipitation or aggregation of the hormonal receptor. The columns were precooled at 4°C, and elution was performed at the same temperature. The composition of the eluate was the same as that of the pre-equilibration medium. Under these conditions, 1.2 ml of eluate was necessary to exclude 90% of the bound radioactivity within 25 to 30 min without eluting any free hormone (see Fig. 10). The eluate was collected and counted. All determinations were performed in triplicate; reproducibility was better than 5%. Elution at 4°C prevented dissociation of the hormone-receptor complex during gel filtration. On membrane fractions, the dissociation-rate constant was lowered by reducing the temperature [9]. The same was true after solubilization of the hormonal receptor. When the [^{3}H] vasopressin-receptor complex was solubilized and stored at 4°C in the presence of a large excess of unlabeled vasopressin, the amount of bound radioactivity recovered after 36 hr was still 61% of that measured immediately after solubilization. Blanks corresponding to the samples, treated as described, but containing no protein, were included in each experimental series. The amount of radioactivity eluted from blanks was < 0.06% of the radioactivity layered at the top of the column. It was < 10% of the specific binding obtained when [^{3}H] vasopressin was used at a concentration of 2 × 10^{-8} M. Recovery in the 1.2-ml eluate of Dextran Blue layered at the top of the column was 79.6 ± 5.5% (mean ± SD of 12 determinations).

Nonspecific binding increased linearly together with the tritiated peptide concentration. The contribution of nonspecific binding to total binding was negligible for [^{3}H] LVP concentrations below 10^{-7} M. However, for the highest doses tested, its contribution to total binding was much greater. Addition of bovine serum albumin 1% or vasopressin 10^{-6} M to the medium used for pre-equilibration and elution of the Bio-gel columns failed to

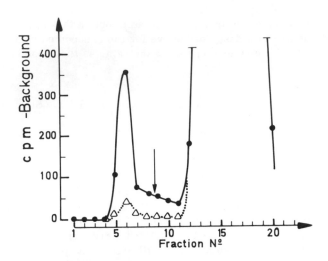

FIG. 10.   Elution pattern of vasopressin bound to soluble receptors. Separation of the hormone-receptor complex from free hormone. Membranes
were solubilized in the presence of 100 mM tris-HCl, pH 8.0; 10 mM MgCl$_2$;
and 0.5% (vol/vol) Triton X-100 at 4°C under continuous stirring. After
centrifugation at 226,000 g for 70 min at 4°C in a Beckman centrifuge
(rotor 50 Ti, 50,000 rpm), 75 µl of the supernatant (total volume 105 µl)
were then incubated at 30°C for 20 min with 3×10^{-8} M [^{3}H]vasopressin
(measurement of total binding: ●). Nonspecific binding was determined
under identical experimental conditions, except that the incubation medium
contained 10^{-5} M unlabeled hormone (△). At the end of the incubation
period, samples were cooled and a 100-µl aliquot layered at the top of a
Bio-gel P-30 column pre-equilibrated at 4°C in 100 mM tris-HCl, pH 8.0;
10 mM MgCl$_2$; and 0.36% Triton X-100. After the sample had penetrated
into the gel, eluant was added; the composition of the eluant medium was
identical to that of the equilibration medium of the columns. Elution was
then performed at 4°C and 10-drop fractions were collected and counted.
Modified from Ref. 52, p. 7888.

reduce the share of nonspecific binding in total binding. Other studies had
shown that tritiated vasopressin was able to bind to bovine serum albumin
[57], to hemoglobin, and to Dextran Blue.

D.   Characterization of Soluble Vasopressin Receptors

To avoid possible differences among membrane preparations, the same
preparation was used for comparing soluble and membraneous receptors.

When the soluble extract was incubated at 30°C in the presence of an inframaximal dose of tritiated vasopressin (2×10^{-8} M) the amount of radioactivity bound at equilibrium did not decrease with time. After 5, 10, 15, and 30 min incubation, the amounts of vasopressin bound were, respectively, 0.145, 0.155, 0.143, and 0.167 pmol/mg protein. This observation indicated that no major inactivation of the hormone occurred in the soluble extract.

Vasopressin binding on the soluble extract was dose-dependent and saturable. For the most sensitive soluble extract, apparent Km for hormone binding was close to that measured on membrane fractions. However, apparent affinity usually decreased (highest apparent Km for binding measured = 1.7×10^{-7} M). Even when affinity decreased, hormonal binding was still cooperative (see Table 3, n: Hill coefficient = 1.39 ± 0.06).

The solubilization yield was 30%, despite the fact that all binding activity had disappeared from the residual pellet of detergent-treated membranes. This might be due to the interaction of detergent or of some other component in the medium with the hormonal receptor. It was observed that low detergent concentrations (0.01%) induced a 40% drop in membrane binding capacity without appearance of any soluble receptor.

TABLE 3. Comparison of Membrane-Bound and Solubilized
Vasopressin Receptors

	Membrane receptor	Soluble receptor
Apparent Km (M)	2×10^{-8}	2×10^{-8}-1.7×10^{-7} (four preparations)
Hill coefficient	1.52 ± 0.11[a]	1.39 ± 0.06[a]
Oxytocin/vasopressin Km ratio	10	10
Dissociation rate constant = k_{-1} (mn^{-1})	0.020 0.035 0.036	0.040 0.042
Maximal binding capacity (pmol/mg protein)	0.8-1.0	0.9-1.2 (free receptor) 3 -3.3 (hormone receptor complex

[a]Standard error on the slope of the linear regression line.

As observed on intact membranes, the soluble receptor was still able to discriminate between different but structurally related neurohypophysial peptides. The oxytocin concentration inducing 50% inhibition of tritiated vasopressin binding (5×10^{-8} M) was 10 times higher than the vasopressin concentration eliciting the same effect. Both oxytocin and vasopressin were able to induce the same maximum inhibition. Taking into account the fact that both specificity of the soluble receptor for neurohypophysial peptides and hormonal binding cooperativity were maintained, it was concluded that no major denaturation of the vasopressin receptor occurred during solubilization.

In addition, the cellular specificity of vasopressin binding was demonstrated at the level of soluble membrane extracts. The same experiment as that described already was carried out using liver plasma membranes prepared and solubilized in exactly the same way as the kidney plasma membranes. Soluble liver extract was able to bind [³H]vasopressin (see Table 4). Very large amounts of unlabeled vasopressin or oxytocin were necessary to induce slight inhibition of [³H]vasopressin binding. Each of the two peptides induced different maximum inhibitions. The [³H]vasopressin binding observed on soluble liver extract probably corresponds to the nonspecific binding observed on kidney plasma membrane extract.

The solubilization yield of hormone-receptor complex formed prior to the addition of detergent to the membranes was almost 100%, whatever the initial level of receptor occupancy. However, when the soluble hormone-receptor complex was further incubated at 30°C, i.e., under conditions

TABLE 4.   [³H]Vasopressin Binding to Liver Membrane-Soluble Extract

Unlabeled peptide added (Molarity)	pmoles [³H]Vasopressin bound per mg protein in presence of:	
	Vasopressin	Oxytocin
0	0.141	0.141
1×10^{-8}	0.118	0.147
2×10^{-8}	0.134	0.126
5×10^{-8}	0.134	0.131
1×10^{-7}	0.124	0.137
1×10^{-6}	0.135	0.096
1×10^{-5}	0.079	0.088
1×10^{-4}	0.052	0.100

TABLE 5. Specific and Nonspecific Binding Activities Present in Separated or Mixed Phases: Solubilization of Free Receptor or Hormone–Complex Receptor[a],[b]

Phase	Binding activity	pmoles [³H]Vasopressin bound per ml			
		Solubilization of free receptor		Solubilization of hormone–receptor complex	
Upper	Total	0.008	0.005[c]	0.517	0.310[c]
	Nonspecific	0.007		0.050	
Lower	Total	0.170	0.238[c]	4.495	6.293[c]
	Nonspecific	0.043		0.364	
Nonseparated	Total	0.042	0.084[c]	2.269	4.538[c]
	Nonspecific	0.033		0.237	

[a] Before solubilization of the hormone–receptor complex, membranes were incubated at 30°C in the presence of 4×10^{-8} M [³H]vasopressin. After solubilization and centrifugation, samples were kept at 4°C. When hormonal receptor was solubilized in the absence of labeled hormone, binding was studied in the presence of 2×10^{-8} M [³H]vasopressin. Incubation was carried out at 30°C for 20 min.

[b] Modified from Ref. 52, p. 7890.

[c] Total amount present in the phase (pmol): lower phase, 1.4 ml; upper phase, 0.6 ml.

permitting reversibility of the hormone-receptor interaction, a spontaneous 70% drop was observed in the maximum binding capacity of the soluble receptor. At equilibrium, the apparent solubilization yield was 30%, a value similar to that obtained after solubilization of the free receptor.

The dissociation-rate constant of the soluble vasopressin-receptor complex was measured in the presence of an excess of unlabeled vasopressin. It was found to be very close to the constant measured for the hormone-receptor complex within the membrane (see Table 3).

From all these results, it seems reasonable to conclude that: (1) Treatment of membranes with Triton X-100 led to complete extraction of the vasopressin receptor. (2) Two forms of receptor appeared during solubilization, one was accessible to the hormone and the other was inaccessible. Neither of these forms was convertible into the other, since even at a high hormonal concentration it was not possible to restore full binding capacity. (3) Previous occupation of the receptor by the hormone prevented the appearance of the inaccessible form of receptor, provided the turnover of bound hormonal molecules was slowed down by lowering the temperature. The appearance of the inaccessible form of receptor might be due to interaction with one or several of the components present in the incubation medium. In connection with this possibility, Table 5 clearly indicates that the concentration of the hormone-receptor complex was higher in the lower phase than in the upper one. Furthermore, when the two phases were mixed, the amount of hormone-receptor complex recovered was only 70% of the amount expected on the basis of measurements performed separately on each phase. In the case of free receptor, the apparent loss in binding capacity due to mixing was much more pronounced (35% recovery only). The composition of the two phases was shown to differ as regards their protein, phospholipid, and cholesterol contents [52]. These observations strongly suggest the presence of a component, mainly located in the upper phase, whose interaction with the receptor would account for the drop in both apparent affinity and maximum binding capacity of the soluble receptor.

ACKNOWLEDGMENTS

The work reported in this chapter was supported by grant No. 220 from the Centre National de la Recherche Scientifique and grant No. 73.3.1206 from the Délégation Générale a la Recherche Scientifique et Technique.

REFERENCES

1. F. Bastide and S. Jard, Biochim. Biophys. Acta, 150:113 (1968).

2. W. I. Baba, A. J. Smith, and M. M. Townshend, Quart. J. Exptl. Physiol., 52:416 (1967).

3. J. Orloff and J. S. Handler, J. Clin. Invest., 41:702 (1962).

4. J. J. Grantham and M. B. Burg, Amer. J. Physiol., 211:255 (1966).

5. E. Brown, D. L. Clarke, V. Roux, and D. H. Sherman, J. Biol. Chem., 238:P.C.852 (1963).

6. W. A. Anderson and E. Brown, Biochim. Biophys. Acta, 67:674 (1963).

7. L. R. Chase and G. D. Aurbach, Science, 159:545 (1968).

8. T. Dousa, O. Hechter, I. L. Schwartz, and R. Walter, Proc. Natl. Acad. Sci. U.S.A., 68:1693 (1971).

9. J. Bockaert, C. Roy, R. Rajerison, and S. Jard, J. Biol. Chem., 248:5922 (1973).

10. B. J. Campbell, G. Woodward, and V. Bord Berg, J. Biol. Chem., 247:6167 (1972).

11. S. Hynie and G. W. G. Sharp, Biochim. Biophys. Acta, 230:40 (1971).

12. H. P. Bär, O. Hechter, I. L. Schwartz, and R. Walter, Proc. Natl. Acad. Sci. U.S.A., 67:7 (1970).

13. J. Bockaert, C. Roy, and S. Jard, J. Biol. Chem., 247:7073 (1972).

14. P. Cuatrecasas, Biochem. Rev., 43:169 (1974).

15. C. Roy, T. Barth, and S. Jard, J. Biol. Chem., 250:3149 (1975).

16. C. Roy, T. Barth, and S. Jard, J. Biol. Chem., 250:3157 (1975).

17. S. Jard, C. Roy, R. Rajerison, T. Barth, and J. Bockaert, Second International Conference on cyclic AMP, Vancouver, July 1974, Advances in cyclic nucleotide research, Raven Press, New York, Vol 5:31 (1975).

18. E. E. Thompson, P. Freychet, and J. Roth, Endocrinology, 91:1199 (1972).

19. J. Marchetti, Experientia, 29:351 (1973).

20. C. T. O. Fong, L. Silver, D. R. Christman, and I. L. Schwartz, Proc. Natl. Acad. Sci. U.S.A., 46:1273 (1960).

21. V. du Vigneaud, C. H. Schneider, J. E. Stouffer, V. V. S. Murti, J. P. Aroskar, and G. Winestock, J. Am. Chem. Soc., 84:409 (1962).

22. C. T. O. Fong, I. L. Schwartz, E. A. Popende, L. Silver, and M. A. Schoessler, J. Am. Chem. Soc., 81:2592 (1959).

23. K. E. Wilzbach, J. Am. Chem. Soc., 79:1013 (1957).

24. I. Sjöholm and L. Carlsson, J. Labelled Compds., 3:3 (1967).

25. L. Carlsson and I. Sjöholm, Acta Chem. Scand., 20:259 (1966).

26. Y. Agishi and J. F. Dingman, Biochem. Biophys. Res. Commun., 18:92 (1965).

27. P. Pradelles, J. L. Morgat, P. Fromageot, M. Camier, D. Bonne, P. Cohen, J. Bockaert, and S. Jard, FEBS Lett., 26:189 (1972).

28. B. J. Campbell, G. Woodward, and V. Borberg, J. Biol. Chem., 247:6167 (1972).

29. J. L. Morgat, H. Lam Thanh, R. Cardinaud, P. Fromageot, J. Bockaert, M. Imbert, and F. Morel, J. Labelled Compds., 3:276 (1970).

30. J. L. Morgat and P. Fromageot, in Radio Pharmaceuticals and Labelled Compounds, Vol. 2, International Atomic Energy Agency, Vienna, 1973, pp. 109–119.

31. J. L. Morgat, H. Lam Thanh, and P. Fromageot, Biochim. Biophys. Acta, 207:374 (1970).

32. M. Camier, R. Alazard, P. Pradelles, J. L. Morgat, P. Fromageot, and P. Cohen, Eur. J. Biochem., 32:207 (1973).

33. R. Axen and S. Ernback, Eur. J. Biochem., 18:351 (1971).

34. P. Cuatrecasas, J. Biol. Chem., 255:3059 (1970).

35. O. H. Lowry, N. J. Rosebrough, A. L. Farr, and R. J. Randall, J. Biol. Chem., 193:265 (1961).

36. E. Stürmer, in Neurohypophysial Hormones and Similar Polypeptides (B. Berde, ed.), Handbook of experimental pharmakologie, Vol. 23, Springer-Verlag, Berlin, 1968, pp. 180–189.

37. G. M. Farquhar and G. E. Palade, Proc. Natl. Acad. Sci. U.S.A., 51:569 (1964).

38. J. K. Choi, J. Cell. Biol., 25:175 (1963).

39. R. M. Hays, M. D. B. Singer, and S. Malamed, J. Cell. Biol., 25:195 (1965).

40. M. Parisi, P. Ripoche, and J. Bourguet, Pflügers Arch., 309:59 (1969).

41. R. M. Rajerison, M. Montegut, S. Jard, and F. Morel, Pflügers Arch., 233:302 (1972).

42. J. Aceves and D. Erlij, J. Physiol. (London), 212:195 (1971).

43. N. Carasso, P. Favard, S. Jard, and R. Rajerison, J. Microscop., 10:315 (1971).

44. J. Bockaert, M. Imbert, S. Jard, and F. Morel, Mol. Pharmacol., 8:230 (1972).

45. E. J. Ariens, J. M. Van Rossum, and P. C. Koopman, Arch. Intern. Pharmacodyn., 127:459 (1960).

46. J. Bockaert, S. Jard, F. Morel, and M. Montegut, Am. J. Physiol., 219:1514 (1970).

47. T. Barth, S. Jard, F. Morel, and M. Montegut, Experientia, 28:962 (1972).

48. P. Emmelot, C. J. Bos, E. L. Benedetti, and P. Rumke, Biochim. Biophys. Acta, 90:126 (1964).

49. D. F. Fitzpatrick, G. R. Davenport, L. Forte, and E. J. Landon, J. Biol. Chem., 244:3561 (1969).

50. J. Ramachandran and V. Lee, Biochem. Biophys. Res. Commun., 41:358 (1970).

51. C. Roy, J. Bockaert, R. Rajerison, and S. Jard, FEBS Lett., 30:329 (1973).

52. C. Roy, R. Rajerison, J. Bockaert, and S. Jard, J. Biol. Chem., 250:7885 (1975).

53. J. P. Changeux, M. Kasai, M. Huchet, and J. C. Meunier, C. R. Acad. Sci., Paris, 270:2864 (1970).

54. P. Cuatrecasas, J. Biol. Chem., 247:1980 (1972).

55. M. L. Dufau, E. H. Charreau, and K. J. Catt, J. Biol. Chem., 248:6973 (1973).

56. A. Helenius and H. Söderlund, Biochim. Biophys. Acta, 307:287 (1973).

57. F. B. Edwards, R. B. Rombauer, and B. J. Campbell, Biochim. Biophys. Acta, 194:234 (1969).

AUTHOR INDEX

Numbers in parentheses are reference numbers and indicate that an author's work is referred to although his name is not cited in text. Underlined numbers give the page on which the complete reference is listed.

Aaronson, S. A., 82(29), 95(29), 97
Ablad, E., 57(33), 71
Abraham, S., 528(44,50), 531
Aceves, J., 678, 703
Achong, B. C., 306(43), 375
Adair, W. L., 481, 483(8), 487, 488(8), 489(8), 490(8), 492(8), 493(8), 494
Adamkiewicz, V. W., 319(83), 377
Adams, R. A., 305, 375
Adelman, R. C., 392(75), 400(75), 412(75), 414(75), 417(75), 425
Agishi, Y., 512(3), 529, 669(26), 676(26), 702
Agre, P., 87(47), 90(47), 98
Ahlquist, R. P., 54(8), 70
Airhart, J., 276, 297
Alazard, R., 672(32), 702
Albert, A., 114(21), 118
Alexander, N. M., 44(15), 51
Alexander, P., 319 (82), 377
Alexander, R. W., 54(7), 59(7,36), 62(7), 70, 71
Allan, D., 490(28), 495
Allan, R., 490(27), 491(27), 495
Alonso, A., 191(42), 196(42), 246, 253(31), 294
Altamirano, M., 3(12), 32

Amer, M. S., 548, 563
Ames, B. N., 237(102), 250
Amherdt, M., 367(192), 383
Amir, S. M., 642(7), 651(7), 654(7), 658(7), 661(7), 662(7), 663
Andersen, N. H., 604(13), 613
Anderson, C. R., 3(6), 32
Anderson, W. A., 668(6), 701
Andreasen, P. A., 411(125), 428
Andreatta, R., 44(18), 52
Andres, G. V., 23(63), 35
Andrews, E. D., 458(53), 475
Andrews, E. P., 152(25), 157, 486(19), 487(19), 495
Anfinsen, C. B., 489(24), 495, 589(43), 590(44), 598, 636(50), 639
Angerwall, L., 318(80), 365(80), 377
Anoddy, H. P., 168(22), 174
Antonioli, J. A., 316(74), 377
Aquaron, R., 645(18), 664
Aragona, C., 567(16), 575(16), 596
Archer, J. A., 253(28), 294, 303(8,14), 313(8), 321(8), 333(8), 335(8), 336(8), 339(8),

(Archer, J. A.)
　340(8), 356(8), 366(14), 369(195,
　196), 370(200), 374, 383, 392(47,
　49,50), 396(47), 397(47,49,50),
　398(47,49,50), 399(47,49), 400
　(109), 402(109), 403(47), 407(47,
　49), 408(47), 410(47,49), 411(47,
　49), 412(109), 414(109), 417(47,
　109), 420(49,50,109,133), 424,
　427, 428, 465(75), 476, 659(40),
　665
Ariens, E. J., 681(45), 703
Armstrong, K. J., 460(59), 475
Arnaud, C. D., 548(29), 549(29),
　552(29), 556(29), 557(29), 561
　(29), 563
Arnberg, H., 14(42), 34
Arnold, A., 54(10), 55(10,11), 70
Aronow, L., 437(15), 473
Aroskar, J. P., 669(21), 676(21),
　702
Arquilla, E. R., 325(101,102,103),
　378, 388(20), 389(20,35,36),
　394(35,36), 423
Ashbrook, J. D., 211(65), 248,
　348(140), 350(140), 380
Ashitaka, Y., 177(19), 191(19), 192
　(19), 245
Ashton, W. D., 372(154), 381
Ashwell, G., 262(61), 281(112,113,
　114), 282(112,113), 295, 298,
　650(26), 664
Assan, R., 47(27), 52, 338(119),
　379, 415(129), 428
Astaldi, A., 319(81), 365(81), 377
Astaldi, G., 319(81), 365(81), 377
Atlas, D., 66(41), 71
Attallah, A. A., 601(10), 613
Auger, J., 490(27), 491(27), 495
Aurbach, G., 56(20,21), 70
Aurbach, G. D., 66(42), 72, 218(88),
　225(98), 249, 303(11), 347(11),
　366(11), 374, 415(128), 428, 535
　(5), 536(5), 538(5), 546(20), 548
　(30), 549(30), 550(32), 552(42),

(Aurbach, G. D.)
　555, 556(42), 560, 561(30),
　562, 563, 564, 668(7), 701
Aurbach, G. O., 457(52), 474
Avruch, J. A., 160(10), 173
Axelrod, J., 54(3), 70
Axen, R., 672, 702

Baba, W. I., 668(2), 701
Bachhawat, 282(117), 298
Bahl, O. P., 262(64), 267, 268
　(64,76), 269, 282(64,123), 296,
　297, 298
Baird, C. E., 600(3), 613, 616
　(1), 637
Bale, W. F., 388(24), 394(79),
　423, 426
Banerjee, S. P., 466(78), 476
Bankal, A., 662(45), 665
Bär, H. P., 55(18), 70, 668(12),
　701
Bar, R. S., 370(200), 383
Baraille, D. P., 171(29), 174
Bargia, G. R., 319(81), 365(81),
　377
Barham, F. W., 392(72), 396
　(72), 398(72), 410(72), 417
　(72), 425, 451(41), 453(41),
　474, 595(46), 598
Barnabei, O., 120(10), 121(10),
　141, 144(4), 156
Barnard, E. A., 31(72), 35
Barr, Y. M., 303(22), 306(43),
　374, 375
Barrantes, F. J., 504(12), 510
Bartels, E., 4(16,18), 5(16), 8
　(18), 33
Barth, T., 669(15,16,17), 681
　(47), 688(15), 689(15,16), 691
　(16,17), 692(17), 701, 703
Bastide, F., 668(1), 701
Bataille, D., 367(192), 383, 395
　(84), 426
Bataille, P., 46(23), 47(23), 52

Bates, R. W., 392(48), 400(48), 412(48), 414(48), 420(48), 424
Bauer, S., 396(91), 426
Baukal, A., 229(100), 237(100), 241(100,106), 243(100), 249, 250
Baukal, A. J., 218(86), 249, 628(44), 639
Baulieu, E. E., 211(64), 248, 340 (126), 380, 418(131), 428
Bauman, A. J., 145(14), 157
Bauminger, S., 616(13), 637
Baxter, J. W. M., 520(32), 530
Beall, R. J., 595(49), 598
Becker, C., 317(69), 377
Becker, J. W., 323(93), 378
Beckman, B., 82(37), 92(37), 97
Bekesi, J. G., 484(13), 494
Bell, J., 200(52), 247
Bellisario, R., 262(64), 267, 268(64), 282(64), 296
Benda, P., 29(71), 35
Benedetti, E. L., 653(32), 664, 682 (48), 703
Ben Haim, D., 3(7), 32
Benjamin, T. L., 481(7), 494
Bennett, G. M., 5(22), 33
Bennett, M. V. L., 2(3), 32
Bennett, V., 74(4,5,6,10), 77(4,10), 82(5,10,33,36), 85(5), 88, 90(5, 10,33), 91(33), 92(36), 93, 94(5, 36), 95(33,36), 96, 97, 392(65), 396(65), 407(65), 425, 437(12), 439(12), 473
Bentley, P. J., 515(15), 519(26), 529, 530
Benyesh-Melnick, M., 304(26), 374
Benzonana, G., 131, 132, 141
Berger, E., 520(30), 530
Bergeron, J. J. M., 387(12), 401 (12), 412(12), 414(12), 422
Berkson, J., 372(153,155), 381
Berman, M., 211(76), 213(76), 248
Bernhardt, S. A., 356(167), 382
Bernstein, J., 20(60), 35
Berry, M. N., 396, 426

Berson, S. A., 47(26,27), 52, 211(60,62), 247, 248, 254(39), 255(39), 294, 330(105), 338 (119), 340(124), 348(124), 379, 380, 387, 388(21), 389(15), 390(15), 391, 395(21), 403(21), 415(129), 422, 423, 424, 428, 645(17), 664
Bertino, R. E., 211(71), 248
Bertrand, J., 392(77), 425, 626 (35), 630(35), 638
Bethel, R. A., 610(18), 613
Bhalla, V. K., 100(2,4,6), 101 (2,4), 109(14), 113(2,6), 115 (6), 116(6,14), 117, 120(6), 140, 200(51), 247, 262(63), 268(70), 295, 296
Bianco, A. R., 303(6,7), 312(6), 313, 314(7), 315(7), 356(177), 357(177), 364(177), 367(6,177), 369(7), 371(177), 373(177), 373, 382, 397(99,100), 427
Bicking, J. B., 611(20), 614
Biener, J., 395(83), 426
Biesecker, G., 14(35,44), 18(44), 33, 34
Bihler, D. A., 389(34), 423
Bikle, D., 534(1), 562
Bilzekian, J. P., 56(20,21), 70
Birkinshaw, M., 566, 572, 596
Birnbaumer, L., 121(14), 122 (14), 136(29), 141, 142, 144 (3), 147(15), 156, 157, 160(1, 2,3,4,5,6,7,8), 163(2), 164 (2), 165(2), 166(4), 167(4), 168(2,4), 169(4,5,24,25), 171 (4,25), 172(31), 173, 174, 218 (89), 249, 253(23,25), 255(46), 293, 295, 316(68), 332(108), 377, 379, 400(106), 401(106), 411(123), 427, 428, 521(33), 530, 557(47), 561(47), 564, 595(47), 598, 657(37), 662 (37), 664
Bitensky, M. W., 168(21), 174

Blanchett-Mackie, J., 38(7), 51
Blaszó, G., 320(87), 378
Blecher, M., 121, 123(18,19), 135
(27), 137(16), 141, 142, 269(81),
270(81), 296, 402(120), 403(120),
428, 586(39), 597
Bliss, C. I., 111(18), 118
Blondel, B., 367(192), 383
Blumenfeld, O. O., 487(20), 488,
495
Blundell, T. L., 389(37), 418(37),
423
Bockaert, J., 253(34), 294, 512(2),
516(20), 529, 530, 668(9,13),
669(17,27,29), 670(27,29), 671
(29), 672(27,29), 673(27), 674
(27), 676(44), 677(27,29), 679
(44), 680(44), 681(44,46), 682
(9), 684(9,13), 685(9,51), 686
(9), 690(9), 691(17), 692(17),
693(52), 695(9), 696(52), 699
(52), 700(52), 701, 702, 703
Bockman, R. S., 466(79), 476
Bodansky, O., 265(66), 266(66), 296
Bode, J., 18(55), 34
Boesman, M., 77(24), 97
Bogard, M., 57(33), 71
Bohlen, P., 22(64), 35, 581(38), 597
Bohn, H., 44(18), 52
Bohonos, N., 451(35), 474
Bolen, R. J., 270(98), 297
Bonne, D., 669(27), 670(27), 672
(27), 673(27), 674(27), 677(27),
702
Boquet, P., 13(33), 33, 459(57), 475
Borberg, V., 617(30), 638, 669(28),
676(28), 702
Bord Berg, V., 668(10), 682(10), 701
Boroff, D. A., 14(46), 34
Borris, D. P., 504(12), 510
Bos, C. J., 653(32), 664, 682(48),
703
Boshell, B. R., 392(73), 400(73),
412(73), 414(73), 425
Bosmann, H. B., 91(53), 98

Boucher, M. E., 168(18,19,23),
173, 174, 388(25), 423
Boue, A., 283(129), 299
Boue, J. G., 283(129), 299
Bourguet, J., 678(40), 703
Bourke, J. R., 642(9,10), 650
(10), 651(10), 655(10), 657(10),
661(10), 662(10), 663(47), 663,
665
Bourne, H. R., 316(55), 366(55),
370, 376
Bourrillon, R., 490(25), 495
Boyd, L. F., 367(182,183), 382
Boyd, N. R. H., (36), 530
Boyd, W. C., 480(1), 494
Boyer, P., 400(112), 427
Boyett, J. D., 318(79), 377
Boyle, I. T., 534(2), 562
Boyle, J. M., 74(12), 96
Boyle, W., 523, 530
Boyüm, A., 311, 312, 376, 397
(98), 426
Bradley, C., 567(17), 575(17),
596
Bradley, R. M., 82(29), 95(29),
97
Bradshaw, R. A., 367(182,183),
382
Brady, R. N., 14(45), 18(45), 34
Brady, R. O., 82(27,29,30,31),
95(27,29,30), 97
Brand, J. S., 547(23), 548(23),
550(35), 563
Brandenburg, D., 389(40), 390
(40), 395(83), 400(40), 403(40),
406(40), 408(40), 412(40), 414
(40), 418(40), 424, 426
Brange, J., 388(27), 423
Braunstein, G. D., 287(130), 291
(134), 299
Brenner, M., (23), 141
Bretscher, M. S., 152(24), 157
Bricker, L. A., 544(18), 546(18),
550(18), 562
Broder, S. W., 307(50), 308, 376

Brodie, B. B., 49(28), 50(28), 52, 164(15), 173, 608(15), 613

Broer, Y., 389(42), 390(42), 396 (42), 397(42, 93), 399(42), 403 (42), 407(42), 408(42), 409(42), 410(42, 93), 411(42), 417(42), 424, 426

Bromer, W. W., 168(22, 23), 173, 174, 388(25), 423

Brown, E., 668(5, 6), 701

Brown, G., 313(59), 376

Brown, T. G., 54(10), 55(10, 11), 70

Brown, W. E. L., 371, 372, 381

Brundish, D. E., 46, 52

Buchanan, K. D., 127(22), 141

Buell, D. N., 253(28), 294, 303(8, 11, 25), 304(30), 306(25, 30), 307 (25), 308(30, 52), 309, 310, 311, 313(8), 321(8), 323(95), 324(25, 95), 331(30), 333(8), 335(8), 336 (8), 339(8, 121), 340(8, 122), 347 (11), 356(8), 366(11), 369(199), 374, 375, 376, 378, 379, 383, 392(47, 53), 396(47), 397(47, 53, 96, 97), 398(47, 53, 96, 97), 399(47), 402(96, 97), 403(47), 406(96, 97), 407(47, 53), 408(47), 410(47), 411 (47), 415(96, 97), 417(47), 424, 426, 458(54), 465(75), 475, 476, 659(40), 665

Bunzli, H., 471(99, 100), 477

Burg, M. B., 668(4), 701

Burgen, A. S. V., 54(1), 70

Burger, H. G., 177(3), 190(3), 216 (3), 217(3), 245, 262(60), 295

Burger, M. M., 281(110), 298, 480 (3, 4), 481(7), 482(11), 483(11), 486(11), 487(11), 488(11), 489(11), 494, 91(52), 98

Burk, D. J., 346, 380

Burke, G., (6), 616(10), 637

Burleigh, B. D., 208(57), 247

Butcher, R. W., 55(17), 70, 120(1), 140, 144(1), 156, 252(20), 293,

(Butcher, R. W.)
600(3), 613, 616(1, 5), 637

Butel, J. S., 304(26), 374

Cadenas, E. H., 451(44), 474

Calek, A., Jr., 316(67), 377

Calin, H., 451(45), 474

Callop, P. M., 487(20), 488(20), 495

Camier, M., 669(27), 670(27), 672(27, 32), 673(27), 674(27), 677(27), 702

Campbell, B. J., 617, 638, 668 (10), 669(28), 676(28), 682, 696(57), 701, 702, 703

Canfield, R. E., 177(14), 245, 252(5), 259(5), 270(5, 93), 293, 297

Canterbury, J. M., 544(18), 546 (18), 550(18), 562

Carafoli, E., 616(22), 638

Carasso, N., 679(43), 703

Carbone, P. P., 291(134), 299

Cardinaud, R., 512(2), 529, 669 (29), 670(29), 671(29), 672(29), 677(29), 702

Carlsen, R. B., 643(11), 663

Carlson, S., 252(14), 253(14), 293

Carlsson, L., 669(24, 25), 676 (24), 702

Caron, M., 54(4), 58(4), 59(4, 35, 36), 62(4), 65(4), 70, 71

Caron, M. G., 54(5), 55(5), 56 (5), 58(5), 59(5), 62(5), 64(5), 69(47), 70, 72

Carpenter, C. C. J., 74(14), 96

Carraway, T. F., Jr., 642(7), 651(7), 654(7), 658(7), 661(7), 662(7), 663

Carroll, R. C., 18(58), 35

Cash, W. D., 630(43), 639

Cashman, D. C., 282(116), 298

Castro, A., 177(2), 191(2), 196

(Castro, A.)
  (2), <u>245</u>
Castro, A. E., 177(4), 191(4,42),
  196(4,42), <u>245</u>, <u>246</u>, 253(30,31),
  <u>294</u>
Catt, K. J., 177(3,5,6,7,10,11,18,
  20), 178(5), 179(5,31), 180(32),
  181(32,33,34), 188(18,35,36),
  190(3,5,37), 192(11,37), 193(33,
  46), 195(5,10), 197(5,11,20,37,
  48), 199(18), 200(34), 203(5,7,
  10,18,20,53), 205(32,37), 206
  (48), 208(10,55), 211(78,79),
  213(78,79), 216(3), 217(3,79,84),
  218(79,86), 219(18,20,33,79),
  221(10), 222(10,79), 223(90,91,
  92,93,94,95,96,97), 225(5,10,
  90,91,93), 226(90,91), 228(91,
  97), 229(7,18,31,53,91,93,94,
  100), 230(91), 231(91,94,97),
  233(93), 235(93,94), 237(100),
  239(92,96), 241(32,92,94,100,
  106), 243(33,93,100), <u>245</u>, <u>246</u>,
  <u>247</u>, <u>248</u>, <u>249</u>, <u>250</u>, 252(10,11),
  253(11), 262(57,58,60), 268(10,
  75), 269(84), 270(97,99), 275(99),
  278(99), 281(111), 282(124,125),
  <u>293</u>, <u>295</u>, <u>296</u>, <u>297</u>, <u>298</u>, <u>299</u>,
  (141), 356(161), <u>380</u>, <u>381</u>, 595
  (50), <u>598</u>, 628(44), <u>639</u>, 662(45),
  <u>665</u>, 693(55), <u>703</u>
Causton, A., 544(17), <u>562</u>
Cava, M. P., 6, <u>33</u>
Cha, S., 13(34), <u>33</u>
Chace, N. M., 483(12), 484(12),
  485(12), 486(12), 487(12), 490
  (12), <u>494</u>
Chadwick, A., 574(26), <u>597</u>
Chaikoff, I. L., 528(44), <u>531</u>
Chambaut, A. M., 401(118), <u>428</u>
Chan, J., 576(32), <u>597</u>
Chan, W. Y., 515(18), <u>529</u>
Chance, R. E., 388(28), <u>423</u>
Chander, M. L., 337(118), <u>379</u>
Chang, H. W., 14(40), 18(40), 25

(Chang, H. W.)
  (40), <u>34</u>, 69(44), <u>72</u>
Chang, K.-J., 57(28), <u>71</u>, 82(33),
  90(33), 91, 95(33), <u>97</u>, 437(12),
  439(12,19), 440(20), 441(25),
  442(27), <u>473</u>
Chang, L. L., 616(10), <u>637</u>
Changeaux, J. P., 241(104), <u>250</u>
Changeaux, J.-P., 3(11), 13(33),
  14(36), 15(49,50), 16(52), 18
  (36), 25(36), 26(66), 29(71),
  31, <u>32</u>, <u>33</u>, <u>34</u>, <u>35</u>, 356(151,
  152), 371, <u>381</u>, 459(57), <u>475</u>,
  693(53), <u>703</u>
Channing, C. P., 177(21), 191
  (39), <u>245</u>, <u>246</u>, 252(5,7,19),
  259(5,7), 270(5,94), <u>293</u>, <u>297</u>
Chard, T., 522(34), (36), <u>530</u>
Charreau, E. H., 223(91,92,93,
  94), 225(91,93), 226(91), 228
  (91), 229(91,93,94), 230(91),
  231(91,94), 233(93), 235(93,
  94), 239(92), 241(92,94), 243
  (93,94), <u>249</u>, 269(84), <u>296</u>,
  693(55), <u>703</u>
Charveau, E. H., 270(99), 275
  (99), 278(99), <u>297</u>
Chase, L. R., 171(28), <u>174</u>, 668
  (7), <u>701</u>
Chessin, L. N., 304(28), <u>375</u>
Chino, T. H., 463(63), <u>475</u>
Cho, M. I., 262(55), <u>295</u>
Cho, T. M., 437(14), <u>473</u>, 504
  (12), <u>510</u>
Chobsieng, P., 616(13), <u>637</u>
Choi, J. K., 675(38), <u>702</u>
Chorlton, B., 544(17), <u>562</u>
Chou, J. Y., 316(88), 366(88),
  367(88), <u>378</u>
Christ, E. J., 600(2), <u>613</u>
Christiansen, A. H., 388(27),
  <u>423</u>
Christman, D. R., 669(20), 676
  (20), <u>701</u>
Chuang, J., 536(8), 543(8), 553

(Chuang, J.)
  (45), 556(45), 557(45), 559(45),
  561(45), 562, 564
Cirillo, V. J., 600(4, 5), 610(4, 17,
  19), 613, 614, 616(3), 637
Civen, M., 38(2), 51
Clark, A. J., 431(1, 2), 472
Clark, D. G., 13(32), 14(32), 33
Clarke, D. L., 668(5), 701
Clarkson, B., 303(20), 374
Clemmons, D. R., 392(64), 397(64),
  406(64), 407(64), 425, 471(91),
  476
Clifford, P., 307(46), 375
Cline, M. J., 313(65), 315(65), 377
Closset, J., 643(12, 13), 646(22),
  660(42), 661(42), 663, 664, 665
Coates, C. W., 3(12), 32
Cochin, J., 500, 510
Cohen, J. B., 16(52), 34
Cohen, P., 669(27), 670(27), 672
  (27), 673(27), 674(27), 677(27),
  702
Cohn, D., 535(6), 562
Cole, F., 252(6), 259(6), 268(73),
  293, 296
Colella, D. F., 55(11), 70
Coleman, J. S., 211(59), 247, 348
  (136), 380
Colquhoun, D., 3(8), 32
Colton, T., 111(16), 117
Colwell, J. A., 550(37), 563
Connell, G. E., 282(115), 298
Connolly, T. N., 330(107), 379
Conway, A., 356(165), 382
Cooper, D., 14(39), 18(39), 34
Cooper, J., 372(156), 381, 579(36),
  597
Cooperstein, S. J., 43(14), 51, 265
  (67), 266(67), 296
Coulam, C. B., 268(71), 270(71),
  296
Coulson, P., 262(59), 295
Courtney, K. D., 23(63), 35
Coverstone, M., 54(4, 5, 6), 55(5),

(Coverstone, M.)
  56(5), 58(4, 5, 6), 59(4, 5, 6),
  62(4, 5, 6), 64(5), 65(4), 70
Cowburn, D. A., 8(25), 9(26), 10
  (26, 27), 11(26, 28), 12(26, 28),
  15(26, 48b), 16(26), 18(26),
  26(25, 26), 27(26), 28(25, 26,
  27), 33, 34
Cowie, A. T., 566(3), 574(3),
  596
Coy, E., 513(6), 529
Cragoe, E. J., 611(20), 614
Craig, L. C., 535, 562
Craig, S., 95(55), 98
Crepy, O., 68(43), 72
Crofford, O. B., 172(32), 174
Crosby, W. H., 313(66), 377
Crovetti, F., 616(22), 638
Crumpton, M. J., 490(27, 28, 29),
  491(27), 492(29), 495
Csapo, A. I., 520(31), 530
Cuatrecasas, P., 57(28, 29), 69
  (45), 71, 72, 74(4, 5, 6, 7, 8, 9,
  10), 76(22), 77(4, 9, 10, 22), 79,
  81, 82(5, 7, 9, 10, 33, 34, 35, 36),
  83(7, 22), 84(7, 22, 42, 43, 45,
  46), 85(5, 7), 86(7, 43), 87(7,
  42, 47), 88, 89, 90(5, 10, 33,
  42, 47, 48, 49), 91(33), 92(7,
  36, 42), 93, 94(5, 34, 36), 95
  (33, 36, 55), 96, 97, 98, 120
  (3), 137(30), 140, 142, 225
  (99), 241(105), 249, 250, 253
  (37), 269(82), 270(87, 89), 275
  (87), 294, 296, 297, 313(57),
  323(57, 92), 337(113), 340(113),
  348(186, 187), 376, 378, 379,
  381, 383, 386(2, 9), 392(2, 57,
  58, 59, 60, 61, 63, 65, 66, 67),
  396(57, 60, 65, 67, 89), 397(66,
  95), 398(57, 60, 66, 95), 399
  (57, 66), 400(58, 61, 102, 103),
  401(59, 103), 402(61, 63), 403
  (2, 57, 58, 59, 61, 63), 406(61,
  63), 407(57, 58, 59, 60, 61, 63,

(Cuatrecasas, P.)
65, 67, 89), 408(57, 58), 410(57,
66), 411(57, 95), 412(2, 58, 59),
414(58, 59), 415(61, 63), 417(57,
58, 59, 61, 63), 422, 425, 426,
427, 431(4, 5), 433(4), 434(4),
435(10), 436(10), 437(4, 10, 12),
438(10, 16, 17), 439(12, 18, 19),
440(20), 441(10, 25), 442(4, 27),
443, 444(28, 29), 446, 447, 448
(10), 449(10), 450(28), 451(39,
40, 42), 452(39), 453(29, 39, 40,
42, 47), 454(39, 42), 455(29, 40,
47, 49, 50, 51), 457(51), 458(47,
51), 459(51), 460(51, 58, 61, 62),
461(47), 462(47), 463(58, 62, 64,
65), 464(49, 50), 465(73), 466
(73, 77, 78), 467(73, 77, 81, 82, 83),
468, 469(83), 470(83, 90), 471
(16, 49), 472, 473, 474, 475, 476,
489, 495, 507. 510, 566(2), 575
(2), 580, 581, 588, 589(43), 590
(44), 595(2), 596, 597, 598, 636
(50), 639, 659(39), 665, 668(14),
672, 693(54), 701, 702, 703
Culp, B., 29(70), 30(70), 35
Cumar, F. A., 82(27), 95(27), 97
Cunningham, B. A., 323(93), 378
Curnow, R. T., 630(40), 638
Curran, P. F., 342(130), 380
Cutfield, J. F., 389(37), 418(37),
423
Cutfield, S. M., 389(37), 418(37),
423
Czech, M. P., 451(38), 474
Czernik, A. J., 630(43), 639

Dairman, W., 22(64), 35, 581(38),
597
Dakuhara, Y., 460(60), 463(60), 475
Daly, J. W., 500, 510
Daniel, C. W., 528(49), 531
Daniel, E. E., 400(115), 427
Danzo, B. J., 177(22), 245, 259(54),

(Danzo, B. J.)
266(68), 270(95), 295, 296,
297
Daughaday, W. H., 111(15), 117,
253(27), 294, 392(62), 400(62),
403(62), 407(62), 412(62), 414
(62), 417(62), 425, 450(34),
451(34), 474
Davenport, G. R., 551(41), 564,
682(49), 703
David, G. S., 463(63), 475, 645
(16), 664
Davis, B. J., 592, 598
Dawson, B. F., 535(5), 536(5),
538(5), 546(20), 562, 563
Dazord, A., 46(23), 47(23), 52,
626(35), 630(35), 638
Deal, W., 4(18), 7(21), 8(18, 21),
9(21), 33
Deana, A. A., 6(24), 33
DeCarlin, M., 504(12), 510
Dedman, M. L., 44, 52
De Falco, R. J., 319(85), 378
Deftos, L. J., 535(5), 536(5),
538(5), 562
de Harven, E., 303(20), 374
Dekker, A., 616(4), 637
de Krestser, D. M., 262(60),
295
DeKretser, D. M., 177(3, 6),
190(3), 216(3), 217(3), 245,
252(11), 253(11), 293
Delaney, R., 77(24), 97
DeLuca, H. F., 534(2), 562
De Meyts, P., 211(77), 213(77),
215(77), 248, 356(177), 357
(176, 177, 178, 179, 180, 181),
359(176), 361(176), 362, 364
(176, 177, 178, 179, 180, 181),
365(179), 366, 367(176, 177),
369(199), 370(200), 371(177),
373(176, 177), 382, 383, 392
(51, 53), 397(51, 53), 398(53),
407(53), 408(51), 417(51), 418
(132), 424, 428, 448, 474,

(De Meyts, P.)
  660(41), 665
Demura, H. , 253(38), 256(38), 294
Den, H. , 82(28), 95(28), 97
DeOme, K. B. , 528(49), 531
deRobertis, E. , 504, 510
DeRubertis, F. R. , 630(40), 638
Desbuquois, B. , 84(45), 98, 225(98),
  249, 270(89), 297, 392(59), 400
  (102), 401(59), 403(59), 407(59),
  412(59), 414(59), 415(128), 417
  (59), 425, 427, 428, 444(28), 446
  (28), 450(28), 451(28), 457(52),
  471(95, 96), 473, 474, 477
Desjardin, C. , 107(13), 108(13), 117
De Zoeten, L. W. , 388(22), 389(31),
  392(22), 423
DiBella, F. , 548, 549(29), 552, 556,
  557, 561, 563
Dievard, J. C. , 490(25), 495
Dill, I. K. , 451(35), 474
Dingman, J. F. , 512(3), 529, 669
  (26), 676(26), 702
Dionne, V. E. , 3(8), 32
Dixon, J. E. , 508(17), 510
Dodge, J. T. , 486, 495
Dodson, E. J. , 389(37), 418(37),
  423
Dodson, G. G. , 389(37), 418(37),
  423
Dole, W. P. , 507(15), 510
Dolly, J. O. , 31(72), 35
Douglas, S. D. , 304(28), 375
Dousa, T. P. , 548(29), 549(29),
  552(29), 556(29), 557(29), 561
  (29), 563, 668(8), 701
Dreyer, W. J. , 137, 142
Duchon, G. , 400(115), 427
Dufau, M. L. , 177(5, 7, 10, 11, 18,
  20), 178(5), 179(5, 31), 180(32),
  181(32, 33), 188(18, 35, 36), 190
  (5, 37), 192(11, 37), 193(33, 46),
  195(5, 10), 197(5, 11, 20, 37, 48),
  199(18), 203(5, 7, 10, 18, 20, 53),
  205(32, 37), 206(48), 208(10, 55),

(Dufau, M. L.)
  219(18, 20, 33), 221(10), 222
  (10), 223(90, 91, 92, 93, 94, 95,
  96, 97), 225(5, 10, 90, 91, 93),
  226(90, 91), 228(91, 97), 229
  (7, 18, 31, 53, 91, 93, 94, 100),
  230(91), 231(91, 94, 97), 233
  (93), 235(93, 94), 237(100),
  239(92, 96), 241(32, 92, 94, 100,
  106), 243(33, 93, 94, 100), 245,
  246, 247, 249, 250, 252(10),
  262(57, 58), 268(10, 75), 269
  (84), 270(97, 99), 275(99), 278
  (99), 281(111), 282(124, 125),
  293, 295, 296, 297, 298, 299,
  (141), 380, 595(50), 598, 693
  (55), 703
Duguid, J. R. , 16(51, 53), 34
Dulak, N. C. , 464(71), 471(93,
  94), 475, 477
Dumm, M. E. , 317(70), 377
Dumont, J. , 441(24), 473, 642(4),
  663
Dunham, E. , 468(87), 476
Dunlop, D. , 55(12), 70
Dunnick, J. , 56(22), 71, 120(10),
  121(10, 13), 141
Dunning, H. N. , 270(98), 297
du Vigneaud, V. , 669(21), 676
  (21), 702
Dwiggins, C. W. , Jr. , 270(98),
  297
Dziak, R. , 550(35), 563

Eagle, H. , 651(27), 664
Eaker, D. , 14(42), 34
Eakins, K. E. , 610(18), 613
Earle, W. R. , 467(86), 476
Ebner, K. E. , (47), 531
Eckert, I. , 282(118), 298
Edelhoch, E. , 388(30), 423
Edelhoch, H. , 356(169), 357(174),
  382
Edelman, I. , 498(1), 502(1), 506

(Edelman, I.)
  (1, 14), 509, 510
Edelman, P. M., 388(17), 395(17),
  422
Edelstein, S. J., 18(58), 35
Edwards, F. B., 696(57), 703
Edwards, P., 396(91), 426
Egan, S. M., 517, 530
Eisen, H. J., 395(87), 398(87), 426
Eisen, S. A., 313(58), 376
Eisman, J. A., 547(25), 549(25, 31),
  554(25), 555(46), 556(46), 558(25,
  46), 560(25), 561(25), 563, 564
Ek, L., 57(33), 71
Ekins, R. P., 211(61), 247
El-Allawy, R. M. M., 396(90), 426,
  451(43), 453(43), 474
Eldefrawi, A. T., 18(57), 25(57), 34
Eldefrawi, M. R., 18(57, 58), 25(57),
  34, 35
Ellman, G. L., 20, 23, 35
Elmore, D. T., 127(22), 141
Emmelot, P., 653, 664, 682, 703
Enders, J. F., 304(27), 375
Engel, W., 177(23), 245
Englander, T., 319(82), 377
Entlicher, G., 490(26), 492(26), 495
Epstein, M. A., 303(22), 306(43),
  374, 375
Erlij, D., 678, 703
Ernback, S., 672, 702
Eshkol, A., 177(1), 244
Esmann, V., 317(72), 318(72), 377
Espeland, D. H., 177(13), 191(13),
  245
Evans, W. H., 387(12), 401(12),
  412(12), 414(12), 422
Exton, J. H., 164(14), 173
Eylan, E., 319(82), 377
Eylar, E. H., 281(104), 297

Fahey, J. L., 304(30), 305(34), 306
  (30), 308(30), 331(30), 375
Fain, J. N., 451(37, 38), (48), 474,

(Fain, J. N.)
  630(43), 639
Fairbanks, G., 26, 27, 28, 35,
  276(102), 297
Falconer, I. R., 566, 572, 596
Faloona, G. R., 171(26), 174
Farber, S., 305(36), 375
Farmer, T. H., 44(17), 52
Farquhar, G. M., 675(37), 702
Farr, A. L., 42(12), 51, 135(28),
  142, 256(48), 259(48), 295,
  503(11), 510, 523(39), 530,
  538(9), 562, 568(22), 580(22),
  597, 617(31), 638, 675(35),
  702
Farr, N. J., 23(62), 35
Favard, P., 679(43), 703
Fayet, G., 642(5, 6), 646(19, 20,
  21, 22), 647(23), 651(5, 6), 652
  (6, 20, 21, 29), 655(6), 658(5, 6,
  38), 660(42), 661(6, 38, 42),
  662(23), 663(46), 663, 664, 665
Featherstone, R. M., 23(63), 35
Fedak, S. A., 66(42), 72, 552
  (42), 556(42), 564
Feigelson, P., 282(120), 298
Feinstein, H., 56(23), 71
Felber, J. P., 316(74), 377
Feldman, H., 211(69), 213(69),
  248
Feldman, H. A., 211(70), 213
  (70), 248, 348(137), 380
Felix, J. M., 389(33), 394(33),
  423
Fellows, R. E., 576(33), 597
Fenzi, G., 663(46), 665
Ferguson, K. A., 151, 154, 157
Ferguson, R. N., 356(169), 382
Fialkow, P. J., 307(46), 375
Field, J., 317(71), 377, 616(4),
  637
Field, J. B., 144(5), 156, 642(2),
  654(2, 34), 655(2, 34), 663, 664
Field, M., 74(3, 13), 96
Figarova, V., 191(38), 246

Filler, R., 616(26), 638

Filmer, D., 356(162), 357(162), 381

Finegold, I., 305(34), 375

Finkelstein, R. A., 74(1), 77(1,24), 82(1), 83(39), 96, 97, 98

Finn, F. M., 40(9,10), 41(9,10), 43(9,10), 46(9), 51(9,10,29,30, 31), 51, 52

Finney, D. H., 515, 529

Finney, D. J., 111(17), 118

Fischman, D. A., 487(23), 493(23), 495

Fishman, P. H., 74(10), 77(10), 82 (10,29,31), 90(10), 95(29), 96, 97

Fitzpatrick, D. F., 551, 564, 682, 703

Fitzpatrick, R. J., 515(15,17), 529

Flack, J. D., 616(2), 637

Flanagan, R. W. J., 127(22), 141

Flatters, M., 515(16), 529

Fleck, U., 14(46), 34

Fleischer, S., 486(18), 495, 616 (16), 630(16), 637

Fletcher, J. E., 211(65), 248, 348 (140), 350(140), 380

Fletcher, M. A., 121(11), 141, 144 (12,13), 148(13), 152(26), 156, 157

Flores, J., 82(37), 92(37), 97

Foley, G. E., 305(36), 375

Follet, B. K., 515, 529

Folley, S. J., 522(35), 530, 574(26, 27), 597

Fong, C. T. O., 669(20,22), 676 (20), 701, 702

Forgue, E., 387(13), 400(13,114), 401(13,114), 402(13,114), 403 (114), 407(114), 408(114), 412 (114), 414(114), 417(114), 420 (13,114), 421(13,114), 422, 427

Forsling, M. L., 522(34), (36), 530

Forsyth, I. A., 574(26,27), 597

Forte, L., 551(41), 564, 682 (49), 703

Fouchereau, M., 389(42), 390 (42), 396(42), 397(42,93), 399 (42), 403(42), 407(42), 408 (42), 409(42), 410(42,93), 411 (42), 417(42), 424, 426

Fowlkes, B. J., 323(95), 324(95), 378

Franchimont, P., 330(106), 379

Frank, B. H., 168(19), 174

Frank, R. N., 372(157), 381

Franklin, G. I., 14(37), 34

Franklin, H. A., 303(17), 374

Franks, D. J., 630(42), 638

Frantz, W. L., 566(12), 569, 596, 597

Frazier, G. R., 348(139), 380

Frazier, W. A., 367(182,183), 382

Freeman, C., 392(75), 400(75), 412(75), 414(75), 417(75), 425

Freychet, P., 171(29), 174, 218 (85), 249, 255(43), 268(78), 269(78), 294, 296, 302(5), 303 (5), 312(5), 313(5), 321(90,91), 324(91), 334(112), 336(112), 337(112), 338(91), 339(112), 340(90,112), 348(112), 356 (112), 357(178), 364(178), 366 (178), 367(192), 369(197), 370 (200), (98), 373, 378, 379, 382. 383, 386(4), 387(13,14), 388(26), 389(14,26,38,39,40, 41,42,43), 390(26,38,39,40, 41,43), 391(26,42,43), 392 (38,41,45,52), 393(26,38), 394(38,41,52,78), 395(84), 396(14,26,42), 397(42,43,45, 93), 398(45), 399(38,42,43, 45), 400(4,13,14,26,38,39, 40,41,52,78,108,113,114), 401(13,14,114,117), 402(13, 39,108,113,114), 403(14,40, 42,45,78,114), 405(14,41,122),

(Freychet, P.)
406(40,41,52,122), 407(38,39,
41,42,45,52,78,114,122), 408
(38,40,42,52,78,114), 409(42),
410(42,93), 411(41,42,45), 412
(14,26,38,39,40,41,52,78,108,
114,122), 414(14,26,38,39,40,41,
52,78,108,114,122), 415(52),
416(41), 417(38,39,41,42,52,78,
114), 418(14,39,40,41,52,122,
132), 420(13,39,41,108,114,134,
135), 421(13,113,114), 422, 423,
424, 425, 426, 427, 428, 444(30,
31,32), 448(32), 450(32), 465
(74), 474, 476, 512(1), 529, 669
(18), 701
Frieden, C., 357(172), 382
Friend, D. S., 396, 426
Friesen, H. G., 120(5,8), 140,
241(107), 250, 252(16), 257(52),
293, 295, 392(69), 400(69), 403
(69), 407(69), 412(69), 414(69),
425, 433(8), 447(8), 471(97,98),
473, 477, 566(7,8,9,10,11),
567(11,13,14,15,16,17,19), 568
(8), 570(8), 571(8), 573(7,8),
574(7,8), 575(7,10,11,13,15,16,
17,28,29), 576(7,30,31,32,34),
579(9), 584(9), 585(9), 586(9),
587(9), 589(9), 591(9), 593(9),
596, 597
Fritz, H., 282(118), 298
Froesch, E. R., 406(121), 428,
471(99,100), 477
Fromageot, P., 13(33), 33, 459(57),
475, 512(2), 529, 669(27,29,30),
670(27,29-31), 671(29), 672(27,
29,32), 673(27), 674(27), 677
(27,29), 702
Frost, S., 630(43), 639
Frowein, J., 177(23), 245
Fuchs, S., 636(50), 639
Fudenberg, H. H., 304(28), 375
Fujino, M., 44(19), 52
Fujiwara, R., 44(19), 52

Fuller, R. W., 168(22), 174
Fulpius, B., 13, 33
Fulpuis, B. W., 14(39), 18(39),
34

Gagne, H. T., 528(50), 531
Galli, C., 145(14), 157
Gammeltoft, S., 84(44), 86(44),
98, 392(74,76), 396(74), 398
(74,76,101), 399(74), 403(74),
406(76), 407(74), 408(74), 410
(74,76), 411(74,76,124,125),
418(74,76), 425, 427, 428, 434
(9), 439(9), 473, 595(48), 598
Gandy, H. M., 253(38), 256(38),
294
Gardner, J. D., 74(12), 96, 318
(78), 377, 392(46), 398(46),
403(46), 407(46), 410(46), 411
(46), 424, 467(80), 476
Garrett, C. J., 388(18,23), 395
(18), 423
Garrison, M. M., 392(48), 400
(48), 412(48), 414(48), 420
(48), 424
Garwin, J. L., 463(66), 475
Gavin, J. R., 211(77), 213(77),
215(77), 248
Gavin, J. R., Jr., 465(74), 468
(74), 476
Gavin, J. R., III, 253(28), 270
(88), 275(88), 294, 297, 302,
303(5,8,9,10,11,14,16,25),
306(25), 307(25), 308, 309,
310, 311, 312, 313(5,8), 321
(8,10), 323, 324(25), 325(9,
10), 333(8), 334(10), 335, 336
(10), 339(10,121), 340(8,10,
122), 347(10,11), 348(10), 356
(8), 357(176,179), 359(176),
361(176), 362(176), 364(176,
179), 365(179), 366(11,14,16),
367(176), 369(195,199), 370
(200), 373(10,176), 373, 374,

(Gavin, J. R., III)
379, 382, 383, 392(45,47,49 50,51,53), 396(47), 397(45,47, 49,50,51,53,96,97), 398(45,47, 49,50,53,96,97), 399(45,47,49), 402(96,97), 403(45,47), 406(96, 97), 407(45,47,49,53), 408(47, 51), 410(47,49), 411(45,47,49), 415(96,97), 417(47,51), 420(49, 50,133), 424, 426, 428, 448(33), 458(54), 465(75), 474, 475, 476, 659(40), 660(41), 665

Gay, V. L., 108(24), 118

Geary, W. L., 252(6), 259(6), 268 (73), 293, 296

Gelehrter, T. D., 463(66), (88), 475, 476

Gemershausen, J., 395(86), 426

Gemzell, C. A., 288(132), 299

Gerber, P., 303(18), 374

Germershausen, J., 464(69), 475

Gerner, R. E., 303(17), 305(35), 374, 375

Geschwind, I. I., 387(12), 401(12), 412(12), 414(12), 422

Gey, G. O., 464(70), 475

Giblett, E. R., 307(46), 375

Gibson, Q. H., 358(185), 383

Gilman, A. G., 57(32), 71

Ginsberg, B. H., 316(89), 367(89), 378

Ginsburg, V., 480(6), 494

Giordano, N. D., 47(25), 52

Giorgio, N. A., 123(18,19), 135(27), 141, 142, 402(120), 403(120), 428, 586(39), 597

Giraud, A., 646(21), 652(21), 663 (46), 664, 665

Glade, P. R., 303(19,23), 304(28), 305, 306(23), 307(50), 308, 374, 375, 376

Gliemann, J., 84(44), 86(44), 98, 392(74,76), 396(74,90), 398(74, 76,101), 399(74), 403(74), 406 (76), 407(74), 408(74), 410(74,

(Gliemann, J.)
76), 411(74,76,125), 418(74, 76), 425, 426, 427, 428, 434 (9), 439(9), 451(43), 453(43), 473, 474, 595(48), 598

Glinsmann, W. H., 395(87), 398 (87), 426

Glossman, H., 218(86,88), 249, 553(44), 564, 628(44), 639, 662(45), 665

Glover, J. S., 105(26), 118, 650 (24), 664

Goff, M. M., 325(103), 378

Goldberg, N. D., 468(87), 476

Goldbeter, A., 356(163), 381

Goldenberg, R. L., 191(40), 192 (43), 246

Goldfien, A., 270(92), 297

Goldfine, I. D., 255(46), 295, 318(78), 370(200), 377, 383, 392(46,48,54), 395(87), 398 (46,54,87), 399(54), 400(48, 109), 402(109), 403(46,54), 407(46,54), 410(46,54), 411 (46,54), 412(48,109), 414(48, 109), 417(54,109), 420(48,54, 109), 421(54), 424, 426, 127, 467(80), 471(101), 476, 477

Goldmann, P. H., 57(32), 71

Goldstein, A., 437(15), 473, 498, 501, 502, 504(5), 509, 510

Goldstein, S., 464(72), 475

Good, N. E., 330(107), 379

Good, R. A., 318(77a), 377

Goodfriend, T., 302(2), 373, 386 (6), 452

Goodman, D. B. P., 534(1), 562

Gorden, P., 120(5), 140, 255(47), 295, 303(8,9,10,13,14,16), 313(8), 321(8,10), 325(9,10), 333(8), 334(10), 335(8), 336 (8,10), 339(8,10), 340(8,10), 347(10), 348(10), 356(8), 366 913,14,16,188), 369(195,196, 197), 370(200), 373(10), 374,

(Gorden, P.)
  383, 389(39), 390(39), 392(47,
  49,50), 396(47), 397(47,49,50),
  398(47,49,50), 399(47,49), 400
  (39,108,109), 402(39,108,109),
  403(47), 407(39,47,49), 408(47),
  410(47,49), 411(47,49), 412(39,
  108,109), 414(39,108,109), 417
  (39,47,109), 418(39), 420(39,
  49,50,109,133,135), 424, 427,
  428, 465(75), 476, 659(40), 665
Gorman, R. E., 168(21), 174
Gorman, R. R., 608, 613, 616(15),
  626(15), 630(15), 637
Gorski, J. L., 262(59), 295
Gospodarowicz, D., 177(24), 221
  (24), 246, 252(8,9), 259(8,9),
  267(8), 268, 293
Gothosker, B., 307(46), 375
Gotti, G., 319(81), 365(81), 377
Graf, A., 21(61), 35
Granger, H., 305(34), 375
Grantham, J. J., 668(4), 701
Gray, E. G., 501, 506(7), 510
Gray, R. W., 534(2), 562
Greaves, M. F., 308(53), 313(59),
  376
Green, K., 621, 638
Green, R., 317(69), 377
Green, W. L., 151(17), 157
Greenbaum, A. L., 595(53), 598
Greene, L. A., 466(78), 476
Greenough, W. B., 74(14), 84(40,
  41), 96, 98
Greenwood, F. C., 83(38), 98, 105,
  118, 124, 141, 147(27), 157, 166,
  173, 254(40), 294, 324, 325(97),
  378, 388(29), 389, 423, 431, 472,
  569, 597, 650(24), 664
Gregoriadis, G., 262(61), 295
Grollman, A. P., 58(34), 71
Groth, J., 506(14), 510
Groves, T. D. D., 538(48), 531
Grundfest, H., 3(12), 32
Grunfeld, C., 58(34), 71

Guldberg, C. M., 343(132), 380
Gunther, G. R., 323(93), 378
Gwyne, J. T., 487(21), 495

Haber, E., 56(24,25,26), 67(25),
  68(25), 69(25), 71, 270(91),
  297
Hadden, E. M., 318(77a), 377
Hadden, J. W., 318(77a), 377,
  468(87), 476
Haddox, M. K., 468(87), 476
Hageman, E. C., (47), 531
Hakomori, S., 82(32), 95(32), 97
Hall, R., 655(35,36), 663(36),
  664
Hallund, O., 388(27), 423
Ham, E. A., 600(4,5), 610(4,17,
  19), 613, 614, 616(3), 637
Hamlin, J. L., 325(101), 378,
  389(36), 394(36), 423
Hammerstrom, S., 616(24), 620
  (24), 638
Hammond, J. M., 177(9), 245,
  253(27), 294, 392(62), 400(62),
  403(62), 407(62), 412(62), 414
  (62), 417(62), 425, 450(34),
  451(34), 474
Han, S., 192(44), 247, 262, 295
Hanahan, D. J., 486(17), 495
Handler, J. S., 668(3), 701
Handwerger, B. S., 303(6,7),
  312(6), 313(6,7), 314(7), 315
  (7), 367(6), 369(7), 373, 397
  (99,100), 427, 576(33), 597
Hanks, J. H., 467(85), 476, 526
  (41), 531
Hanoune, J., 401(118), 428
Hansen, B., 325(104), 378
Haour, F., 120(7), 140, 199(50),
  206(50,54), 247, 252(1), 259
  (1), 266(1), 267(1), 268(1),
  270(1), 272(1), 276(1), 278(1),
  280(1), 292, 392(77), 425
Harbon, S., 630(38), 638

Harper, E. T., 350(143), 381
Hartwig, J., 318(76), 377
Hasan, S. H., 120(7), 140, 199(50), 206(50), 247
Hatanaka, C., 44(19), 52
Haugaard, N., 388(16), 395(16), 422
Hauser, D., 66(42), 72
Havinga, E., 389(31), 423
Hawker, C., 548(26), 563
Hawker, R. W., 642(9,10), 650(10), 651(10), 655(10), 657(10), 661 (10), 662(10), 663(47), 663, 665
Hayes, R. L., 528(53), 531
Haymand, M. J., 490(29), 492(29), 495
Hays, R. L., 514, 529
Hays, R. M., 678(39), 702
Hazelbauer, G. L., 15(50), 31, 34
Heath, D., 548(30), 549(30), 560, 561(30), 563
Hechter, O., 316(67), 377, 451(45), 474, 668(8,12), 701
Heding, L. G., 388(27), 423
Hedrick, J. L., 152(19), 157
Heilbronn, E., 18(56), 34
Helenius, A., 693, 703
Hellerstein, E. E., 305(36), 375
Hellman, A., 307(49), 376
Hendrick, J. C., 330(106), 379
Hendricks, C., 303(14), 366(14), 374, 420(133), 428
Hendricks, C. M., 120(5), 140, 303(13), 366(13), 374
Henle, G., 306(42), 375
Henle, W., 306(42), 375
Hennen, G., 642(5), 643(12,13,14), 645(14), 646(22), 651(5), 658(5), 660(42), 661(42), 663, 664, 665
Henney, C. S., 316(55), 366(55), 370(55), 376
Hepp, K. D., 401(116), 427, 463(67), 475
Hersch, E. M., 313(63), 376
Hertzfeld, J., 356(164), 381
Herzenberg, L. A., 313(60), 376

Hickman, J., 203(53), 229(53), 247, 262(61), 281(111), 295, 298
Hickman, J. W., 281(114), 298
Hilbert, N., 528(45), 531
Hill, A. V., 350, 371(144), 372, 381
Hiller, J. M., 498(1,4), 502(1), 506(1,14), 507(15), 509, 510
Hintz, R. L., 392(64), 396(64), 397(64), 406(64), 407(64), 425, 471(91), 476
Hiromichi, T., 337(115), 379
Hirschhorn, K., 303(19,23), 305, 306(23), 374
Hirshfield, A. N., 192(44,45), 247, 262(55,56), 295
Hodgkin, D. C., 389(37), 418(37), 423
Hoffert, J. F., 318(79), 377
Hofmann, K., 40(9,10), 41(9,10), 43(9,10), 44(18), 46(9), 51(9, 10,29,30,31), 51, 52
Holick, M. F., 534(2), 562
Holland, J. B., 252(6), 259(6), 268(73), 293, 296
Holland, J. F., 484(13), 494
Hollenberg, M. D., 74(10), 76 (22), 77(22), 82(10,35), 83(22), 84(22), 90(10), 96, 97, 269, 296, 323(92), 378, 431(5), 435 (10), 436(10), 437(10,12), 438 (10,17), 439(12), 441(10), 448 (10), 449(10), 466(77), 467(77, 81,82,83,84), 468, 469(83), 470(83,90), 472, 473, 476
Holloway, P. W., 586, 598
Holmgren, J., 74(11,16,17), 77 (23,26), 82(26), 83(23), 90(26), 96, 97
Holmlund, C. E., 451(35), 474
Holohan, K. N., 127, 141
Hoover, C. R., (47), 531
Horejsi, J., 279(103), 297
Hourani, B. T., 483(12), 484(12),

(Hourani, B. T.)
485(12), 486, 487(12), 490(12), 494

House, P. D. R., 392(70,71), 400 (70,71), 401(119), 412(70,71), 414(70), 425, 428

Hovi, T., 468(89), 476

Howe, C., 487(20), 488(20), 495

Huang, D., 442(27), 473

Huchet, M., 16(52), 34, 693(53), 703

Huckins, C., 196(47), 247

Hughes, W. L., 255(42), 294

Humbel, R. E., 406(121), 428, 471 (99,100), 477

Humes, J. L., 600(4,5,7), 601(12), 610(4,17,19), 613, 614, 616(3, 21), 620(21), 626(21), 637

Hummel, J. P., 137(32), 142

Hung, L. T., 512(2), 529

Hunston, D. L., 211(66), 213(66), 248, 340(125), 348(125), 380

Hunter, M. J., 539, 562

Hunter, W. M., 83(38), 98, 105(26), 118, 124(21), 141, 147(27), 157, 166, 173, 254(40), 294, 324, 325 (97), 378, 388(29), 389, 423, 431, 472, 481, 494, 569, 597, 650(24), 664

Hurley, T., 576(33), 597

Hutt, D. M., 372(158), 381

Huunan-Seppala, A., 63(39), 66(39), 71

Hwang, P., 579(35), 597

Hynie, S., 668(11), 701

Ide, M., 38(6), 51

Illiano, G., 392(60), 396(60), 398 (60), 400(103), 401(103), 407(60), 425, 427, 451(42), 453(42), 454 (42), 474

Imbert, M., 512(2), 529, 669(29), 670(29), 671(29), 672(29), 676 (44), 677(29), 679(44), 680(44),

(Imbert, M.)
681(44), 702, 703

Ingham, K. C., 357(174), 382

Irvine, R. A., 281(112), 282(112), 298

Iseri, O. A., 544(16), 548(16), 562

Isselbacher, K. J., 74(13), 96

Ito, E., 303(21), 318(21), 333(21), 374

Iverson, L. L., 54(1), 70

Izawa, S., 330(107), 379

Izzo, J. L., 388(24), 394(79), 423, 426

Izzo, M. J., 388(24), 394(79), 423, 426

Jackson, R. L., 152(25), 157

Jacobs, S., 440(20), 441(25), 473, 538(10,11), 562

Jacquemin, Cl., 389(32,33), 394 (32,33), 395(32), 423

James, M. A. R., 522(34), 530

Jamieson, J. D., 567(21), 596

Jansen, F. K., 395(83), 426

Jansons, V. K., 481(10), 482(11), 483(11), 486(11), 487(11), 488 (11), 489(11), 494

Jaquet, P., 642(5), 643(14), 645 (14), 651(5), 658(5), 663

Jard, S., 216(82), 249, 253(34), 294, 516(20), 530, 668(1,9,13), 669(15,16,17,27), 670(27), 672(27), 673(27), 674(27), 676 (44), 677(27), 678(41), 679 (41,43,44), 680(44), 681(44, 46,47), 682(9), 684(9,13), 685(9,13,51), 686(9), 688(15), 689(15,16), 690(9), 691(16,17), 692(17), 693(52), 695(9), 696 (52), 699(52), 700(52), 701, 702, 703

Jarett, L., 253(26,27), 293, 294, 367(191), 383, 392(62), 395

(Jarett, L.)
(85), 400(62), 403(62), 407(62),
412(62), 414(62), 417(62), 425,
426, 427, 450(39), 451(34), 474
Jarett, R. J., 388(18), 395(18), 423
Jen, P., 302(5), 303(5), 312(5), 313
(5), 373, 392(45), 396(56), 397
(45), 398(45), 399(45), 403(45,
56), 407(45), 410(56), 411(45,56),
417(56), 418(56), 424, 425, 465
(74), 468(74), 476
Jessup, R., 616(2), 637
Jiang, N. S., 268(71), 270(71), 296
Johansson, B. G., 179(30), 246,
325(100), 378, 433(7), 472, 568,
597, 643, 663
Johnson, C. A., 487(22), 495
Johnson, C. B., 121, 123(18, 19, 20),
135(27), 137(16), 141, 142, 269
(81), 270(81), 296, 402(120), 403
(120), 428, 586(39), 597
Johnson, J., 396(91), 426
Johnston, G. G., 550(34), 563
Jondal, M., 306(44, 45), 307(44),
375
Jones, A. B., 630(39), 638, 642(3),
654(3), 655(3), 657(3), 662(3),
663
Jorgensen, K. H., 388(27), 423
Julius, M. H., 313(60), 376
Jung, H., 520(29), 530

Kadohama, N., 252(15), 293, 566
(12), 596
Kahn, C. R., 161(13), 163(13), 173,
302(4), 303(7, 14, 16), 313(7), 314
(7), 315(7), 316(4, 89), 321(4, 91),
324(4, 91), 325(4), 334(112), 336
(112), 337(91, 112), 338(91), 339
(112), 340(111, 112), 341(111),
347(4), 348(4, 12), 355(4), 356
(112), 366(14, 16, 188), 367(89,
194), 369(7, 197, 198), 370(200),
373, 374, 378, 379, 383, 386(3),

(Kahn, C. R.)
387(3, 11), 389(3, 39), 390(39),
392(3, 48, 50, 52, 54), 394(3, 52),
395(3), 396(11), 397(50, 100),
398(3, 50, 54), 399(54), 400(3,
11, 39, 48, 52, 107, 108, 109, 110),
401(3, 11, 107), 402(3, 11, 39,
107, 108, 109), 403(54), 406(3,
52, 121), 407(3, 11, 39, 52, 54),
408(52), 410(54), 411(54), 412
(11, 39, 48, 52, 108, 109), 414
(11, 39, 48, 52, 108, 109, 110,
126, 127), 415(52), 417(11, 39,
52, 54, 109, 110, 126, 127), 418
(3, 39, 52, 127), 420(3, 11, 39,
48, 50, 54, 107, 108, 109, 126,
127, 133), 421(3, 11, 54, 127),
422, 424, 427, 428
Kahn, R., 218(85), 249, 268(78),
269(78), 296, 333(109), 379,
389(38), 390(38), 392(38), 393
(38), 394(38, 78), 399(38), 400
(38, 78), 403(78), 407(38, 78),
408(38, 78), 412(38, 78), 414
(38, 78), 417(38, 78), 420(135),
424, 425, 428, 444(32), 448
(32), 450(32), 474
Kaji, H., 451(44), 474
Kalant, N., 317(73), 377
Kalman, S. M., 437(15), 473
Kammerman, S., 177(14, 21),
191(39), 245, 246, 252(5, 7, 19),
259(5, 7), 270(5, 93, 94), 293,
297
Kaneko, T., 616(4), 637
Kaplan, N. M., 616(7), 637
Kaplan, N. O., 508(17), 510
Karlin, A., 2(1), 3(10), 4(10, 15,
16, 17, 18), 5(10, 16, 17, 20),
7(10, 21), 8(18, 21, 25), 9(10,
21, 26), 10(26, 27), 11(10, 26,
28), 12(26, 28), 15(26, 47, 48,
48b), 16(1, 26, 47, 48), 17(54),
18(26, 47, 48), 22(47, 48), 24
(47), 25(36, 47, 48), 26(25, 26,

(Karlin, A.)
  48), 27(26), 28(25,26,27,47,48),
  31(47), <u>32</u>, <u>33</u>, <u>34</u>
Karlsson, E., 13(30), 14, <u>33</u>, <u>34</u>
Karoly, K., 392(75), 400(75), 412
  (75), 414(75), 417(75), <u>425</u>
Kasai, M., 3(11), 13(11), 15(49),
  <u>32</u>, <u>34</u>, 693(53), <u>703</u>
Katchalsky, A., 342(130), <u>380</u>
Kathan, R. H., 487(22), <u>495</u>
Katz, B., 3(4,5), <u>32</u>
Katzen, H. M., 33(117), <u>379</u>, 387
  (10), 395(86), <u>422</u>, <u>426</u>, 464(69),
  <u>475</u>
Kauman, A., 169(25), 171(25), <u>174</u>
Kaumann, A. J., 316(68), <u>377</u>
Keen, H., 388(18), 395(18), <u>423</u>
Keller, D., 270(92), <u>297</u>
Kelly, L. A., 38(5), <u>51</u>
Kelly, P. A., 120(8), <u>140</u>, 257(52),
  <u>295</u>, 392(69), 400(69), 403(69),
  407(69), 412(69), 414(69), <u>425</u>,
  471(97), <u>477</u>, 566(7,10,11),
  567(11,13,14,15,17), 573(7),
  574(7), 575(7,10,11,13,15,17,
  29), 576(7,30,31), <u>596</u>, <u>597</u>
Kemp, G., 31, <u>35</u>
Kenny, A. D., 544(16), 548(16), <u>562</u>
Kenny, A. G., 551(40), <u>564</u>
Kerkof, P. R., 528(50), <u>531</u>
Kerr, M. A., 551(40), <u>564</u>
Kesselring, P., 211(72), <u>248</u>, 348
  (138), <u>380</u>
Ketelslegers, J.-M., 181(34), 190
  (37), 192(37), 197(37), 200(34),
  205(37), 211(79), 213(79), 217
  (79,84), 218(79), 219(79), 222
  (79), <u>246</u>, <u>248</u>, <u>249</u>, 356(161),
  <u>381</u>
Keutmann, H. T., 218(88), <u>249</u>, 535,
  536, 538, 546(20), <u>562</u>, <u>563</u>
Keynes, R. D., 3(13), <u>32</u>
Khairallah, E. A., 276(101), <u>297</u>
Kidwai, A. M., 400, <u>427</u>
Killander, J., 232, <u>250</u>, 458, <u>475</u>

Kimball, F. A., 616(27,28), 620
  (27,28), <u>638</u>
Kimelberg, H., 55(15), <u>70</u>
King, C. A., 74(15), 77(25), <u>96</u>,
  <u>97</u>
Kirton, K. T., 616(17,28), 620
  (28), <u>637</u>, <u>638</u>
Kitabgi, P. E., 171(29), <u>174</u>
Kitamura, H., 304(29), 305(29),
  <u>375</u>
Kitau, M. J., 522(34), <u>530</u>
Klee, W., 502, <u>510</u>
Klein, G., 306(41,44,45), 307
  (44,46), <u>375</u>
Klein, I., 121(11), <u>141</u>, 144(10,
  12,13), 148(13), <u>156</u>
Kleinsmith, L. J., 259(54), <u>295</u>
Klett, R., 13(34), <u>33</u>
Klett, R. P., 14(39), 18(39), <u>34</u>
Klotz, I. M., 211(66), 213(66),
  <u>248</u>, 340(125), 348(125), <u>380</u>,
  441(22), <u>473</u>
Knott, G. D., 211(73,74,79),
  213(73,74,79), 217(73,74,79,
  84), 218(79), 219(79), 222(79),
  <u>248</u>, <u>249</u>, 356(161), <u>381</u>
Kobayashi, Y., 269(85), <u>297</u>
Koch, Y., 616(13), <u>637</u>
Kocourek, J., 490(26), 492(26),
  <u>495</u>
Koffenberger, J. F., 168(18),
  <u>173</u>
Kohn, L. D., 253(36), <u>294</u>, 367
  (184), <u>382</u>, 642(7), 650(25),
  651(7), 654(7), 658(7), 661(7),
  662(7), <u>663</u>, <u>664</u>
Kohn, L. S., 661(43), <u>665</u>
Koide, S. S., 177(19), 191(19),
  192(19), <u>245</u>
Kolb, H. J., 463(67), <u>475</u>
Kolena, J., 252(5), 259(5), 270
  (5), <u>293</u>
Kollander, S., 252(14), 253(14),
  <u>293</u>
Kolodny, E. H., 82(27), 95(27),

(Kolodny, E. H.)
97
Koltai, M., 320(87), 378
Kong, Y. C., 44(20), 52
Kono, T. J., 386(8), 392(72), 396
(72), 398(72), 410(72), 417(72),
422, 425, 451(36,41), 452(36),
453(36,41), 474, 595(46), 598
Koopman, P. C., 681(45), 703
Kopelovich, L., 528(44), 531
Koretz, S., 56(22), 71
Koritz, S. B., 38(5), 51
Korneman, S. G., 137(31), 142
Kornfeld, R., 490(16), 494
Kornfeld, S., 481, 483(8), 487, 488
(8), 489(8), 490(8,16), 492(8),
493(8), 494
Kortez, S., 120(10), 121(10,13), 141
Koshland, D. E., Jr., 356(162,165,
166), 357(162), 381, 382
Kozlovskis, P. L., 544(18), 546(18),
550(18), 562
Kozyreff, V., 144(3), 156, 160(7),
173
Krans, H. M. J., 136(29), 142, 144
(3), 147(15), 156, 157, 160(4,5,6,
7), 166(4), 167(4), 168(4), 169(4,
5), 171(4), 172(31), 173, 174, 218
(89), 249, 332(108), 379, 411(123),
428, 521(33), 530, 557(47), 561
(47), 565, 657(37), 662(37), 664
Krishna, G., 49, 50(28), 52, 164,
173, 608(15), 613
Kristensen, P., 282(119), 298
Kritchevsky, G., 145(14), 157
Krug, F., 84(45), 98, 270(89), 297,
313, 323(57), 376, 392(59,66),
397(66), 398(66), 399(66), 400
(102), 401(59), 403(59), 407(59),
410(66), 412(59), 414(59), 417
(59), 425, 427, 444(28), 446(28),
450(28), 451(28), 465(73), 466(73),
467(73), 473, 476
Krug, U., 313, 323(57), 376, 392
(66), 397(66), 398(66), 399(66),

(Krug, U.)
410(66), 425, 465(73), 466(73),
467(73), 476
Kubanek, J., 490(26), 492(26),
495
Kuehl, F. A., Jr., 600(4,5,7),
601(12), 610(4,17,19), 613,
614, 616(3,21), 620(21), 626
(21), 637
Kumar, S., 44(21), 52
Kuo, J. R., 451(35), 474
Kurzrok, R., 600(1), 610(1), 613

Laburthe, M., 420(134), 428
Lacorbiere, M., 281(109), 298
Lafferty, M. A., 609(16), 613
Lambert, B., 389(32,33), 394
(32,33), 395(32), 423
Lamprecht, S. A., 616(13), 637
Lam Thanh, H., 669(29), 670
(29,31), 671(29), 672(29), 677
(29), 702
Landau, E. M., 3(7), 32
Landesman, R., 288(131,133),
299
Landon, E. J., 551(41), 564,
682(49), 703
Landon, J., 522(34), (36), 530
Lands, A. M., 54(10), 55(10),
70
Lane, K., 546(21), 548(21), 549
(21), 563
Langer, B., 21(61), 35
Langmuir, I., 345, 380
Larson, B. L., (47), 528(48,52),
531
La Rue, M. K., 77(24), 97
Laryea, J. B., 282(116), 298
Lasfargues, E. Y., (46), 531
Lasser, M., 56(23), 71
LaTorre, J. L., 504(12), 510
Laudat, M. H., 369(197), 383,
389(39), 390(39), 400(39,113),
402(39,113), 407(39), 412(39),

(Laudat, M. H.)
414(39), 417(39), 418(39), 420
(39), 421(113), 424, 427, 471
(95), 477
Laudat, Ph., 369(197), 383, 389
(39), 390(39), 400(39,112,113),
402(39,113), 407(39), 412(39),
414(39), 417(39), 418(39), 420
(39), 421(113), 424, 427, 471
(95), 477
Lauersen, N. H., 268(72), 296
Laurent, T. C., 232, 250, 458, 475
Lauter, C. J., 91(50), 98, 653(33),
664
Lavis, V. R., 451(46), 474
Lawson, G. F., 100(3,4), 101(4),
117
Lawson, G. M., 208(56), 247
Lazar, P., 283(129), 299
Lazarow, A., 43(14), 51, 265(67),
266(67), 296
Lazdunski, M., 356(168), 382
Le Cam, A., 389(43), 390(43), 391
(43), 397(43), 399(43), 424
Lee, C. H., 252(4), 259(4), 268(71),
270(4,71), 293, 296
Lee, C. Y., 3(9,11), 13(9,11), 32,
177(8,15,26), 199(49), 218(87),
221(15), 222(26), 245, 246, 247,
249, 259(53), 262, 268(62), 276
(100), 282(122), 295, 297, 298
Lee, L. T., 487(20), 488(20), 495
Lee, V., 684, 703
Lefkowitz, R. J., 38(4), 44(22), 51,
52, 54(4,5,6,7), 55(5,14,19), 56
(5,24,25,26,27), 57(30), 58(4,5,
6), 59(4,5,6,7,35,36), 62(4,5,
6,7), 63(37,40), 64(5), 65(4),
66(37), 67(25), 68(25), 69(25,46,
47), 70, 71, 72, 120(4), 140, 255
(44), 270(91), 294, 297, 302(1),
303(12), 373, 374, 386(5), 422
Lehrer, R. I., 313(65), 315(65), 377
Leibold, W., 306(44), 307(44), 375
Leidenberger, F., 100(1,3,5,7),

(Leidenberger, F.)
117, 177(16), 208(56), 245,
247, 283(128), 291(135), 299
Leimgruber, W., 22(64), 35,
581(38), 597
Lenoir, P., 389(43), 390(43),
391(43), 397(43), 399(43), 424
Leon, M. A., 323, 378
Leray, F., 401(118), 428
Lesniak, M. A., 120(5), 140, 211
(77), 213(77), 215(77), 248,
255(47), 295, 303(9,10,13,14),
321(10), 325(9,10), 334, 336
(10), 339(10), 340(10), 347(10),
348, 357(176), 359(176), 361
(176), 362(176), 364(176), 366
(13,14), 367(176), 369(195),
370(200), 373(10,176), 374,
382, 383, 392(49,51), 397(49,
51), 398(49), 399(49), 407(49),
408(51), 410(49), 411(49), 417
(51), 420(49,133), 424, 428,
660(41), 665
Levely, G. S., 544(18), 546(18),
550(18), 562
Leventhal, B. G., 313(63), 376
Levey, G. S., 121, 141, 144(6,7,
8,9,10,11,12,13), 148(13),
156, 253(24), 270(90), 293,
297
Levine, D., 211(69), 213(69),
248
Levitzki, A., 66, 72, 356(166),
357(173,175), 367(175,193),
369, 382, 383
Levy, B., 55(13), 70
Li, C. H., 318(77b), 377
Li, C. Y., 313(66), 377
Liao, T. H., 28(69), 35, 643(11),
663
Lichtash, N., 616(26), 638
Lichtenstein, L. M., 316(55),
366(55), 370(55), 376
Lieb, C. C., 600(1), 610(1), 613
Limbird, L., 63(40), 71

Lin, F. , 396(91), 426
Lin, M. C. , 662(44), 665
Lin, S. Y. , 302(2), 373, 386(6), 422
Lindahl, T. , 306(44), 307(44), 375
Linde, S. , 325(104), 378
Lindholm, L. , 74(11), 96
Lindner, H. R. , 616(13), 637
Lindstrom, J. , 14(41), 18(41), 29 (70), 30(70), 34, 35
Lineweaver, H. , 346, 380
Lipsett, M. B. , 107(11), 117, 254 (41), 255(41,45), 294
Lis, H. , 480(2), 494
Lissitzky, S. , 642(5,6), 643(14), 645(14,18), 646(20,21,22), 647 (23), 651(5,6), 652(6,20,21,29), 655(6), 658(5,6,38), 660(42), 661 (6,38,42), 662(23), 663(46), 663, 664, 665
Littlefield, J. W. , 464(72), 475
Litwack, G. , 616(26), 638
Liu, T. C. , 262(59), 295
Liu, W.-K. , 208(57), 247
Livesey, S. J. , 549(31), 555(46), 556(46), 558(46), 563, 564
Livingston, A. , 517, 530
Livingston, J. N. , 392(67), 396(67), 407(67), 425, 439(18), 473
Lockwood, D. H. , 392(67), 396(67), 407(67), 425, 439(18), 473
Loh, H. H. , 437(14), 473, 504, 510
Loken, S. C. , 451(37), 474
Long, D. A. , 319(84), 377
Long, M. , 56(23), 71
Lonnroth, I. , 74(11,16,17), 77(23), 83(23), 96, 97
Lopez, C. , 468(87), 476
Losee, K. , 20(60), 35
LoSpalluto, J. J. , 83(39), 98
Loten, E. G. , 616(12), 637
Lowery, P. J. , 498(5), 501(5), 504 (5), 510
Lowney, L. I. , 498(5), 501(5), 502 (9), 504, 510

Lowry, O. H. , 23(62), 35, 42, 51, 135, 142, 256, 259(48), 295, 503, 510, 523, 530, 538, 562, 568, 580, 597, 617, 638, 673, 702
Luduena, F. L. , 54(10), 55(10), 70
Ludwig, M. L. , 539, 562
Lundin, P. M. , 318(80), 365(80), 377
Lunenfeld, B. , 177(1), 244
Lutz, R. A. , 211(72), 248, 348 (138), 380

McArthur, J. W. , 111(16), 117
McAuliff, J. P. , 54(10), 55(10, 11), 70
Macchia, V. , 386(7), 422, 642 (1), 663
McFarland, V. W. , 82(27), 95 (27), 97
McGrath, H. , 528(44), 531
McGuire, E. J. , 281(107), 298
McHugh, R. B. , 211(63), 248
MacIndoe, J. H. , 252(15), 293, 566(12), 596
McKeel, D. W. , 253(26), 293, 400, 427
McKinney, G. R. , 317(69), 377
MacManus, J. P. , 630(42), 638
McMillan, J. , 29(70), 30(70), 35
McNamee, M. G. , 11(28), 12(28), 15(47,48), 16(47,48), 18(47, 48), 22(47,48), 24(47), 25(47, 48), 26(48), 28(47,48), 31(47), 33, 34
McNeilly, A. S. , 522(35,38), (36), 530
Magee, W. E. , 616(20), 637
Maguire, M. E. , 57(32), 71
Maizel, J. V. , Jr. , 152(20), 157
Majumder, G. C. , 252(15), 293, 566(12), 595(52), 596, 598
Makino, S. , 26(65b), 35, 459(56),

(Makino, S.)
475
Malaisse-Lagae, F., 367(192), 383
Malamed, S., 678(39), 702
Malbon, C. C., 553(45), 556, 557
(45), 559(45), 560, 561, 564
Mancini, J., 191(42), 196(42), 246
Mancini, R. E., 177(2,4), 191(2,4),
196(2,4), 245, 253(30,31), 294
Mandel, L. R., 600(7), 610(19),
613, 614
Manley, S. W., 642(9,10), 650(10),
651(10), 655(10), 657(10), 661(10),
662(10), 663(47), 663, 665
Mann, D. L., 270(88), 275(88), 297,
340(122), 379, 397(96), 398(96),
402(96), 406(96), 415(96), 426
Manning, M., 513(6), 520(32), 529,
530
Maor, D., 319(82), 377
March, S., 463(65), 475
Marchalonis, J. J., 179(29), 246,
325(99), 378, 547, 549, 563
Marchesi, V. T., 152(25), 157, 458
(53), 475, 486, 487(19), 495
Marchetti, J., 669(19), 701
Marcus, R., 550(32), 555, 563
Margolis, F., 282(120), 298
Marinetti, G. V., 56(22), 71, 120
(10), 121(10,13), 141, 394(80,81),
396(81), 400(80,81), 420(81), 426
Mariz, I. K., 253(27), 294, 392(62),
400(62), 403(62), 407(62), 412
(62), 414(62), 417(62), 425, 450
(34), 451(34), 474
Maroko, P. R., 508(17), 510
Marsh, J. M., 252(21,22), 289(21,
22), 293, 616(8), 628(8), 630(8),
632(8), 637
Marshall, J. M., 520(30,31), 530
Martin, M. M., 392(50), 397(50),
398(50), 420(50), 424
Martin, N., 400(112), 427
Martin, R. G., 237(102), 250
Martin, S. P., 317(69), 377

Martin, T. J., 547(25), 549(25,
31), 554(25), 555, 556(46),
558(25,46), 560(25), 561(25),
563, 564
Martins-Ferreira, H., 3(13), 32
Marx, S. J., 218(88), 249, 303
(11), 347(11), 366(11), 374,
552, 556, 564
Marz, L., 268(76), 282(123), 296,
298
Mason, R. J., 318(75,76), 377
Matsuoka, Y., 307(47), 376
Matthews, B. W., 356(167), 382
Mattson, C., 18(56), 34
Maurer, W., 576(33), 597
Mautner, H., 4(18), 8(18), 33
May, M., 55(15), 70
Means, A. R., 177(17), 196(47),
245, 247, 252(12), 253(12),
256(12), 293
Means, G. E., 14(43), 34, 40(11),
46(11), 51
Meardi, G., 319(81), 365(81),
377
Mecklenburg, R. S., 255(45), 294
Megyesi, K., 366(188), 370(200),
383, 406(121), 428
Meinert, C. L., 211(63), 248
Meites, J., 567(17), 575(17), 596
Melcher, U. K., 339(120), 379
Meldolesi, J., 567, 596
Melmon, K. L., 316(55), 366(55),
370(55), 376
Mendelson, C., 188(36), 190(37),
192(37), 197(37), 205(37), 229
(100), 237(100), 241(100), 243
(100), 246, 249
Menez, A., 13(33), 33, 459(57),
475
Menézes, J., 306(44), 307(44),
375
Menon, K. M. J., 266(68), 296
Menon, T., 144(2), 156
Menten, M. L., 345, 380
Merchant, D. J., 333(109), 379

Mercola, D. A., 389(37), 418(37), 423

Mercola, K., 388(20), 389(20), 423

Meunier, J.-C., 13, 14(36), 18(36), 25(36), 26(66), 29(71), 33, 35, 241 (104), 250, 459(57), 475, 693(53), 703

Michaelis, L., 345, 380

Michallson, D., 18(55), 34

Michel-Béchet, M., 646(20), 652 (20), 664

Mickey, J., 63(40), 71

Midgley, A. R., 108(12), 117, 177 (27), 191(27,41), 192(27,44,45), 246, 247, 266(68), 269(136), 296, 299

Midgley, A. R., Jr., 108(24), 118, 252(17), 253(17,29), 259(54), 262 (55,56), 293, 294, 295, 342(128b), 380, 517(23), 530

Miledi, R., 3(4,5), 13, 14(31), 32, 33

Miles, A. A., 319(84), 377

Miller, G., 306(40), 375

Miller, O. V., 608, 613, 616(15,20), 625(15), 630(15), 637

Miller, S. S., 548(29), 549(29), 552 (29), 556(29), 557(29), 561(29), 563

Minker, E., 320(87), 378

Minowada, J., 303(24), 307(48), 324(48), 374, 376

Miravet, L., 534(2), 562

Mirsky, I. A., 337(114), 379

Mitchell, C., 486(17), 495

Mitchell, M. J., 6(24), 33

Miyachi, Y., 107, 117, 254(41), 255 (41,45), 294

Modolell, J. B., 92(54), 98

Moenkemeyer, H., 575(28), 597

Molinoff, P., 13(31), 14(31), 33, 57(31), 71

Monod, J., 356(151), 381

Monroe, J. H., 303(18), 374

Monroe, S. E., 253(29), 294

Montegut, M., 516(20), 530, 678 (41), 679(41), 681(46,47), 703

Montibeller, J. A., 51(29,31), 52

Moody, T., 18(55), 25(65a), 34, 35

Moon, I. C., 192(44), 247

Moore, G., 303(24), 307(48), 324 (48), 374, 376

Moore, G. E., 303(17,21), 304, 305(29,31,35), 307(47,51), 308, 318(21), 333(21), 374, 375, 376

Moore, R. O., 92(54), 98

Moore, W. J., 215(80), 248

Moore, W. V., 600(9), 613, 616 (11), 619, 620(11), 628(45), 630(11), 637, 639, 642(8), 651 (8), 661(8), 662(8), 663

Moorhead, P. S., 305(32), 375

Mora, P. T., 82(27,30,31), 95 (27,30), 97

Moran, J. F., 55(15), 70

Morel, F., 253(34), 294, 512(2), 516(20), 529, 530, 669(29), 670(29), 671(29), 672(29), 676 (44), 677(29), 678(41), 679(41, 44), 680(44), 681(44,46,47), 702, 703

Morell, A. G., 262, 281(112), 282(112), 295, 298, 650, 664

Morera, A. M., 46(23), 47(23), 52, 626(35), 630(35), 638

Morgat, J. L., 512(2), 529, 669 (27,29,30), 670(27,30,31), 671(29), 672(27,29,32), 673 (27), 674(27), 677(27,29), 702

Morley, J. S., 44(16), 52

Moroder, L., 44(18), 52

Morris, C. J. O. R., 44(17), 52

Morris, J. W. S., 389(34), 423

Morris, P., 262(59), 295

Morrison, M., 514(8), 515(8), 516(8), 529, 616(19), 637

Moseley, J. M., 549(31), 563

Moses, H. L., 304(28), 375
Moyle, W. R., 44(20), 52, 268(76),
    269(85), 283, 296, 297, 299, 351
    (160), 372(160), 381
Mukherjee, C., 54(4,5), 55(5), 56
    (5), 58(4,5), 59(4,5,36), 62(4,5),
    64(5), 65(4), 70, 71
Muller, E. R. A., 252(14), 253(14),
    293
Mully, K., 471(100), 477
Munsick, R. A., 513(4), 529
Munson, P. L., 544(16), 546(19),
    548, 562, 563
Munston, D. L., 441(22), 473
Murad, R., 318(75), 377
Murphy, R. F., 127(22), 141
Murphy, W. H., 333(109), 379
Murti, V. V. S., 669(21), 676(21),
    702
Muth, K., 6(24), 33

Nachmansohn, D., 3(12), 32
Naftolin, F., 177(13), 191(13), 245
Naim, E., 56(23), 71
Nakamura, M., 38(6), 51
Nakayama, R., 44(19), 52
Narahara, H. T., 337(115), 379,
    388(19), 395(19), 423
Naspitz, C. K., 480(5), 494
Nazaki, Y., 26(65b), 35
Neer, E. J., 132, 142
Némethy, G., 356(162), 381
Neoh, S. H., 77(24), 97
Neri, G., 483(14), 485(14), 488(14),
    490(14), 494
Neuman, M. W., 546(21), 548(21),
    549(21), 563
Neuman, W. F., 535(6), 546(21),
    547(23), 548(21,23), 549(21),
    562, 563
Neville, D. M., Jr., 122, 152(22),
    141, 157, 161(11,12,13), 162(11),
    163(12,13), 173, 211(77), 213(77),
    215(77), 218(85), 248, 249, 255

(Neville, D. M., Jr.)
    (43), 263, 268(78), 269(78),
    294, 296, 303(14,16), 318(78),
    321(90,91), 324(91), 334(112),
    336(112), 337(91,112), 338(91),
    339(112), 340(90,111,112),
    341, 348(112), 356(112), 357
    (176,178,179), 359(176), 361
    (176), 362(176), 364(176,178,
    179), 365(179), 366(14,16,178),
    367(176,194), 369(198,199),
    370(200), 373(176), (98), 374,
    377, 378, 379, 382, 383, 387
    (11,14), 388(26), 389(14,26,
    38), 390(26,38), 391(26), 392
    (38,46,48,50,51,52,53,54),
    393(26,38), 394(38,52,78),
    396(1,14,26), 397(50,51,53),
    398(46,50,53,54), 399(38,54),
    400(11,14,26,38,48,52,78,
    104,105,107,108,109,110),
    401(11,14,107), 402(11,107,
    108,109), 403(14,46,54,78),
    405(14), 406(52,121), 407(11,
    38,46,52,53,54,78), 408(38,
    51,52,78), 410(46,54), 411
    (46,54), 412(11,14,26,38,48,
    52, 78, 108, 109), 414(11,14,
    26,38,48,52,78,108,109,110,
    126,127), 415(52), 417(11,38,
    51,52,54,78,109,110,126,127),
    418(14,52,127,132), 420(11,
    48,50,54,107,108,109,126,
    127,133), 421(11,54,127),
    422, 423, 424, 427, 428, 444
    (30-32), 448(32,33), 450(32),
    467(80), 474, 476, 553(43,44),
    564, 567, 596, 653, 660(41),
    664, 665
Newerly, K., 388(21), 395(21),
    403(21), 423
Newman, G. B., 211(61), 247
Niall, H. D., 535(5), 536(5),
    538(5), 562
Nicander, L., 38(8), 51

Nichol, L. W., 441(23), 473
Nicholas, A. G., 269(81), 270(81), 296
Nichols, G., 550(36), 563
Nicholson, G. L., 281(109), 298
Nickerson, M., 55(16), 70
Nicolson, G. L., 367(190), 383
Niederwieser, A., (23), 141
Niemann, I., 548, 563
Nieschlag, E., 107(11), 117, 254 (41), 255(41), 294
Nilsson, K., 306(44), 307(44), 375
Nirenberg, M., 502, 510
Nishimura, O., 44(19), 52
Niswender, G. D., 108(24), 118
Noall, M. W., 460(59), 475
Nola, E., 460(62), 463(62), 475
Nonoyama, M., 306(39), 375
Noonan, K. D., 480(4), 494
Nordling, S., 468(89), 476
Nozaki, Y., 459(56), 475
Nutley, M. L., 337(115), 379

O'Connell, M., 515(18), 529
O'Connor, W. V., 55(11), 70
Odell, W. D., 111(15), 117
Oelz, O., 471(99, 100), 477
Ogata, E., 548(26), 563
Ogston, A. G., 441(23), 473
O'Hara, D., 56(25, 27), 67(25), 68(25), 69(25, 46), 71, 72, 270 (91), 297
Oka, T., 397(94), 426, 463(68), 475
Okabayashi, T., 38(6), 51
O'Keefe, E., 74(21), 82(34, 36), 92 (36), 93, 94(34, 36), 95(36), 97, 397(95), 398(95), 411(95), 426, 470(90), 476
Olefsky, J. M., 313, 326(61), 376, 396(56, 91), 397(55), 403(55, 56), 410(55, 56), 411(55, 56), 417(55, 56), 418(56), 424, 425, 426, 465, 476
Olsen, R., 14(36), 18(36), 25(36), 33

Olsen, R. W., 13(33), 26(66), 33, 35, 241(104), 250, 459 (57), 475
Ong, D. E., 14(45), 18(45), 34
Ono, M., 460(60), 463(60), 475
Ontjes, D., 546(19), 563
Ooms, H., 388(20), 389(20), 423
Oppenheim, J. J., 313(63), 376
Orci, L., 367(192), 383, 395(84), 426
O'Riordan, J. L. H., 211(61), 247
Orloff, J., 668(3), 701
Osborn, M., 152(21), 157
Osborn, R. H., 151(16), 157
Oseroff, A. R., 91(52), 98
Osterlind, K., 84(44), 86(44), 98, 411(124, 125), 428, 434(9), 439(9), 473
Ottlecz, A., 320(87), 378
Owenn, J. J. T., 308(53), 376
Oxman, M. N., 307(49), 376

Pacheco, H., 646(19), 664
Packer, L., 486(18), 495
Pagano, J., 306(39), 375
Pairault, J., 400(112), 427
Pal, B. K., 502(9), 510
Palade, G. E., 567(21), 596, 675(37), 702
Palmer, J. S., 66(42), 72
Paltrowitz, I. M., 303(19), 374
Pandian, M. R., 269(85), 297
Parick, I., 57(28), 71
Parikh, I., 76(22), 77(22), 83(22), 84(22), 97, 460(62), 463(62, 65), 475
Parisi, M., 678(40), 703
Park, C. R., 164(14), 173, 451 (44), 474
Park, K., 270, 297
Parker, C. W., 311, 313(58), 316(54), 366(54), 376
Parlow, A. F., 113(19), 118,

(Parlow, A. F.)
  257(49), 292(49), 295
Partridge, S. M., 513(5), 529
Pastan, I., 38(4,6), 44(4,22), 51,
  52, 120(4), 140, 302(1), 303(12),
  373, 374, 386(5,7), 422, 642(1),
  663
Pasternak, G., 501, 506, 510
Patel, B. C., 481(10), 494
Paton, W. D. M., 431(3), 472
Patrick, J., 14(41), 18(41), 29(70),
  30, 34, 35
Patterson, J. M., 168(19,20,23),
  174, 388(25), 423
Paulsen, C. A., 114(21), 118, 177
  (6,13), 191(13), 245, 252(11),
  253(11), 293
Pearson, J., 498(4), 510
Peck, W., 550(33), 563
Pekar, A. H., 168(19), 174
Pennisi, F., 547, 563
Perlman, W. H., 68(43), 72
Perrelet, A., 367(192), 383
Perrenoud, M. L., 401(118), 428
Perry, W. L. M., 319(84), 377
Pert, C. B., 498(2), 501, 502(2),
  503, 506, 509, 510
Peterson, R. E., 253(38), 256(38),
  294
Phelps, C. P., 281(105), 297
Phillips, H. J., 333(110), 379
Pierce, J. G., 643, 663
Pierce, N. F., 74(14,18), 77(18),
  84(40,41), 96, 97, 98
Pierson, R. W., Jr., 464(71), 471
  (92), 475, 477
Pilczyk, R., 547(25), 549(25), 554
  (25), 558(25), 560(25), 561(25),
  563
Pinchera, A., 663(46), 665
Pincus, J. H., 483(12), 484(12),
  485(12), 486(12), 487(12), 490
  (12), 494
Pitelka, D. R., 528(50), 531
Planells, R., 646(22), 664

Platt, T., 12(29), 27(29), 33
Podesta, E., 223(96), 229(100),
  237(100), 239(96), 241(100),
  243(100), 249
Podskalny, J. M., 316(88), 366
  (88), 367(88), 378, 471(101),
  477
Pohl, S. L., 120(9), 121, 122,
  136(29), 141, 142, 144(3), 147
  (15), 156, 157, 160(1,2,3,4,5,
  6,7,8,9,10), 163(2), 164(2),
  165(2), 166(4), 167(4), 168(2,
  4), 169(4,5,24,25), 171(4,25,
  28), 172(30,31,32), 173, 174,
  218(89), 249, 253(25), 293,
  316(68), 332(108), 377, 379,
  400(106), 401(106), 411(123),
  427, 428, 521(33), 530, 557
  (47), 561(47), 564, 595(47),
  598, 657(37), 662(37), 664
Pohley, F. M., 106(22), 118,
  257, 295
Pollack, R., 307(49), 376
Pomeroy, S. R., 515(18), 529
Popende, E. A., 669(22), 702
Posner, B. I., 392(68,69), 400
  (68,69), 403(68,69), 407(68,
  69), 412(68,69), 414(68,69),
  417(68), 425, 566(10,11), 567
  (11,13,14,15), 575(10,11,13,
  29), 596, 597
Pospisil, J., 191(38), 246
Possani, L. D., 14(39), 18(39),
  34
Pothier, L., 305(36), 375
Potter, L. T., 13(31), 14(31,37),
  33, 34, 63(38), 66(38), 71
Potts, J. T., Jr., 535(5), 536
  (5), 538(5), 546(20), 562, 563
Poulis, P., 401(119), 428
Powell, A. E., 323, 378
Powell, C. E., 54(9), 70
Powell, W. S., 616(24), 620(24),
  638
Pradelles, P., 669(27), 670, 672

(Pradelles, P.)
  (32), 673(27), 674(27), 677(27),
  702
Presl, J., 191(38), 246
Pressman, D., 307(47), 376
Pricer, W., 38(4,7), 44(4), 51,
  255(44), 294, 386(5), 422
Pricer, W. E., Jr., 281(113), 282
  (113), 298
Prigogine, I., 342(131), 380
Prives, J., 7(21), 8(21), 9(21), 33
Prives, J. M., 8(25), 15(48b), 26
  (25), 28(25), 33, 34
Psychoyos, S., 630(43), 639
Puca, G. A., 460(62), 463(62), 475
Pulliam, M. W., 367(183), 382

Rabinowitz, D., 200(52), 247, 323
  (95), 324, 378
Rabkin, R., 550(37), 563
Racker, E., 31, 35
Radcliffe, M. A., 400(115), 427
Raff, M. C., 308(53), 376
Raftery, M. A., 13, 14(32,38), 16
  (51,53), 18(55), 25(65a), 33, 34
Raisz, L. G., 547(23), 548(23), 563
Raizada, M. M. S., 330(107), 379
Rajaniemi, H. J., 108(12), 117, 177
  (12,28), 191(12), 192(44,45), 245,
  246, 247, 252(2), 259(2), 262(55,
  56), 270(2,96), 292, 295, 297,
  342(128b), 380
Rajerison, R., 668(9), 669(17), 678
  (41), 679(41,43), 682(9), 684(9),
  685(9,51), 686(9), 690(9), 691
  (17), 692(17), 693(52), 695(9),
  696(52), 699(52), 700(52), 701,
  703
Rall, T. W., 144(2), 156
Ramachandran, J., 44(20), 52, 164,
  165, 173, 283, 299, 351(160),
  372(160), 381, 684, 703
Ramachandran, S., 121(11), 141
Ramsey, R. B., 101(23), 116(23), 118

Ramwell, P. W., 616(2), 637
Rançon, F., 389(42), 390(42),
  396(42), 397(42,93), 399(42),
  403(42), 407(42), 408(42), 409
  (42), 410(42,93), 411(42), 417
  (42), 420(134), 424, 426, 428
Rand, H. P., 2(2), 32
Randall, A. L., 23(62), 35
Randall, R. J., 42(12), 51, 135
  (28), 142, 256(48), 259(48),
  295, 503(11), 510, 523(39),
  530, 538(9), 562, 568(22), 580
  (22), 597, 617(31), 638, 673
  (35), 702
Rang, H. P., 431(3), 472
Rao, Ch. V., 177(25), 191(25),
  246, 252(3), 257(3), 259(3),
  262(3), 263(3), 268(79), 270
  (3), 280(79), 281(79), 282, 292,
  296, 600(8), 613, 616(9,14,23),
  617(29), 622(33), 623(36), 624
  (36), 625(36), 627(36), 629(36),
  630(33,36), 631(36,46), 635
  (47,48), 637, 638, 639
Rapin, A. M. C., 480(3), 494
Rasmussen, H., 451(44), 474,
  534(1), 535, 548, 562, 563
Ray, T. K., 56(22), 71, 120(10),
  121(10,13), 141, 653(30), 664
Rayford, P. L., 372(156), 381,
  579(36), 597
Raynaud, J.-P., 211(64), 248,
  340(126), 380, 418(131), 428
Raz, A., 601(11), 613
Reaven, G. M., 313, 326(61),
  376, 396(56), 397(55), 403(55,
  56), 410(55,56), 411(55,56),
  417(55,56), 418(56), 424, 425,
  465, 476
Rechler, M. M., 316(88), 366
  (88), 367(88), 378, 471(101),
  477
Reddy, W. J., 392(73), 400(73),
  412(73), 414(73), 425
Redwood, W. R., 481(10), 494

Reece, D. K., 211(73), 213(73), 217(73), 248
Reed, L. J., 372(155), 381
Reeke, G. N., Jr., 323(93), 378
Rees, H., 518(24), 530
Rees Midgley, A., Jr., 107(13), 108(13), 117
Reich, E., 13(34), 14(39), 18(39), 33, 34
Reichert, L. E., Jr., 100(1,2,3,4, 5,6,7), 101(2,4,8,9,23), 107(10, 13), 108(13,24), 109(14), 113(2, 6,19,20), 115(6), 116(6,14,20, 23), 117, 118, 120(6), 140, 177 (16), 191(41), 200(51), 208(56), 245, 246, 247, 262(63), 268(70), 283(128), 291(135), 295, 296, 298, 342(128b), 380
Reichnitz, S., 200(52), 247
Reilly, K., 394(81), 396(81), 400 (81), 420(81), 426
Reisfeld, R. A., 463(63), 475
Reiss, E., 544(18), 546(18), 550(18), 562
Reiter, E. O., 191(40), 246
Reiter, M. J., 8(25), 15(48b), 26 (25), 28(25), 33, 34
Renner, R., 463(67), 475
Repke, D. W., 538(12), 541(15), 544, 550(39), 562, 564
Rethy, A., 120(10), 121(10), 141, 144(4), 156
Reuter, A., 330(106), 379
Reuter, M., 253(26), 293
Reynolds, J. A., 26(65b), 27(68), 35, 152(23), 157, 459(56), 475
Rice, B. F., 252(6,22), 259(6), 268(73), 289(22), 293, 296
Rice, R. H., 14(43), 34, 40(11), 46(11), 51
Richards, J., 108(12), 117, 342 (128b), 380
Richardson, M. C., 38(3), 51
Richter, M., 480(5), 494
Riordan, J. R., 636(49), 639

Ripoche, P., 678(40), 703
Risser, W. L., (88), 476
Ritschard, W. J., 471(99,100), 477
Robbins, J., 356(169), 382
Robbins, P. W., 91(52), 98
Roberts, J. S., 522(37), 530
Robertson, H. A., 576(31), 597
Robertson, M. C., 576(34), 597
Robinson, C. A., Jr., 392(73), 400(73), 412(73), 414(73), 425
Robinson, G. A., 55(17), 70, 120(1), 140, 144(1), 156, 252 (20), 293, 616(5), 637
Robinson, G. W., 28(69), 35
Rochman, H., 44(16), 52
Rodbard, D., 111(25), 118, 211 (69,71,78), 213(69,78), 216 (81,83), 218(81), 248, 249, 340(127,128a), 346(127), 348 (139), 349(127), 350(128a), 354(160), 355(127), 372(156, 157,158,159,160), 380, 381, 417(130), 418(130), 428, 579 (36), 595(51), 597, 598
Rodbell, J., 144(3), 156
Rodbell, M., 120, 121(14), 122 (14), 136, 141, 142, 147, 157, 160(1,2,3,4,5,6,7,8), 163(2), 164(2), 165(2), 166(4), 167(4), 168(2,4), 169(4,5), 171(4), 172(31), 173, 174, 218(89), 249, 253(23,25), 293, 332, 379, 396, 400(106), 401(106), 411(123), 426, 427, 428, 442, 449, 473, 521(33), 530, 557, 561, 564, 600, 601, 613, 657, 662(37,44), 664, 665
Rodgers, P., 550(36), 563
Rolland, M., 645(18), 664
Romaldini, J. H., 663(46), 665
Rombauer, R. B., 696(57), 703
Roncone, A., 388(24), 394(79), 423, 426
Rosa, V., 547, 563

Rosal, T. P., 288(133), <u>299</u>
Rose, G. A., 544(17), <u>562</u>
Rosebrough, N. J., 23(62), <u>35</u>, 42
    (12), <u>51</u>, 135(28), <u>142</u>, 256(48),
    259(48), <u>295</u>, 503(11), <u>510</u>, 523
    (39), <u>530</u>, 538(9), <u>562</u>, 568(22),
    580(22), <u>597</u>, 617(31), <u>638</u>, 673
    (35), <u>702</u>
Roseman, S., 82(28), 95(28), <u>97</u>,
    281(107), <u>298</u>
Rosemberg, E., 114(21), <u>118</u>
Rosen, O. M., 58(34), <u>71</u>
Rosenfield, S., 616(26), <u>638</u>
Rosenthal, H. E., 527, <u>531</u>
Rosenthal, J. W., (48), <u>474</u>
Rosenthal, S. L., 388(17), 395(17),
    <u>422</u>
Ross, G., 177(9), <u>245</u>
Ross, G. T., 114(21), <u>118</u>, 191(40),
    192(43), <u>246</u>, 281(114), 287(130),
    291(134), <u>298</u>, <u>299</u>, 372(156),
    <u>381</u>, 579(36), <u>597</u>
Rosselin, G., 47(27), <u>52</u>, 171(29),
    <u>174</u>, 338(119), 369(197), <u>379</u>,
    <u>383</u>, 389(39, 42), 390(39, 42), 396
    (42), 397(42, 93), 399(42), 400
    (39), 401(117), 402(39), 403(42),
    405(122), 406(122), 407(39, 42),
    408(42, 122), 409(42), 410(42, 93),
    411(42), 412(39, 122), 414(39,
    122), 415(129), 417(39, 42), 418
    (39, 122), 420(39, 134), <u>424</u>, <u>426</u>,
    <u>427</u>, <u>428</u>
Roth, J., 38(4), 44(4, 22), <u>51</u>, <u>52</u>,
    120(2, 4, 5), <u>140</u>, 211(77), 213
    (77), 215(77), 218(85), <u>248</u>, <u>249</u>,
    253(28), 255(43, 44, 46, 47), 268
    (74, 78), 269(74, 78), 270(88),
    275(88), <u>294</u>, <u>295</u>, <u>296</u>, <u>297</u>, 302
    (13), 303(5, 8, 9, 10, 12, 13, 14, 15,
    16), 312(5), 313(5, 8), 316(89),
    321(8, 10, 90, 91), 324(3, 91, 96),
    325(3, 9, 10), 326(96), 333(8),
    334(10, 112), 335(8), 336(8, 10,
    112), 337(91, 112), 338(91), 339

(Roth, J.)
    (8, 10, 112, 121), 340(8, 10, 90,
    111, 112, 122), 341(111), 342,
    347(10), 348(10, 112), 356(8,
    112, 177), 357(176, 177, 178,
    179), 359(176), 361(176), 362
    (176), 364(176, 177, 178, 179),
    365(179), 366(13, 14, 15, 16,
    178, 188, 189), 367(89, 176, 177),
    369(195, 196, 197, 198, 199),
    370(200), 371(177), 373(10,
    176, 177), (98), <u>373</u>, <u>374</u>, <u>378</u>,
    <u>379</u>, <u>380</u>, <u>382</u>, <u>383</u>, 386(1, 5,
    7), 387(11, 14), 388(26), 389
    (1, 14, 26, 38, 39), 390(26, 38,
    39), 391(26), 392(1, 38, 45, 47,
    48, 49, 50, 51, 52, 53, 54), 393
    (26, 38), 394(38, 52, 78), 396
    (11, 14, 26, 47), 397(45, 47, 49,
    50, 51, 53, 96, 97), 398(45, 47,
    49, 50, 53, 54, 96, 97), 399(38,
    45, 47, 49, 54), 400(11, 14, 26,
    38, 39, 48, 52, 78, 108, 109, 110),
    401(11, 14), 402(11, 39, 96, 97,
    108, 109), 403(14, 45, 47, 54,
    78), 405(14), 406(52, 96, 97,
    121), 407(11, 38, 39, 45, 47, 49,
    52, 53, 54, 78), 408(38, 47, 51,
    52, 78), 410(47, 49, 54), 411
    (45, 47, 49, 54), 412(11, 14, 26,
    38, 39, 48, 52, 78, 108, 109), 414
    (11, 14, 26, 38, 39, 48, 52, 78,
    108, 109, 110, 127), 415(52, 96,
    97), 417(11, 38, 39, 47, 51, 52,
    54, 78, 109, 110, 127), 418(14,
    39, 52, 127, 132), 420(11, 39,
    48, 49, 50, 54, 108, 109, 127,
    133, 135), 421(11, 54, 127),
    <u>422</u>, <u>423</u>, <u>424</u>, <u>426</u>, <u>427</u>, <u>428</u>,
    444(30, 31, 32), 448(32, 33),
    450(32), 458(54), 465(74, 75),
    468(74), <u>474</u>, <u>475</u>, <u>476</u>, 512
    (1), <u>529</u>, 566(1), 575(1), <u>596</u>,
    642(1), 659(40), 660(41), <u>663</u>,
    <u>665</u>, 669(18), <u>701</u>

Roth, S., 281(107,108), <u>298</u>
Roughton, F. J. W., 358(185), <u>383</u>
Rouser, G., 145, <u>157</u>
Roux, V., 668(5), <u>701</u>
Roy, C., 668(9,13), 669(15,16,17),
    682(9), 684(9,13), 685(9,13,51),
    686(9), 688(15), 689(15,16), 690
    (9), 691(16,17), 692(17), 693(52),
    695(9), 696(52), 699(52), 700
    (52), <u>701</u>, <u>703</u>
Rubenstein, A. H., 550(37), <u>563</u>
Rubin, M. M., 356(152), 371(152),
    <u>381</u>
Rufener, C., 367(192), <u>383</u>
Ruiz, E., 121(11), <u>141</u>, 144(13),
    148(13), <u>156</u>, 544(18), 546(18),
    550(18), <u>562</u>
Rumke, P., 653(32), <u>664</u>, 682(48),
    <u>703</u>
Ruoslahti, E., 468(89), <u>476</u>
Ryan, D., 179(31), 223(92,94), 229
    (31,94,100), 231(94), 235(94),
    237(100), 239(92), 241(92,94,
    100,106), 243(94,100), <u>246</u>, <u>249</u>,
    <u>250</u>
Ryan, R. J., 114(21), <u>118</u>, 121, <u>141</u>,
    177)8,15,26), 199(49), 218(87),
    221(15), 222(26), <u>245</u>, <u>246</u>, <u>247</u>,
    <u>249</u>, 252(4), 259(4,53), 262, 268
    (62,71), 270(4,71), 276(100),
    282(122), <u>293</u>, <u>295</u>, <u>296</u>, <u>297</u>,
    <u>298</u>

Sachs, L., 82(28), 95(28), <u>97</u>
Saez, J. M., 46, 47, <u>52</u>, 626(35),
    630(35), <u>638</u>
Saffran, M., 253(35), <u>294</u>, 514(7,
    8), 515(7,8), 516(7,8), 517(7),
    <u>529</u>
St. Arneault, G., 484(13), <u>494</u>
Saito, T., 252(13,18), <u>293</u>
Sallis, J. D., 536(7), <u>562</u>
Salnikow, J., 28(69), <u>35</u>
Salomon, Y., 662(44), <u>665</u>

Sammon, P. J., 546(21), 547,
    548(21), 549(21), <u>563</u>
Samuelsson, B., 616(24), 620(24),
    621, <u>638</u>
Sandberg, A. A., 303(21), 318
    (21), 333(21), <u>374</u>
Sanders, H., 276(101), <u>297</u>
Sapag-Hagar, M., 595(53), <u>598</u>
Sar, M., 517(22), 518(24,25),
    <u>530</u>
Saraswathi, S., 282(117), <u>298</u>
Saroff, H. A., 356(169), 357(170,
    171,174), <u>382</u>
Saruta, T., 616(7), <u>637</u>
Sato, G. H., 38(1), <u>51</u>
Savard, K., 252(22), 289(22),
    <u>293</u>
Sawyer, W. H., 513(6), 520(32),
    <u>529</u>, <u>530</u>
Saxena, B. B., 120(7), <u>140</u>, 177
    (25), 191(25), 199(50), 206(50,
    54), <u>246</u>, <u>247</u>, 252(1,3,13,18),
    253(38), 256(38), 257(3), 259
    (1,3), 262(3), 263(3), 266(1),
    267(1), 268(1,72,77), 270(1,
    3), 272(1), 276(1), 278(1), 280
    (1), 282, 288(131,133), <u>292</u>,
    <u>293</u>, <u>294</u>, <u>296</u>, <u>297</u>, <u>299</u>
Sayers, G., 44(21), 47(25), <u>52</u>,
    269(83), <u>296</u>, 550(38), <u>563</u>,
    595(49), <u>598</u>
Scatchard, G., 211(58,59), <u>247</u>,
    267(69), <u>296</u>, 340(123), 348
    (136), <u>379</u>, <u>380</u>, 436, 441,
    <u>473</u>, 527, <u>531</u>, 587, <u>598</u>, 626,
    <u>638</u>
Schachman, H. K., 237(103), <u>250</u>
Schaumburg, B. P., 411(125),
    <u>428</u>, 630(41), <u>638</u>
Scheinberg, I. H., 262(61), 281
    (112), 282(112), <u>295</u>, <u>298</u>
Schemberg, I. H., 650(26), <u>664</u>
Schenk, A., 121(11), <u>141</u>, 144
    (13), 148(13), <u>156</u>
Schildknecht, J., 211(72), <u>248</u>,

(Schildknecht, J.)
   348(178), 380
Schimmer, B. P., 38(1), 51
Schlessinger, J., 357(173), 382
Schlichtkrull, J., 388(27), 423
Schmidt, J., 13(32), 14(32,38), 18
   (55), 25(65a), 33, 34, 35
Schmidt-Gollwitzer, M., 120(7),
   140, 199(50), 206(50), 247
Schneider, C. H., 669(21), 676(21),
   702
Schneider, G. T., 252(6), 259(6),
   268(73), 293, 296
Schneider, J. A., 306(37), 307(37),
   375
Schoessler, M. A., 669(22), 702
Schoffeniels, E., 3, 32
Schramm, M., 56(23), 71
Schucher, R., 317(73), 377
Schulster, D., 38(3), 51
Schulz, K., 498(5), 501(5), 504(5),
   510
Schussler, G. C., 601(10), 613
Schuurs, A. H. W. M., 253(32,33),
   294
Schwartz, I. L., 388(17), 395(17),
   422, 668(8,12), 669(20,22), 676
   (20), 701, 702
Schwartz, R. H., 303(6,7), 312(6),
   313, 314, 315, 367(6), 369(7),
   373, 397(99,100), 427
Schwartz, S., 200(52), 247
Sealock, R., 14(36), 18(36), 25(36),
   33
Seelig, S., 44(21), 52, 269(83),
   297, 595(49), 598
Segel, L. A., 367(193), 383
Segrest, J. P., 152(25), 157
Seiguer, A. C., 177(2,4), 191(2,4),
   196(2,4), 245, 253(30), 294
Sela, B.-A., 82(28), 95(28), 97
Selinger, R. C. L., 38(2), 51
Sell, K. W., 308(52), 376
Seltzman, T. P., 40(10), 41(10),
   43(10), 51(10), 51

Severson, A. R., 550(34), 563
Shanks, R. G., 55(12), 70
Shapiro, A. L., 152(20), 157
Share, L., 522(37), 530
Sharma, O. P., 528(53), 531
Sharon, N., 480(2), 494
Sharp, G. W. G., 56(26), 71,
   74(2), 82(37), 92(37), 96, 98,
   668(11), 701
Shearer, G. M., 316(55), 366(55),
   370(55), 376
Shen, A. L., 348(136), 380
Sherman, D. H., 668(5), 701
Sheth, A. R., 266(68), 296
Shirasu, H., 548(26), 563
Shitaka, M., 44(19), 52
Shiu, R. P. C., 120(8), 140, 241
   (107), 250, 252(16), 257(52),
   293, 295, 392(69), 400(69),
   403(69), 407(69), 412(69), 414
   (69), 425, 433(8), 447(8), 471
   (97), 473, 477, 566(7,8,9,10),
   567(14,17), 568(8), 570(8),
   571(8), 573(7,8), 574(7,8),
   575(7,10,17), 576(7,30,31),
   579(9), 584(9), 585(9), 586(9),
   587(9), 589(9), 591(9), 593(9),
   596, 597
Shlatz, L., 394(80,81), 396(81),
   400(80,81), 420(81), 426
Shrager, R. I., 211(74,75), 213
   (74,75), 217(74), 248
Sibiga, S., 276(101), 297
Sica, V., 57(28), 71, 460(62),
   463(62), 475
Silman, H. I., 17(54), 34
Silman, I., 5(20), 33
Silver, L., 669(20,22), 676(20),
   701, 702
Simon, E. J., 498(1,4), 502(1),
   506(1,14), 507(15), 509, 510
Simon, G., 145(14), 157
Simon, J., 405(122), 406(122),
   408(122), 412(122), 414(122),
   418(122), 428

Simon, W., 546(21), 548(21), 549
  (21), 563
Simpson, E., 313(60), 376
Simpson, T. H., 151(16), 157
Singer, M. D. B., 678(39), 702
Singer, S. J., 5(19), 33, 367(190),
  383, 539, 562
Singh, A., 508(18), 510
Sips, R., 351(145), 381
Sjöholm, I., 669(24, 25), 676(24),
  702
Sken, A. L., 211(59), 247
Slater, R. H., 54(9), 70
Smetana, R., 279(103), 297
Smigel, M., 616(16), 630(16), 637
Smith, A. J., 152(19), 157, 668(2),
  701
Smith, B. R., 655(35, 36), 663(36),
  664
Smith, D. F., 483(14), 485(14),
  488(14), 490(14), 494
Smith, D. M., 550(34), 563
Smith, G. C., 177(3), 190(3), 216
  (3), 217(3), 245, 262(60), 295
Smith, G. D., 441(23), 473
Smith, M., 14(39), 18(39), 34
Smith, R. L., 611(20), 614
Smith, R. M., 253(26), 293, 367
  (191), 383, 395(85), 426
Smith, R. W., 308(52), 376
Smith, S., 528(50), 531
Sneyd, J. G. T., 616(12), 637
Snyder, S. H., 437(13), 466(78),
  473, 476, 498(2), 501(8), 502(2),
  503, 506(8), 509, 510
Söderlund, H., 693, 703
Soderman, D. D., 395(86), 426,
  464(69), 475
Sodoyez, J. C., 325(102, 103), 378,
  389(35), 394(35), 423
Sodoyez-Goffaux, F., 325(102),
  378, 389(35), 394(35), 423
Sokolovsky, M., 636(49), 639
Soll, A. H., 340(111), 341(111),
  379, 370(200), 383, 392(54),

(Soll, A. H.)
  398(54), 399(54), 400(109, 110),
  402(109), 403(54), 407(54),
  410(54), 411(54), 412(109),
  414(109, 110, 126, 127), 417
  (54, 109, 110, 126, 127), 418
  (127), 420(54, 109, 126, 127),
  421(54, 127), 424, 427, 428
Soll, A. S., 367(194), 383
Soloff, M. S., 253(35), 294, 514
  (7, 8, 9, 10, 11), 515(7, 8), 516
  (7, 8), 517(7), 518(9, 10, 11,
  24), 519(9, 10), 520(9, 10), 521
  (10), 527(9, 10, 11), 529, 530,
  616(19), 637
Solyom, A., 91(50), 98, 653(33),
  664
Somlyo, A. F., 519(27), 530
Somlyo, A. V., 519(27), 530
Sonenberg, M., 121(15), 141,
  466(79), 476
Song, C. S., 265(66), 266(66),
  296
Sox, H. C., 304(30), 306(30),
  308(30), 331(30), 375
Spector, A. A., 211(65), 248,
  348(140), 350(140), 380
Spillman, C. H., 616(18, 28),
  620(28), 637, 638
Stadie, W. C., 388(16), 395(16),
  422
Stagg, B. H., 44(16), 52
Stanbury, J. B., 609, 613
Stanley, H. E., 356(164), 381
Steck, T. L., 26(67), 27(67),
  28(67), 35, 487(23), 493(23),
  495
Stedman, E., 5(23), 33
Steelman, S., 106(22), 118, 257,
  295
Steer, M. L., 66(41), 71, 367
  (193), 383
Stein, S., 22(64), 35, 581(38),
  597
Steinbach, J. H., 3(8), 32

Steinberg, A. H., 514(11), 518(11), 527(11), 529

Sternlieb, I., 281(112), 282(112), 298

Steroid, J., 46(23), 47(23), 52

Stevens, C. F., 3(6,8), 32

Stock, T. L., 276(102), 297

Storm, D. R., 121, 141

Stossel, T. P., 318(75,76), 377

Stouffer, J. E., 460(59), 475, 669 (21), 676(21), 702

Strife, A., 303(20), 374

Stumpf, W. E., 517(22), 518(24,25), 530

Stürmer, E., 674(36), 702

Sugiyama, H., 29(71), 35

Sullivan, T. J., 311(54), 316(54), 366(54), 376

Sundström, C., 306(44), 307(44), 375

Sutcliffe, H. S., 547, 549, 554, 558, 560, 561(25), 563

Sutherland, E. W., 55(17), 70, 120 (1), 140, 144(1,2), 156, 252(20), 293, 616(5), 637

Sutter, B. Ch. J., 389(32), 394(32), 395(32), 423

Suzuki, F., 460(60), 463(60), 475

Svennerholm, L., 74(16,17), 75, 81, 96, 97, 98

Svensmark, O., 282(119), 298

Swallow, R. L., 47(25), 52

Swartz, T. L., 253(35), 294, 514 (7,8,9,10,11), 515(7,8), 516(7, 8), 517(7), 518(9,10,11), 519(9, 10), 520(9,10), 521(10), 527(9, 10,11), 529, 616(19), 637

Swillens, S., 441(24), 473

Swislocki, N. I., 121, 141

Szabo, M., 616(10), 637

Szewchuk, A., 282(115), 298

Szutowicz, A., 367(183), 382

Takeda, Y., 460(60), 463(60), 475

Tanaka, A., 38(6), 51

Tanford, C., 26(65b), 27(68), 35, 152(23), 157, 459(56), 475, 487(21), 495

Tarnoff, J., 610(17), 613, 616(3), 637

Tashjian, A., 546(19), 563

Taylor, S. I., 441(21), 473

Tell, G. P. E., 57(28,29), 71, (187), 383, 455(49), 464(49), 471(49), 474

Temin, H. M., 464(71), 471(92, 93,94), 475, 477

Temperley, J. M., 44(16), 52

Terenius, L., 498(3), 502(3), 509

Terry, W. D., 308(52), 376

Terryberry, J. E., 333(110), 379

Thalhimer, W., 464(70), 475

Thompson, E. E., 512(1), 529, 669(18), 701

Thompson, G. E., 319(85,86), 378

Thorell, J. I., 179(30), 246, 325 (100), 378, 433(7), 472, 568, 597, 643, 663

Thornton, E. R., 508(18), 510

Tierney, J., 121(15), 141

Tietze, F., 337(117), 379

Tindal, J. S., 566(3), 574(3), 596

Todaro, G. J., 82(29), 95(29), 97

Tomasi, V., 56(22), 71, 120(10), 121, 141, 144(4), 156

Tomchick, R., 54(3), 70

Tomizawa, H. H., 337(115,116), 379

Tong, W., 651, 664

Topper, Y. J., 397(94), 426, 463(68), 475

Torresani, J., 646(21), 652(21), 664

Toshima, S., 304(29), 305(29), 375

Townshend, M. M., 668(2), 701
Toxier, R., 646(19), 664
Trams, E. G., 91(50), 98, 653 (33), 664
Tregear, G. W., 549(31), 555(46), 556(46), 558(46), 563, 564
Trevisani, A., 120(10), 121(10), 141, 144(4), 156
Triggle, D. J., 55(15), 70
Trowbridge, C. G., 100(1,3,4), 101(4), 117, 208(56), 247, 283 (128), 299
Troxler, F., 66(42), 72
Tshushima, T., 471(98), 477
Tsong, Y. Y., 177(19), 191(19), 192(19), 245
Tsuruhara, T., 177(5,7,10,11,18), 178(5), 179(5), 180(32), 181(32, 33), 188(19,35), 190(5,37), 192 (11,37), 193(33,46), 195(5,10), 197(5,11,37), 199(18), 203(5,7, 10,18,53), 205(32,37), 208(10,55), 219(18,33), 221(10), 222(10), 225 (5,10), 229(7,18,53), 241(32), 243(33), 245, 246, 247, 252(10), 262(57,58), 268(10,75), 270(97), 281(111), 282(124), 293, 295, 296, 297, 298, (141), 380, 595 (50), 598
Tsushima, T., 120(5), 140, 566(11), 567(11,14), 575(11), 576(30), 596, 597
Tuppy, H., 282(121), 298
Turba, F., 528(45), 531
Turkington, R. W., 252(15), 257 (51), 293, 295, 528(51), 531, 566 (12), 567(18), 569, 575(18), 595 (52), 596, 597, 598
Turner, R. S., 281(110), 298
Twarog, J. M., 528(52), 531
Tyrode, M. V., 514, 529

Udenfriend, S., 22(64), 35, 581(38), 597

Ueda, K., 38(1), 51
Uhr, J. W., 339(120), 379
Ulrich, K., 303(21), 318(21), 333 (21), 374
Underwood, L. E., 392(64), 396 (64), 397(64), 406(64), 407(64), 425, 471(91), 476
Unger, R. H., 171(26,27), 174
Ushijima, Y., 51(29), 52

Vaheri, A., 468(89), 476
Vaitukaitis, J. L., 107(11), 117, 177(9,17), 191(40), 192(43), 197(48), 206(48), 245, 246, 247, 252(12), 253(12), 254(41), 255(41), 256(12), 281(114), 287(130), 291(134), 293, 294, 298, 299
Vakakis, N., 555(46), 556(46), 558(46), 564
Vallee, B. L., 636(49), 639
Van Cauter, E., 441(24), 473
Van der Hamer, C. J. A., 650 (26), 664
Vandlen, R., 18(55), 25(65a), 34, 35
Van Dongen, C. G., 514, 529
vanDorp, D. A., 600(2), 613
Van Hall, E. V., 177(18), 188(18), 199(18), 203(18), 219(18), 229 (18), 245, 281(114), 298
Vanha-Perttula, T., 177(12), 191(12), 245
Vanha-Pertulla, T., 177(28), 246
van Heyningen, S., 74(20), 77(20, 25), 97
van Heyningen, W. E., 74(14,15, 19), 96, 97
Vanka-Perrtulas, T., 252(2), 259(2), 270(2), 292
Vannotti, A., 316(74), 377
Van Rossum, J. M., 681(45), 703
Van Strick, R., 388(22), 392(22),

(Van Strick, R.)
  423
Van Weeman, B. K., 253(32,33),
  294
Van Wyk, J. J., 392(64), 396(64),
  397(64), 406(64), 407(64), 425,
  471(91), 476
Varandani, P. T., 337(118), 379
Vassent, G., 211(67,68), 216(82),
  248, 249
Vatner, D., 63(37), 66(37), 71
Vaughan, M., 84(40,41), 98, 318
  (75,76), 377, 388(16), 395(16),
  422
Venter, J. C., 508, 510
Verrier, B., 642(5,6), 646(21),
  651(5,6), 652(6,21), 655(6), 658
  (5,6,38), 660(42), 661(6,38,42),
  663(46), 663, 664, 665
Vesin, M. F., 630(38), 638
Vinten, J., 84(44), 86(44), 98, 398
  (101), 411(124,125), 427, 428,
  434(9), 439(9), 473
Vinuela, E., 152(20), 157
Vitetta, E. S., 339(120), 379
Vlahakes, G. J., 387(10), 422
VonEuler, U. S., 54(2), 70

Waage, P., 343(132), 380
Wade, R., 46, 52
Wagner, V., 191(38), 246
Wakeling, A. E., 616(17,18,25),
  620(25), 630(37), 637, 638
Walbach, D. F. H., 276(102), 297
Walborg, E. F., Jr., 483(14), 485
  (14,15), 488(14), 490(14,16),
  494
Walker, W. A., 74(13), 96
Wallace, R. E., 467(85), 476
Wallach, D. F. H., 26(67), 27(67),
  28(67), 35
Walter, L., 484(13), 494
Walter, R., 668(8,12), 701
Wang, J. L., 323(93), 378

Ward, D. N., 208(57), 247
Wardlaw, S., 268(72), 296
Warner, C. E., 31(72), 35
Warshaw, J., 56(27), 71
Wasserman, M. A., 55(13), 70
Watanabe, K., 282(125), 299,
  595(50), 598
Way, E. L., 437(14), 473, 504
  (13), 510
Weaver, R. A., 523, 530
Weber, G., 504(12), 510
Weber, H. G., 211(72), 248, 348
  (138), 380
Weber, K., 12(29), 27(29), 33,
  152(21), 157
Weber, M., 16(52), 34
Wedner, H. J., 311(54), 313(58),
  316(54), 366(54), 376
Weed, J. C., 252(6), 259(6),
  268(73), 293, 296
Weidemann, M. J., 392(70), 400
  (70), 401(119), 412(70), 414
  (70), 425, 428
Weigele, M., 22(64), 35, 581
  (38), 597
Weill, C. L., 15(47,48), 16(47,
  48), 18(47,48), 22(47,48), 24
  (47), 25(47,48), 26(48), 28
  (47,48), 31(47), 34
Weinberg, A. N., 317(71), 377
Weinstein, Y., 316(55), 366(55),
  370(55), 376
Weisbauer, V., 282(121), 298
Weise, H.-C., 177(23), 245
Weiss, B., 49(28), 50(28), 52,
  164(15), 173, 608(15), 613
Weiss, G. H., 216(83), 249
Weiss, L., 463(67), 475
Weiss, M., 211(76), 213(76), 248
Weissman, B., 282(116), 298
Well, C. A., 471(101), 477
Werle, E., 282(118), 298
Westheimer, F. H., 508, 510
White, D., 281(108), 298
Whitfield, J. F., 630(42), 638

Whittaker, V. P., 501, 506(7), 510
Wicker, J. V., 609(16), 613
Wide, L., 288(132), 299
Widnell, C. C., 40(9,10), 41(9,10),
  42(13), 43(9,10), 44(13), 46(9),
  51(9,10), 51, 91(51), 98
Wieland, O., 463(67), 475
Wiener, A. M., 12(29), 27(29), 33
Wilchek, M., 489(24), 495, 589(43),
  598
Wilfong, R. F., 553(43), 564
Williams, L. T., 54(7), 59(7,36),
  62(7), 70, 71
Williams, R. H., 337(115), 379,
  451(46), 474
Willis, G. H., 5(22), 33
Wilson, E. E., 318(77a), 377
Wilzbach, K. E., 130, 141, 669,
  702
Winand, R., 253(36), 294, 367(184),
  382, 642(7), 650(25), 651(7),
  654(7), 658(7), 661(7,43), 662
  (7), 663, 664, 665
Winestock, G., 669(21), 676(21),
  702
Wingender, W., 51(30), 52
Winget, G. D., 330(107), 379
Winnik, M., 4(17), 5(17), 7(21), 8
  (21), 9(21), 33
Winter, B. A., 509, 510
Winter, W., 330(107), 379
Winterburn, P. J., 281(105), 297
Wintersberger, E., 282(121), 298
Wintrobe, M. M., 313(64), 376
Winzler, R. J., 281(106), 298, 487
  (22), 495
Witkum, P., 82(37), 92(37), 97
Wofsey, L., 539, 562
Wohltmann, H. J., 388(19), 395
  (19), 423
Wolcott, R. G., 13(32), 14(32), 33
Wolfe, B. M., 57(31), 71
Wolff, J., 600(9), 613, 616(11),
  619, 620(11), 628(45), 630(11,
  39), 637, 638, 639, 642(3,8),

(Wolff, J.)
  651(8), 654(3), 655(3), 657(3),
  661(8,43), 662(3,8), 663, 665
Wollmet, A., 389(40), 390(40),
  400(40), 403(40), 406(40), 408
  (40), 412(40), 414(40), 418
  (40), 424
Wong, M., 534(1), 562
Woo, C., 519(27), 530
Woodard, C. J., 66(42), 72
Woodward, C., 218(88), 249
Woodward, G., 617(30), 638,
  668(10), 669(28), 676(28), 682
  (10), 701, 702
Woolfolk, B. J., 152(26), 157
Wray, V. P., 485(15), 490(16),
  494
Wu, Y. C., 437(14), 473, 504
  (13), 510
Wuu, T. C., 520(32), 530
Wyman, J., 347(147), 356(151),
  371, 381
Wyngarden, L. J., 616(17,25,27,
  28), 620(25,27,28), 630(37),
  637, 638

Yagi, Y., 307(47), 376
Yalow, R. S., 47(26,27), 52, 211
  (60,62), 247, 248, 254(39),
  255(39), 294, 330(105), 338
  (119), 340(124), 348(124), 379,
  380, 387, 389(15), 390(15),
  391, 415(129), 422, 424, 428,
  645(17), 664
Yam, L. T., 313(66), 377
Yamamoto, A., 145(14), 157
Yamashita, K., 144(5), 156, 642
  (2), 654(2,34), 655(2,34), 663,
  664
Yang, K.-P., 208(57), 247
Yip, C. Y., 394(82), 400(82),
  426
Yolcin, B., 319(81), 365(81),
  377

Yong, M. S., 55(16), 70
Yu, J., 487, 493(23), 495

Zanetti, M. E., 610(9), 614
Zapf, J., 406(121), 428
Zeleski, A. J., 269(136), 299
Zeleznik, A., 107(13), 108(12,13),
    117, 191(41), 246, 342(128b), 380
Zenser, T. V., 630(40), 638

Zirrolli, J. A., 57(31), 71
Zor, V., 616(4,13), 637
Zucker-Franklin, D., 313(62),
    376
Zull, J. E., 536(8), 538(12), 541
    (15), 543(8), 544(18), 546(18),
    550(18,39), 553(45), 556(45),
    557(45), 559(45), 560, 561(45),
    562, 564
Zur Hausen, H., 306(38), 375

SUBJECT INDEX

Acetamidination of parathyroid
539-547
Acetamidino lysine, 539-540
Acetic anhydride, 636
Acetylcholine receptors, 1-35
  affinity chromatography, 17-24
  assay by affinity labeling, 5-13
  assay by binding of α-neurotox-
    ins, 13-15
  characterization of purified recep-
    tors, 24, 32
    gel electrophoresis, 26-29
    immunological methods, 29-31
    initial characteristics, 24-26
    reconstitution of membrane,
      31-32
  isolation of, 15-24
  probing in intact cells, 2-5
    electroplax, 3-5
    general approaches, 2-3
  purification of, 15-24
  Triton X-100, 27
N-Acetylgalactosamine, 74
N-Acetylglucosamine, 489
N-Acetylneuraminic acid, 74
Acrylamide gel electrophoresis,
  29-30
ACTH, 130, 541-542, 600
  [^{125}]ACTH, 386
  amino acid sequence of, 44, 45
  iodination of, 126-127

ACTH-sensitive adrenocortical
  membranes, 37-52
  adenylate cyclase assay, 48-51
  criteria of homogeneity, 42-44
  electron microscopy, 43-44
  marker enzymes, 42-43
  hormone-receptor interaction,
    44-48
    binding studies, 47-48
    labeling the hormone, 44-47
    radioactivity, 46-47
  preparation of membranes, 38-
    42
Acute myelogenous leukemia, 309
Adenosine 3',5'-monophosphate
  (see cAMP)
Adenosine triphosphate (see ATP)
Adenylate cyclase, 83, 94, 95,
  144, 608-609, 683-685
  activation of, 92, 166
  assay, 48-51, 164-166
  -containing membrane fractions,
    58-59
  factors affecting activity, 662-
    663
  solubilization of, 694
Adipocytes, 600
Adipose tissue, prostaglandin
  receptors in, 599-614
  application of the binding re-
    action, 609-611

(Adipose tissue)
  binding to intact lipocytes, 601-602
  binding to receptor preparation,
    601-606
  lipocyte preparation, 600-601
  preparation for quantitation, 606-
    608
  properties of the preparation,
    608-609
beta-Adrenergic receptors, 53-72
  approaches to purification, 67-69
    affinity chromatography, 69
    solubilization, 67-68
  binding assay for [^{3}H] (-)-alpren-
    olol, 57-62
    compared to other methods, 66-67
    interpretation of results, 62
    potential pitfalls, 62-65
  [^{3}H]catacholamine binding, 56-57
Adrenocortical membranes, ACTH-
    sensitive, 37-52
  adenylate cyclase assay, 48-51
  criteria of homogeneity, 42-44
    electron microscopy, 43-44
    marker enzymes, 42-43
  hormone-receptor interaction, 44-
    48
    binding studies, 47-48
    labeling the hormone, 44-47
    radioactivity, 46-47
  preparation of membranes, 38-42
Acrenocorticotropic hormone
  (see ACTH)
Adrenocorticotropin, displacement
    by, 445
Affi-Gel 401, 17
Affinity adsorbent, preparation of,
    587-588
Affinity chromatography
  acetylcholine receptors, 17-24
  beta-adrenergic receptor purifi-
    cation, 69
  fractionation, 488-489
  gonadotropin receptors, 275-
    278

(Affinity chromatography)
  purification of solubilized,
    241-244
  opiate receptors, 506-508
  purification of prolactin recep-
    tors, 588-592
Affinity gel, 17-20
Affinity labeling
  acetylcholine receptors, 5-13
  opiate receptors, 508-509
Agarose, 17, 18, 38, 69, 76
Agarose beads, 180, 181
Agglutination, inhibition of, 480-
    481
Albumin, 226, 447, 452
(-)-Alprenolol, 60, 62, 63
(+)-Alprenolol, 62
[^{3}H] (-)-Alprenolol, 53-72
  binding, 57-62
    compared to other methods,
      66-67
    incubation conditions, 59-60
    interpretation of results, 62
    potential pitfalls, 62-65
    structural formula, 57
    Triton X-100, 68
Amino acid
  protein analysis, 276, 277
  sequence of ACTH, 44, 45
p-Amino-N, N-dimethylbenzyl-
    amine, 5
Ammonium acetate, 274-275
cAMP, 144, 160, 164, 165, 182,
    600, 612, 661
  dibutyryl, 652
  formation of, 252
  inhibition of, 282
  phosphodiesterase, 609
  purification of, 165-166
AMP, determinations for, 49-50
[^{125}]Angiotensin, 386
Antigens, 305
Apoferritin, 226
Arginine, 539-540
Aspartic acid, 276

Association rates of insulin receptors, 433-434
ATPase membrane, 609
ATP regenerating system, 49-50
Autoradiography of oxytocin receptors, 517-518

B-cell, 324
B-cell lines, 308-310
Benzenes, 507
Benzoquinonium, 17
Binding
  acetylcholine receptors, 13-15
  [^{3}H](-)-alprenolol, 57-62
    compared to other methods, 66-67
    incubation conditions, 59-60
    interpretation of results, 62
    potential pitfalls, 62-65
  [^{3}H]catecholamine, 56-57
  etorphine, 504, 505
  follicle-stimulating hormone, 200-202, 261-262
  [^{125}I]glucagon assay, 148
  gonadotropin receptors, 188-189, 209-223
    site of subcellular, 192-193
  growth hormone receptors
    isotherm for, 343-346
    kinetics of, 355-356
    steady-state, 333-355
  hormone assays, 136-140
  hormone-receptor interaction, 47-48
  human chorionic gonadotropin, 197-199, 261-262
  [^{125}I]human chorionic gonadotropin characteristics, 267-268
  Hummel-Dreyer assay, 138-139
  inhibition of, 481
  insulin, 313-316
    Hill plot, 350-355
    Lineweaver-Burk plot, 346
    nonspecific, 434-435

(Binding)
  pH effect, 336
  Scatchard plot, 346-350
  specific, 434-438
  steady-state, 333-340
  insulin receptors, 403-418
    analysis of data, 440-441
    cell membranes, 412-414
    expression of results, 415-418
    general problems, 403-409
    intact cells, 409-411
    solubilization, 415
  to intact lipocytes, 601, 602
  luteinizing hormone, 197-199, 261-262
  measurement of labeled glucagon, 169-171
  naloxone, 504, 506
  naltrexone, 505
  α-neurotoxins, 13-15
  nonspecific, 111, 112, 340-341, 361
  oxytocin receptors, 518-528
    by isolated mammary gland cells, 523-528
    metal ions and, 519-520
    pH and, 519-520
  parathyroid hormone receptors, 556-561
    pH in, 560
  [^{125}I]peptide, 416
  to plasma membranes, 136-137
  prolactin, 572-575
    specific, 261-262
    subcellular particle preparation, 567-568
    testing activity, 569-570
  prostaglandin receptors in adipose tissue
    application of the reaction, 609-611
    intact lipocytes, 601, 602
    receptor preparation, 601-606
  prostaglandin receptors in

(Binding)
  corpora lutea
  assay for, 617-620
  conditions for, 622-625
  constants, 626-630
  effect of chemibal modification of
    membrane proteins on, 635-
    636
  to solubilized hormone receptors,
    137-140
  specific, 111, 340-341
    follicle-stimulating hormone,
      261-262
    human chorionic gonadotropin,
      261-262
    insulin, 434-438
    luteinizing hormone, 261-262
    prolactin, 261-262
  stereospecific opiate, 502-505
    to brain cerebrosides, 504
    centrifugation techniques, 502
    filtration technique, 503-505
    in lipid extracts, 504
    morphine-receptor assay, 503
  thyrotropin receptors, 656-658
    crude particulate fractions, 657-
      658
    intact cells, 656
    plasma membranes, 657-658
  tissue preparations for opiate
    receptor studies, 499-501
  vasopressin, 685-692, 695-700
Bio-Gel A-15, 38
Bio-Gel P-60, 102
Bisquaternary activators, 4
Blood mononuclear cells, periph-
  eral, 311-316
Blue Dextran, 138, 226, 231, 232,
  234
Borohydride, tritiated, 650
Bovine serum albumin (BSA), 256,
  257, 409, 410, 414, 481
Brain cerebrosides, stereospecific
  narcotic binding, 504
Brij-35, 272-273

Bromoacetylcholine bromide, 5
Bungarotoxin, 541-542
Burkitt's lymphoma, 309, 311

Calcitonin, 541-542
Carbamylcholine, 13, 17, 31-32
Carbohydrates in gonadotropin
  receptor interaction, 281-283
Carbowax 6000, 457
Carboxymethylcellulose chromatography in parathyroid hormone receptors, 535-538
p-Carboxyphenyltrimethylam-
  monium, 20
p-Carboxyphenyltrimethylam-
  monium iodide, 20-21
Cardiac glucagon receptors, 143-
  157
  dissociable glucagon-receptor
    site, 148-151
  [^{125}I] glucagon binding assay,
    148
  iodination of glucagon, 147-148
  molecular weight estimation of
    [^{125}I] glucagon, 151-156
  phosphatidylinositol isolation,
    145-147
  phosphatidylserine isolation,
    145-146
Carrier-free monoiodination,
  324-325
[^{3}H] Catecholamine binding, 56-57
Cell counts, 333
Cell membranes
  insulin receptor binding, 412-
    414
  insulin receptor preparation,
    399-402
  interaction of [^{125}I] choleragen
    and choleragenoid, 84-90
  particulate preparation, 567-579
  distribution of activity in sub-
    cellular fractions, 570-572
  labeled hormone preparation,

(Cell membranes)
568–569
prolactin-binding subcellular
particle preparation, 567–568
properties of, 572–575
radioreceptor assay, 575–579
testing prolactin-binding activity, 569–570
tissue source, 567
prostaglandin receptor preparation, 616–618
Cellulose, 38
Cellulose chromatography of
[^{125}I] insulin, 392–393
Cell viability, 333
Cerebrosides, 79, 504
Chediak-Higashi syndrome, 305
Chloramine-T, 83, 124, 325, 390
iodination, 101–107
radioiodination, 178–179
p-Chloromercuribenzoate, 636
Choleragen, 79–80
interaction of ^{125}I-labeled with
cells and cell membranes,
84–90
interaction of ^{125}I-labeled with
membrane components, 92–
95
radioiodination of, 82–84
use of ^{125}I-labeled as plasma
membrane markers, 90–92
Choleragenoid, 74–80
interaction of ^{125}I-labeled with
cells and cell membranes,
84–90
radioiodination of, 82–84
use of ^{125}I-labeled as plasma
markers, 90–92
Cholera toxin receptors, 73–98
choleragen, 74–80
interaction of ^{125}I-labeled
with cells and cell mem-
branes, 84–90
interaction of ^{125}I-labeled
with membrane components,

(Cholera toxin receptors)
92–95
radioiodination of, 82–84
use of ^{125}I-labeled as plasma
membrane markers, 90–92
choleragenoid, 74–80
interaction of ^{125}I-labeled
with cells and cell mem-
branes, 84–90
radioiodination of, 82–84
use of ^{125}I-labeled as plasma
membrane markers, 90–92
Cholesterol, 280–281
hChorionic gonadotropin (hCG),
177, 178, 241–244, 283–292
binding, 197–199, 261–262
cellular localization of, 190–191
labeling, 255–256
measurement of activity, 203–
206
structure-function relation,
207–208
testicular receptors for, 193–
195
[^{125}I] hChorionic gonadotropin,
182, 185–187, 190, 231–237
binding characteristics, 267–
268
[^{131}I] hChorionic gonadotropin,
185–187, 190, 231–237
Chromatoelectrophoresis, 256
Chromatography
affinity
acetylcholine receptors, 17–24
beta-adrenergic receptor
purification, 69
fractionation, 488–489
gonadotropin receptors, 275–
278
opiate receptors, 506–508
purification of prolactin receptors by, 588–592
purification of solubilized
gonadotropin receptors, 241–
244

(Chromatography)
  carboxymethylcellulose in para-
    thyroid hormone receptors,
    535-538
  cellulose, of [^{125}I] insulin, 392-
    393
  column, fractionation, 488
  thin layer
    [^{125}I] glucagon, 167-168
    opiates, 499, 500
    [^{3}II] prostaglandin F_1, 620-621
    purity of iodinated hormones,
      129-130
Chromosomal abnormalities, 305
Chronic myelogenous leukemia,
    309
Chymotrypsinogen, 633, 634
Column chromatography, frac-
    tionation, 488
Concanavalin A, 180, 181, 365,
    455, 465
  transformation by, 323-324
Corpora lutea, prostaglandin re-
    ceptors in, 615-639
  binding
    assay for, 617-620
    conditions for, 622-625
    constants, 626-630
    effect of chemical modification
      of membrane proteins on, 635-
      636
  macromolecular nature of, 632-
    635
  preparation of cell membranes,
    616-618
  specificity of, 631-632
  thin layer chromatography, 620-
    621
Critical micellar concentration of
    Lubrol-PX, 131, 132, 134
Cysteic acid, 276
Cystine, 276
Cytochrome-C, 265-266
Cytochrome-C oxidase, 194
Cytochrome oxidase, 43

Dansylation, 276
DEAE, 145-147, 167
Decamethonium, 4
Deoxycholate, 272
Desoctapeptide insulin, displace-
    ment, by, 446
Detergent (see also names of
    detergents):
  -containing buffer, 227
  elution in the presence of, 489
  elution without, 489
  nonionic
    solubilization with, 92-95
    testicular receptors solubilized
      with, 228-238
  [^{125}I] prolactin and, 583-587
  purification of, 272-274
Dextran, 486
Dextrorphan, 502, 504
Diazotization, 507-508
Dibutyryl cAMP, 652
Diiodotyrosine, 645
p-Dimethylaminobenzoic acid,
    20-21
N'-(4-N, N-Dimethylamino-
    benzyl)maleamic acid, 5-6
Dimethylformide hexafluoro-
    isopropanol, 458
Dimethylsulfoxide, 458
Dinitrofluorobenzene, 635-636
Disk gel electrophoresis, pro-
    lactin receptor analysis by,
    592, 593
Dissociation rates of insulin re-
    ceptors, 433-434
5, 5'-Dithio(2-nitrobenzoic acid),
    5
Dithiothreitol (DTT), 4-5, 8-12,
    536, 547, 636
DNase, 633, 634
Dose-response curve, 361-364

EDTA, 10, 12, 15-17, 23-27
Electrolytic iodination, 548-549

Electron microscopy
  ACTH-sensitive adrenocortical
    membranes, 43-44
  gonadotropin receptors, 259-261
Electrophoresis
  disk gel, prolactin receptor anal-
    ysis by, 592, 593
  gel
    acetylcholine receptors, 26-29
    acrylamide, 29-30
    gonadotropic hormones, 227-
      228, 238
    polyacrylamide, 151-156, 239,
      276-278
Electroplax
  labeling receptor in, 8-9
  probind in intact cells, 3-5
Elution
  in the presence of detergent,
    489
  [^{125}I]proinsulin, 392
  without detergent, 489
Enzymatic probes of insulin-re-
    ceptor interactions, 451-455
Enzymes
  instability of, 43
  marker, 42-43
  mitochondrial, 43
  proteolytic, in isolation of sur-
    face material, 485-486
Epidermal growth factor (EGF),
    467-470
Epinephrine, 451-453, 600
Epstein-Barr virus (EBV), 305-
    307
Estrogen, 515
Ethanol, 274-275
N-Ethylmaleimide, 5, 636
Ethylnorlevorphanol, 509
Etorphine
  binding, 504, 505
  thin layer chromatography,
    500
  tritium-labeled, 498

Fat cells, measurements in,
    442-451
Ferguson plots, 154-155
Fibroblasts, insulin receptors in,
    467-471
Ficoll, 311
Ficoll-Hypaque gradient, 311-312
Fluoroscein, 95
Follicle-stimulating hormone
    (FSH), 99-118, 176-177, 284
  applications of tissue receptor
    assay, 116
  binding, 200-202
    specific, 261-262
  calculation of assay results,
    109-113
  cellular localization of, 191-192
  characteristics of the assay,
    113-115
  preparation of the radioligand,
    101-108
  preparation of rat testes tubule
    homogenate, 108-109
  procedure for tissue receptor
    assay, 109
  testicular receptors for, 195-
    196
  [^{125}I]hFollicle-stimulating hor-
    mone, 183, 186-189
  hFollicle-stimulating hormone,
    labeling of, 256
Formaldehyde, methylation with,
    46-47
Fractionation
  affinity chromatography, 488-
    489
  column chromatography, 488
  of the crude lipid fraction, 280-
    281
  glycopeptides, 488
  isolation of wheat germ agglu-
    tinin, 488-489
  oxytocin receptors, 524-525
  plasma membranes, 488

Galactose, 454
Galactose-ceramide, 74
Galactose-galactose-ceramide, 74
β-Galactosidase, 453-455
Gel electrophoresis
  acetylcholine receptors, 26-29
  acrylamide, 29-30
  disk, prolactin receptor analysis
    by, 592, 593
  gonadotropic hormones, 227-228,
    238
  polyacrylamide, 151-156, 239,
    276-278
Gel filtration, 26, 231-233, 242,
    455, 456, 559, 581, 582
  columns, 137-138
Gel isoelectric focusing, pro-
    lactin receptor analysis by,
    592, 594
γ-Globulin, 226
Glucagon, 130, 136, 137, 139,
    600
  displacement by, 445-446
  estimation of inactivation of,
    172
  iodination of, 124-126, 147-148
  labeled
    measurement of binding of,
      169-171
    storage of, 168
  labeling with radioiodine, 166-
    168
[^{125}I] Glucagon, 139-140, 144-
    145
  -binding assay, 148
  biological characterization of,
    167-168
  chemical characterization of,
    167-168
  molecular weight estimation,
    151-156
  thin layer chromatography,
    167-168
Glucagon receptors
  binding, 136-140

(Glucagon receptors)
  cardiac, 143-157
    dissociable glucagon-receptor
      site, 148-151
    [^{125}I] glucagon binding assay,
      148
    iodination of glucagon, 147-148
    molecular weight estimation of
      [^{125}I] glucagon, 151-156
    phosphatidylinositol isolation,
      145-147
    phosphatidylserine isolation,
      145-146
  isolation of proteins, 119-142
    hormone-binding assays, 136-
      140
    purity of radioactive ligands,
      124-130
    rat liver plasma membranes,
      122-123
    solubilization of, 130-136
  in plasma membranes, 159-174
    assay of adenylate cyclase,
      164-166
    estimation of inactivation of
      glucagon, 172
    labeling glucagon with radio-
      iodine, 166-168
    measurement of binding of
      labeled glucagon, 169-171
    purification method, 160-164
Glucopyranoside, 180
Glucose, 452-454
[^{125}I] Glucose, 128-129
Glucose-ceramide, 74
Glutamic acid, 276
Glycolipids, 78, 281-282
Glycopeptides, 76
  fractionation, 188
  releasing surface, 485-486
Glycoproteins, 281-282
  purification of radioiodinated,
    179-184
Glycosphingolipids, 74, 78-79
Gonadotropic hormones, 175-250

(Gonadotropic hormones)
  characterization of, 177–189
  determination of binding constants,
    209–223
  gel electrophoresis, 227–228, 238
  preparation of, 177–189
  radioligand-receptor assay, 196–
    202
    applications of, 203–208
  testicular receptors solubilized
    with nonionic detergents,
    228–238
  Triton X-100, 227, 228, 235-237,
    239, 241
Gonadotropin receptors, 251–299
  affinity chromatography, 275–278
    purification of solubilized, 241–
    244
  application in biology and medi-
    cine, 283–292
  binding, 188–189, 209–223
  site of subcellular, 192–193
  carbohydrate role in interaction,
    281–283
  cellular localization of, 190–
    193
  characterization of, 263–280
    ovarian, 238–241
    solubles, 223–228
  electron microscopy, 259–261
  extraction of solubles, 223–228
  lipid role in interaction, 280–
    281
  localization in vitro, 259–263
  localization in vivo, 257–259
  molecular weight, 237
  preparation of hormones as
    ligands, 253–257
  preparation of particulate, 190–
    196
  purification of, 263–280
  solubilization of, 263–280
    ovarian, 238–241
  testicular receptors
    for follicle-stimulating hor-

(Gonadotropin receptors)
    mone, 195–196
    for human chorionic gonado-
      tropin, 193–195
    for luteinizing hormone, 193–
      195
    Triton X-100, 272–273, 277
Gonadotropins (see also hChori-
    onic gonadotropin):
  evaluation of physical properties,
    184
  labeled
    characterization of, 177–190
    preparation of, 177–190
  radioiodination
    chloramine-T method, 178–179
    lactoperoxidase method, 179
    purification, 179–184
  structure-function relation,
    207–208
Gramicidin A, 31
Growth hormone
  degradation, 338–339
  displacement by, 445–446
  iodination of, 568
[^{125}I] Growth hormone, 574, 584–
    585, 587–590
Growth hormone receptors, 301–
    383
  cell preparations, 303–324
    biological relevance on
      lymphocytes and monocytes,
      316–324
    cultured lymphoid cell lines,
      303–311
    peripheral blood mononuclear
      cells, 311–316
  cooperative interactions, 356–
    365
    controls of the absence of re-
      binding, 360–361
    definitions, 356–357
    dose-response curve, 361–364
    fractional saturation, 364
    kinetic method to access, 357–

(Growth hormone receptors)
360
negative cooperativity, 364-365
nonspecific binding, 361
degradation, 339-340
labeling hormones, 324-330
molecular pathology of insulin-
resistant states, 369-370
molecular topochemistry, 366
new models of hormone action,
367-369
radioreceptor assay, 365-366
reaction of hormones with, 330-
356
Hill plot, 350-355
isotherm for binding, 343-346
kinetics of binding, 355-356
Lineweaver-Burk plot, 346
in optimal conditions, 330-333
Scatchard plot, 346-350
steady-state binding, 333-355
search for new biological actions,
366
target cell sensitivity, 366-367
Guanidine hydrochloride, 588
Guanidine-HCl
purification of, 270-272
solubilization, 487

Hemoglobin, 368
Hexamethonium, 4, 5, 17
Hill plot, 350-355
Histidine, 276
oxidation of, 44
Hormones (see also names of hormones; types of hormones)
degradation, 337-339, 407-408
labeled, 341
characterization of, 184-189
preparation of, 568-569
speciric activity of, 256-257
labeling, 324-330
ACTH-sensitive adrenocortical
membranes, 44-47

(Hormones)
with radioactive iodine, 254
preparation as ligands, 253-257
purity of iodinated, 129-130
radioreceptor assay of, 365-366
reaction with growth hormone
receptors, 330-356
Hill plot, 350-355
isotherm for binding, 343-346
kinetics of binding, 355-356
Lineweaver-Burk plot, 346
in optimal conditions, 330-333
Scatchard plot, 346-350
steady-state binding, 333-355
-receptor interaction, 44-48
binding studies, 47-48
iodination, 44-46
labeling the hormone, 44-47
radioactivity, 46-47
-responsive subcellular system,
682
separation of bound from free,
170, 332-333
$[^{125}I]$ Hormones, 136, 138, 340
recovery of, 128-129
specific radioactivity of, 128-
129
Hummel-Dreyer binding assay,
138-139
N-2-Hydroxyethylpiperaxine-N'-
2-ethanesulfonic acid (HEPES),
330, 410, 656
Hydroxylbenzylpindolol, 67
Hypaque, 312
Hypotonic extraction, 482-485

Igepal-630, 272-273
Immunization with plasma mem-
brane proteins, 279-280
Immunoglobulins, 306
Immunology, characterization of
purified receptors, 29-31
Infectious mononucleosis,
309

Inhibition
  of agglutination, 480-481
  of cAMP, 282
  of binding, 481
  of [^{125}I] insulin, 404
  of [^{3}H] thymidine, 490
Insulin, 130, 136, 241, 301-383,
    541-542
  binding, 313-316
    Hill plot, 350-355
    Lineweaver-Burk plot, 346
    nonspecific, 434-435
    pH effect, 336
    Scatchard plot, 346-350
    specific, 434-438
    steady-state, 333-340
  -binding cells, 312-313
  cell-bound, 410
  degradation, 337-338
  displacement by, 445-446
  dose-response curve, 361-364
  effect on leucocytes, 317-320
  iodination of, 126-127
  kinetic aspect of, 408-409
  labeled
    quality control, 393-394
    storage of, 393-394
  macromolecular derivatives,
    460-464
  membrane-bound, 412
  nonreceptor interactions, 434-439
  quantitative aspect of, 406-409
  radioactive derivates, prepara-
    tion of, 431-433
  radiolabeled, 387-395
  relative potencies, 405
  -resistant states, 369-370
  screening of existing cell lines
    for, 308, 311
  [^{125}I] Insulin, 323, 330, 336, 339,
    392, 442-447
    cellulose chromatography, 392-
      393
    displacement of, 445-446
    dissociation of, 360-363

([^{125}I] Insulin)
  inhibition of, 404
  preparation of, 389-394
  purification of, 390, 391
[^{127}I] Insulin, 390
Insulin receptors, 301-428
  applications of studies, 418-421
    pathological states, 420-421
    structure-function relation-
      ships, 419-420
  binding, 403-418
    analysis of data, 440-441
    cell membranes, 412-414
    expression of results, 415-418
    general problems, 403-409
    intact cells, 409-411
    solubilization, 415
  biochemical identification of,
    429-477
  analysis of binding data, 440-
    441
  association rates, 433-434
  dissociation rates, 433-434
  identification problem, 434-439
  measurement of interactions,
    439-440
  nonreceptor insulin inter-
    actions, 434-439
  number and affinity of recep-
    tors, 431
  preparation of radioactive in-
    sulin derivatives, 431-433
  degradation, 407-408
  in fibroblasts, 467-471
  interaction of insulin with mem-
    brane receptors, 442-471
    in cultured cells, 464-471
    enzymatic probes, 451-455
    fat cell measurements, 442-
      451
    macromolecular insulin de-
      rivatives, 460-464
    solubilization, 455-459
    in lymphocytes, 465-467
    proparations, 395-403

(Insulin receptors)
  cell membranes, 399-402
  intact cells, 396-399
  intact organs, 395
  isolation, 396-402
  solubilization, 402-403
  tissue pieces, 395
  structural specificity, 321-322
  Triton X-100, 402, 455-459
$[^{131}I]$ Iodide, 389
Iodination
  ACTH, 126-127
  chemistry, 254-255
  chloramine-T, 101-107
  electrolytic, 548-549
  glucagon, 124-126, 147-148
  growth hormone, 568
  hormone receptor, 44-46
  insulin, 126-127
  lactoperoxidase, 107-108, 127-
    128, 394
    catalyzed, 549, 643-649
  oxytocin, 669-670
  parathyroid hormones, 538,
    547-549
  procedure for, 390, 391
  prolactin, 568
  protocols for, 326-330
  secretin, 124-126
    lactoperoxidase method, 127-
    128
  vasoactive intestinal peptide,
    124-126
  vasopressin, 669-670
Iodine
  radioactive, labeling of hormones
    with, 254
  separation of gound from free,
    102
  -tritium substitution technique,
    669-672
Iodoacetamide, 636
Iodo-oxytocin, 669-672
Iodovasopressin, 669-672
Isolation

(Isolation)
  acetylcholine receptors, 15-24
  insulin receptors, 396-402
  membrane fractions, 15-16
  mitogenic lectin receptors in
    lymphocytes, 490
  phosphatidylinositol, 145-147
  phosphatidylserine, 145-146
  plasma membranes, 122-123,
    486
  proteins, 119-142
    hormone-binding assays, 136-
    140
    purity of radioactive ligands,
    124-130
    rat liver plasma membranes,
    122-123
    solubilization of, 130-136
  surface material using proteo-
    lytic enzymes, 485-486
  wheat germ agglutinin, 482-489
(-)-Isomers, 56, 57
(+)-Isomers, 56, 57
(-)-Isoproterenol, 65

Krebs-Ringer bicarbonate (KRB),
  410, 412, 414, 447, 452
Krebs-Ringer phosphate (KRP),
  409, 410, 412, 413

Lactoperoxidase, 433
  iodination, 107-108, 127-128, 394
    catalyzed, 549, 643-649
  labeling method, 255-256
  radioiodination, 179
Lectin receptors, 479-495
  assays for wheat germ agglutinin,
    480-481
    inhibition of agglutination, 480-
    481
    inhibition of binding, 481
  isolation of wheat germ agglu-
    tinin, 482-489

(Lectin receptors)
    fractionation, 488-489
    preparation of subcellular fractions, 482-486
    procedures for, 491-492
    solubilization, 486-487
    mitogenic lectin receptors in lymphocytes, 490
    Triton X-100, 489
Leucine, 276
Leucocytes
    effect of insulin on, 317-320
    mononuclear, 312-314
Leukemia, 304, 305, 309
Levorphanol, 502, 504
    thin layer chromatography, 500
Ligand receptor interactions, 431-441
    analysis of binding data, 440-441
    association rates, 433-434
    dissociation rates, 433-434
    identification problem, 434-439
    measurement of interactions, 439-440
    nonreceptor insulin interactions, 434-439
    number and affinity of receptors, 431
    preparation of radioactive insulin derivatives, 431-433
Ligands
    labeled
      preparation of, 498-499
      purification of, 498-499
    preparation of hormones as, 253-257
    radioactive, purity of, 124-130
Lineweaver-Burk plot, 346
Lipase, 633, 634
Lipids
    fractionation of the crude fraction, 280-281
    in gonadotropin receptor interaction, 280-281
    stereospecific binding assay, 504

Lipocytes
    binding to intact, 601, 602
    preparation of, 600-601
Lithium diiodosalicylate (LIS), 458
    solubilization, 486-487
Long-acting thyroid stimulator (LATS), 662-663
Lubrol-PX, 68, 82, 92-94, 144, 235, 237, 239, 402, 458
    determination of critical micellar concentration, 131-132, 134
    spectra of methyl orange, 133
[^{14}C] Lubrol-PX, purification of, 130-131
Lubrol-WX, 68, 235, 237, 239
Lucerne, 655
Luteal cells, preparation of subcellular fractions, 259, 260
Luteinizing hormone (LH), 100, 176-178, 241, 244, 283-292
    binding, 197-199
      specific, 261-262
    cellular localization of, 190-191
    measurement of activity, 203-206
    structure-function relation, 207-208
    testicular receptors for, 193-195
hLuteinizing hormone (hLH), labeling, 255-256
Lymphoblastic leukemia, 309
Lymphoblastoid cells, 304
Lymphocytes, 313
    as biohazards, 307
    biological relevance of growth hormone receptors on, 316-324
    cultured, 330-337
    insulin receptors in, 465-467
    mitogenic lectin receptors in, 490
    transformation, 323-324
B-Lymphocytes, 313
Lymphoid cells, cultured lines, 303-311

Lysine, 539–540

Maleimide, 5
4-(N-Maleimido)benzyltrimethyl-
    ammonium iodide (MBTA),
    5–7, 25–26
  assay, 11–13
  labeling receptor with, 7–8
4-(N-Maleimido)benzyltri-
    [^{3}H]methylammonium
    iodide, 6–7
4-(N'-Maleimido)-N, N-dimethyl-
    benzylamide, 6
Mannopyranoside, 180
Marker enzymes, 42–43
Membrane fractions
  adenylate cyclase-containing,
    58–59
  isolation of, 15–16
  labeling, 9–10
  purification of, 15–16
Membrane receptors, interaction
    of insulin with, 442–471
  in cultured cells, 464–471
  enzymatic probes, 451–455
  fat cell measurements, 442–451
  macromolecular insulin deriva-
    tives, 460–464
  solubilization, 455–459
Mercaptoethanol, 636
Metabisulfite, 325
Metal ions, oxytocin receptor
    binding and, 519–520
Methionine, 276
  oxidation of, 44, 255
Methyl [^{3}H]acetimidate, 540–542
  labeling with, 541–542
N-Methyl tryptophan, 44
Methylation with formaldehyde,
    46–47
Microcentrifugation assay, 557–558
Mitochondrial enzymes, 43
Mitogenic lectin receptors in
    lymphocytes, 490

Molecular weight
  estimation of [^{125}I]glucagon,
    151–156
  gonadotropin receptor, 237
Monocytes
  biological relevance of growth
    hormone receptors on, 316–
    324
  counts, 313–316
Monoiodination
  carrier-free, 324–325
  stoichiometric, 324–330
Monoiodoinsulin, 325
  preparation of, 388–389
  properties of, 388–389
Monoiodotyrosine, 645
Mononuclear leucocytes, 312–314
Monophosphatidylinositol, 144
Monosialogangliosides, 82
G$_{M1}$Monosialogangliosides, 74–
    76, 80
G$_{M3}$Monosialogangliosides, 74, 80
Morphine
  -receptor assay in cultured cells,
    503
  -Sepharose beads, 507
  thin layer chromatography, 500
  tritium-labeled, 498–499
Myeloma, 309
Myoglobin, 226

Naloxone
  binding, 504, 506
  thin layer chromatography, 500
  tritium-labeled, 498–499
Naltrexone, 506
  binding, 505
  thin layer chromatography, 500
  tritium-labeled, 498
Neoplasms, capacity to form,
    305–306
Neuraminidase, 453–454, 633, 634
Neurohypophysial peptide, prepara-
    tion of, 669–675

(Neurohypophysial peptide)
  characterization of final product,
    672-675
  iodine-tritium substitution tech-
    nique, 669-672
  review of methods, 669
α-Neurotoxins, 25
  assay by binding of, 13-15
p-Nitrobenzoyl chloride, 508
p-Nitro-N, N-dimethylbenzyl-
    amine, 5
p-Nitrophenol, 20-21
o-Nitrophenylsulfenyl tryptophan,
    44
Nonionic detergent
  solubilization with, 92-95
  testicular receptors solubilized
    with, 228-238
Norepinephrine, 69
(-)-Norepinephrine, 65
[³H]Norepinephrine, 144
5'-Nucleotidase, 42-43, 194, 195,
    265-266, 570, 571
  cytochemical localization of, 44

Oligosaccharide, 76
Opiate receptors, 497-510
  affinity chromatography, 506-
    508
  affinity labeling, 508-509
  agonist and antagonist properties
    of opiates, 506
  preparation of labeled ligands,
    498-499
  purification of labeled ligands,
    498-499
  stereospecific binding, 502-505
    to brain cerebrosides, 504
    centrifugation techniques, 502
    filtration technique, 503-505
    in lipid extracts, 504
    morphine-receptor assay, 503
  tissue preparations for binding
    studies, 499-501

Opiates, thin layer chromato-
    graphy, 499, 500
Organon, 241
Ovarian gonadotropin receptors
  characterization of, 238-241
  solubilization of, 238-241
Oxidation
  of histidine, 44
  of methionine, 44, 255
  of peroxide, 44
  of serine, 44
  of tryptophan, 44
Oxyhemoglobin, 350
Oxytocin
  analogs, 513-514
  biological assays, 674-675
  characterization of, 675-677
  displacement by, 445
  iodination of, 669-670
  metabolism of, 520-521
  purification of, 669-670, 672
  radioactivity, 672-673
  radioimmunoassay for, 522
  tritiation, 670-672
[³H]Oxytocin, 512-513, 679-681
  radioactivity from, 514-517
  uptake of, 514-517
Oxytocin receptors, 511-531
  autoradiography, 517-518
  binding, 518-528
    by isolated mammary gland
      cells, 523-528
    metal ions and, 519-520
    pH and, 519-520
  characterization on intact
    epithelial cells, 675-681
  fractionation of, 524-525
  limitations of tissue uptake
    studies, 517
  mammary tissue, 514-515, 528
  uterus, 515-516

Papain to release surface glyco-
    peptides, 485

Parathyroid hormone, 533–564
  acetamidination of, 539–547
  iodination, 538, 547–549
  labeled preparations, 549–550
  purification of, 535–538
  tritiated acetamidino, 544–547
Parathyroid hormone receptors,
    533–564
  binding, 556–561
    pH in, 560
  carboxymethylcellulose chromato-
    graphy, 535–538
  preparations, 550–556
  kidney membrane, 551–556
Penicillin, 308
Peptides
  displacement by, 445–446, 459
  neurohypophysial preparation,
    669–675
    characterization of final pro-
      duct, 672–675
    iodine-tritium substitution tech-
      nique, 669–672
    review of methods, 669
  tryptophyl bonds, 55
  vasoactive intestinal, 130, 136,
    137
  iodination of, 124–126
[^{125}I] Peptides, binding, 416
Peroxidases, 255
Peroxide, oxidation of, 44
pH
  in insulin binding, 336
  in oxytocin receptor binding,
    519–520
  in parathyroid hormone receptor
    binding, 560
  in prostaglandin receptor binding,
    622–625
Phenol solubilization, 487
Phenylalanine, 44
[^{14}C] Phenylalanine, 47
Phosphatidylinositol, isolation of,
    145–147
Phosphatidylserine, 144

(Phosphatidylserine)
  isolation of, 145–146
Phosphodiesterase cAMP, 609
Phospholipase, 453–454
Phospholipase A, 229, 633, 634
Phospholipase C, 229, 633, 634
Phospholipase D, 633, 634
Phospholipids, 280–281, 454
Plasma membranes
  binding, 136–137
  fractionation, 488
  glucagon receptor in, 159–174
    assay of adenylate cyclase,
      164–166
    estimation of inactivation of
      glucagon, 172
    labeling glucagon with radio-
      iodine, 166–168
    measurement of binding of
      labeled glucagon, 169–171
    purification method, 160–164
  isolation of, 122–123, 486
  preparation of, 263–266
  proteins, immunization with,
    279–280
  purification of, 270–274
  solubilization of, 270
  thyrotropin receptors
    binding, 657–658
    interactions, 658–661
    preparations, 652–655
  use of [^{125}I] choleragen and
    choleragenoid, 90–92
Polyacrylamide, 38
Polyacrylamide gel electrophor-
    esis, 151–156, 239, 276, 278
Polyethylene glycol (PEG), 274–
    275, 457, 486, 581–584
Pregnyl, 241
[^{125}I] Proinsulin, 391
  elution profile, 392
Proinsulin, displacement by, 446
Prolactin, 241, 252, 286
  binding, 572–575
    specific, 261–262

(Prolactin)
 subcellular particle preparation, 567-568
 testing activity, 569-570
 displacement by, 445
 iodination of, 568
 radioreceptor assay for, 575-579
hProlactin, 284, 285
 labeling, 255-256
[^{125}I] Prolactin, 570-572
 detergent and, 583-587
[^{125}I] hProlactin, 572-574, 584
[^{125}I] oProlactin, 583-587
Prolactin receptors, 565-598
 particulate cell membrane preparation, 567-579
 distribution of activity in subcellular fractions, 570-572
 labeled hormone preparation, 568-569
 prolactin-binding subcellular particle preparation, 567-568
 properties of, 572-575
 radioreceptor assay, 575, 579
 testing prolactin-binding activity, 569-570
 tissue source, 567
 soluble, 579-592
 affinity adsorbent preparation, 587-588
 detection of activity, 581-583
 disk gel electrophoresis analysis, 592, 593
 gel isoelectric focusing analysis, 592, 594
 problem of [^{125}I] prolactin with detergent, 583-587
 protein determination, 580-581
 purification by affinity chromatography, 588-592
 solubilization of membrane proteins, 580
 Triton X-100, 580-581, 585-587
Pronase, 633, 634
(-)-Propranolol, 58, 60

[^{3}H] Propranolol, 66
Propylthiouracil, 655
Prostaglandin E$_1$, 600-612, 616
Prostaglandin E$_2$, 608-612, 616
[^{3}H] Prostaglandin E$_1$, 601-611
 binding assay for, 617-620
 binding conditions, 622-625
 binding constants, 626-630
 separation of bound and free, 619-620
 thin layer chromatography, 620-621
Prostaglandin receptors
 in adipose tissue, 599-614
 application of the binding reaction, 609-611
 binding to intact lipocytes, 601-602
 binding to receptor preparation, 601-606
 lipocyte preparation, 600-601
 preparation for quantitation, 606-608
 properties of the preparation, 608-609
 in corpora lutea, 615-639
 binding assay for, 617-620
 binding conditions, 622-625
 binding constants, 626-630
 effect of chemical modification of membrane proteins on binding, 635-636
 macromolecular nature of, 632-635
 preparation of cell membranes, 616-618
 specificity of, 631-632
 thin layer chromatography, 620-621
Protein
 amino acid analysis, 276, 277
 concentration of membrane-rich fractions, 41, 42
 determination, 259, 580-581
 effect of chemical modification

(Protein)
  of, 635–636
  isolation of, 119–142
    hormone-binding assays, 136–
      140
    purity of radioactive ligands,
      124–130
    rat liver plasma membranes,
      122–123
    solubilization of, 130–136
  plasma membrane, immunization
    with, 279–280
  solubilization, 580
Proteolytic enzymes in isolation of
    surface material, 485–486
Purification
  acetylcholine receptors, 15–24
  beta-adrenergic receptors, 67–
    69
    affinity chromatography, 69
    solubilization, 67–68
  cAMP, 165–166
  detergents, 272–274
  glucagon receptors, 160–164
  glycoprotein, radioiodinated,
    179–184
  gonadotropin receptors, 263–
    280
    solubilized, 241, 244
  guanidine-HCl, 270–272
  [^{125}I] insulin, 390, 391
  labeled ligands, 498–499
  [^{14}C] Lubrol-PX, 130–131
  membrane fractions, 15–16
  oxytocin, 669–670, 672
  parathyroid hormones, 535–538
  plasma membranes, 270–274
  prolactin receptors, 588–592
  thyrotropins, 643–650
  toxins, 14
  vasopressin, 669–670, 672
Pychosine, 79
Pyridine, 458
  solubilization, 487
Pyronin Y, 27

Radioactive insulin derivatives,
    preparation of, 431–433
Radioactive iodine, labeling of
    hormones with, 254
Radioactive ligands, purity of,
    124–130
Radioactivity
  bound, 332–333
  counting of, 103
  free, 332
  hormone-receptor interaction,
    46–47
  oxytocin, 672–673
  [^{3}H] oxytocin, 514–517
  specific
    calculation of, 103
    of [^{125}I] hormones, 128–129
    measurement of, 107
  total, 332
  vasopressin, 672–673
Radioimmunoassay, 365–366, 405
  for oxytocin, 522
Radioiodination, 324, 650
  choleragen, 82–84
  choleragenoid, 82–84
  gonadotropins
    chloramine-T method, 178–179
    lactoperoxidase method, 179
    purification, 179–184
Radioiodine, labeling glucagon
    with, 166–168
Radiolabeled insulin, 387–395
Radiolabeled thyrotropin, 642–650
Radioligand receptor, gonadotropic
    hormone assay, 196–202
  applications of, 203–208
Radioligands
  preparation of, 101–108
  stability of, 103–107
Receptor assay
  growth hormone receptor, 365–
    366
  prolactin, 575–579
Rebinding, controls of the ab-
    sence of, 360–361

Rhodamine, 95
RNase, 633, 634

Scatchard plot, 345-350
Secretin, 130, 136, 137
  iodination of, 124-126
    lactoperoxidase method, 127-128
Sephadex G-25, 46
Sephadex G-50, 179, 234, 455, 644, 645
Sephadex G-100, 102-104, 148-151, 180, 181, 585
Sephadex G-200, 231, 233, 644, 645
Sepharose, 180, 181, 184
  -morphine beads, 507
Sepharose 4B, 277
Sepharose 6B, 92-94, 231-237, 240, 242, 277, 461
Serine, oxidation of, 44
Sialic acid, 74-82, 454-455
Sodium deoxycholate, 68
Sodium dodecyl sulfate (SDS), 26-27, 151-156, 272, 276-278
Sodium dodecylfulfate, 458
Sodium metabisulfite, 101
Solubilization
  adenylate cyclase, 694
  glucagon receptors, 130-136
  gonadotropic receptors, 263-280
    ovarian, 2380241
  guanidine-HCl, 487
  insulin receptors, 402-403, 455-459
  isolation of wheat germ agglutinin, 486-487
  lithium diiodosalicylate, 486-487
  membrane vasopressin receptors, 693-699
  with nonionic detergents, 92-95
  phenol, 487

(Solubilization)
  plasma membranes, 270
  proteins, 580
  purification of beta-adrenergic receptors, 67-68
  pyridine, 487
  testes particles, 225
  testicular receptors with nonionic detergents, 228-238
  Triton X-100, 487
Solution, labeling in, 10-11
Sphingomyelin, 79
Steady-state binding
  growth hormone receptors, 333-355
  insulin, 333-340
Stereospecific opiate binding, 502-505
  to brain cerebrosides, 504
  centrifugation techniques, 502
  filtration technique, 503-505
  in lipid extracts, 504
  morphine-receptor assay, 503
Steroidogenesis, 38
Stoichiometric monoiodination, 324-330
Streptomycin, 308
Succinylmorphine, 507
Sucrose, 123, 266, 449-450
  density gradient, 235, 236, 240
    centrifugation, 522-525
    sedimentation, 22-24

T-cell
  lines, 308-311
  transformant of, 324
Testes, solubilization of particles, 225
Testes tubule tissue receptor assay, 99-118
Testicular receptors
  for follicle-stimulating hormone, 195-196
  for human chorionic gonado-

(Testicular receptors)
    tropin, 193-195
  for luteinizing hormone, 193-195
  solubilized with nonionic deter-
    gents, 228-238
Tetranitromethane, 635-636
Thin layer chromatography
  [^{125}I]glucagon, 167-168
  opiates, 499, 500
  [^{3}H]prostaglandin E$_1$, 620-621
  purity of iodinated hormones,
    129-130
[^{3}H] Thymidine, inhibition of, 490
Thymidine, stimulation of, 468,
    469
Thyroglobulin, 226
Thyroid cells
  thyrotropin receptor interactions,
    658-661
  thyrotropin receptor prepara-
    tions, 651-652
Thyroid-stimulating hormone
    (TSH), 642-663
Thyrotropin
  nature and properties of, 643
  preparation of, 643-650
  purification of, 643-650
  radiolabeled, 642-650
  tritiated, 650
Thyrotropin receptors, 641-665
  binding, 656-658
    crude particulate fractions,
      657-658
    intact cells, 656
    plasma membranes, 657-658
  interactions, 658-661
  preparations, 651-656
    crude particulate, 655-656
    intact thyroid cells, 651-652
    plasma membranes, 652-655
  quantitative aspects of inter-
    action, 658-663
L-Thyroxine, 655
Tissue receptor assay (TRA),
    99-118

(Tissue receptor assay (TRA))
  applications of, 116
  calculation of results, 109-113
  characteristics of, 113-115
  preparation of the homogenate,
    108-109
  preparation of the radioligand,
    101-108
  procedure of, 109
Toxin
  purification of, 14
  tritiation of, 14
Trasylol, 136, 228
Trichloroacetic acid, 432-433
Triethylamine, 508
Tritiated acetamidino para-
    thyroid hormone, 544-547
Tritiated borohydride, 650
Tritiated thyrotropin, 650
Tritiation
  oxytocin, 670-672
  toxin, 14
  vasopressin, 670-672
Tritium, 498-499
  -iodine substitution technique,
    669-672
  -labeled etorphine, 498
  -labeled morphine, 498-499
  -labeled naloxone, 498-499
  -labeled naltrexone, 498
  stability of, 544-547
Tritium gas handling apparatus,
    670-672
Triton X-100
  acetylcholine receptors, 27
  [^{3}H] (-)-alprenolol, 68
  gonadotropic hormones, 227,
    228, 235-237, 239, 241
  gonadotropin receptors, 272-
    273, 277
  insulin receptors, 402, 455-459
  lectin receptors, 489
  prolactin receptors, 580-581,
    585, 587
  solubilization, 487

(Triton X-100)
vasopressin receptors, 693-696,
699
Trypsin, 228, 229, 340, 451-454,
633, 634
to release surface glycopeptides,
485-486
Trypsinogen, 633, 634
Tryptophan, 276
oxidation of, 44
Tryptophyl peptide bonds, 44
(+)-Tubocurarine, 13, 17
Tween-80, 272
[^{3}H] Tyrosine, 679

Uterus, oxytocin receptors,
515-516

Vasoactive intestinal peptide
(VIP), 130, 136, 137
iodination of, 124-126
Vasopressin
binding, 685-692, 695-700
biological assays, 674-675
characterization of, 675-677
displacement by, 445
iodination of, 669-670
purification of, 669-670, 672
radioactivity, 672-673
tritiation, 670-672
[^{3}H] Vasopressin, 685-692, 698

Vasopressin receptors, 667-703
characterization in membrane
fractions, 681-693
characterization of oxytocin receptors on intact epithelial
cells, 675-681
neurohypophysial peptide preparation, 669-675
characterization of final product, 672-675
iodine-tritium substitution
technique, 669-672
review of methods, 669
solubilization of membrane,
693-699
Triton X-100, 693-696, 699

Wheat germ agglutinin (WGA), 471
assays for activity, 480-481
inhibition of agglutination,
480-481
inhibition of binding, 481
isolation of, 482-489
fractionation, 488-489
preparation of subcellular
fractions, 482-486
procedures for, 491-492
solubilization, 486-487
[^{125}I] Wheat germ agglutinin,
preparation of, 481

Zonal centrifugation, 39-42